BlackBerry

iPhone / iPad

◎ Harden's 21st
EDITION

London Restaurants
2012

"Gastronomes' bible"
Evening Standard

Survey driven reviews of over 1,800 restaurants

Put us in your client's pocket!

Branded editions for BlackBerry and iPhone
call to discuss the options on 020 7839 4763.

© **Harden's Limited 2011**

ISBN 978-1-873721-96-4

British Library Cataloguing-in-Publication data:
a catalogue record for this book is available from
the British Library.

Printed in Italy by Legoprint

Research assistants: Helen Teschauer, Gilles Talarek, Tom Kochavi

Harden's Limited
14 Buckingham Street
London WC2N 6DF

Would restaurateurs (and PRs) please address
communications to 'Editorial' at the above address,
or ideally by email to: editorial@hardens.com

CONTENTS

RATINGS & PRICES

Ratings

Our rating system is unlike those found in other guides (most of which tell you nothing more helpful than that expensive restaurants are, as a general rule, better than cheap ones).

What we do is to compare each restaurant's performance – as judged by the average ratings awarded by reporters in the survey – with other restaurants in the same price-bracket.

This approach has the advantage that it helps you find – whatever your budget for any particular meal – where you will get the best 'bang for your buck'.

The following qualities are assessed:

F — Food
S — Service
A — Ambience

The rating indicates that, *in comparison with other restaurants in the same price-bracket*, performance is...

❶ — Exceptional
❷ — Very good
❸ — Good
④ — Average
⑤ — Poor

Prices

The price shown for each restaurant is the cost for one (1) person of an average three-course dinner with half a bottle of house wine and coffee, any cover charge, service and VAT. Lunch is often cheaper. With BYO restaurants, we have assumed that two people share a £5 bottle of off-license wine.

Telephone number – all numbers should be prefixed with '020' if dialling from outside the London area.

Map reference – shown immediately after the telephone number.

Rated on Editors' visit – indicates ratings have been determined by the Editors personally, based on their visit, rather than derived from the survey.

Website – the first entry in the small print (after any note about Editors' visit)

Last orders time – listed after the website (if applicable); Sunday may be up to 90 minutes earlier.

Opening hours – unless otherwise stated, restaurants are open for lunch and dinner seven days a week.

Credit and debit cards – unless otherwise stated, Mastercard, Visa, Amex and Maestro are accepted.

Dress – where appropriate, the management's preferences concerning patrons' dress are given.

Special menus – if we know of a particularly good value set menu we note this (e.g. "set weekday L"), together with its formula price (FP) calculated exactly as in 'Prices' above. Details change, so always check ahead.

HOW THIS GUIDE IS WRITTEN

Survey

This guide is based on our 21st annual survey of what 'ordinary' diners-out think of London's restaurants. In 1998, we extended the survey to cover restaurants across the rest of the UK; it is by far the most detailed annual survey of its type. Out-of-town results are published in our UK guide.

This year, the total number of reporters in our combined London/UK survey, conducted mainly online, exceeded 8,000, and, between them, they contributed some 85,000 individual reports. This is a vast exercise, and we are grateful to Rémy Martin Fine Champagne Cognac for continuing to support it.

How we determine the ratings

In the great majority of cases, ratings are arrived at statistically. This essentially involves 'ranking' the average survey rating each restaurant achieves in the survey – for each of food, service and ambience – against the average ratings of the other establishments which fall in the same price-bracket. (This is essentially like football leagues, with the most expensive restaurants going in the top league and the cheaper ones in lower leagues. Where the restaurant is ranked *within its own particular league* determines its ratings.)

How we write the reviews

The tenor of each review and the ratings are very largely determined by the ranking of the establishment concerned, which we have derived as described above. At the margin, we may also pay some regard to the proportion of positive nominations (such as for 'favourite restaurant') compared to negative nominations (such as for 'most overpriced').

To explain why a restaurant has been rated as it has, we extract snippets from survey comments ("enclosed in double quotes"). On larger restaurants, we receive several hundred reports, and a short summary cannot possibly do individual justice to all of them.

What we seek to do – *without any regard to our own personal opinions* – is to illustrate the key themes which have emerged in our analysis of the collective view. The only exception to this is the newest restaurants, where survey views are either few or non-existent, and where we may be obliged to rely on our own opinions. Unless the review carries the small-print note "Rated on Editors' visit", however, the ratings awarded are still our best analysis of the survey view, not our own impressions.

Richard Harden   **Peter Harden**

RÉMY MARTIN®

FINE CHAMPAGNE COGNAC

Few business partnerships last as long as the co-operation between Rémy Martin and Harden's. This is based on many things, but particularly on authenticity, integrity and reliability, which are important to both of us.

Harden's derives its authenticity from its annual nationwide survey of restaurant-goers, leading to the creation of the UK's definitive democratic restaurant guides. For Rémy Martin, it comes from three centuries of tradition, our origins in the heart of Cognac and the unique know-how of our cellar-master.

Since 1724, Rémy Martin – the only large cognac house still in family ownership – has produced cognacs of exceptional quality and taste. Alone, we source 100% of our grapes from the very 'heart of Cognac'. The "heart" has its own official designation: 'Appellation Fine Champagne Contrôllée'. "Fine Champagne" indicates a blend of cognac from the two best areas in the centre of the Cognac region, Grande Champagne (at least half the blend) and Petite Champagne.

Champagne lends its name to these two Cognac areas because, like the famous sparkling wine region, the region is typfied by undulating hills and a chalky soil. Over 80% of all the Fine Champagne cognac produced in this designated area is used in Rémy Martin Fine Champagne cognacs.

Such unrivalled provenance results in three main characteristics which distinguish Rémy Martin; the harmony between the complex aromas and the sweetness of the flavours; the elegant richness of the aromas and palate; and the supreme length of the finish.

This is why we believe that Rémy Martin captures the very heart of Cognac and it is this unswerving dedication to quality over nearly three centuries that has led Rémy Martin to become the worldwide leader in the most premium of cognacs.

The Restaurant Rémys

There are three tiers of recognition to the Restaurant Rémys. The first is the Rémy Martin VSOP Award for the Best-Rated Newcomer, which remains the industry's most coveted recognition of up and coming restaurants and Rémy Martin is once again proud to be associated with the development of such a dynamic category.

The second is the Coeur de Cognac Award for Top Dessert – a much overlooked, yet sublime aspect to a complete dining experience. And the last, but by no means the least, is the Rémy Martin XO Excellence Award for the Best All-Round Restaurant. This award is the result of painstaking analysis of the survey results to identify the true crème de la crème among London's ever more competitive restaurant world.

SURVEY RESTAURANT REMYS

In conjunction with our sponsors Rémy Martin Fine Champagne Cognac, last year we introduced three new awards based on the results of the survey.
(Last year's position is given in brackets.)

Rémy Martin XO Award
Best All-Round Restaurant

Winner
  1   **Le Gavroche (2)**
Runners-up
  2   The Ledbury (4)
  3   The Ritz (6=)
  4   Chez Bruce (5)
  5   Min Jiang (-)
  6   Trinity (10)
  7   Marcus Wareing (1)
  8   Clos Maggiore (-)
  9   Scott's (-)
 10 La Trompette (-)

Coeur de Cognac Award
Best Dessert

Winner
  1   **Marcus Wareing (1)**
      (Custard Tart)
Runners-up
  2   Dinner – *Tipsy Cake (c1810) with spit-roast pineapple* (-)
  3   Chez Bruce – *Cheeseboard* (3)
  4   Le Gavroche – *Tarte Tatin* (-)
  5   Ledbury – *Gingerbread soufflé* (-)

Rémy Martin VSOP Award
Best-rated Newcomer

Winner
  1   **Dinner**
Runners-up
  2   Morito
  3   Yashin
  4   Pollen Street Social
  5   Brawn

SURVEY MOST MENTIONED

These are the restaurants which were most frequently mentioned by reporters. (Last year's position is given in brackets.) An asterisk* indicates the first appearance in the list of a recently-opened restaurant.

1	J Sheekey (1)
2	Scott's (2)
3	Marcus Wareing At The Berkeley (4)
4	Chez Bruce (3)
5	Le Gavroche (5)
6	The Ledbury (10)
7=	Clos Maggiore (13)
7=	Galvin Bistrot de Luxe (8)
9	The Wolseley (6)
10	Les Deux Salons*

11	Terroirs (11)
12	Bleeding Heart (8)
13	The Cinnamon Club (15)
14	The Square (20)
15	Bar Boulud*
16	La Trompette (12)
17	Le Caprice (16)
18	Galvin La Chapelle (36)
19	Oxo Tower (Rest') (19)
20	La Poule au Pot (18)

21	The Ivy (14)
22	Benares (29)
23	The River Café (22)
24=	Dinner*
24=	Bocca Di Lupo (21)
26	Zuma (26)
27	Amaya (35)
28	Koffmann's*
29	Gordon Ramsay (17)
30	Andrew Edmunds (24)

31	Moro (30)
32=	L'Atelier de Joel Robuchon (32)
32=	Gordon Ramsay at Claridge's (25)
34	Bistrot Bruno Loubet (-)
35	Pied à Terre (-)
36	Murano (33)
37	Yauatcha (36)
38	Arbutus (23)
39	Galvin at Windows (31)
40	The Anchor & Hope (27)

SURVEY NOMINATIONS

Top gastronomic experience

1   Marcus Wareing At The Berkeley (1)
2   Le Gavroche (2)
3   The Ledbury (3=)
4   Chez Bruce (3=)
5   Dinner*
6   La Trompette (5=)
7= The Square (7)
7= Pied à Terre (-)
9   Viajante (-)
10 Gordon Ramsay (5=)

Favourite

1   Chez Bruce (1)
2   The Wolseley (5)
3   Le Caprice (3)
4   Galvin Bistrot de Luxe (2)
5   The Ledbury (9)
6   La Trompette (3)
7   Le Gavroche (-)
8   Marcus Wareing At The Berkeley (-)
9   J.Sheekey (6)
10 Trinity (-)

Best for business

1   The Wolseley (1)
2   The Don (5)
3   The Square (3)
4   Bleeding Heart (4)
5   Galvin La Chapelle (9)
6   Coq d'Argent (2)
7   L'Anima (6)
8= Galvin Bistrot de Luxe (7)
8= Scott's (8)
10 The Ivy (10)

Best for romance

1   Clos Maggiore (2)
2   La Poule au Pot (1)
3   Andrew Edmunds (3)
4   Bleeding Heart (4)
5   Chez Bruce (6)
6   Galvin at Windows (5)
7   Le Caprice (9)
8   Le Gavroche (10)
9   The Ledbury (-)
10 Oxo Tower (Rest') (-)

Best breakfast/brunch

1. The Wolseley (1)
2. Roast (3)
3. Smiths (Ground Floor) (-)
4. Cecconi's (4)
5. Automat (9)
6. Simpsons-in-the-Strand (5)
7. Caravan (-)
8. The Goring Hotel (9)
9. Providores (Tapa Room) (-)
10. Tom's Kitchen (8)

Best bar/pub food

1. The Anchor & Hope (1)
2. Harwood Arms (2)
3. Bull & Last (3)
4. Canton Arms*
5. The Orange (8)
6. The Gun (-)
7. The Anglesea Arms (4)
8. The Thomas Cubitt (6)
9. The Eagle (8)
10. The Pantechnicon (-)

Most disappointing cooking

1. Gordon Ramsay at Claridge's (2)
2. Oxo Tower (Rest') (1)
3. The Ivy (4)
4. Marcus Wareing at the Berkeley (-)
5. Gordon Ramsay (3)
6. Les Deux Salons*
7. The Wolseley (-)
8= Skylon (-)
8= Hibiscus (-)
8= maze (-)

Most overpriced restaurant

1. Oxo Tower (1)
2. Gordon Ramsay at Claridge's (2)
3. Gordon Ramsay (3)
4. Marcus Wareing at the Berkeley (-)
5. The River Café (5)
6. Hakkasan (6)
7. Alain Ducasse (7)
8= maze (10)
8= Le Gavroche
10. Nobu (-)

SURVEY HIGHEST RATINGS

FOOD

SERVICE

£85+

	FOOD		SERVICE
1	The Ledbury	1	Le Gavroche
2	Le Gavroche	2	The Ledbury
3	One-O-One	3	The Ritz Restaurant
4	The Square	4	Marcus Wareing
5	Marcus Wareing	5	The Square

£65-£84

	FOOD		SERVICE
1	Chez Bruce	1	Chez Bruce
2	Zuma	2	The Goring Hotel
3	Min Jiang	3	Angelus
4	Gauthier Soho	4	Texture
5	Yauatcha	5	Le Caprice

£50-£64

	FOOD		SERVICE
1	Morgan M	1	Oslo Court
2	Hunan	2	Trinity
3	Trinity	3	La Trompette
4	La Trompette	4	Brula
5	Pollen Street Social	5	Pollen Street Social

£40-£49

	FOOD		SERVICE
1	Dinings	1	Upstairs Bar
2	Sushi-Say	2	Caraffini
3	Buen Ayre	3	Sushi-Say
4	Sukho Fine Thai Cuisine	4	Emile's
5	Barrafina	5	About Thyme

£39 or less

	FOOD		SERVICE
1	Café Japan	1	Uli
2	Ragam	2	Yoshino
3	New Tayyabs	3	Kaffeine
4	Pham Sushi	4	Adams Café
5	500	5	Tinello

SURVEY HIGHEST RATINGS

AMBIENCE

OVERALL

AMBIENCE	OVERALL
1 The Ritz Restaurant	1 Le Gavroche
2 Le Gavroche	2 The Ledbury
3 The Ledbury	3 The Ritz Restaurant
4 L'Atelier de Joel Robuchon	4 Marcus Wareing
5 Marcus Wareing	5 Dinner
1 Min Jiang	1 Chez Bruce
2 Les Trois Garçons	2 Min Jiang
3 Paramount	3 Scott's
4 Scott's	4 J Sheekey
5 Belvedere	5 The Goring Hotel
1 Clos Maggiore	1 Trinity
2 La Poule au Pot	2 Clos Maggiore
3 Café du Marché	3 Pollen Street Social
4 The Wallace	4 La Trompette
5 Galvin La Chapelle	5 Galvin La Chapelle
1 Wapping Food	1 Upstairs Bar
2 Andrew Edmunds	2 Barrafina
3 Upstairs Bar	3 J Sheekey Oyster Bar
4 The Oak	4 Sushi-Say
5 Barrafina	5 Babur
1 Gordon's Wine Bar	1 Kaffeine
2 Paradise	2 Paradise
3 El Pirata	3 Ganapati
4 La Buvette	4 500
5 Polpetto	5 Tinello

SURVEY BEST BY CUISINE

These are the restaurants which received the best average food ratings (excluding establishments with a small or notably local following).

Where the most common types of cuisine are concerned, we present the results in two price-brackets. For less common cuisines, we list the top three, regardless of price.

For further information about restaurants which are particularly notable for their food, see the cuisine lists starting on page 246. These indicate, using an asterisk*, restaurants which offer exceptional or very good food.

British, Modern

£50 and over		Under £50	
1	The Ledbury	1	Inside
2	Chez Bruce	2	Tom Ilic
3	Trinity	3	Lamberts
4	Pollen Street Social	4	Emile's
5	The Glasshouse	5	The Sands End

French

£50 and over		Under £50	
1	Le Gavroche	1	Upstairs Bar
2	Pied à Terre	2	Brawn
3	Morgan M	3	Bistrot Bruno Loubet
4	La Trompette	4	Le Cercle
5	The Square	5	Comptoir Gascon

Italian/Mediterranean

£50 and over		Under £50	
1	Murano	1	Zucca
2	The River Café	2	500
3	Assaggi	3	Dehesa
4	Enoteca Turi	4	Le Querce
5	Bocca Di Lupo	5	Latium

Indian & Pakistani

£50 and over		Under £50	
1	Zaika	1	Ragam
2	Amaya	2	Babur
3	Trishna	3	New Tayyabs
4	Café Spice Namaste	4	Indian Zing
5	The Cinnamon Club	5	Lahore Kebab House

Chinese

£50 and over
1. Hunan
2. Min Jiang
3. Yauatcha
4. Kai Mayfair
5. Royal China Club

Under £50
1. Taiwan Village
2. Pearl Liang
3. Ba Shan
4. Barshu
5. Ken Lo's Memories

Japanese

£50 and over
1. Roka W1
2. Zuma
3. Umu
4. Yashin
5. Nobu

Under £50
1. Dinings
2. Café Japan
3. Sushi-Say
4. Jin Kichi
5. Pham Sushi

British, Traditional
1. Dinner
2. Scott's
3. Bull & Last

Vegetarian
1. Vanilla Black
2. Roussillon
3. Mildred's

Burgers, etc
1. Lucky Seven
2. Automat
3. Joe Allen

Pizza
1. Franco Manca
2. Santa Maria
3. Donna Margherita

Fish & Chips
1. Golden Hind
2. Toff's
3. Two Brothers

Thai
1. Sukho Fine Thai Cuisine
2. Nahm
3. Isarn

Steaks & Grills
1. Buen Ayre
2. Hawksmoor
3. Goodman City

Fish & Seafood
1. One-O-One
2. J.Sheekey
3. Scott's

Fusion
1. Viajante
2. E&O
3. Caravan

Spanish
1. Barrafina
2. Dehesa
3. El Parador

Turkish
1. Mangal 1
2. Cyprus Mangal
3. Gem

Lebanese
1. Maroush
2. Yalla Yalla
3. Al-Waha

TOP SPECIAL DEALS

The following menus allow you to eat in the restaurants concerned at a significant discount when compared to their evening à la carte prices.

The prices used are calculated in accordance with our usual formula (i.e. three courses with house wine, coffee and tip).

Special menus are by their nature susceptible to change – please check that they are still available.

Weekday lunch

£60+ Gordon Ramsay
Hélène Darroze
Marcus Wareing
Rib Room

£55+ L'Atelier de Joel Robuchon
Dinner
Sketch (Lecture Rm)
The Square

£50+ The Bingham
The Capital Restaurant
Dorchester Grill
Le Gavroche
Gordon Ramsay at Claridge's
Hibiscus
Kai Mayfair
maze
maze Grill
Murano
Rasoi
Roussillon

£45+ Blakes
Cassis Bistro
The Greenhouse
Pearl
Pied à Terre
Roux At Parliament Square
Texture
Viajante

£40+ Athenaeum
Babylon
Belvedere
China Tang
Galvin at Windows
Kicca
Paramount
Quaglino's
Rhodes W1 Restaurant
Seven Park Place
Spice Market

£35+ Criterion
Daphne's
Frederick's
Goodman
High Timber
Kitchen W8
Little Italy

Lucio
Mitsukoshi
Momo
Mon Plaisir
Montpeliano
Notting Hill Brasserie
Pellicano
Tamarind
Les Trois Garçons
Verta
The Warrington

£30+ Arbutus
The Ark
L'Aventure
Bistro K
Bocca Di Lupo
Café Luc
Caponata
Chabrot Bistrot d'Amis
Charlotte's Bistro
Charlotte's Place
Cinnamon Kitchen
City Miyama
Colony
Le Deuxième
Essenza
Fish Place
The Forge
Frantoio
Harrison's
Kiku
The Meat & Wine Co
Rock & Rose
Suk Saran
Timo
Verru

£25+ Admiral Codrington
Ambassador
Benja
Café des Amis
Cantina del Ponte
Carnevale
Chez Patrick
Les Deux Salons
Electric Brasserie
Franklins
Fratelli la Bufala
Gastro
Grumbles

Hix Oyster & Chop House
The Hoxton Grill
Lots Road
Market
Polish Club
Ozer
Princess Victoria
The Rose & Crown
Rossopomodoro
Sonny's
Sophie's Steakhouse
Venosi
Wine Gallery
XO
Zayna

Origin Asia
La Petite Auberge
El Pirata
Le Sacré-Coeur
Sapori
Seasons Dining Room
Tentazioni
Thali
Woodlands
Yming

£20+ Al Forno
Chez Lindsay
Cocotte
Ganapati
Gessler at Daquise
Giraffe
Mogul
Naga
The Old Bull & Bush

£15+ The Bountiful Cow
Café Japan
Fairuz
54 Farringdon Road
Fish in a Tie
Galicia
Kolossi Grill
Mona Lisa
Sagar

£10+ Inshoku
Mirch Masala

Pre/post theatre (and early evening)

£55+ Pied à Terre

Quo Vadis
Zaika

£50+ L'Atelier de Joel Robuchon
Galvin at Windows
Massimo
maze Grill

£30+ The Almeida
Arbutus
Bocca Di Lupo
Le Deuxième
L'Escargot
The Forge
Mon Plaisir

£40+ Indigo
Spice Market

£35+ The Avenue
Bank Westminster
Brasserie Joël
Brasserie Roux
Christopher's
Circus
Criterion
Daphne's
Dean Street Townhouse
Franco's
Frederick's
Little Italy
Orso

£25+ Les Deux Salons
54 Farringdon Road
Grumbles
Hix
Menier Chocolate Factory
Ozer

£20+ Yming

Sunday lunch

£60+ The Capital Restaurant

£45+ Launceston Place

£30+ Como Lario
The Spread Eagle

£25+ Elephant Royale
Lots Road

THE RESTAURANT SCENE

Openings finally show the strain

This year we record 107 openings, well down on last year (140) and somewhat below the range generally observed during the 'noughties' (120 to 142). At 71, however, closings are barely changed from last year (72), and well within the usual range. (See lists on pages 22 and 23.)

The ratio of openings to closings stands at an historically low level of 1.5:1. If the normal five year trough-to-trough cycle we have observed for the past two decades is followed, however, next year looks set to see an even lower ratio of openings to closings. In short, in purely numerical terms, things may get worse before they get better.

... as diners turn away from hype and celebrity, and towards quality

Let's not get too hung up on the numbers, though: the most important thing about the current restaurant scene is that it's maturing, and maturing in a very good way too.

Back in the '90s, the restaurants 'everyone' was talking about were Sir Terence Conran's big, brash 'gastrodromes'. This was an age when the food pages talked a lot about 'Modern British' cooking, and every dish came with a raspberry coulis. The fad soon passed.

Then, in the early noughties, Gordon Ramsay hogged the limelight. His bright idea was to perfect and popularise – but not much to advance – classic 'haute cuisine'. We found ourselves fretting in this introduction five years ago about the f-word chef's dominance at the top end of the market; potentially stultifying, we said. As it turns out, his dominance of the London market was then at a high point from which it has subsequently rapidly receded.

There were other interesting developments, of course, such as the march of gastropubs, and the 'grass roots' trends in British cooking, often twinned with a focus on sustainability and provenance. But many of the supposed improvements in the quality of London dining were of style rather than substance.

But now London's restaurateurs seem to be doing some serious work. One emblematic trend is the gradual reclaiming of Covent Garden as a 'proper' restaurant destination. Another is the remedying of one of London's longest-standing and most puzzling deficiencies – the (until recently) remarkably poor steakhouse scene.

But most significantly, there's a tangible growth in the pursuit of 'real cooking'. Take a glance at our Editor's top ten picks on the page opposite. With the exception of the *Riding House Café* – none the worse for being a 'fashionable' debut – this year has been all about serious food-led operations. These restaurants are about pursuing the best ingredients, and doing something imaginative with them. London has lagged appallingly on that front. Perhaps 2012 will be remembered for Olympian achievements in the kitchen as well as on the track!

Market trends

The following seem to us to be the trends of the moment:

● London is seeing the launch of a wave of high-class restaurants which emphasise innovative cooking of high quality. Examples include such new openings as *Dinner, Galoupet, Hedone, Medlar, Pollen Street Social* and *Roganic*

● Hotels are investing a lot to make their restaurants relevant to wider audiences. Many are succeeding – four out of the five recent openings debuting on our most-mentioned list (p11) are in hotels

● 'Petits-plats' formulae are becoming so common as to be unremarkable, especially at the upper end of the market

● The most popular flavour for new restaurants, especially in the mid-range, is London's original restaurant comfort-cuisine: Italian

● The culinary spotlight appears to be turning away from 'new' areas, and towards the rejuvenation of long-established restaurant areas, and especially Covent Garden

● The steakhouse boom continues. The more we are told we should eat less meat for the good of the planet, the more of it London diners seem determined to consume.

● America, and in particular New York, is the origin of, or provides the inspiration for, many recent and forthcoming openings – these include *Balthazar, Bar Boulud, Cut* and *Sushisamba,* as well as Russell Norman's *Polpo* empire

● Some variety of the brasserie format remains popular in the middle market, perhaps with most obvious success at *Les Deux Salons* and the *Riding House Café*.

Every year, we select what seem to us personally to be the ten most significant openings of the preceding 12 months. This year, our selection is as follows:

Brawn	Medlar
Les Deux Salons	Pollen Street Social
Dinner	Riding House Cafe
Galoupet	Roganic
Hedone	Yashin

This is a very strong field. Difficult economic conditions have not impacted adversely on the quality of new openings.

Prices

The average price of dinner for one at establishments listed in the guide is £45.01. Prices have risen by an unprecedented 11.1% in the past 12 months. Just over 2% of this may be attributed to the January 2011 increase in the rate of VAT. Pre-tax prices are therefore up some 9% year-on-year. This extraordinary rise has to be seen as a 'rebound' after a very marginal (0.3%) increase in pre-tax prices the year before: if we look back at the past *two* years together, prices are seen to have risen by 'only' 4.5% per annum over the period.

OPENINGS AND CLOSURES

Openings (107)

Alyn Williams
Amaranto
Anokha Restaurant (EC4)
Antidote
Aurelia
Balthazar
Benito's Hat (W1)
Bennett Oyster Bar & Brasserie
Bistro du Vin (W1, EC1)
Boisdale of Canary Wharf
Brawn
Bread Street Kitchen
Caffè Vergnano (EC4)
Canonbury Kitchen
Canta Napoli (N12)
Cantinetta
Capote Y Toros
Casa Malevo
Cavallino
Cây Tre (W1)
Chabrot Bistrot d'Amis
Charm
Chiswell Street Dining Rooms
Le Cigalon
Cocorino (W1)
Cocotte
Corner Room
Cut
da Polpo
La Delizia (SW18)
Dragoncello
E l l even Park Walk
Eighty-Six Bar and Restaurant
The English Pig
Entrée
Fish Place
Four Seasons (W1)
Fox & Grapes
Frankie's Italian Bar & Grill (SW6)
Fulham Wine Rooms
The Gallery
Galoupet
Geales Chelsea Green (SW3)
Gilbert Scott
The Grand Imperial
Grazing Goat
Hawksmoor (EC2)
Hedone
The Henry Root
Homa
Ibérica (E14)
Ilia
Inamo (SW1)
Indian Zilla
Jam Tree (SW6)
José
Kateh
Kazan (Cafe) (SW1)
Kentish Canteen
Kerbisher & Malt
Kimchee
Kopapa
Ladurée (WC2)
Lahore Kebab House (SW16)
Lupita
Made In Camden
Mar I Terra (W1)
Massimo
Medlar
Mill Lane Bistro
Morito
Nizuni
Nopi
Nordic Bakery (W1)
Novikov
Opera Tavern
Otto Pizza
Pizarro
Pizza East Portobello
Pollen Street Social
Quantus
Le Querce (SE3)
Quince
Raoul's Café & Deli (W6)
Riding House Café
Rocca Di Papa (SE21)
Roganic
Roots At N1
Samarqand
Smith Square Bar & Restaurant
La Sophia

Openings (cont'd)

Spice Market
Spuntino
Sushisamba
Tempo
Thali
34 Grosvenor Square
Tsuru *(EC4)*
Union Street Café
Venosi

Verru
Verta
Vinoteca Seymour
  Place *(W1)*
Watatsumi
Yalla Yalla *(W1)*
Yashin

Closures (71)

Artisan
Arturo
Atma
Aubergine
Baretto
Battery
Bermondsey Kitchen
Blue Elephant
Bombay Bicycle Club
  (SW10, NW3)
Café Mozart
Cantina Italia
Carpaccio's
Chez Kristof
Coast
Cocoon
Donzoko
Eastside Inn
Emni
Faro
Fat Badger
Fish Shop
Frankie's Italian
  Bar & Grill *(W4)*
Friends
Fung Shing
Garbo's
Gem & I
Gilmour's
Green & Red Bar & Cantina
Green Chilli
Izakaya Aki
Just St James
Kastoori
Kazan *(EC3)*
Konstam

L-Restaurant & Bar
Langan's Coq d'Or Bar
  & Grill
Locale
Ma Cuisine *(TW1,TW9)*
Maroush III *(W1)*
Metrogusto
Michael Moore
Monsieur M.
More
101 Pimlico Road
Osteria Emilia
Otarian
Red Pepper
Rooburoo
Rosemary Lane
The Rye
S & M Café *(SE10)*
Sargasso
Seaport
Seasons Dining Room
Story Deli
Sushi-Hiro
Taman Gang
Tampopo
Tartufo Trattoria
Taste of McClements
La Trouvaille
Urban Turban
Via Condotti
Villandry Kitchen *(WC1,W4)*
Vineria
W55
Wine Factory
Wódka

EATING IN LONDON FAQs

How should I use this guide?

You will often wish to use this guide in a practical way.
At heart, the issue will usually be geographical – where can
we eat near…? To answer such questions, the Maps (from
page 300) and Area Overviews (from page 262) are the
place to start. The latter tell you all the key facts about the
restaurants – perhaps dozens of 'em – in a particular area in
the space of a couple of pages. These Area Overviews are
unique, so please do spend a second to have a look!

This section, though, is about seeking out new places when
you want to be inspired to make a culinary adventure for its
own sake, or you need to find a venue for a special event.

What makes London special?

Each year in recent times we've had to re-write this section!
In the old days, the answer was always easy. London was like
New York: it offered lots of cuisines (good), but few done
especially well (bad). It was the very opposite of Paris, where
essentially one cuisine was endlessly elaborated.

Nowadays, the London story is both more interesting and
more positive. Not only is there cosmopolitanism, there is also
quality. It is the combination of the two which – at long last –
is making London a city which can genuinely claim to be one of
the world's best places to eat. We'll cover some culinary fields
particularly worth exploring on the following two pages, but
first let's dispose of that hoary old chestnut…

Which is London's best restaurant?

It's getting more and more difficult to say, because the old
certainties are breaking down. But let's stick with the
traditional 'haute cuisine' definition. On that basis, the safest
choice is the oldest – Le Gavroche is London's original grand
restaurant of the modern era, and it remains the very best
place to eat in the centre of town.

The second best restaurant – The Ledbury – is interesting
precisely because it's everything that the Gavroche is not.
The chef is Antipodean, not of French descent. It is in
Notting Hill, not Mayfair. The style is svelte and modern, not
the very essence of classicism. The Ledbury, in short, is a
worthy champion of the newer style that has begun to
transform London's restaurant scene of late.

For our third choice, though, we go back in time to The Ritz.
It has always been famous for its Louis XVI-style interior
but improving food is beginning to make this a destination
for any sort of celebration, not just for romance.

For other truly tip-top suggestions, please use the lists on
pages 14-15.

What about something a little more reasonably priced?

Although no one would say that London is a cheap place to eat, it is getting much easier to find food well worth eating without paying a fortune for it.

Most notable in this category is the group formed around 'London's favourite restaurant' for the 7th successive year, *Chez Bruce* (Wandsworth), plus its siblings *La Trompette* (Chiswick) and the *Glasshouse* (Kew). (That group also includes the Ledbury, mentioned on the previous page.)

Other hidden jewels out in Zones 2 and 3 include *Chez Liline* (Finsbury Park), *Morgan M* (Islington), *Trinity* (Clapham), *Lambert's* (Balham) and that wonderful '70s period-piece, *Oslo Court* (St John's Wood)

What about some really good suggestions in the heart of the West End?

It used to be practically impossible to find a really good meal in the heart of London at any reasonable cost! No longer, fortunately.

Names particularly to consider include *Arbutus*, *Giaconda Dining Room*, *Galvin Bistrot de Luxe* and *Wild Honey*. If you're happy to eat more in tapas style, add to this list *Barrafina* (be prepared to queue), *Bocca di Lupo*, *Dehesa*, *Polpo* and *Terroirs*.

If you want a little more comfort and style, as well as pretty good food you're unlikely to go far wrong at the restaurant which attracts most survey attention, *J Sheekey*, a fish specialist hidden-away in the very heart of Theatreland, or at *Scott's*, a celebrity magnet on one of the grandest streets in Mayfair. These last are hardly bargain suggestions, but they do offer all-round value. For pure theatre, a visitor should probably try to eat at the *Wolseley* – the nation's 'grand café', by the Ritz – at some point. Breakfast or tea provide excellent opportunities!

It is a symbol of the recent improvements in Covent Garden that *Clos Maggiore* – newly-crowned as 'London's most romantic restaurant', and with an extraordinary wine list – is on full public view just a few paces from the market itself! A more recent opening of note is the *Opera Tavern*.

And don't forget to lunch!

Lunch in London can be a great bargain. Restaurants don't come much grander than *Le Gavroche*, for example, and it famously offers a superb-value all-in lunch – even including some very decent wine – for less than many relatively run-of-the-mill establishments end up charging for a basic dinner. For further top value suggestion, see the list on pages 18 and 19.

And for the best of British?

British food – long confined to a sort of tourist ghetto – has recently become very fashionable. The change all began with the Smithfield restaurant *St John*, whose bravery and dedication to old-fashioned (and usually offal-heavy) British cooking has won it international acclaim. The trend that St John kicked off when it opened back in 1994 has recently culminated in the opening of Heston Blumenthal's much-heralded *Dinner* (Knightsbridge) – it is not meant as a backhanded compliment to describe it as an opening which has almost lived up to the hype! Tables do need to be booked weeks, and possibly months, ahead.

Other restaurants which may to be said to be from the school of St John include *Magdalen* (South Bank), *Great Queen Street* (Covent Garden), *Hereford Road* (Bayswater) and *St John Bread & Wine* (Shoreditch). In a different idiom, the recently opened *Gilbert Scott* reflects another 'take' on the reviving interest in more obscure British recipes.

But a lot of 'British' cooking is taking place in gastropubs...

What are gastropubs?

These are essentially bistros in pub premises. They come in a variety of styles. What many people think of as the original gastropub (*The Eagle*, 1991) still looks very much like a pub with a food counter. At the other end of the scale, however, the 'pub' element is almost redundant, and the business is really just a restaurant housed in premises that happen once to have been a pub.

Few of the best gastropubs are particularly central. The handy location of the *Anchor & Hope*, on the South Bank, is no doubt part of the reason for its great popularity. Other stars include the *Bull & Last* (Kentish Town), the *Canton Arms* (Stockwell) and the *Harwood Arms* (Fulham).

Isn't London supposed to be a top place for curry?

London has a reasonable claim to being the world's top Indian restaurant city. Leading lights such as *Amaya*, *The Painted Heron*, *The Cinnamon Kitchen*, *Benares*, *Rasoi*, *Trishna* and *Zaika* are pushing back the frontiers, but – perfectly reasonably – charge the same as their European equivalents.

What's more exciting in terms of value are the many Indian restaurants where you can eat much more cheaply than you could eat European. There are too many of them to list here – search out the asterisked restaurants in the Indian and Pakistani lists commencing on pages 257 and 259 respectively.

Two top names in the East End are, however, almost legendary 'value' experiences – the *Lahore Kebab House* and *New Tayyabs*. The *Rasa* group also includes some very good value options.

Any money-saving tips?

● The top tip, already noted, is to lunch not dine. If you're a visitor, you'll find that it's better for your wallet, as well as your digestion, to have your main meal in the middle of the day. In the centre of town, it's one of the best ways you can be sure of eating 'properly' at reasonable cost. See the spread on pages 18 and 19.

● Think ethnic – for a food 'experience' at modest cost, you'll almost always be better off going Indian, Thai, Chinese or Vietnamese (to choose four of the most obvious cuisines) than French, English or Italian. The days when there was any sort of assumption that ethnic restaurants were – in terms of comfort, service and décor – in any way inferior to European ones is long gone, but they do still tend to be cheaper.

● Don't assume the West End is the obvious destination. That's not to say that – armed with this book – you shouldn't be able to eat well in the heart of things, but you'll almost certainly do better in value terms outside the Circle line. Many of the best and cheapest restaurants in this guide are easily accessible by tube. Use the maps at the back of this book to identify restaurants near tube stations on a line that's handy for you.

● If you must dine in the West End, try to find either pre-theatre (generally before 7 pm) or post-theatre (generally after 10 pm) menus. You will generally save at least the cost of a cinema ticket, compared to dining à la carte. Many of the more upmarket restaurants in Theatreland do such deals. For some of our top suggestions, see page 19.

● Use this book! Don't take pot luck, when you can benefit from the pre-digested views of thousands of other diners-out. Choose a place with a ❶ or ❷ for food, and you're very likely to eat much better than if you walk in somewhere 'on spec' – this is good advice anywhere, but is most particularly so in the West End.

● Once you have decided that you want to eat within a particular area, use the Area Overviews (starting on p262) to identify the restaurants that are offering top value. We have gone to a lot of trouble to boil down a huge amount of data into the results which are handily summarised in such lists. Please use them! You are unlikely to regret it.

● Visit our website, www.hardens.com for the latest reviews, and restaurant news, and to sign up for our annual spring survey.

DIRECTORY

Comments in "double quotation-marks" were made
by reporters.

Establishments which we judge to be particularly
notable have their NAME IN CAPITALS.

A Cena TW1 £48 ❷❷❷
418 Richmond Rd   8288 0108   1–4A
One of the best restaurants round Richmond, this "first-class local Italian", in St Margaret's, combines a "delightful" setting and "superb" service, with "enjoyable" food and an "impressive" selection of "well-priced" wine. / www.acena.co.uk; 10 pm; closed Mon L & Sun D; booking: max 6, Fri & Sat.

A La Cruz EC1 £49 ❸❸④
42 Northampton Rd   7837 1999   9–1A
"Superb steak, awesome chips and outstanding red wine" – all help inspire enthusiasm for this "good-value" Argentinian parilla, in Farringdon. / www.alacruz.com; 10pm, Sat & Sun 9.30pm; closed weekday L; no Amex.

The Abbeville SW4 £45 ④❸❷
67-69 Abbeville Rd   8675 2201   10–2D
An "exceptionally welcoming" Clapham local, which draws fans from numerous nearby postcodes with its "lovely" ambience; the food is "frustratingly variable", but "more often good than bad". / www.renaissancepubs.co.uk; 10.30 pm, Sun 9 pm.

Abeno £36 ❸❷④
47 Museum St, WC1   7405 3211   2–1C
17-18 Great Newport St, WC2   7379 1160   4–3B
"Having the food cooked at your table is a fun bonus", at these rather "different" okonomi-yaki (fancy Japanese omelettes) parlours in the West End – "friendly little places", and in "handy" locations too; they can, though, "get a bit hot and crowded". / www.abeno.co.uk; 10 pm-midnight; WC2 no booking.

The Abingdon W8 £52 ❸❷❷
54 Abingdon Rd   7937 3339   5–2A
"Perfectly suiting the needs of its locale", this "gently buzzing" pub-conversion, off Kensington High Street, offers food "at the finer end of gastropub", and "accommodating" service too; it makes a great choice for a "casual" meal – try to book a booth at the back. / www.theabingdon.co.uk; Mon 10.30 pm, Sun 9.30 pm.

Abokado £16 ④❸④
16 Newman St, W1   7636 9218   2–1B
160 Drury Ln, WC2   7242 5600   4–2D
The Lexington, 40-56 City Rd, EC1   7608 2620   12–1A
63 Cowcross St, EC1   7490 4303   9–1A
33 Fleet St, EC4   7353 8284   9–2A
"A novel and interesting lunchtime option" – these good alternatives to Pret offer "no-hassle, healthy bites" (udon-noodle soups, wraps, and so on) to "eat on the run". / www.abokado.com; 7.30 pm; no Amex; no booking.

About Thyme SW1 £45 ❷❶④
82 Wilton Rd   7821 7504   2–4B
"Classy" by local standards, this Pimlico restaurant serves an "enjoyable mix" of Spanish-influenced dishes, and some "superb regional wines"; tables are rather "packed-in", but staff are particularly "friendly and professional". / www.aboutthyme.co.uk; 10.30 pm; closed Sun.

L'Absinthe NW1 £38 ❸❶❷
40 Chalcot Rd   7483 4848   8–3B
"So French it hurts!"; service that's authentic "almost to the point of parody" breathes character into this "delightful" Primrose Hill corner spot, which serves a sensibly "limited" menu of "good-value" bistro fare. / www.labsinthe.co.uk; 10.30 pm, Sun 9.30 pm; closed Mon.

Abu Zaad W12 £24 ❸❸④
29 Uxbridge Rd 8749 5107 7–1C
"A long-running Syrian favourite", near Shepherd's Bush Market;
its "fresh and beautifully-prepared" dishes – including "super grills
and juices", and excellent mezze – offer "great value".
/ www.abuzaad.co.uk; 11 pm; no Amex.

L'Accento Italiano W2 £42 ❸②❸
16 Garway Rd 7243 2201 6–1B
"Genuine family-Italian cooking", a "well-chosen fixed-price menu"
and a "decent" wine list – the features which continue to satisfy the
small fan club of this "solid" Bayswater fixture, recently revamped.
/ www.laccentorestaurant.co.uk; 11 pm, Sun 6 pm; closed Sun L.

Acorn House WC1 £45 ④④⑤
69 Swinton St 7812 1842 8–3D
In "an odd location on a busy Bloomsbury road", an "interesting little
organic place", where eco-consciousness is a theme, and "excellent
seasonal ingredients are the focus"; even fans feel the cooking "needs
to sharpen up", though, and the "squashed-in" dining room, in the
style of a "railway carriage", is no particular advantage.
/ www.acornhouserestaurant.com; 10 pm; closed Sat L & Sun.

Adam Street WC2 £60 ④④❷
9 Adam St 7379 8000 4–4D
It's the relaxing and enjoyable vibe of this "discreet" private members'
club, "tucked-away off the Strand", which makes it a handy venue for
business lunches (and the wine list is pretty good too) – the food
"is not impressive". / www.adamstreet.co.uk; L only, closed Sat & Sun.

Adams Café W12 £29 ❸❶❷
77 Askew Rd 8743 0572 7–1B
"Delicious" tagines, couscous and grills in "plentiful" quantities have
made a firm "local favourite" of this "super-friendly" Tunisian café,
in the backwoods of Shepherd's Bush; by day, it's a greasy spoon;
licensed, or you can BYO (£3 corkage). / www.adamscafe.co.uk; 11 pm;
closed Sun.

Addie's Thai Café SW5 £30 ❷❷❸
121 Earl's Court Rd 7259 2620 5–2A
A "fast and furious" joint, near Earl's Court tube, worth seeking out
for its "extraordinarily good Thai food", and "at bargain prices too".
/ www.addiesthai.co.uk; 11 pm; closed Sat L & Sun L; no Amex.

Admiral Codrington SW3 £47 ❸④❸
17 Mossop St 7581 0005 5–2C
"Excellent" steaks are a "surprise menu highlight" at this airy and
"pleasant" dining room attached to a "noisy" (and perennially
fashionable) Chelsea pub; with its sliding roof, it makes a "delightful
summer location" too. / www.theadmiralcodrington.co.uk; 11 pm;
set weekday L £29 (FP).

Afghan Kitchen N1 £21 ❷④④
35 Islington Grn 7359 8019 8–3D
A "teeny" café, by Islington Green, serving a "limited menu"
of "cheap and delicious" Afghani curries; service can be "short",
and the interior is very "cramped" and "crowded", so "take-away
is an option worth bearing in mind". / 11 pm; closed Mon & Sun;
no credit cards.

Aglio e Olio SW10 £37 ❸❸❸
194 Fulham Rd   7351 0070   5–3B
"A jam-packed" café, by the Chelsea & Westminster Hospital, that's "the epitome of cheap 'n' cheerful"; "it may be noisy and cramped", but – "year in, year out" – it serves "outstanding" pasta, and other reliable fare. / 11.30 pm.

Al Duca SW1 £45 ❹❹❺
4-5 Duke of York St   7839 3090   3–3D
Prepare yourself for "small portions", "tightly-packed tables" and a "lack of atmosphere", but the "simple, modern food" on offer at this low-key Italian comes at bargain prices – well, St James's-style bargain prices anyway. / www.alduca-restaurant.co.uk; 11 pm; closed Sun.

Al Forno £39 ❸❷❷
349 Upper Richmond Rd, SW15   8878 7522   10–2A
2a King's Rd, SW19   8540 5710   10–2B
"Hilarious staff and cosy surroundings" all contribute to the "quirky" experience of visiting these busy traditional Italians – "a perfect place with friends", and "excellent for kids" too, with "biiiggg pizza" the star of the "tasty" menu. / SW15 11 pm; SW19 11.30 pm, Sun & Mon 10.30 pm; set weekday L £23 (FP).

Al Hamra W1 £46 ❹❺❹
31-33 Shepherd Mkt   7493 1954   3–4B
"For a true taste of Lebanon", say fans, seek out this Shepherd Market "classic" (which benefits from some fine al fresco tables); as ever, though, it can seem "seriously overpriced", and service is sometimes "terrible". / www.alhamrarestaurant.co.uk; 11.30 pm.

Al Sultan W1 £43 ❷❸❺
51-52 Hertford St   7408 1155   3–4B
"Let the wonderful Lebanese food beguile you", when you visit this "professional" little place, near Shepherd Market; if you're looking for atmosphere, though, you might want to try elsewhere. / www.alsultan.co.uk; midnight.

Al Volo
The Old Truman Brewery E1 £32 ❷❹❸
Hanbury St   7377 0808   12–2C
A "perennial favourite", in the heart of Brick Lane; this trendy Italian café "continues to serve up delicious food at very reasonable prices" – cognoscenti go for the calzone. / www.alvolo.co.uk; Sun-Wed 10 pm, Thu-Sat 11 pm.

Al-Waha W2 £42 ❷❸❹
75 Westbourne Grove   7229 0806   6–1B
"Squashed" and anonymous-looking the premises may be, but this Bayswater "stand-out" offers "unexpectedly fabulous" Lebanese food, and at "affordable prices" too. / www.alwaharestaurant.com; 11 pm; no Amex.

Alain Ducasse
Dorchester W1 £111 ❹❹❹
53 Park Ln   7629 8866   3–3A
"How is this three Michelin Stars?"; the notion that this opulent but "slightly dead" Mayfair dining room is one of London's best is a joke – reporters do have some "fabulous" experiences, of course, but there are far too many visits which "lack flair"; either way, your wallet is pretty much guaranteed "a heart attack". / www.alainducasse-dorchester.com; 10 pm; closed Mon, Sat L & Sun; jacket.

Alba EC1 £52 ❸②④
107 Whitecross St 7588 1798 12–2A
*"Precise Piedmontese cooking", a "very good Italian wine list",
and "the friendliest service" have won a super-loyal following for this
"upmarket" (but slightly "sterile") stalwart, especially as a "business
lunch and post-Barbican stand-by". / www.albarestaurant.com; 11 pm;
closed Sat & Sun.*

Albannach WC2 £51 ⑤⑤⑤
66 Trafalgar Sq 7930 0066 2–3C
*As a cocktail bar it's fine, but the food at this Scottish-themed venue,
on Trafalgar Square, can be "quite dreadful"; service is "slow" too,
and don't expect to hear any Caledonian accents among the kilted
staff! / www.albannach.co.uk; 10.45 pm, Sun 6 pm; closed Sun D.*

Albertine W12 £33 ④②⓿
1 Wood Ln 8743 9593 7–1C
*OK, it's "more a wine bar with food than a restaurant with wine",
but this "cramped" fixture makes a "quirky" and "Bohemian" refuge
from "the urban desert of Shepherd's Bush Green"; there are "lots of
interesting bottles" on offer too. / 10.30 pm; closed Sat L & Sun; no Amex.*

The Albion N1 £42 ④④❷
10 Thornhill Rd 7607 7450 8–3D
*"In a quiet and leafy part of Islington", this "lovely" boozer is famous
for its "wonderful" garden; otherwise, though, it's pretty ordinary –
service can be "slow", and the food is only "moderately good".
/ www.the-albion.co.uk; 10 pm, Sun 9 pm.*

Albion E2 £44 ❸❸❷
2-4 Boundary St 7729 1051 12–1B
*"A Formica heaven for the casual scoffer!" – Sir Terence Conran's
"brilliant" neighbourhood caff "fits like a glove into Shoreditch",
and succeeds in "accommodating mums in prams and local arty
types alike"; its "ribsticking British food" is "unpretentious, and tasty"
too. / www.albioncaff.co.uk; 11 pm.*

Ali Baba NW1 £19 ❸②❸
32 Ivor Pl 7723 5805 2–1A
*"Recently the TV has been focused on current affairs" –
understandable enough, at this "family-run and very authentic"
Egyptian, in a front room behind a Marylebone take-away; BYO.
/ midnight; no credit cards.*

Alisan HA9 £35 ⓿②④
The Junction, Engineers Way, Wembley 8903 3888 1–1A
*"Granted, it's not the best location" – "in an industrial estate,
opposite Wembley Stadium" – but this contemporary-style Chinese
is worth a trip for its "very interesting and different dim sum";
and there's "free, easy parking" too! / www.alisan.co.uk; 11 pm,
Sat 11.30 pm, Sun 10.30 pm; closed Tue.*

All Star Lanes £45 ④⑤❸
Victoria Hs, Bloomsbury Pl, WC1 7025 2676 2–1D
Whiteley's, 6 Porchester Gdns, W2 7313 8363 6–1C
Old Truman Brewery, 95 Brick Ln, E1 7426 9200 12–2C
*"Considering the food is incidental to the bowling", the cooking
at these "fun" 10-pin venues could be a lot worse, with "fab burgers"
the top tip; they are "a little overpriced", though, and the waiters
"don't have a great attitude". / www.allstarlanes.co.uk; WC1 10.30 pm,
Fri & Sat midnight, Sun 9 pm; E1 10 pm; W2 10.30 pm, Fri-Sun 11 pm;
WC1 & W2 closed L Mon-Thu.*

Alloro W1   £57   ❸❸❸
19-20 Dover St   7495 4768   3–3C
"Ideal for business", this *"smart"* and *"spacious"* Mayfair Italian offers a *"high standard"* of cooking; the downside? – it can seem a little *"dull"*. / www.alloro-restaurant.co.uk; 10.30 pm; closed Sat L & Sun.

Alma SW18   £39   ❹❺❸
499 Old York Rd   8870 2537   10–2B
The year that's seen the revamp of this *"madly-popular"* Wandsworth boozer has inspired very mixed feedback – let's hope for fewer reports of *"disastrous"* meals next year! / www.thealma.co.uk; 10.30 pm, Sun 9 pm.

The Almeida N1   £59   ❹❸❹
30 Almeida St   7354 4777   8–2D
"One of the D&D stable's better restaurants", this large Islington dining room is a *"civilised"* venue, serving *"competent"* Gallic fare, and as a pre-theatre option – prior to a show opposite – it works perfectly; on the downside, the decor can seem *"cold"*, and the cooking *"mediocre, for the price"*. / www.almeida-restaurant.co.uk; 10.30 pm; closed Mon L & Sun D; set pre theatre £33 (FP).

Alounak   £27   ❸❹❸
10 Russell Gdns, W14   7603 1130   7–1D
44 Westbourne Grove, W2   7229 0416   6–1B
"Superb" kebabs and other *"lovely, fresh Persian dishes"*, all in *"ample portions"*, help explain the *"regular queues"* for these *"inexpensive"* BYO Iranian cafés, in Bayswater and Olympia. / 11.30 pm; no Amex.

Alyn Williams
Westbury Hotel W1 NEW
Bond St   7629 7755   3–2C
Good omens for this late-2011 'fine dining' opening, in Mayfair; until recently, Williams headed up Marcus Wareing's kitchen, and the hotel seems to have had quite a success with its other recent dining debut, the Gallery. / www.westburymayfair.com.

Amaranth SW18   £30   ❷❷❸
346 Garratt Ln   8874 9036   10–2B
"Always a winner" – this *"busy"* Thai café, in Earlsfield, makes *"a great cheap and cheerful place to eat"*, with *"ever-fresh"* dishes and *"helpful"* staff; you can BYO too (corkage £2.50). / 10.30 pm; D only, closed Sun; no Amex.

Amaranto
Four Seasons Hotel W1 NEW   £75
Hamilton Pl   7319 5206   3–4A
Reporter excitement about this luxurious new Mayfair dining room seems to be in inverse proportion to the vast expenditure on its blingy decor – too little, in fact, even for a rating; such feedback as there is is talks of *"flappy"* service of Italian food that's *"fussy"* and *"overpriced"*. / www.fourseasons.com; 10.30 pm.

Amaya SW1   £63   ❶❷❷
Halkin Arc, 19 Motcomb St   7823 1166   5–1D
"Style and flair" abound at this *"simply outstanding"* nouvelle Indian – one of London's best – tucked-away in Belgravia; many of its *"innovative"*, *"light"* and *"flavourful"* tapas-style dishes come from a central grill. / www.realindianfood.com; 11.30 pm, Sun 10.30 pm.

Ambassador EC1 £41 ❸❸❸
55 Exmouth Mkt 7837 0009 9–1A
With its "stripped-down bistro look", this Clerkenwell venture strikes
harsher reporters as looking "a little uncared-for"; "it does what
it does well", though, including "solid and flavourful" dishes,
and "well-matched wine". / www.theambassadorcafe.co.uk; 10.15 pm;
set weekday L £26 (FP).

Amerigo Vespucci E14 £43 ❹❹❸
25 Cabot Sq 7513 0288 11–1C
A "decent" traditional Italian which has particular attractions for
Canary Wharf chain-o-phobes – "the best thing going for it is that it's
not part of a larger group". / www.amerigovespucci.co.uk; 11 pm; closed
Sat L & Sun L.

Amico Bio EC1 £37 ❹❹❹
43-44 Cloth Fair 7600 7778 9–2B
"Tucked-away behind Bart's", this meat-free Italian is "such a good
concept"; it's a "shame, then, that it doesn't quite deliver" – the food
"may sound fantastic", but the results can be "rather patchy".
/ www.amicobio.co.uk; 10.30 pm; closed Sat L & Sun.

Anarkali W6 £32 ❸❷❸
303-305 King St 8748 1760 7–2B
"At last it's back, and back on form!"; to the relief of regulars,
this Hammersmith curry classic has re-opened following a flood –
"I've been going for over 30 years, and the food's even better than
before". / www.anarkalirestaurant.co.uk; midnight, Sun 11.30 pm.

The Anchor & Hope SE1 £39 ❶❸❷
36 The Cut 7928 9898 9–4A
"Other gastropubs pale in comparison", say fans of London's No.1
boozer, near the Old Vic – "a winner on many levels",
but most importantly for the "exciting twist" it puts on "big-flavoured"
British dishes (many with offal); arrive early – "its popularity is its own
worst enemy!" / 10.30 pm; closed Mon L & Sun D; no Amex; no booking.

Andrew Edmunds W1 £43 ❸❷❶
46 Lexington St 7437 5708 3–2D
"Gorgeously scruffy, yet atmospheric", this delightfully "quirky"
candlelit Soho favourite is as perfect as ever for "an intimate tête-à-
tête" – sit upstairs if you can; the "simple" food is reasonably
"inventive", but it's the "superb" wines that offer "outstanding value".
/ 10.30 pm; no Amex; booking: max 6.

Angels & Gypsies
Church Street Hotel SE5 £38 ❷❸❷
29-33 Camberwell Church St 7703 5984 1–3C
"A surprise find in a Camberwell hotel!" – this "cool" but "friendly"
hang-out is "well worth a detour" for its "super-fresh and interesting"
tapas, plus a range of other "fairly-priced" Spanish "classics".
/ www.churchstreethotel.com; 10.30 pm; closed Mon L.

Angelus W2 £78 ❷❶❸
4 Bathurst St 7402 0083 6–2D
"On the way to classic status" – this "cosy" ex-pub, near Lancaster
Gate, is a "very Gallic" and "intimate" spot, serving many "brilliant"
dishes; service is at its best when patron Thierry Thomasin
("the sommelier's sommelier") is there, presiding over his "fantastic"
wine list. / www.angelusrestaurant.co.uk; 11 pm, Sun 10 pm.

The Anglesea Arms SW7   £40   ❸④❷
15 Sellwood Ter   7373 7960   5–2B
A very "buzzy" South Kensington hostelry, which boats a "cosy back restaurant", but is perhaps best known for its bijou terrace; the food's "good value" too… "and all the better for not being at all 'gastro-'"!
/ www.angleseaarms.com; 10 pm, Sun 9.30 pm.

The Anglesea Arms W6   £45   ❷④❷
35 Wingate Rd   8749 1291   7–1B
"It's great now you can book!", say fans of this "unfussy" tavern, near Ravenscourt Park – one of London's original gastropubs and still, for most reporters, "one of the best"; the occasional report of "appalling" meals this year, however, denied it an 'outstanding' food rating. / Mon 10 pm, Tue-Sat 10.30 pm, Sun 9.30 pm; no Amex; no booking.

Anglo Asian Tandoori N16   £34   ❷①❷
60-62 Stoke Newington Church St   7254 3633   1–1C
"Still a cut above most Indian restaurants" – this surprisingly romantic Stoke Newington veteran is showing impressive longevity! / 11.45 pm.

L'Anima EC2   £69   ❸❸❸
1 Snowden St   7422 7000   12–2B
With its "clean" and "craftsmanlike" cooking, Francesco Mazzei's "slick" and "airy" Italian is undoubtedly "a great City restaurant"; of late, however, it's "gone slightly off the boil", and is taking ever more flak for "inconsistent" food and a rather "corporate" ambience.
/ www.lanima.co.uk; 10.30 pm; closed Sat L & Sun.

Annie's   £45   ④❷❷
162 Thames Rd, W4   8994 9080   1–3A
36-38 White Hart Ln, SW13   8878 2020   10–1A
"For a lazy weekend brunch" – in the company of "kids of all ages" – these "cosy" and "eclectically-furnished" havens of shabby-chic, in Chiswick and Barnes, come in to their own; "filling" food of a "comfort" nature plays something of a supporting role.
/ www.anniesrestaurant.co.uk; 10 pm, Sat 10.30 pm, Sun 9.30 pm.

Anokha Restaurant   £42   ❷❸❸
2 Creechurch Lane, EC3   7283 7729   9–2D
4 Burgeon St, EC4   7236 3999   9–3B NEW
These small Indian restaurants – one in a basement near Fenchurch Street station, the other "hidden-away between St Paul's and Blackfriars" – offer some "brilliant" cooking. / 11 pm; EC3 closed Sat-Sun; EC4 closed Sat L and Sun.

Antelope SW17   £36   ❷❸❷
76 Mitcham Rd   8672 3888   10–2C
The Victorian-style dining room at this Tooting pub, recently relaunched, makes "a surprisingly good find", and wins praise for its "interesting" menu, well-chosen wine and "great" beers; the staff attitude is "accommodating" too. / www.antic-ltd.com/antelope; 10.30 pm; closed Mon-Fri L & Sun D; no Amex.

Antidote W1 NEW   £45   ❸④❸
12a Newburgh St   7287 8488   3–2C
The tucked-away Soho site of La Trouvaille (RIP) has now been relaunched (same owners) as a simple and very Gallic wine bar; the food is decent enough, and there's an entertaining list of 'biodynamique' wines, but service on our own early-days visit was Clouseau-meets-Keystone Kops. / Rated on Editors' visit; www.antidotewinebar.com; 10.30 pm; closed Sun D.

Antipasto & Pasta SW11 £38 ❸❷❸
511 Battersea Park Rd 7223 9765 10–1C
"Nothing is too much hassle" for staff at this "manically busy but
entertaining" Battersea Italian, which offers "great food at very
reasonable prices". / 11.30 pm, Sun 11 pm; need 4+ to book.

Apostrophe £17 ❹❸❸
Branches throughout London
A Gallic café-multiple that's still often seen as "a cut above other
coffee house chains", thanks not least to its "terrific coffee" and its
"interesting" snacks; sliding ratings, however, support those who say
it's "not quite at the level it once was". / www.apostropheuk.com;
most branches 6 pm, Sat 5.30 pm; no booking.

Applebee's Cafe SE1 £40 ❷❸❹
5 Stoney St 7407 5777 9–4C
A wet fish counter as you enter advertises the "specialist" attractions
of this "friendly" Borough Market fixture, where the dishes are
"wonderfully fresh and well-prepared". / www.applebeesfish.com; 10 pm,
Fri 10.30 pm.

Apsleys
Lanesborough Hotel SW1 £90 ❸❷❸
1 Lanesborough Pl 7333 7254 5–1D
This "opulent" dining room by Hyde Park Corner, governed from afar
by hot-shot Roman chef Heinz Beck, is starting to win more acclaim;
critics still find it "unexciting" and "nose-bleedingly expensive", but on
many accounts the Italian cooking – pasta in particular – is "simply
incredible". / www.apsleys.co.uk; 10.30 pm; booking: max 12.

aqua kyoto W1 £72 ❸❸❶
240 Regent St (entrance 30 Argyll St) 7478 0540 3–2C
"Set in a beautifully cool, black and red space" – and with
a "wonderful rooftop terrace" – this "lovely" (if "touristy") Japanese
is definitely the better part of this rooftop complex, near Oxford
Circus; the food is "pretty pricey", but usually matches up.
/ www.aqua-london.com; Mon-Wed 10.45 pm, Thu-Sat 11.15pm; closed Sun.

aqua nueva W1 £62 ❹❹❹
240 Regent St (entrance 30 Argyll St) 7478 0540 3–2C
"For the amazing roof terrace" alone, it's worth a visit to this "large"
and "glamorous" – but sometimes "lifeless" – venue, near Oxford
Circus (sibling to 'aqua kyoto', see also); more generally, though,
the standards – including of the Spanish cuisine – are indifferent.
/ www.aqua-london.com; 11 pm.

Arbutus W1 £52 ❷❷❸
63-64 Frith St 7734 4545 4–2A
This "thoroughly accomplished" Soho bistro has won a big name with
its "no-nonsense" dishes, often based on cheaper cuts, plus "stunning
wines" (by the glass or carafe), and all at very "sensible" prices
(particularly at lunch); the interior is rather "dull", but it does get
a boost from "lots of happy diners". / www.arbutusrestaurant.co.uk;
set weekday L £32 (FP), set dinner & pre-theatre £34 (FP).

Archduke Wine Bar SE1 £46 ❺❹❹
Concert Hall Approach, South Bank 7928 9370 2–3D
New owners the Black & Blue group don't seem hugely to have
changed the spirit of this South Bank 'institution' (their word), which
inhabits atmospheric railway arches near the Festival Hall – it's still
"not a foodie destination", but "good live jazz" adds to its "reliable"
pre-concert appeal. / www.thearchduke.co.uk; Sun-Wed 11 pm, Fri & Sat
1 am.

The Arches NW6   £41   ④❸❷
7 Fairhazel Gdns   7624 1867   8–2A
*"You go for the vino more than anything else" (a marvellous
list at miraculous prices), when you seek out this "electric and
wonderful" Swiss Cottage wine bar; "OK" food plays a supporting
role. / 10.30 pm; no Amex.*

Archipelago W1   £56   ❸❸❶
110 Whitfield St   7383 3346   2–1B
*"Exotic" decor contributes to the "magical" aura of this "eccentric
and fun little venue", near the Telecom Tower – "a must-do if your
life will be incomplete never having eaten pan-fried zebra, or gnu
Stroganoff". / www.archipelago-restaurant.co.uk; 10.15 pm; closed
Sat L & Sun.*

The Ark W8   £55   ❸❸❷
122 Palace Gardens Ter   7229 4024   6–2B
*"Perfect for a romantic night out" – this tightly-packed Italian, just off
Notting Hill Gate, inspires only limited feedback, but fans applaud its
cosy style and its "refined" cooking. / www.ark-restaurant.com; 10.30 pm;
closed Mon L & Sun; set weekday L £32 (FP).*

Ark Fish E18   £46   ❶❷④
142 Hermon Hill   8989 5345   1–1D
*"Quality is unsurpassed, and quantity more than adequate" –
this brilliant fish restaurant, in South Woodford, is sometimes claimed
as "the best place on the London/Essex borders"; "no booking,
so arrive early and expect a wait". / www.arkfishrestaurant.co.uk; Tue-Thu
9.45 pm, Fri & Sat 10.15 pm, Sun 8.45 pm; closed Mon; no Amex.*

L'Art du Fromage SW10   £47   ❸❷④
1a Langton St   7352 2759   5–3B
*"Cheese, cheese... and more cheese", from "wonderful fondues"
to "a good variety on the board" – the "brilliant" formula, say fans,
of this year-old World's End venture, where service which
is "so knowledgeable" takes the edge off a rather "basic" setting.
/ www.artdufromage.co.uk; 10.30 pm; closed Mon L & Sun.*

Artigiano NW3   £48   ④❸④
12a Belsize Ter   7794 4288   8–2A
*This Belsize Park Italian inspires a variety of opinions – on the
downside, it's "fairly standard" and "rather pricey", but the overall
verdict is that it's "worth looking out for... if you're in the area".
/ www.etruscarestaurants.com; 10.30 pm, Sun 10 pm; closed Mon L.*

L'Artista NW11   £36   ④④❸
917 Finchley Rd   8731 7501   1–1B
*This "buzzing" Italian may have a "grim location (under the tube
bridge by Golder's Green station)", but it "always puts a smile on your
face", thanks to its "cheerful" ("cheesy") style and its "huge, tasty
pizzas" – "fantastic for a family outing!" / www.lartistapizzeria.com;
midnight.*

L'Artiste Musclé W1   £39   ④❸❸
1 Shepherd Mkt   7493 6150   3–4B
*"A super-secret little bistro in Mayfair's Shepherd Market", which
is "quite stylish, in a falling-down sort of way" – "as in Paris,
the ambience makes you feel the food is better than it is!" / 10.30 pm;
closed Sun L.*

F S A

Asadal WC1   £46   ❸④④
227 High Holborn   7430 9006   2–1D
A "spacious" cellar, under Holborn tube, which offers "simple but well-cooked" Korean food – "a huge surprise, given the grotty entrance and unpromising location". / www.asadal.co.uk; 11 pm; closed Sun L.

Asakusa NW1   £33   ❶④④
265 Eversholt St   7388 8533   8–3C
"It may not look much from the outside" ("or the inside, for that matter!"), but this "authentically Japanese-feeling" establishment, near Euston Station, is worth seeking out for its "amazing, cheap food". / 11.30 pm, Sat 11 pm; D only, closed Sun.

Asia de Cuba
St Martin's Lane Hotel WC2   £91   ④⑤④
45 St Martin's Ln   7300 5588   4–4C
A "funky" haunt of (surprisingly) long standing, which still has a fan club, who applaud its "vibrant" style and its fusion fare "to die for"; for sceptics, though, it's "past its prime" – "blindingly expensive for food that's only moderately OK, and snootily served too". / www.stmartinslane.com; midnight, Sun 11 pm.

Ask   £36   ⑤④④
Branches throughout London
An ongoing refurbishment programme aims to recapture the "lost reputation" of this pizza-multiple; no uptick in ratings just yet, though – they average out somewhere "between OK and dreadful". / www.askcentral.co.uk; most branches 11 pm, Fri & Sat 11.30 pm; some booking restrictions apply.

Assaggi W2   £69   ❷❷❸
39 Chepstow Pl   7792 5501   6–1B
"My favourite London Italian!" – still how many reporters feel about this famously "unglitzy" room, over a Bayswater pub, which has won renown for "simple" dishes, "brilliantly" executed, and wonderfully "warm" service too; in recent times, however, even some of its most dedicated fans have found it "slightly below usual standards". / 11 pm; closed Sun; no Amex.

Les Associés N8   £41   ④❷④
172 Park Rd   8348 8944   1–1C
Long-established in a Crouch End front room, this very Gallic outfit is still "always reliable, and really great value", says its fans; doubters, though, say "they've let things slip", and that it's now "really ordinary". / www.lesassocies.co.uk; 10 pm; closed Mon, Tue L, Sat L & Sun D; 24 hr notice for L bookings.

Atari-Ya   £28   ❶❷④
20 James St, W1   7491 1178   3–1A
1 Station Pde, W5   8896 3175   1–3A **NEW**
31 Vivian Ave, NW4   8202 2789   1–1B
75 Fairfax Road, London, NW6   7328 5338   8–2A
Some of the best sushi in London is to be found at these "busy" and "utilitarian" café/take-aways, which are usually packed with Japanese diners; the new Ealing branch takes over where Sushi Hiro (RIP) left off, but regulars still "cry with pleasure" – it's so "amazing". / www.atariya.co.uk; W1 8.30 pm, NW4 9.30 pm, NW6 10.30 pm, W5 9 pm; NW4 closed Mon.

L'ATELIER DE JOEL ROBUCHON WC2 £90   ❷❸❷
13-15 West St   7010 8600   4—2B
*"Sitting at the bar, watching the expert chefs at work" adds to the
frisson of "the amazing taste sensations" delivered by the "magical"
small plates on offer at Joël Robuchon's "chic" Covent Garden
outpost (which has a "more formal" dining room upstairs); "go for
the set lunch, unless you want a heart attack when the bill arrives…"
/ www.joelrobuchon.co.uk; 10.45 pm, Sun 10.30 pm; no trainers;
set pre-theatre £52 (FP), set weekday L £58 (FP).*

Athenaeum
Athenaeum Hotel W1   £69   ❷❷❸
116 Piccadilly   7499 3464   3—4B
*This little-sung Mayfair dining room is winning quite a following
among reporters, especially as a business rendezvous; service
is "attentive", the food "delicious", the Art Deco-ish decor
is "classy"… and "during the week, the set menu really is excellent!"
/ www.athenaeumhotel.com; 10.30 pm; set weekday L £40 (FP).*

The Atlas SW6   £41   ❷❸❸
16 Seagrave Rd   7385 9129   5—3A
*"Imaginative" and "gutsy" Mediterranean cuisine has helped win
a widespread fan club for this "bustling" boozer (with garden),
"tucked-away" near Earl's Court 2. / www.theatlaspub.co.uk; 10 pm.*

Aubaine   £53   ④④④
4 Heddon St, W1   7440 2510   3—2C
260-262 Brompton Rd, SW3   7052 0100   5—2C
37-45 Kensington High St, W8   7368 0950   5—1A **NEW**
*Morning visitors to this trendy bakery/bistro chain are rewarded
by "outstanding" pastries, and a "great atmosphere" too; later on,
however, the experience is much more "ordinary" – it doesn't help
that "you almost have to pay to breath". / www.aubaine.co.uk;
SW3 10 pm; W1 11 pm, W1A 9 pm, W8 10 pm, Sun 6 pm; W8 no booking.*

Aurelia W1   **NEW**
13-14 Cork St   awaiting tel   3—3C
*The owners of Zuma, Roka and so on only 'do' quality productions,
so this Mayfair newcomer – scheduled to open around the publication
date of this guide – should be one to watch; following in the footsteps
of one of their other properties, La Petite Maison, it's to be a
Mediterranean petits-plats affair.*

Aurora W1   £45   ❸❸❷
49 Lexington St   7494 0514   3—2D
*A "lovely" Soho spot, with a "great courtyard" – it's eclipsed
in popularity by Andrew Edmunds (opposite), but this is also
a "romantic" place, and has a similarly "decent" food offer too.
/ 10.30 pm, Sun 9 pm.*

Automat W1   £59   ④④④
33 Dover St   7499 3033   3—3C
*A "charismatic" but "noisy" American "diner-style-restaurant", in the
heart of Mayfair, which draws a "lively" crowd; it's a big hit for
breakfast, and for "great hamburgers" too, but it does have critics,
who say it's "more a useful rendezvous than a place you'd actually
choose to eat!" / www.automat-london.com; midnight; closed Sat D & Sun D.*

L'Autre Pied W1 £62 ❷❷❸
5-7 Blandford St   7486 9696   2–1A
"The superb little sister of Pied à Terre" – a "serious but fun"
Marylebone venture founded on a small-plate formula
of "adventurous" and "exquisite" dishes; the set lunch, in particular,
is "a steal". / www.lautrepied.co.uk; 10.45 pm; closed Sun D;
set weekday L & pre theatre £37 (FP).

Avalon SW12 £40 ❹❸❷
16 Balham Hill   8675 8613   10–2C
It's the "incredible" outside space that really sets this large and trendy
Balham gastroboozer apart, even if its supporters do insist that the
food is "a notch above the usual". / www.theavalonlondon.co.uk;
10.30 pm, Sun 9 pm.

L'Aventure NW8 £56 ❷❷❶
3 Blenheim Ter   7624 6232   8–3A
St John's Wood's "little piece of France" is an "unfailing" and
"romantic" classic – especially the "blissful terrace on a balmy
summer's evening"; its "unashamedly traditional" cuisine is dished
up under the "ever-watchful eye" of owner Catherine Parisot. / 11 pm;
closed Sat L & Sun; set weekday L £34 (FP).

The Avenue SW1 £55 ❹❸❸
7-9 St James's St   7321 2111   3–4D
"A stunning legacy of '90s restaurant design", this "light" and "airy"
– "Manhattan-esque" – St James's brasserie remains a popular
business choice; not everyone's impressed though – it can still seem
a "soulless" and "incredibly noisy" place, where the food is simply
"dull". / www.theavenue-restaurant.co.uk; 10.30 pm; closed Sat L & Sun;
set pre theatre £36 (FP).

Awana SW3 £56 ❹❹❹
85 Sloane Ave   7584 8880   5–2C
London's most upscale Malaysian, in Chelsea, is still "very busy";
reporters, though, can't really discern why – prices are "sky high",
service can "border on rude", and the food is often rather "average".
/ www.awana.co.uk; Mon-Wed 11 pm, Thu-Sat 11.30 pm, Sun 10.30 pm.

Axis
One Aldwych Hotel WC2 £57 ❹❷❹
1 Aldwych   7300 0300   2–2D
A grand Covent Garden basement that makes a "useful" spot for
a "competent" business or pre-theatre meal; despite the best efforts
of the "very helpful staff", though, ambience can seem "lacking".
/ www.onealdwych.com; 10.30 pm; closed Sat & Sun.

Azou W6 £33 ❸❸❷
375 King St   8563 7266   7–2B
An appearance on the 'f-word' boosted the profile of this tiny family-
run Hammersmith café; it remains a "lovely" and "intimate" spot,
serving "large helpings" of Moroccan fare in a manner that's
"cordial", "endearing" and "occasionally chaotic". / www.azou.co.uk;
11 pm; no Amex.

Ba Shan W1 £34 ❷❹❸
24 Romilly St   7287 3266   4–3A
"Just as good as Bar Shu… but cheaper!" – a spin-off from the
restaurant opposite, this Soho café dishes up some "blisteringly hot
and unusual" Sichuanese dishes, with "real Chinese flavours". / 11 pm,
Fri 11.30 pm.

Babbo W1 £70 ④④⑤
39 Albermarle St   3205 1099   3–3C
*"Why so expensive?" – the prices at this "crushed" Mayfair Italian
(unrelated to the famous NYC establishment of the same name)
leave reporters mystified; all it really has going for it is a "great
location", not far from the Ritz.* / www.babborestaurant.co.uk; 11 pm;
closed Sun.

Babur SE23 £41 ❶❶❷
119 Brockley Rise   8291 2400   1–4D
*"Thank you Harden's for helping us discover Babur!" – this Honor
Oak Park "star" continues to offer "extraordinarily imaginative and
interesting" Indian cooking, a "great wine list", and "fantastic" service
too… for "about half the cost you'd pay in the West End"!*
/ www.babur.info; 11 pm, 10.30 pm.

Babylon
Kensington Roof Gardens W8 £69 ④④❷
99 Kensington High St   7368 3993   5–1A
*"A sense of drama" heightens a visit to this eighth-floor "haven" –
"the most wonderful spot", with "super views", and also, of course,
"huge roof gardens for a romantic pre-prandial stroll"; shame
it "trades on its location", though – the food is "dull", and the prices
are "daylight robbery".* / www.virgin.com/roofgardens; 10.30 pm; closed
Sun D; set weekday L £41 (FP).

Il Bacio £42 ❸④④
61 Stoke Newington Church St, N16   7249 3833   1–1C
178-184 Blackstock Rd, N5   7226 3339   8–1D
*Those in search of a "great family hang-out" in Highbury or Stoke
Newington should seek out these "frantic" Sardinians; topping the
menu: "super pizzas in massive portions".* / www.ilbaciohighbury.co.uk;
10 pm-11 pm; N5, Mon-Fri L; no Amex.

Back to Basics W1 £48 ❷❷④
21a Foley St   7436 2181   2–1B
*A "cramped and bustling" Marylebone corner-spot, whose "simple
but great-tasting fish" makes it "a real find" – especially if you can
get a pavement table; "the day's specials on the blackboard are
particularly interesting".* / www.backtobasics.uk.com; 10.30 pm.

Baker & Spice £41 ❸❸❷
54-56 Elizabeth St, SW1   7730 5524   2–4A
47 Denyer St, SW3   7225 3417   5–2D
20 Clifton Rd, W9   7289 2499   8–4A
*"The best baked goods", "divine scrambled eggs" and light bites
"so nutritious you can almost feel the vitamins" make these
"informal" deli/bakeries popular with many reporters – even those
who find the product "outstanding", though, may feel prices are
so high that it just "isn't worth it".* / www.bakerandspice.uk.com; 7 pm,
Sun 5 pm-6 pm; closed D; no Amex; no booking.

Balans £44 ④❸❸
34 Old Compton St, W1   7439 3309   4–2A
60 Old Compton St, W1   7439 2183   4–3A
239 Old Brompton Rd, SW5   7244 8838   5–3A
Westfield, Ariel Way, W12   8600 3320   7–1C
214 Chiswick High Rd, W4   8742 1435   7–2A
187 Kensington High St, W8   7376 0115   5–1A
These "buzzy" diners go on till late, and are really all about the vibe
("almost like a club") and the "people-watching" – nowhere more
so than at the 24/7 heart-of-gay-Soho HQ; food quality can be a
"roller coaster", but the "good-value" brunch is a highpoint.
/ www.balans.co.uk; midnight-2 am; 34 Old Compton St 24 hrs; some booking
restrictions apply.

Bald Faced Stag N2 £43 ❸❷❷
69 High Rd   8442 1201   1–1B
"A delicious meal is guaranteed", say the many fans of East Finchley's
"fantastic local gastropub", which goes "from strength to strength".
/ www.thebaldfacedstagn2.co.uk; 10.30 pm, Sun 9.30 pm; no Amex.

Balthazar WC2 NEW
4-6 Russell St   awaiting tel   4–3D
Englishman in New York Keith McNally has established his famous
SoHo brasserie as a Big Apple perennial; in conjunction with Richard
Caring, he's to launch a London offshoot in 2012 – which may well
cement the revival of Covent Garden as a fashionable restaurant
destination.

Baltic SE1 £45 ④④④
74 Blackfriars Rd   7928 1111   9–4A
For a "fun night out" – "as long as the vodka keeps on flowing" –
this "spacious" and "airy" post-industrial venue, by Southwark tube,
still has many fans; it "seems to have lost direction", though – it feels
more "barn-like" nowadays, and the "unusual Baltic-inspired" food
seems no better than incidental. / www.balticrestaurant.co.uk; 11.15 pm,
Sun 10.15 pm.

Bam-Bou W1 £48 ❸❸❷
1 Percy St   7323 9130   2–1C
It's the "colonial styling" and the "buzzy and fun" vibe that make this
seductive Fitzrovia townhouse such an ideal spot for romance (or a
party), but the Franco-Vietnamese food is "interesting" too, even if
some say "you pay a bit over the odds" for it. / www.bam-bou.co.uk;
midnight; closed Sat L & Sun; booking: max 6.

The Banana Tree Canteen £32 ❸❷❸
103 Wardour St, W1   7479 4790   3–2D NEW
21-23 Westbourne Grove, W2   7221 4085   6–1C
166 Randolph Ave, W9   7286 3869   8–3A NEW
237 West End Ln, NW6   7431 7808   1–1B
75-79 Battersea Rise, SW11   7228 2828   10–2C
412-416 St John St, EC1   7278 7565   8–3D
"A lovely oriental mini-chain"; you may have to endure
"uncomfortable bench-seating", but the fare is "reliable, tasty and
inexpensive". / 11 pm, Sun 10.30 pm; booking: min 6.

Bangalore Express £34 ④❸❷
103-107 Waterloo Rd, SE1   7021 0886   9–4A
1 Corbet Ct, EC3   7220 9195   9–3C
"Fun table-booths up ladders" (SE1) is just part of the "interesting concept" of these "buzzy" modern Indians, which feature "Indian fish 'n' chips with tangy mushy peas" alongside traditional thalis; most reporters feel they're "good value", but the occasional disastrous report on EC3 drags ratings down overall. / www.bangaloreexpress.co.uk; 11 pm; closed Sun.

Bangkok SW7 £35 ❷❷❸
9 Bute St   7584 8529   5–2B
"They've been doing the same thing for pretty much 30 years, and they do it pretty well" – the UK's oldest Thai restaurant continues to satisfy and, for somewhere in South Kensington, it's very "reasonably priced" too. / 10.45 pm; no Amex.

Bank Westminster
St James Court Hotel SW1 £59 ④❸④
45 Buckingham Gate   7630 6644   2–4B
"There's not a lot of competition round here", so this large but "unexciting" joint has established itself as the undoubted "staple" of the Victoria Street business crowd; "sunny-day tables in the conservatory" are the most sought-after. / www.bankrestaurants.com; 10.30 pm; closed Sat L & Sun; set pre theatre £37 (FP).

Banners N8 £43 ④④❸
21 Park Rd   8348 2930   1–1C
"The food's only OK, the service snarky, and the setting authentically shabby, but I could eat here every week!" – this world-food bistro is an 'institution' in Crouch End; famously, it's at its best for breakfast and/or with kids; indeed, "it's almost too family-friendly". / www.bannersrestaurant.com; 11.30 pm, Fri & Sat midnight, Sun 11 pm; no Amex.

Baozi Inn WC2 £17 ❷⑤④
25 Newport Ct   7287 6877   4–3B
"It's a bit rough 'n' ready, in-and-out" – and with "hilariously rude" staff too – but this pint-sized Chinatown three-year-old serves up Sichuan bites that are both "cheap" and "incredibly tasty". / 10 pm, Fri-Sat 10.30 pm; no credit cards; no booking.

BAR BOULUD
MANDARIN ORIENTAL SW1 £50 ❷❷❸
66 Knightsbridge   7201 3899   5–1D
Daniel B's "buzzy" NYC-import is proving a "great addition to the London scene" – an "efficient" basement operation that's "good-value" too (especially by Knightsbridge standards); "divine" burgers are – perhaps curiously – the highlight of its "old-fashioned and unfussy" French menu, on which "fine charcuterie" also rates a mention. / www.barboulud.com; 10.45 pm Mon-Sat, Sun 9.45 pm.

Bar Italia W1 £28 ❸④❶
22 Frith St   7437 4520   4–2A
A "crazy, old-fashioned Italian coffee bar" that's become the definitive 24/7 Soho institution – "THE place after clubbing for a caffeine shot to get you home". / www.baritaliasoho.co.uk; open 24 hours, Sun 4 am; no Amex; no booking.

Bar Trattoria Semplice W1 £43 ④④⑤
22-23 Woodstock St 7491 8638 3–2B
*The (remarkably inferior) trattoria-style offshoot of Mayfair's Semplice
divides views – fans do insist it offers "simple but tasty" dishes in a
"very informal setting", but there's a fair-sized gang of critics who find
portions "small" and standards "mediocre".*
/ www.bartrattoriasemplice.com; 11 pm, Fri-Sat 11.30 pm, Sun 9.30 pm.

Barbecoa EC4 £58 ④④④
20 New Change Pas 3005 8555 9–2B
*Jamie O has never run a truly impressive upmarket restaurant,
and this "cavernous" and "noisy" City BBQ looks unlikely to break the
mould; the view (St Paul's) may be "unbeatable", and the vibe may
be "fun", but – for too many reporters – it's a "vacuous" and
"overpriced" operation that's "worth giving a miss".*
/ www.barbecoa.com; 11 pm.

La Barca SE1 £58 ④❸❷
80-81 Lower Marsh 7928 2226 9–4A
*Near Waterloo, an "old-established Italian with a loyal following";
critics may find it "old-fashioned", and "pricey" for what it is,
but devotees prefer to think of it as "a wonderful throw-back to the
'60s and '70s". / www.labarca-ristorante.com; 11.15 pm; closed Sat L & Sun.*

Il Baretto W1 £55 ❷④④
43 Blandford St 7486 7340 2–1A
*An "improved" Marylebone Italian, whose "simple and delicious"
dishes are generally reckoned to be worth their "high" prices;
the service can be a touch "variable", though, and the "noisy"
basement setting is something of a drawback. / www.ilbaretto.co.uk;
10.45 pm, Sun 10 pm; closed Sun.*

The Barnsbury N1 £42 ❸④❸
209-211 Liverpool Rd 7607 5519 8–2D
*A "friendly" and "relaxed" gastroboozer (with garden) that's "worth
the walk from Upper Street"; Sunday lunch is a particular highlight.
/ www.thebarnsbury.co.uk; 10 pm, Sun 8 pm; closed Sun D.*

Barrafina W1 £40 ❶❶❷
54 Frith St 7813 8016 4–2A
*"Still the go-to place in the West End"; the Hart brothers' inspired
take-off of Barcelona's famous Cal Pep is an ongoing blockbuster,
with "a wonderful vibe" and "zen-perfect" tapas ("zingy seafood" the
highlight); NB: only 23 seats, so consider "dining solo" – "you can
sometimes jump the queue!" / www.barrafina.co.uk; 11 pm, Sun 10.30 pm;
no booking.*

Barrica W1 £30 ❸❸❷
62 Goodge St 7436 9448 2–1B
*"Vibrant", but sometimes "chaotic" – this Fitzrovia yearling "feels as if
it has been airlifted straight from Barcelona"; it offers some
"outstanding" dishes and "an ample, well-chosen wine list",
all "at reasonable prices". / www.barrica.co.uk; 10.30 pm; closed Sun.*

Bar Shu W1 £46 ❷④❸
28 Frith St 7287 6688 4–3A
*"Give your tongue a kicking", at this Soho café, whose "mouth-
numbing" Sichuanese cuisine is arguably "the best of its type
in London"; the culinary experience may be "amazing", but sadly the
"moody" service is "average at best". / www.bar-shu.co.uk; 11 pm, Fri-Sat
11.30 pm.*

Basilico £32 ❷❸❹
690 Fulham Rd, SW6   0800 028 3531   10–1B
26 Penton St, N1   0800 093 4224   8–3D
51 Park Rd, N8   8616 0290   1–1C **NEW**
515 Finchley Rd, NW3   0800 316 2656   1–1B
175 Lavender Hill, SW11   0800 389 9770   10–2C
178 Upper Richmond Rd, SW14   0800 096 8202   10–2B
"It's impossible to contemplate ordering any other take-away pizza",
say fans of this "excellent" chain, and its "awesome, thin and crispy"
offerings. / www.basilico.co.uk; 11 pm; no booking.

Bayee Village SW19 £36 ❸❸❷
24 High St   8947 3533   10–2B
In the chain-hell which is Wimbledon Village, this "efficient" operation
is all the more worth knowing about – it offers "solid" Chinese
cooking ("with a few interesting specialities too"). / www.bayee.co.uk;
11 pm.

Beach Blanket Babylon £62 ⑤⑤❶
45 Ledbury Rd, W11   7229 2907   6–1B
19-23 Bethnal Green Rd, E1   7749 3540   12–1C
"Worth a visit for the decor alone" – these "exotic" and "fun"
Gaudiesque hang-outs, in Notting Hill and Shoreditch, offer "divine"
cocktails, and plenty of scope for romance too; the food, though,
can be "truly awful". / www.beachblanket.co.uk; 10 pm; W2 some booking
restrictions apply Fri & Sat.

Bedlington Café W4 £25 ④❷⑤
24 Fauconberg Rd   8994 1965   7–2A
"Sound" cooking and friendly service – plus a BYO policy – ensure
a devoted following for this little Thai caff in deepest Chiswick; no one
minds too much about its "unchanging" menu, or the "dreary" decor.
/ 10 pm; closed Sun L; no credit cards.

Beirut Express £39 ❷④④
65 Old Brompton Rd, SW7   7591 0123   5–2B
112-114 Edgware Rd, W2   7724 2700   6–1D
"Authentic fresh cuisine" – lovely shawarmas and zingy mezze,
in "generous portions" – makes these "reasonably-priced" Lebanese
cafés, in South Kensington and Bayswater, well worth seeking out.
/ www.maroush.com; W2 2 am; SW7 midnight.

Beiteddine SW1 £46 ❸④⑤
8 Harriet St   7235 3969   5–1D
A "very good basic Lebanese"; having avoided the glitzification that's
engulfed the area, this rather dowdy veteran remains – by the
standards of Sloane Street – notably modestly-priced.
/ www.beiteddine.com; midnight.

Belgo £37 ④④❸
50 Earlham St, WC2   7813 2233   4–2C
67 Kingsway, WC2   7242 7469   2–2D
72 Chalk Farm Rd, NW1   7267 0718   8–2B
44-48 Clapham High Rd, SW4   7720 1118   10–2D
"Stick to the moules, frites and beers", and you can have a "fun"
time at this "basic" but "bustling" Belgian chain (where the waiters
dress as monks); when it comes to more adventurous fare, however
"the law of diminishing returns" quickly sets in.
/ www.belgo-restaurants.co.uk; most branches 10.30 pm-11.30 pm;
SW4 midnight, Thu 1 am, Fri & Sat 2 am, Sun 12.30 am.

FSA

Bellamy's W1 £70 ❸❷❸
18-18a Bruton Pl 7491 2727 3–2B
"Quiet and luxurious, in a nicely old-fashioned way" – this "discreet" Mayfair mews operation is a "well-spaced" room with service that's "friendly without being familiar", and it offers Gallic fare that's "reliable but not too adventurous". / www.bellamysrestaurant.co.uk; 10.15 pm; closed Sat L & Sun.

Bellevue Rendez-Vous SW17 £40 ❷❷❷
218 Trinity Rd 8767 5810 10–2C
"A perfect local"; "straightforward French classics" are "done well and without pretensions", at this "reliably enjoyable" and "reasonably-priced" family-run spot, near Wandsworth Common. / www.bellevuerendezvous.com; 10.30 pm; closed Mon L; no Amex.

Belvedere W8 £68 ❹❸❶
Holland Pk, off Abbotsbury Rd 7602 1238 7–1D
"Looks like a Hollywood film set!"; this "delightful" Art Deco "gem" is certainly very "plush", and it enjoys a "really stunning" setting, actually in Holland Park – shame the cooking is no more than "fairly reliable". / www.belvedererestaurant.co.uk; 10.30 pm; closed Sun D; set weekday L £40 (FP).

Benares W1 £75 ❷❷❸
12a Berkeley Square Hs, Berkeley Sq 7629 8886 3–3B
"Nobody uses spices better than Atul Kochar", and his "new slant on Indian cuisine" helps create some "intense" and "totally harmonious" dishes at this "sleek" Mayfair dining room; it's "very pricey", though, and can seem slightly "soulless". / www.benaresrestaurant.co.uk; 10.45 pm, Sun 10.15 pm; no trainers.

Bengal Clipper SE1 £39 ❸❹❸
Shad Thames 7357 9001 9–4D
"One of the Butler's Wharf pioneers", this South Bank Indian is "still serving remarkably good food, 15 years on" (and the Sunday buffet, in particular, is "an incredible bargain"); "aloof service lets it down" though – it can "kill the ambience of what's otherwise a classy room". / www.bengalclipper.co.uk; 11.30 pm, Sun 11 pm.

Benihana £61 ❹❸❸
37 Sackville St, W1 7494 2525 3–3D
77 King's Rd, SW3 7376 7799 5–3D
"Go in a big group of family and friends" – especially with teens – to get the most out of this "fun" US-style teppan-yaki chain, whose "entertaining" staff include knife-wielding chefs who cook at your table; the food is "actually quite good", if "expensive" for what it is. / www.benihana.co.uk; 10.30 pm, Sun 10 pm.

Benito's Hat £20 ❸❷❹
12 Great Castle St, W1 7636 6560 3–1C **NEW**
56 Goodge St, W1 7637 3732 2–1B
19 New Row, WC2 awaiting tel 4–3C
"Hats off to you, Señor Benito!"; these "efficient" Mexican operations have "lovely" staff, and offer "outstanding" made-to-order burritos and tacos at "fair prices"; "arrive early, or the queue can be long". / 10 pm, Thu-Sat 11 pm.

Benja W1 £47 ❷❷❸
17 Beak St 7287 0555 3–2D
Just off Regent Street, but oddly little-known, this lavishly-furnished (but quite cramped) townhouse-Thai is of special note for its "outstanding-value" prix-fixe lunch. / www.benjarestaurant.com; 10.45 pm; closed Sun; set weekday L £28 (FP).

Bennett Oyster Bar & Brasserie SW11 NEW £50 ④⑤④
7-9 Battersea Sq   7223 5545   10–1C
Battersea reporters are torn between delight that "this graveyard site has finally re-opened" and concern that its latest incarnation as a smart seafood brasserie still has "a lot of work to do"; our own visit confirmed that standards leave lots of scope for 'tightening up'. / bennettsbrasserie.com; 10 pm, Fri-Sat 10.30 pm.

Bentley's W1   £67   ❷❸❸
11-15 Swallow St   7734 4756   3–3D
Richard Corrigan's "polished" seafood dishes – amongst the capital's best – have put this "civilised" stalwart, near Piccadilly Circus, back on the map in recent years; the "glamorous yet informal" oyster bar downstairs (with great outside seats) is, however, a better bet than the "rather stuffy" dining room above. / www.bentleys.org; 10.30 pm; no jeans; booking: max 8.

Bento Cafe NW1   £32   ❷❷④
9 Parkway   7482 3990   8–3B
"Stuff yourself silly at a thoroughly reasonable price" – this "always-busy" but "efficient" Camden Town pit stop serves "sushi and noodles a-plenty". / bentocafe.co.uk; 10.15 pm, Fri-Sat 11 pm.

Benugo   £34   ④⑤❸
14 Curzon St, W1   7629 6246   3–4B
23-25 Gt Portland St, W1   7631 5052   3–1C
V&A Museum, Cromwell Rd, SW7   7581 2159   5–2C
Natural History Museum, Cromwell Rd, SW7   7942 5011   5–2B NEW
Westfield, Unit 1070 Ariel Way, W12   8746 9490   7–1C
St Pancras International, , NW1   7833 0201   8–3C
BFI Southbank, Belvedere Rd, SE1   7401 9000   2–3D
116 St John St, EC1   7253 3499   9–1A
82 City Rd, EC1   7253 1295   12–1A
These potentially classy cafés occupy some great sites, such as the "terrific space" in the V&A, and the "happening" BFI branch; too often, however, the setting is a "wasted asset", given the "awful" service, and food (from sarnies and coffee to grander fare) that's "so ordinary and expensive". / www.benugo.com; 4 pm-10 pm; W1 & EC1 branches closed Sat & Sun; W1 & EC1 branches, no credit cards.

Bertorelli   £46   ⑤⑤⑤
5 Argyll St, W1   7437 2503   3–1C NEW
37 St Martin's Ln, WC2   7836 5837   4–4C
15 Mincing Ln, EC3   7283 3028   9–3D NEW
"Why does it still exist when it's so consistently bad?" – a question too often on the lips of reporters on this middle-of-the-road Italian chain; the raison d'être of the West End branches is particularly hard to discern. / www.bertorelli.co.uk; 10 pm; EC3 closed Sat & Sun; booking: W1 max 10, WC2 max 6; set always available £30 (FP).

Best Mangal   £31   ❸❸❸
104 North End Rd, W14   7610 1050   7–2D
66 North End Rd, W14   7602 0212   7–2D
619 Fulham Rd, SW6   7610 0009   5–4A
"Fantastic for a regular meat-fest", these "buzzing" Turkish joints, near West Kensington tube, serve "well-charred, super-moist kebabs" cooked in front of you on the charcoal BBQ; there's also a Fulham branch. / www.bestmangal.com; midnight, Sat 1 am; no Amex.

Bevis Marks EC3 £63 ❸❸❸
Bevis Marks   7283 2220   9–2D
An intriguing annex to London's oldest synagogue houses this "high-quality" kosher venture; it is "perfect for business discussions" and makes "an interesting change from other City restaurants"... although "it is a little expensive for what it is".
/ www.bevismarkstherestaurant.com; 8.30 pm; closed Fri D, Sat & Sun.

Beyoglu NW3 £34 ❸④④
72 Belsize Ln   7435 7733   8–2A
"In an area not well served by restaurants" (Belsize Park), an establishment whose "very tasty" and affordable Turkish food ensures consistent popularity. / www.beyoglu.co.uk; 11 pm; no Amex.

Bibendum SW3 £79 ❸❷❷
81 Fulham Rd   7581 5817   5–2C
"The airy beauty of the space" – "fantastic on a sunny day" – has made this first-floor Brompton Cross dining room a modern-day classic; "professional" service and notable wine also play their part but, of late, the "superior Gallic cuisine" has played rather a supporting role. / www.bibendum.co.uk; 11 pm, Sun 10.30 pm; booking: max 12 at L, 10 at D.

Bibendum Oyster Bar SW3 £63 ❸❷❷
81 Fulham Rd   7589 1480   5–2C
"Lovely fruits-de-mer" in Art Deco surroundings – the makings of a treat at this Brompton Cross fixture, albeit one which comes "at a price"; "get a table in the original space", though, "not in the lobby of the Conran Shop". / www.bibendum.co.uk; 10.30 pm, Sun 10 pm; no booking.

Big Easy SW3 £51 ④④❷
332-334 King's Rd   7352 4071   5–3C
This "roll-up-your-sleeves" American 'crab shack' in Chelsea – jazzed up with live music some evenings – is "a great place to go with friends", and it serves "huge portions" of ribs, steak and seafood; some long-term fans do feel, though, that it has "gone downhill" of late. / www.bigeasy.uk.com; Mon-Thu 11 pm, Fri & Sat 11.30 pm Sun 10.30 pm.

Bincho Yakitori W1 £33 ❸④④
16 Old Compton St   7287 9111   4–2A
Even fans may admit "you need to choose carefully", but this Soho Japanese skewer-specialist pleases most reporters with its dainty dishes – "the tiny lamb chops are particularly good".
/ www.bincho.co.uk; 11.30 pm, Sun 10.30 pm; closed Mon L.

The Bingham TW10 £85 ④④❸
61-63 Petersham Rd   8940 0902   1–4A
"Gorgeous" Thames views (and a "lovely terrace") set an "elegant" tone at this "handsome" dining room, near Richmond Bridge; fans say it's a "perfect all-rounder", but critics complain that it's a "formal" sort of place, with "fussy, fussy" food and "unfocused" service. / www.thebingham.co.uk; 10 pm; closed Sun D; no trainers; set weekday L £50 (FP).

Bistro 1 £20 ④❸④
27 Frith St, W1   7734 6204   4–3A
75 Beak St, W1   7287 1840   3–2D
33 Southampton St, WC2   7379 7585   4–3D
"Nothing fancy, but all good!"; this "no-nonsense" chain may be a bit "humdrum", but – if you're on a budget – it's hard to beat "for a quick and well-priced Mediterranean meal". / www.bistro1.co.uk; midnight.

Bistro Aix N8   £50   ❷❷❷

54 Topsfield Pde, Tottenham Ln   8340 6346   8–1C

"Step through the door, and you're in France" – not Crouch End – at this "very friendly and welcoming" bistro; it's "always full and buzzing", and the food is often "excellent" too. / www.bistroaix.co.uk; midnight; closed Mon, Tue-Fri D only, Sat & Sun open L & D; set always available £29 (FP).

Bistro du Vin   £54   ④❸④

36 Dean St, W1   7432 4800   4–2A **NEW**

40 St John St, EC1   7490 9230   9–1B **NEW**

Take the Hotel du Vin concept, lose the hotel, and... bingo! you have this new Gallic bistro, on the Clerkenwell site of the sadly ill-fated Eastside Inn (RIP); early-day feedback is mixed – for a place that feels like a French-themed hotel coffee shop, prices are certainly high; now in Soho too. / Rated on Editors' visit; Mon-Sat 10.30 pm, Sun 10 pm; W1 closed Sun L.

Bistro K SW7   £50   ④④④

117-119 Old Brompton Rd   7373 7774   5–2B

The Gallic cuisine is "decent" and the setting is "elegant" too – shame, then, that the main impression some reporters take away from this South Kensington yearling is its "astronomical prices". / www.bistro-k.co.uk; 10.30 pm; closed Mon; set weekday L £31 (FP).

Bistrot Bruno Loubet
The Zetter EC1   £47   ❷❷❸

St John's Square 86-88 Clerkenwell Rd   7324 4455   9–1A

Bruno Loubet's "magnificent" cuisine – "gutsy" Gallic bistro fare, with an "Asian-fusion twist" – inspires continuing raves for this "urban-chic" Clerkenwell yearling; main problem? – even fans may fear the place is getting "a bit up itself". / www.thezetter.com; 10.30 pm, Sat & Sun 11 pm.

Bistrotheque E2   £50   ④④❶

23-27 Wadeson St   8983 7900   1–2D

Quite a "mainstream" crowd nowadays frequents this once-edgy East End warehouse-conversion; it "still feels like a bit of a secret", though, and makes a "great venue for brunch" (or, of course, the drag-cabaret). / www.bistrotheque.com; 10.30 pm, Fri 11 pm; closed weekday L; set always available £32 (FP).

Black & Blue   £45   ④④④

37 Berners St, W1   7436 0451   2–1B

90-92 Wigmore St, W1   7486 1912   3–1A

127 King's Rd, SW3   7351 1661   5–3C **NEW**

105 Gloucester Rd, SW7   7244 7666   5–2B

215-217 Kensington Church St, W8   7727 0004   6–2B

1-2 Rochester Walk, SE1   7357 9922   9–4C

"A good stand-by for carnivores"; its branches may rarely set the pulse racing, but this "easy-going" and "no-nonsense" chain offers "reliable steak" and "decent-enough burgers", and at a "decent price" too. / www.blackandbluerestaurant.com; most branches 11 pm, Fri & Sat 11.30 pm; SE1 (South Bank) closed Sun; no booking.

Blakes
Blakes Hotel SW7   £86   ④❸❷

33 Roland Gdns   7370 6701   5–2B

"Hidden-away" in South Kensington, this "quiet and romantic" basement remains a "very sexy" destination for a date; even if its East/West cuisine is "surprisingly good", though, the prices "are enough to quell anyone's ardour". / www.blakeshotels.com; 11.30 pm, Sun 10 pm; set weekday L £49 (FP).

BLEEDING HEART EC1   £60   ❷❷❷
Bleeding Heart Yd, Greville St   7242 8238   9–2A
"For a discreet liaison of a business or romantic nature", this "cosy", "mysterious" and "olde-worlde" den, hidden-way off Holborn, remains phenomenally popular; "high-quality" Gallic fare and "superb" wines are served in a warren or rooms, comprising tavern, bistro and restaurant. / www.bleedingheart.co.uk; 10.30 pm; closed Sun.

Blue Jade SW1   £32   ❸0❸
44 Hugh St   7828 0321   2–4B
This "comfy" Thai, in the backwoods of Pimlico, is a "good, regular neighbourhood spot" par excellence – "it's stuck in a time warp, but the homely food never disappoints, and service is unfailingly charming". / 10.30 pm; closed Sat L & Sun.

Blue Legume N16   £33   ❸❹❷
101 Stoke Newington Church St   7923 1303   1–1C
"For an old-time hippy experience", try this "tiny" but "very busy", Stoke Newington café, long known for its "perfect" breakfasts; it has sprouted a new Islington branch – "a welcome addition to the less exciting end of Upper Street". / 11 pm, Sun 6 pm; no Amex; no bookings Sat & Sun.

Bluebird SW3   £55   ⑤❹❹
350 King's Rd   7559 1000   5–3C
"A total disaster!" – the setting may be "airy" and "glamorous", but this "overpriced" Chelsea landmark continues to dish up "bland bistro-food" of a sometimes "abominable" standard; on a bad day, service is "eye-wateringly poor" too. / www.bluebird-restaurant.co.uk; 10.30 pm.

Bluebird Café SW3   £38   ⑤⑤❹
350 King's Rd   7559 1000   5–3C
"A waste of time and money!" – the D&D group's "notoriously terrible" and "overpriced" King's Road café has "a nice location" (largely al fresco)... "but that's about it". / www.bluebird-restaurant.co.uk; 10 pm, Sun 9.30 pm.

Blueprint Café
Design Museum SE1   £50   ❸❸0
28 Shad Thames, Butler's Wharf   7378 7031   9–4D
"Get a window seat to enjoy one of London's best views" – "impressive even to the well-travelled" – at this Tower Bridge-side operation; as ever, though, there's an odd split in opinion between those who say Jeremy Lee's "seasonal" cuisine really "does the business" and those who find it "underwhelming". / www.danddlondon.com; 10.45 pm; closed Sun D.

Bob Bob Ricard W1   £55   ❹❷❷
1 Upper James St   3145 1000   3–2D
"Glamorous", if "slightly weird" – "imagine Savoy Grill-meets-American diner" – this Soho two-year-old boasts highlights such as "comfy private booths" and "divine" cocktails; the Anglo-Russian "comfort" food is no more than OK... but "how can you not like a place where each table comes complete with its own champagne buzzer?" / www.bobbobricard.com; 11.15 pm; closed Mon & Sun.

Bocca Di Lupo W1   £52   ❷❷❷
12 Archer St   7734 2223   3–2D
*"London's most interesting Italian!"; this "cool" (if "cramped" and
very "clattery") Soho two-year-old is "worth the hype", say fans,
thanks to its "breathtaking" use of "top-class ingredients" to create
"earthy" tapas-style dishes; sitting at the bar is "particularly special".
/ www.boccadilupo.com; 11 pm; closed Sun D; booking: max 10; set weekday
L & pre-theatre £31 (FP).*

Bodean's   £45   ④⑤④
10 Poland St, W1   7287 7575   3–1D
Fulham Broadway, SW6   7610 0440   5–4A
169 Clapham High St, SW4   7622 4248   10–2D
16 Byward St, EC3   7488 3883   9–3D
*"If you like ribs" (not to mention pulled pork and burnt ends), these
"quick and easy", American-style "BBQ-houses" are a rapid route
to "guilty pleasure"; standards are "slipping away", though,
with reports of "faux" food and lacklustre service on the rise.
/ www.bodeansbbq.com; 11 pm, Sun 10.30 pm; EC3 10 pm; 8 or more.*

Boisdale SW1   £61   ④④❷
13-15 Eccleston St   7730 6922   2–4B
*"A top cigar terrace", "an outstanding whisky selection", "blaring
jazz" and "East European girls in kilts" set the scene at this "faux-
Scottish" Belgravian – this may all make for good male-bonding
opportunities, but the "traditional" fare (highlighting steak) can seem
pretty "indifferent", given the "steep" prices. / www.boisdale.co.uk;
11.30 pm; closed Sat L & Sun.*

Boisdale of Bishopsgate EC2   £54   ❸❸❸
202 Bishopsgate, Swedeland Ct   7283 1763   9–2D
*"Top burgers" and "fantastic game in season" are among the pluses
winning praise for this Scottish-themed bar (upstairs)/restaurant
(cellar), near Liverpool Street, which fans say is a "hidden gem".
/ www.boisdale.co.uk; 9 pm; closed Sat & Sun; set always available £35 (FP).*

Boisdale of Canary Wharf E14 NEW   £58   ④④❸
Cabot Pl   7715 5818   11–1C
*This latest addition to laird Ranald Macdonald's faux-Scottish empire
occupies a "large and airy space", with "good views" of Canary
Wharf; its "fun" style and "fabulous" steaks have won it some early-
days praise, but – like the sibling establishments – it's certainly
no bargain. / www.boisdale.co.uk; 11.30 pm; closed Sun.*

The Bolingbroke SW11   £42   ❸❸❸
174 Northcote Rd   7228 4040   10–2C
*"A perfect place to meet with friends, especially with little ones" –
this "reliable" Battersea gastropub is of particular note
as "an absolute must for Sunday lunch". / www.renaissancepubs.co.uk;
10.30 pm, Sun 9 pm.*

Bombay Bicycle Club   £41
128 Holland Park Ave, W11   7727 7335   6–2A
95 Nightingale Ln, SW12   8673 6217   10–2C
*A 'mystery buyer' bought this financially-troubled subcontinental chain
– where standards have sometimes been "dire" of late – in the
summer of 2011; let's hope the new owner can get a grip of what
was once a good-quality operation. / www.thebombaybicycleclub.co.uk;
11 pm, Sun 10.30 pm.*

Bombay Brasserie SW7   £65   ❸❸❸
Courtfield Close, Gloucester Rd   7370 4040   5–2B
*Views divide rather oddly on this vast and once-celebrated South
Kensington Indian, which was refurbished a couple of years ago;
fans find it a "bright and airy" place with "amazing" cuisine –
for detractors, though, "the charm's gone", and food-quality with it.
/ www.bombaybrasserielondon.com; 11.30 pm, Sun 10.30 pm.*

Bombay Palace W2   £44   ❷❷⑤
50 Connaught St   7723 8855   6–1D
*There's certainly "no arty modern presentation", at this "traditional"
Indian veteran, in a quiet Bayswater Square; its "beautifully-spiced"
cuisine, however, "hits the spot time and again".
/ www.bombay-palace.co.uk; 11.30 pm.*

Bonds
Threadneedles Hotel EC2   £62   ④④④
5 Threadneedle St   7657 8088   9–2C
*A "great location" ("right in the middle of the City") helps make the
dining room of this trendy – by local standards – hotel a popular
business lunch destination… even if it "does nothing particularly
well". / www.theetoncollection.com/restaurants/bonds/; 10 pm; closed
Sat & Sun.*

Il Bordello E1   £42   ❷①❷
81 Wapping High St   7481 9950   11–1A
*"Fresh", "no-nonsense" fare is served in "huge" portions, by "fun"
and "personable" staff, at this "traditional" and "relaxed" Wapping
favourite, where "fantastic" pizzas are just one highlight of the
"extensive" menu. / 11 pm, Sun 10.30 pm; closed Sat L.*

La Bota N8   £29   ❸❷❸
31 Broadway Pde   8340 3082   1–1C
*"Bringing a real, rural taste of Spain to Crouch End"; well, the owners
are from Barcelona, and this "noisy" bar is a "comforting" place,
offering consistently "good value for money". / www.labota.co.uk; 11 pm,
Fri-Sun 11.30 pm; no Amex.*

The Botanist SW1   £57   ⑤⑤⑤
7 Sloane Sq   7730 0077   5–2D
*Thanks to its "prime Sloane Square location", the bar area of this
smart, younger-scene hang-out is always "heaving"; avoid the
adjoining restaurant, though – it's "loud" too, with "nonchalant"
service and "bad", "overpriced" cooking.
/ www.thebotanistonsloanesquare.com; 10.30 pm.*

La Bottega   £16   ❸❸❸
20 Ryder St, SW1   7839 5789   3–4C **NEW**
25 Eccleston St, SW1   7730 2730   2–4B
65 Lower Sloane St, SW1   7730 8844   5–2D
14 Gloucester Rd, SW7   7581 6980   5–1B
97 Old Brompton Rd, SW7   7581 6622   5–2B **NEW**
*Springing up in a number of "well-heeled" postcodes, this smart, little
café/deli chain offers "a slice of Italian life" – "simple", "expertly-
sourced" dishes, "delightful" staff… and "great coffee" too.
/ www.labottega65.com; Lower Sloane St 8 pm, Sat 6 pm, Sun 5 pm; Eccleston
St 7 pm; SW7 8 pm; Ryder St closed Sat & Sun; no booking.*

La Bouchée SW7   £48   ❸④❷
56 Old Brompton Rd   7589 1929   5–2B
*"Still a great place to take a date" – this South Kensington bistro
"perennial" continues to exert its very own brand of "crowded" and
"authentically French" charm, and its fare is suitably "solid"; service,
though, can be "haphazard". / www.boudinblanc.co.uk; 10.45 pm.*

Le Bouchon Breton E1 £61 ④⑤⑤
8 Horner Sq   0800 019 1704   12–2B
A Spitalfields venture that's "let down massively" by its "cavernous" quarters – "it's just wrong to put a serious French brasserie in a soulless modern unit"; "hit-and-miss" cooking and "chaotic" service do the place no favours either, but "exceptional cheese" and a huge wine list offer some compensation. / www.lebouchon.co.uk; 10 pm; closed Sun D.

Boudin Blanc W1 £58 ❸④❷
5 Trebeck St   7499 3292   3–4B
"Paris comes to London", at this "cosy and conspiratorial" ("cramped") Shepherd Market fixture, ever-popular for its "buzzing" ambience and its "delicious" (if rather "unadventurous") Gallic cuisine; great al fresco tables. / www.boudinblanc.co.uk; 11 pm.

Boulevard WC2 £38 ⑤⑤④
40 Wellington St   7240 2992   4–3D
Fans tout this "fun" brasserie, in the heart of tourist-ville, as a "cheap" Covent Garden "staple"; even they can concede that service is often "slapdash", however, and harsher critics feel the place is "dire". / www.boulevardbrasserie.co.uk; Mon-Thu 11 pm, Fri & Sat 11.30 pm, Sun 10.30 pm.

The Boundary E2 £63 ❸❸❷
2-4 Boundary St   7729 1051   12–1B
"A Conran classic" – Sir Tel's "cool" and "classy" Shoreditch basement is applauded by most reporters for its "faultless" brasserie-style fare (although, true to form, it's a bit "expensive for what you get"); NB: the rooftop terrace is "the place to be" in summer, but nabbing a table is "a nightmare". / www.theboundary.co.uk; 10.30 pm; closed Mon-Fri L & Sun D.

The Bountiful Cow WC1 £45 ❸④④
51 Eagle St   7404 0200   2–1D
"Superb steaks" and "absolutely fantastic burgers" draw fans to this carnivorous haven near Holborn; service, though, can be "disinterested" and "slow". / www.thebountifulcow.co.uk; 10.30 pm; closed Sun; set weekday L £17 (FP).

Boyd's Brasserie
The Northumberland WC2 £47 ④④④
8 Northumberland Ave   7808 3344   2–3C
It has "such a great location" (just off Trafalgar Square) and hugely "impressive" (marbled) decor too, but this "cavernous" brasserie still feels "impersonal" – it doesn't help that the cooking offers "little in the way of excitement". / www.boydsbrasserie.co.uk; 10 pm; closed Sun.

Bradley's NW3 £53 ④④❸
25 Winchester Rd   7722 3457   8–2A
"Quiet but lovely", say fans, this Swiss Cottage stalwart is an "utterly reliable" choice after a show at the nearby Hampstead Theatre; a crowd of sceptics, though, insist "it's gone right down", offering "very boring" food and "erratic" service too. / www.bradleysnw3.co.uk; 11 pm; closed Sat L & Sun D.

Brady's SW18 £34 ❸❸❸
513 Old York Rd   8877 9599   10–2B
"Exactly how a fish 'n' chip shop should be!"; the "colourful" Mr Brady's "honest and cheerful" Wandsworth bistro offers "excellent" renditions of the national staple (grilled or fried), plus "good, old-fashioned puds". / www.bradysfish.co.uk; 10 pm; closed Mon-Thu L & Sun; no Amex; no booking.

La Brasserie SW3 £48 ⑤④❸
272 Brompton Rd 7581 3089 5–2C
"London's most authentic Parisian brasserie" is – say fans – simply "humming" since the installation of its "impressive" new bar; for critics, though, the fare on offer at this South Kensington fixture is not just "massively overpriced", but "rubbish" too!
/ www.labrasserielondon.co.uk; 11.30 pm; no booking, Sat L & Sun L.

Bar Battu EC2 £42 ❸❸❸
48 Gresham St 7036 6100 9–2B
"A true find in the heart of the City"; thanks to its "esoteric wines at sensible prices" – and its "honest bistro cooking" too – this "vibey" year-old bar/restaurant is already being hailed as "a real lunchtime staple". / 10 pm; closed Sat & Sun.

Brasserie Blanc EC2 £41 ❸❸❸
60 Threadneedle St 7710 9440 9–2C
The "buzzing and competent" EC2 branch of Raymond B's national brasserie chain is "good for business lunches", and handy for "early dinners" too; "it's not fine dining, though, nor an especially warm experience". / www.brasserieblanc.com; 10 pm; closed Sat & Sun.

Brasserie James SW12 £43 ④❸④
47 Balham Hill 8772 0057 10–2C
"A little local brasserie" that's established itself as "a reliable part of Clapham life"; it doesn't attract universal praise, but the "great tasting-menus" have their fans. / www.brasseriejames.com; 10 pm, Sun 9 pm; closed Sun D; no Amex.

Brasserie Joël
Park Plaza Westminster Bridge SE1 £69 ❷④⑤
Westminster Bridge Rd 7620 7272 2–3D
Prices are high, ambience "totally lacking" and service "indifferent", at the dining room of this 1000+ bedroom hotel, at the south end of Westminster Bridge; bizarrely, though, Joël Antunes's Gallic dishes are often "excellent"! / www.brasseriejoel.co.uk; 10.30 pm, Sun 9.30 pm; closed Sat L; set pre theatre £36 (FP).

Brasserie Roux
Sofitel St James SW1 £61 ❸❷❸
8 Pall Mall 7968 2900 2–3C
"It's hard to find decent food at a fair price near Trafalgar Square", so this "convenient" dining room in a "well-spaced" former banking hall is worth knowing about; it offers "genuine" Gallic cooking, "polished" service, and a "civilised" setting (and they do a "fantastic" brunch too). / www.sofitelstjames.com; 11 pm, Sat & Sun 10.30 pm; set pre theatre £36 (FP).

Brasserie St Jacques SW1 £52 ④❸④
33 St James's St 7839 1007 3–4C
"Conveniently located", just off Piccadilly, this "little piece of France" continues to divide opinion; fans love its "comfy" setting, "jovial" maitre d' and "very competent" brasserie fare, but critics just say the whole show is "rubbish". / www.brasseriestjacques.co.uk; 11 pm; closed Sat & Sun; no jeans or trainers.

Brasserie Toulouse-Lautrec SE11 £39 ④❷❷
140 Newington Butts 7582 6800 1–3C
"What it lacks in food" – the Gallic fare is rather "overpriced and average" – is "made up for in atmosphere and jovial service", say fans of this "off-the-beaten-track" Elephant & Castle bistro; it's run by the same family as the Lobster Pot, next door. / www.brasserietoulouselautrec.co.uk; 10.30 pm.

Brawn E2 NEW £43 ❶❷❷
49 Columbia Rd   7729 5692   12–1C
"An East End version of Terroirs... and even better!" – this *"airy"*
corner site has been an instant mega-hit, thanks to its *"gutsy"*
selection of dishes that supporters say are *"a pure joy"*, twinned with
a *"funky"* (and sometimes *"challenging"*) range of 'natural' wines.
/ www.brawn.co; 11 pm; closed Sun D; no Amex.

Bread Street Kitchen EC4 NEW
1 New Change   awaiting tel   9–2B
*Gordon Ramsay's late-2011 debutant opens in a shiny new City mall,
by St Paul's, where there is seemingly much competition (such as
Jamie O's Barbecoa), but nothing yet of real quality – a perfect
opportunity for his new fast-food venture to shine?*

Brick Lane Beigel Bake E1 £7 ❶④⑤
159 Brick Ln   7729 0616   12–1C
"The best beigels in London" (especially the ones *"with huge chunks
of salt beef, slathered in mustard"*) draw crowds night-and-day to this
24/7 East End phenomenon; *"don't worry about the queue, it moves
fast!"* / open 24 hours; no credit cards; no booking.

Brilliant UB2 £37 ❶❷❸
72-76 Western Rd   8574 1928   1–3A
"You have to to go Southall for the real deal", say fans of this huge
and sometimes *"overcrowded"* Indian veteran, who are prepared
to brave a trip to the suburbs for the *"memorable"* curries it offers.
/ www.brilliantrestaurant.com; 11 pm; closed Mon, Sat L & Sun L.

Brinkley's SW10 £50 ⑤④❸
47 Hollywood Rd   7351 1683   5–3B
*A "wonderful courtyard" is the only undoubted plus of this side-street
haunt, whose bar is always packed with Chelsea Lotharios and their
molls – well, it can't be the food, which is "far too expensive for what
it is".* / www.brinkleys.com; 11 pm; closed weekday L.

Brinkley's Kitchen SW17 £44 ④❸❸
35 Bellevue Rd   8672 5888   10–2C
"A reliable destination for a simple dining experience" –
John Brinkley's *"comfortable"* and *"child-friendly"* bistro,
by Wandsworth Common, is an *"ideal local"*; as well as *"a wide and
attractive"* menu, it offers a *"particularly interesting and keenly-priced
wine list"*. / www.brinkleys.com; 11 pm; closed Sun D.

La Brocca NW6 £37 ④④❸
273 West End Ln   7433 1989   1–1B
*Fans of this "cheery" cellar Italian, in West Hampstead, still tout it as
"a great neighbourhood haunt", not least for the quality of its pizza;
the view is growing, however, that it's "not what it used to be"* –
"must try harder!" / www.labrocca.co.uk; 10.30 pm, Fri & Sat 11 pm.

Brompton Bar & Grill SW3 £48 ④❸❸
243 Brompton Rd   7589 8005   5–2C
*A "buzzy" Knightsbridge brasserie whose customer base seems
largely to be drawn from the offspring of those who went there in the
site's "St Quentin" days; a "warm and welcoming" sort of place,
it offers food that's "uncomplicated", but consistently "OK".*
/ www.bromptonbarandgrill.com; 10.30 pm, Sun 10 pm; set always available
£32 (FP).

Brouge £37 ④❸❷
241 Hampton Rd, TW2 8977 2698 1–4A
5 Hill St, TW9 8332 0055 1–4A
A duo of quite "classy-looking" Belgian bistros, in Richmond and Twickenham, serving "solidly-prepared" moules frites in "generous portions", washed down with "excellent" Continental beers. / www.brouge.co.uk; TW2 10 pm; TW9 11 pm; no Amex.

The Brown Dog SW13 £45 ❸❷❷
28 Cross St 8392 2200 10–1A
"In the back streets of what Barnes estate agents call 'Little Chelsea'", this "stylish and dog-friendly" pub is "a firm favourite with families"; the menu may be "limited", but the food is "well-cooked". / www.thebrowndog.co.uk; 10 pm, Sun 9.30 pm.

(Hix at Albemarle)
Brown's Hotel W1 £75 ❸❷❷
Albemarle St 7493 6020 3–3C
For a "quiet environment for a good conversation" – especially on business – you won't do better than this "very professional" and "bustle-free" panelled chamber, in Mayfair; "Mark Hix has created an outstanding menu featuring great British classics alongside many lighter dishes". / www.roccofortecollection.com; 11 pm, 10.30 pm.

(The English Tea Room)
Brown's Hotel W1 £26 ❸❷❶
Albemarle St 7493 6020 3–3C
"Where else would you go for afternoon tea?" – this long-established Mayfair hotel "makes you feel like you're in an Agatha Christie novel", and is well-known for its "elegant" panelled tea room; even fans, though, can find it "expensive". / www.brownshotel.com/dining/english_tea_room.htm; 11 pm; no jeans or trainers; only for afternoon tea.

Browns £42 ⑤④④
2 Cardinal Pl, SW1 7821 1450 2–4B **NEW**
47 Maddox St, W1 7491 4565 3–2C
82-84 St Martin's Ln, WC2 7497 5050 4–3B
9 Islington Grn, N1 7226 2555 8–3D
Butler's Wharf, SE1 7378 1700 9–4D
Hertsmere Rd, E14 7987 9777 11–1C
8 Old Jewry, EC2 7606 6677 9–2C
"Seemingly trading on a combination of past glories and the lovely locations of many of its branches", this national brasserie chain yet again takes a drubbing for food "some school canteens would be ashamed of". / www.browns-restaurants.co.uk; most branches 10 pm-11 pm; EC2 closed Sat & Sun; W1 closed Sun D.

Brula TW1 £51 ❷❶❶
43 Crown Rd 8892 0602 1–4A
"Everything is done beautifully", at this "romantic" and slightly old-fashioned bistro in St Margaret's – service is "utterly delightful" and the "simple" Gallic care is "top-grade". / www.brula.co.uk; 10.30 pm; closed Sun D.

Buen Ayre E8 £45 ❶❸❸
50 Broadway Mkt 7275 9900 1–2D
"I had been a vegetarian for 23 years... but couldn't resist a teeny weeny taste!" – this "barebones" Hackney 'parilla' is acclaimed by all for its "buzzy" vibe, and for steak "so succulent" it's very often hailed as "the best in London". / www.buenayre.co.uk; 10.30 pm; no Amex.

Buenos Aires Cafe £53 ❸❸❸
86 Royal Pde, SE10 8488 6764 1–3D
17 Royal Pde, SE3 8318 5333 1–4D
"For a decent steak" (and also *"good pizza and pasta"*), this *"casual"*
Blackheath Argentinian is just the job, although service can be a bit
"haphazard"; it also has a simpler café/deli sibling, in Greenwich.
/ www.buenosairesltd.com; SE3 10.30 pm; SE10 7 pm, Sat & Sun 6 pm;
no Amex.

The Builders Arms SW3 £41 ❸❸❷
13 Britten St 7349 9040 5–2C
"A neighbourhood treasure"; *"tucked-away"* in Chelsea, this *"warm"*,
"friendly" and *"reliably good"* gastroboozer is the jewel in the crown
of the Geronimo Inns chain. / www.geronimo-inns.co.uk; 10 pm, Sat 11 pm,
Sun 9 pm; no booking.

Bull & Last NW5 £48 ❶❷❷
168 Highgate Rd 7267 3641 8–1B
"Still the best North London gastropub" – this Kentish Town mega-hit
is a *"perfect local"*, where the attractions include *"utterly delicious"*
food, *"humorous"* staff and a *"great location next to the Heath"*;
"the only drawback is that it's always way too loud".
/ www.thebullandlast.co.uk; 10 pm, Sun 9 pm; no Amex.

Bumbles SW1 £48 ❸❷④
16 Buckingham Palace Rd 7828 2903 2–4B
Long written-off as a tourist trap, this *"old-fashioned"* operation near
Buckingham Palace is tipped by fans as a *"hidden gem worthy
of more attention"*; they praise its *"inventive approach to traditional"*
dishes, and especially its *"excellent £10 set lunch"*.
/ www.bumbles1950.com; 10 pm; closed Sat L & Sun.

Bumpkin £47 ⑤④❸
102 Old Brompton Rd, SW7 7341 0802 5–2B
209 Westbourne Park Rd, W11 7243 9818 6–1B
"Underwhelming on all fronts", say critics of these Notting Hill and
South Kensington pub-conversions; fans insist, though, that they're
"congenial" places, and that, if you *"stick to the basics"* of the
"staple" menu, you'll have *"a nice time"*; *"epic"* English breakfasts
are a highlight. / www.bumpkinuk.com; 11 pm.

Buona Sera £36 ❸⓿⓿
289a King's Rd, SW3 7352 8827 5–3C
22 Northcote Rd, SW11 7228 9925 10–2C
"Fun and energetic", this Battersea fixture always delights its family-
centric following with a *"cheerful welcome"* and its *"unfailingly tasty,
good-value fare"*; the Chelsea offshoot (*"perfect pre-cinema"*) benefits
from bizarre two-level seating – a hang-over from its '70s origins
as 'The Jam'. / midnight; WC2 11.30 pm, Sun 10 pm; SW3 closed Mon L.

Busaba Eathai £35 ❸❸❷
35 Panton St, SW1 7930 0088 4–4A
106-110 Wardour St, W1 7255 8686 3–2D
8-13 Bird St, W1 7518 8080 3–1A
22 Store St, WC1 7299 7900 2–1C
Westfield, Ariel Way, W12 3249 1919 7–1C **NEW**
313-319 Old St, EC1 7729 0808 12–1B
"A cut above the Wagamamas of the world" (and notably
"less sterile"), these *"communal"* canteens are *"lovely"* and *"vibrant"*
places, where the *"classic Thai dishes"* deliver *"bags of flavour for
your money"*; perhaps no surprise, then, that *"the queues never seem
to get shorter…"* / www.busaba.co.uk; 11 pm, Fri & Sat 11.30 pm,
Sun 10 pm; W1 no booking; WC1 booking: min 10.

Butcher & Grill £45 ④❸④
39-41 Parkgate Rd, SW11 7924 3999 5–4C
33 High St, SW19 8944 8269 10–2B
*"Stick to the steak 'n' chips", and results can be "first-class", say fans
of these "unfussy" bistro/butchers, in Battersea and Wimbledon;
critics, though, still find the performance resolutely "average".*
*/ www.thebutcherandgrill.com; 11 pm, Sun 9 pm; SW11 closed Sun D;
SW19 closed Mon L.*

Butcher's Hook SW6 £39 ❸❸❸
477 Fulham Rd 7385 4654 5–4A
*"Don't go when Chelsea are playing at home!"… but otherwise this
very decent gastropub, opposite Stamford Bridge, serves "surprisingly
good" food – "nothing complicated, just simple dishes done well".*
/ www.thebutchershook.co.uk; 10.30 pm; no Amex.

Butlers Wharf Chop House SE1 £61 ④④❸
36e Shad Thames 7403 3403 9–4D
*The combination of "iconic" Tower Bridge views and a meaty British
menu helps make this D&D-group venue "a good place to entertain
foreign clients" – hopefully, they won't mind its often "slapdash"
standards; paying your own way? – head for the bar.*
/ www.chophouse.co.uk; 10.45 pm, Sun 9.45 pm.

La Buvette TW9 £37 ❸❷❶
6 Church Walk 8940 6264 1–4A
*"Tucked-away in a church courtyard" (with al fresco dining when
weather permits), this "charming" Gallic bistro, in Richmond, offers
"comforting food, in calm and cosy surroundings", and "good value
for money" too! / www.labuvette.co.uk; 10 pm.*

Byron £31 ❸❸❸
11 Haymarket, SW1 7925 0276 4–4A **NEW**
97-99 Wardour St, W1 7297 9390 3–2D
24-28 Charing Cross Rd, WC2 7557 9830 4–4B **NEW**
33-35 Wellington St, WC2 7420 9850 4–3D
300 King's Rd, SW3 7352 6040 5–3C
242 Earl's Court Rd, SW5 7370 9300 5–2A **NEW**
75 Gloucester Rd, SW7 7244 0700 5–2B
93-95 Old Brompton Rd, SW7 7590 9040 5–2B
Westfield, Ariel Way, W12 8743 7755 7–1C
222 Kensington High St, W8 7361 1717 5–1A
341 Upper St, N1 7704 7620 8–3D
46 Hoxton Sq, N1 3487 1230 12–1B **NEW**
22 Putney High St, SW15 8246 4170 10–2B **NEW**
Cabot Place East, E14 7715 9360 11–1C
7 One New Change, EC2 7246 2580 9–2B **NEW**
*"The new king of burgers!" – this phenomenal chain (part of the
PizzaExpress empire) is achieving massive growth, yet maintaining its
impressive formula of "stylish" decor, "cheery and efficient" staff…
plus "chunky" and "honest" fare that's "full of flavour".*
/ www.byronhamburgers.com.

C London (formerly Cipriani) W1 £88 ⑤⑤④
25 Davies St 7399 0500 3–2B
*"Berlusconi would love it!"; "Eurotrash… WAGs… a scrum through
the paparazzi!" – this "tasteless" but "hilarious" Mayfair Italian
is simply "the worst"; the prices for the "terrible" food and "fake"
service? – "think of a number and double it!" / www.clondon.com;
11.45 pm.*

C&R Cafe £18 ❸④⑤
3-4 Rupert Ct, W1   7434 1128   4–3A
52 Westbourne Grove, W2   7221 7979   6–1B
*"Huge portions of good, cheap Malaysian food" – that's the simple
but compelling proposition of these "authentic" joints, in Chinatown
and Bayswater. / 11 pm.*

The Cabin W4 £42 ④④④
148 Chiswick High Rd   8994 8594   7–2A
*Especially as a daytime or early-evening destination – when 'bargain'
set deals are available – this surf 'n' turf Chiswick diner generally
pleases the locals; as a dinner-destination, though, it doesn't seem
it always measures up. / www.cabinrestaurants.co.uk; 10.30 pm, Fri & Sat
11 pm; no Amex; No toddlers after 7pm; set until 6.30 pm £28 (FP).*

The Cadogan Arms SW3 £48 ❸④❸
298 King's Rd   7352 6500   5–3C
*A "friendly and bustling" Chelsea gastropub, offering "enjoyable" –
and sometimes "outstanding" – fare. / www.thecadoganarmschelsea.com;
10.30 pm, Sun 9 pm.*

Café 209 SW6 £22 ❸❷❷
209 Munster Rd   7385 3625   10–1B
*"Joy, the proprietor, is quite mad, but she tries hard to please";
her BYO café, in deepest Fulham, is "beyond cramped", but the
dishes are "priced cheaper than you could make at home!"
/ 10.30 pm; D only, closed Sun, closed Dec; no Amex.*

**Le Café Anglais
Whiteley's W2** £53 ❸❸❸
8 Porchester Gdns   7221 1415   6–1C
*The new oyster-bar has been "a great addition" to Rowley Leigh's
"airy" Art Deco-style brasserie, above Bayswater's landmark mall –
"one of London's nicer daytime venues", especially for a "family-
friendly" Sunday lunch; a long and "pricey" menu
of "straightforward" classic fare is realised to a reliable standard.
/ www.lecafeanglais.co.uk; 11 pm, Sun 10 pm.*

Café Below EC2 £37 ❸❸❸
St Mary-le-Bow, Cheapside   7329 0789   9–2C
*A "quirky" self-service café in an "atmospheric" crypt, "tucked-away"
under one of Wren's greatest City churches; the food (which has
a veggie slant) can be "surprisingly tasty", especially considering its
"very reasonable" prices. / www.cafebelow.co.uk; 9 pm; closed Sat & Sun;
no Amex.*

Café Bohème W1 £45 ④❷❶
13 Old Compton St   7734 0623   4–2A
*"A great buzz" distinguishes this "very French-feeling"
café/bar/brasserie, in the heart of Soho – a popular all-hours haunt
for anything from a coffee to a full meal. / www.cafeboheme.co.uk;
2.45 am, Sun midnight; booking: max 12.*

Café del Parc N19 £19 ❷❷❷
167 Junction Road   7281 5684   8–1C
*An "utterly improbable and totally fab" find in Tuffnell Park –
a "closely packed" café with "fantastic" staff, producing "brilliant"
tapas "with a twist" from its "very public" kitchen. / www.delparc.co.uk;
10.30 pm; open D only, Wed-Sun; no Amex.*

Café des Amis WC2   £53   ④④④
11-14 Hanover Pl   7379 3444   4–2D
*"It's time they pulled their socks up", at this cutely-located bistro,
by the Royal Opera House – "it's been trading on its old reputation"
for years; the best bet is still the "lively" cellar wine bar.*
/ www.cafedesamis.co.uk; 11.30 pm; closed Sun; set weekday L £29 (FP), set
dinner £33 (FP).

Café du Marché EC1   £52   ❷❷❶
22 Charterhouse Sq   7608 1609   9–1B
*"Down a quaint Smithfield alleyway", this "petit coin de Paris" oozes
"charm and a sense of calm"; its "unabashedly French" cuisine is a
benchmark of consistency, striking just the right note for business
by day, or romance by night (when there's jazz).*
/ www.cafedumarche.co.uk; 10 pm; closed Sat L & Sun; no Amex.

Café Emm W1   £35   ④④❸
17 Frith St   7437 0723   4–2A
*A "bustling" younger-crowd Soho canteen that, say fans, "still can't
be beat for a cheap eat" – it doesn't, however, seem to inspire the
excitement it once did.* / www.cafeemm.com; 11.30 pm, Sun 10.30 pm;
no Amex.

Café España W1   £27   ❸❷❷
63 Old Compton St   7494 1271   4–3A
*"Bustling with tourists and locals nightly" (till late) – this tapas bar
in seediest Soho offers "surprisingly good food for such reasonable
prices" ("and you can't beat a £2 glass of wine to wash it down!").*
/ 11.45 pm, Sun 10.30 pm; closed Mon.

Café in the Crypt
St Martin's in the Fields WC2   £29   ④④❸
Duncannon St   7766 1158   2–2C
*The crypt of Trafalgar Square's great church provides "a lovely and
unusual" setting for this self-service cafeteria; the food may
"look more promising than it is", but fans say that – for somewhere
so central – the prices are "excellent".* / www.smitf.org; Sun 6 pm,
Mon-Tue 8 pm, Wed-Sat 9 pm; no Amex; no booking.

Café Japan NW11   £30   ❶❷④
626 Finchley Rd   8455 6854   1–1B
*"My Japanese wife says this is the best-value sushi in London!" –
the lady is not alone, and this "basic" Golder's Green spot is extolled
by reporters for "fantastic-quality" fare that's among the best,
affordable sushi in town.* / 10 pm; closed Mon; no Amex; only D;
set weekday L £18 (FP).

Café Laville W2   £36   ④④❶
453 Edgware Rd   7706 2620   8–4A
*The "picture perfect" setting – "perched above Regent's Canal" –
creates a "pretty special" atmosphere at this Maida Vale spot;
best go for brunch or a cuppa, though – more substantial fare tends
to be "mediocre".* / 10 pm; no Amex.

Café Luc W1   £56   ④④❷
50 Marylebone High St   7258 9878   2–1A
*An "inviting" setting has helped make this stylish and "buzzing"
yearling a "great addition to Marylebone"; even those who find the
brasserie fare "decent", though, may admit that it's also rather
"unexciting" – brunch is arguably the forte.* / www.cafeluc.com;
10.45 pm; closed weekday L; set weekday L £34 (FP).

Café Pacifico WC2   £43   ⑤④❸
5 Langley St   7379 7728   4–2C
*A "vibrant" Covent Garden cantina of long standing; it survives
by virtue of its "cosy" style, though, rather than its "stereotypical"
Tex-Mex scoff. / www.cafepacifico-laperla.com; 11.45pm, Sun 10.45 pm.*

Café Rouge   £36   ⑤⑤④
Branches throughout London
*With kids in tow (to whom staff can be "lovely"), or for "coffee and
pastries", this faux-Gallic brasserie chain has its uses; in other
respects, though, it feels like a fairly "cynical" operation, whose
guiding principle is too often the lowest common denominator.
/ www.caferouge.co.uk; 11 pm, Sun 10.30 pm.*

Café Spice Namaste E1   £52   ❶❶❸
16 Prescot St   7488 9242   11–1A
*Its debut seemed so path-breaking in the mid-'90s, but – after all
these years – practically every meal at Cyrus & Pervin Todiwala's
"quirky" East End HQ is still "a delight", thanks to "innovative"
Indian-fusion cuisine that's "beyond superb", and "charming" service
too. / www.cafespice.co.uk; 10.30 pm; closed Sat L & Sun.*

Cafe Strudel SW14   £43   ❸④④
429 Upper Richmond Road   8487 9800   1–4A
*Scrumptious coffee and pastries, and some slightly 'different' Austro-
Hungarian food (and wine) make this East Sheen spot a handy local
stand-by. / www.cafestrudel.co.uk; 11 pm, Sun 4 pm; closed Mon & Sun D.*

Caffè Caldesi W1   £53   ④❷❸
118 Marylebone Ln   7487 0754   2–1A
*It's perhaps as a "lovely" lunch venue that this Marylebone Italian –
a "bustling bar" with dining room above – is of most interest;
it attracts little feedback, often to the effect that results are
"average". / www.caldesi.com; 10.30 pm.*

Caffè Nero   £13   ④❸❸
Branches throughout London
*"The most authentic chain coffee" – "close to the genuine Italian
article" – is the special draw to these "friendly and efficient" pit
stops; the pastries and panini, though, are "only standard".
/ most branches 7 pm; City branches earlier; most City branches closed all
or part of weekend; some branches no credit cards; no booking.*

Caffè Vergnano   £12   ④❸❸
62 Charing Cross Rd, WC2   7240 8587   4–3B
Royal Festival Hall, SE1   7921 9339   2–3D
2 New Street Sq, EC4   7936 3404   9–2A   **NEW**
*The "best coffee this side of Italy" makes this Covent Garden café
a "West End stand-out" for caffeine addicts; the larger Royal Festival
Hall outpost – whose offer includes "pasta as an Italian might
recognise it" – is "one of the better places on the South Bank" too.
/ www.caffevergnano.com; SE1 midnight; WC2 8 pm, Fri & Sat midnight,
EC4 11 pm; EC4 Sat & Sun; no Amex.*

La Cage Imaginaire NW3   £43   ④❷❸
16 Flask Walk   7794 6674   8–1A
*A mega-cute Hampstead lane provides the setting for this old-school
Gallic stalwart; the food can seem "ordinary and expensive", but the
overall experience is "very pleasant" nonetheless.
/ www.la-cage-imaginaire.co.uk/; 11 pm.*

Cah-Chi £34 ❸⓿❸
394 Garratt Ln, SW18 8946 8811 10–2B
34 Durham Rd, SW20 8947 1081 10–2B
*These "brilliant" local Koreans, in Earlsfield and Raynes Park,
are "so welcoming"; their food – "including the at-table barbecue" –
is "deliciously fresh" too. / www.cahchi.com; SW18 11 pm, Sat & Sun
11.30 pm; SW20 11 pm; SW20 closed Mon; cash only.*

Cambio de Tercio SW5 £57 ❷❷❷
163 Old Brompton Rd 7244 8970 5–2B
*Hailed by some as "the best Spanish restaurant in the UK!",
this "buzzy" South Kensington "gem" wins adulation for its
"inspiring" – "El Bulli-esque", even! – dishes, and "stunning" wines;
it's "crowded", though, and the two-sittings policy is a continuing
source of complaints. / www.cambiodetercio.co.uk; 11.30 pm.*

Camden Brasserie NW1 £40 ❹❸❹
9-11 Jamestown Rd 7482 2114 8–3B
*A "welcoming" Camden Town stand-by, which has long lived up to its
name; "the best frites" aside, however, its whole performance can
seem a little "anodyne". / www.camdenbrasserie.co.uk; 10.45 pm.*

Camino N1 £44 ❹❺❸
3 Varnishers Yd, Regent Quarter 7841 7331 8–3C
*This "stylish" tapas bar – a couple of minutes' walk from King's Cross
– is one of the best places round the station, and it's "always busy";
drooping ratings, though, support those who say: "popularity has
been its downfall!" / www.camino.uk.com; 11 pm, Sun 10 pm.*

Cannizaro House SW19 £65 ❹❹❸
West Side, Wimbledon Common 8879 1464 10–2A
*A "simply fabulous location" is the trump card of this Wimbledon
Common-side hotel, where the "very expensive" food attains
a standard that's "only OK"; for afternoon tea, however, it is
a "wonderful little secret". / www.cannizarohouse.com; 9.30 pm.*

Canonbury Kitchen N1 NEW £45 ❸❷❹
19 Canonbury Ln 7226 9791 8–2D
*A new Italian, near Highbury & Islington tube, where "a short and
simple rustic menu" comes "well-executed"; ambience-wise, however,
we're talking "sub-PizzaExpress". / www.canonburykitchen.com; 11 pm;
closed Mon-Fri L, Sat D & Sun D; no Amex.*

Canta Napoli £34 ❸❸❹
9 Devonshire Rd, W4 8994 5225 7–2A
932-934 North Finchley, N12 8445 1351 1–1B NEW
*"Italian regionally-themed evenings" are a top time to visit this
Chiswick Neapolitan, which also has quite a name for its pizza;
the harsh view, however, is that it's "an OK local, but doesn't really
stand out"; the North Finchley sibling inspires no feedback.
/ 10.30 pm; no Amex.*

Canteen £39 ❹❹❹
55 Baker St, W1 0845 686 1122 2–1A
Royal Festival Hall, SE1 0845 686 1122 2–3D
Park Pavilion, 40 Canada Sq, E14 0845 686 1122 11–1C
Crispin Pl, Old Spital'ds Mkt, E1 0845 686 1122 12–2B
*"A good formula gone wrong" – fans may like the "simple but
effective" cuisine at these "reinvented British caffs", but more striking
is the number of critics, who complain of "woefully inconsistent"
cooking, sometimes "laughable" service, and "the lack of any real
atmosphere". / www.canteen.co.uk; 11 pm; no booking weekend L.*

Cantina del Ponte SE1   **£46**   ⑤④④
Butler's Wharf Building, 36c Shad Thames   7403 5403   9–4D
*"Lovely views of Tower Bridge" make this D&D-group Italian a useful
South Bank destination for first-time visitors to London; it has its fans
among the natives too, but the feeble overall ratings tend to bolster
those who think its attractions primarily touristic. / www.cantina.co.uk;
11 pm, Sun 10 pm; set weekday L £27 (FP).*

Cantina Laredo WC2   **£45**   ❸④⑤
10 Upper St Martin's Ln   7420 0630   4–3B
*Fans of this US import to Covent Garden, part of an "upmarket
Mexican" chain, hail its dishes as "impressively executed" –
"they make the guacamole at your table!"; for sceptics, though,
the food is "underwhelming", and the interior so "bland" it "feels like
a Travelodge lobby". / www.cantinalaredo.co.uk; 11.30 pm, Sat midnight,
Sun 10.30 pm; over 7 people.*

Cantina Vinopolis
Vinopolis SE1   **£50**   ④④④
1 Bank End   7940 8333   9–3C
*As you might hope at a museum of wine, the wine list at this "bistro-
style" venue – set in attractive South Bank vaults – is "to die for";
otherwise, however, the experience can seem "pricey" and "generic".
/ www.cantinavinopolis.com; 10.30 pm; closed Mon-Wed D & Sun.*

Cantinetta SW15 **NEW**   **£42**   ④⑤❸
162-164 Lower Richmond Rd   8780 3131   10–1A
*"So much potential", as yet unfulfilled, at this Putney newcomer,
formerly called the Phoenix (and under unchanged ownership) –
it may have a "lovely" ambience, but its Italian menu is realised to a
"distinctly average" standard, and service "seemingly can't cope".
/ www.cantinetta.co.uk; 10.30 pm, Fri-Sat 11 pm; closed Sun D; set always
available £28 (FP).*

Canton Arms SW8   **£37**   ❷❷❶
177 South Lambeth Rd   7582 8710   10–1D
*"Just how a gastropub should be" – this Anchor & Hope sibling would
be "a terrific asset" anywhere, but seems particularly "awesome"
in "the Stockwell desert"; its "rough and ready" style only adds to the
ambience, as does the "enthusiastic" service, and the "superb" and
"hearty" British cuisine. / www.cantonarms.com; 10 pm; closed Mon L;
no Amex; no booking.*

Cape Town Fish Market W1   **£49**   ❸④④
5 & 6 Argyll St   7437 1143   3–1C
*Decorated in garish shopping-mall style, this off-beat South African-
backed concept, near Oxford Circus, offers a "quirky" menu ranging
from "traditional" dishes to sushi ; the (few) reports it attracts
suggest the food is "good", if perhaps "overpriced". / www.ctfm.com;
10.45 pm, Fri-Sat 11.15 pm.*

The Capital Restaurant
Capital Hotel SW3   **£92**   ❸④④
22-24 Basil St   7589 5171   5–1D
*"After a slight wobble" on the departure of the previous chef,
this grand but compact Knightsbridge chamber appears to be getting
back on track, and Jerome Ponchelle's cuisine is often "superb";
the atmosphere, though, remains too "library-like" for some tastes.
/ www.capitalhotel.co.uk; 10.30 pm, Sun 10 pm; no jeans or trainers;
set weekday L £54 (FP), set Sun L £60 (FP).*

Caponata NW1   £46   ❸❷❷
3-7 Delancey St   7387 5959   8–3B
"A real surprise in the middle of Camden"; this "modern and airy" restaurant and music venue – laid-out round a glazed courtyard, complete with a 'living wall' – offers some "interesting" and "good-value" Sicilian cooking, and some "lovely" service too. / www.caponatacamden.co.uk; 10.30 pm, Sun 10 pm; set weekday L £30 (FP).

Capote Y Toros SW5 NEW   £39
157 Old Brompton Rd   7373 0567   5–2B
The new tapas bar offshoot of South Kensington's estimable Cambio de Tercio, nearby; it opened too late for much survey commentary (or to receive a rating), but an early reporter hails "great food... but an even better list of sherries". / www.cambiodetercio.co.uk; 11.30 pm; D only, closed Mon & Sun.

LE CAPRICE SW1   £65   ❸❷❷
Arlington Hs, Arlington St   7629 2239   3–4C
"Never putting a foot wrong" has long underpinned the "classic" status of this "swish" and "vibrant" '80s-minimalist brasserie behind the Ritz; it's been "slipping" of late, though – let's hope the major refurbishment in mid-2011 marks a turning point. / www.le-caprice.co.uk; midnight, Sun 11 pm; set always available £43 (FP).

Caraffini SW1   £45   ❸❷❷
61-63 Lower Sloane St   7259 0235   5–2D
"Why change a winning formula?"; ebullient staff greet you "like the Prodigal Son" when you visit this "old-faithful" trattoria, near Sloane Square; the food may be "unadventurous", but it's "always reliable", and "honestly priced" too. / www.caraffini.co.uk; 11.30 pm; closed Sun.

Caravaggio EC3   £60   ④④④
107-112 Leadenhall St   7626 6206   9–2D
"Expense accounts must still be thriving!" – otherwise, reporters are hard put to explain the survival of this "pricey" but "average-all-round" City Italian; or perhaps it has something to do with the "convenient location"? / www.etruscarestaurants.com; 10 pm; closed Sat & Sun; set always available £36 (FP).

Caravan EC1   £39   ❷❷❶
11-13 Exmouth Mkt   7833 8115   9–1A
"Awesome" home-roasted coffee, and "brilliant" Antipodean breakfasts inspire many raves for this "busy" but chilled Clerkenwell café; its main, fusion-tapas menu is also "full of interesting ideas", and realisation – though it can be slightly "hit-and-miss" – is often "top notch". / www.caravanonexmouth.co.uk; Sat 5 pm; closed Sun D; set always available £7 (FP).

Carluccio's   £38   ④④④
Branches throughout London
Love 'em or hate 'em, these "bright" cafés inspire unusually passionate feelings for a chain; to fans, their "snappy fare" makes them a great "cheap 'n' cheerful" stand-by, especially with the family or for brunch – critics just find them "faux-Italian" and "dull". / www.carluccios.com; most branches 11 pm, Sun 10.30 pm; no booking weekday L.

Carnevale EC1   £42   ❸❷④
135 Whitecross St   7250 3452   12–2A
A well-established veggie, by the Barbican, commended by its small fan club for its "original" fare. / www.carnevalerestaurant.co.uk; 11 pm; closed Sat L & Sun; no Amex; set weekday L £26 (FP).

Carob Tree NW5 £32 ④❷④
15 Highgate Rd 7267 9880 8–1B
"Fresh and tasty" dishes win praise for this Greek spot, in Dartmouth Park; of late, however, has it "lost its sparkle"? / 10.30 pm, Sun 9 pm; closed Mon; no Amex.

The Carpenter's Arms W6 £41 ❸④④
91 Black Lion Ln 8741 8386 7–2B
Tucked away in a Hammersmith backwater, this stylishly-converted pub pleases most reporters with its "interesting" and "well-cooked" food; there's a "great" garden too. / 10 pm, Sun 9 pm.

Carvosso's W4 £41 ⑤④❸
210 Chiswick High Rd 8995 9121 7–2A
A "cosy" hang-out – in Chiswick's former police station! – where the stand-out attraction is the "terrific courtyard garden"; well, it certainly isn't the food... / www.carvossosat210.co.uk; 11 pm.

Casa Brindisa SW7 £36 ❸④❸
7-9 Exhibition Rd 7590 0008 5–2C
Yet to be re-badged under the 'Tapas Brindisa' brand, this South Kensington two-year-old is a "high-quality" Spanish operation – even those who feel it's "not in the same league as nearby Tendido Cero" say it's a "fun" spot, offering "decent" fare. / www.casabrindisa.com; 10.45 pm.

Casa Malevo W2 NEW £45 ④④④
23 Connaught St 7402 1988 6–1D
Middling ratings for this Bayswater débutant; most reports applaud a "convivial" joint, offering "good steaks" – to the odd critic, though, it's just a "me-too Argie steakhouse". / www.casamalevo.com; 10.30 pm.

Cassis Bistro SW3 £71 ④④④
232-236 Brompton Rd 8581 1101 5–2C
Marlon Abela's slick new bistro, on the former Knightsbridge site of Oratory (RIP), seduces some reporters with its "crowd-pleasing" Gallic fare – sceptics, however, find its whole style "pretentious", and say prices are "outrageous" too. / 11 pm; set weekday L £45 (FP).

Le Cassoulet CR2 £48 ❸④❸
18 Selsdon Rd 8633 1818 10–2D
"Putting Croydon on the gastronomic map!" – Malcolm John's "honest" and "traditional" Gallic cooking makes this "buzzing" city-centre bistro "the best restaurant for miles around", say fans; cynics, sensing local hype, say the place "doesn't really live up". / www.lecassoulet.co.uk; 10.30 pm, Sat 11 pm, Sun 10 pm.

Catch
Andaz Hotel EC2 £52 ④④④
40 Liverpool St 7618 7200 12–2B
The "beautiful" interior is a high point of this business-friendly fish specialist, that forms part of a Liverpool Street hotel; the food is "good" but it's "overpriced", and the noise from the adjacent bar does little for the atmosphere. / www.andazdining.com; 10.30 pm; closed Sat & Sun.

Cattle Grid £41 ④④④
76 Northcote Rd, SW11 7228 4188 10–2C
1 Balham Station Rd, SW12 8673 9099 10–2C
A small and "relaxed" steak and burger chain that's yet to excite much in the way of reports – such as there are tend to the view that the food is "good, if not great". / www.cattlegridrestaurant.com; 10 pm, Fri & Sat 10.30 pm; no Amex.

Cavallino SW3 NEW £56
4 Sydney St 7352 3435 5–2C
*Jockey Franco Dettori is the PR-friendly backer of this mid-2011
Italian newcomer, in Chelsea; unfortunately we didn't fit in a visit
before this guide went to press, but the overall concept seems rather
similar to the former occupant of the site, Carpaccio's (RIP).
/ www.cavallino-restaurant.com; 11 pm, Sun 10 pm.*

Cây Tre £36 ❷④④
42-43 Dean St, W1 7317 9118 4–2A NEW
301 Old St, EC1 7729 8662 12–1B
*"Confused service doesn't get in the way of some unbelievable
flavours", at this "plastic"-looking Shoreditch Vietnamese; it now has
a stylish café-style Soho sibling, where an early visit found very harsh
acoustics, but dishes of cracking quality. / 11 pm, Fri-Sat 11.30 pm,
Sun 10.30; no Amex.*

Cecconi's W1 £62 ❸❷❶
5a Burlington Gdns 7434 1500 3–3C
*"Hedge-fund-alley-meets-ladies-who-lunch", at this "fun" and
"fashionable" Italian brasserie – a "safe, reliable and very smooth"
hub of Mayfair life, at any time of day (and especially popular for
breakfast). / www.cecconis.co.uk; 1am, Sun midnight.*

Cellar Gascon EC1 £35 ❸❸❷
59 West Smithfield Rd 7600 7561 9–2B
*A slightly "Spartan" spin-off from Farringdon's nearby Club Gascon,
featuring some "unbelievably interesting" SW French wines
to complement its tapas menu; the prix-fixe lunch is "unbeatable
value". / www.cellargascon.com; midnight; closed Sat & Sun.*

Le Cercle SW1 £49 ❷❷❷
1 Wilbraham Pl 7901 9999 5–2D
*"Hits the mark every time!" – this "chic" Gascon basement,
near Sloane Square, is an "elegant" sort of place, offering "eclectic"
tapas-style cuisine and "fascinating" wine; if you grab a booth, it can
be "wonderfully romantic" too. / www.lecercle.co.uk; 10.45 pm; closed
Mon & Sun.*

Cha Cha Moon W1 £29 ④④❸
15-21 Ganton St 7297 9800 3–2C
*It opened to a blaze of hype a couple of years ago, but this "canteen-
style" Cantonese noodle concept – a Chinese Wagamama, if you like
– has never really made waves; "for a quick West End bite", though,
you could do worse. / www.chachamoon.com; 10.30 pm, Fri & Sat
11.20 pm, Sun 10.20 pm.*

Chabrot Bistrot d'Amis SW1 NEW £54 ❸❶❸
9 Knightsbridge Grn 7225 2238 5–1D
*"A truly French feel" distinguishes this "very welcome addition
to Knightsbridge", which wins fans with its "honest" fare, and its
impeccably friendly service; critics can find the food a bit "safe",
though, and the cramped setting "too busy and noisy".
/ www.chabrot.co.uk; 11 pm; closed Sun; set weekday L £33 (FP).*

Chamberlain's EC3 £61 ❸❸④
23-25 Leadenhall Mkt 7648 8690 9–2D
*With its "excellent" fish and "attentive" service, this well-established
City seafood parlour is sometimes said to be "better than expected";
critics, though, insist that "you're just paying for its Leadenhall Market
location". / www.chamberlains.org; 9.15 pm; closed Sat & Sun.*

Chamomile NW3 £28 ❸❷❸
45 England's Ln   7586 4580   8–2B
A "bubbly" café, in the heart of Belsize Park, where "smiley" staff
dish up "the best breakfast in the area", and "great sandwiches and
salads" too. / 6 pm; L only; no Amex.

Champor-Champor SE1 £48 ❷❷❷
62 Weston St   7403 4600   9–4C
Be "magically transported to another world", when you visit this
"weird and wonderful" hide-away, near London Bridge – the staff are
"lovely", and the Malaysian cuisine is usually "intense and complex"
("if occasionally baffling"). / www.champor-champor.com; midnight; D only,
closed Sun.

The Chancery EC4 £50 ❷❸④
9 Cursitor St   7831 4000   9–2A
"Well-considered" cuisine and "fair prices" have made a big,
business-lunching hit of this "professional" joint in the back streets
of legal-land – "one of those rare places where the food is actually
better than it sounds on the menu!" / www.thechancery.co.uk; 10.30 pm;
closed Sat L & Sun.

Chapters SE3 £42 ④❸④
43-45 Montpelier Vale   8333 2666   1–4D
Long a linchpin of the area, this Blackheath brasserie still serves
up "solid" food (including a "stand-out" breakfast); overall, though,
standards are "pretty ordinary nowadays".
/ www.chaptersrestaurants.com; 11 pm, Sun 9 pm.

Le Chardon £46 ④⑤④
65 Lordship Ln, SE22   8299 1921   1–4D
32 Abbeville Rd, SW4   8673 9300   10–2D
A duo of "charming" south London bistros, nowadays in Clapham
as well as East Dulwich; fans praise their "well-executed, traditional
Gallic fare", but even they can find results "variable", and critics slam
"indifferent" food and "appalling" service. / www.lechardon.co.uk; 11 pm.

Charles Lamb N1 £39 ❸❸❷
16 Elia St   7837 5040   8–3D
"A hilarious annual Bastille Day boules tournament" hints at the
"good-humoured" Gallic ownership of this "classic, small
neighbourhood pub", "hidden-away" near Angel – a "charming" place
with "interesting" food, and "well-kept" beer too.
/ www.thecharleslambpub.com; 9.30 pm; closed Mon L, Tue L & Sun D;
no Amex; no booking.

Charlotte's Bistro W4 £50 ④④④
6 Turnham Green Ter   8742 3590   7–2A
This Chiswick yearling inspires mixed feedback – fans proclaim
a "lovely", stylish modern bistro offering "surprisingly interesting"
food, but for sceptics "the cooking looks better than it tastes" and
is "appallingly expensive" for what it is too. / www.charlottes.co.uk;
10.30 pm, Sun 9 pm; set weekday L £31 (FP).

Charlotte's Place W5 £48 ❸❸❸
16 St Matthew's Rd   8567 7541   1–3A
"It's Ealing's best!", say delighted locals, who love this "intimate"
bistro "gem", by the Common, and praise its "imaginative" fare;
bad (ie "awful") days, however, are not entirely unknown.
/ www.charlottes.co.uk; 10 pm, Sun 9 pm; set weekday L £30 (FP).

Charm W6 NEW   £46   ❸❸❷

270-272 King St   8741 8863   7–2B

*"It feels like a Hong Kong bankers' playground", so this "extremely
smart and well-appointed" bar/restaurant makes an odd find on the
mid-market restaurant strip near Ravenscourt Park tube; it's by
no means a bad place, but some critics feel it's "not as good
as others nearby". / 10.30 pm.*

Chella W4   £39   ❸❷❸

142 Chiswick High Rd   8994 6816   7–2A

*"A more interesting take on Middle Eastern food than usual" –
plus attractive decor and "efficient" service – have made this year-old
Iranian "a welcome addition to the Chiswick scene".
/ www.chella-restaurant.co.uk; midnight; no Amex.*

**The Chelsea Brasserie
Sloane Square Hotel SW1**   £54   ④④④

7-12 Sloane Sq   7881 5999   5–2D

*A prime location ("incredibly convenient for the Royal Court") helps
keep this percussive Sloane Square brasserie very busy; the food can
be good too, but those unable to avail themselves of special menus
may find it "overpriced". / www.chelsea-brasserie.co.uk; 10.30 pm;
no Amex.*

Chelsea Bun Diner SW10   £26   ❸❷❸

9a Lamont Rd   7352 3635   5–3B

*The "American-sized" breakfasts at this World's End diner are
legendary in their hang-over-curative properties; indeed, its reputation
for "honest nosh at good and sensible prices" has long made it a
"crowded" destination at any hour; BYO. / www.chelseabun.co.uk; 6 pm;
L only; no Amex; no booking, Sat & Sun.*

The Chelsea Kitchen SW10   £28   ④❸❸

451 Fulham Rd   3055 0088   5–3B

*"Cheap, cheap, cheap… for Chelsea"; this resurrected joint –
relocated to a pub-conversion at the far end of the Royal Borough –
may offer only basic fodder, but fans say it's "still amazing value,
after all these years". / www.chelseakitchen.com; 11.30 pm, Sun 11 pm.*

Cheyne Walk Brasserie SW3   £68   ❸④❸

50 Cheyne Walk   7376 8787   5–3C

*With its "trendy" decor and "fabulous" Gallic food – much of
it cooked on an open grill – this "romantic" Chelsea venture, in a
former pub, can seem quite a "find"; you can think a visit here
"enjoyable", though, and still feel the experience is "no match for the
bill!" / www.cheynewalkbrasserie.com; 10.30 pm; closed Mon L & Sun D.*

CHEZ BRUCE SW17   £68   ❶❶❷

2 Bellevue Rd   8672 0114   10–2C

*For the 7th year, Bruce Poole's "astonishingly consistent"
(yet "reasonably-priced") neighbourhood restaurant, by Wandsworth
Common, is the survey's favourite, thanks to its "artful but unfussy"
cooking, "amazing" wine, "spectacular" cheese and "genuine" staff;
it's "less crowded" too, after the recent expansion.
/ www.chezbruce.co.uk; 10.30 pm, Sun 9.30 pm.*

Chez Gérard £55 ⑤⑤⑤
31 Dover St, W1 7499 8171 3–3C
8 Charlotte St, W1 7636 4975 2–1C
119 Chancery Ln, WC2 7405 0290 2–2D
45 Opera Ter, Covent Garden, WC2 7379 0666 4–3D
9 Belvedere Rd, SE1 7202 8470 2–3D
64 Bishopsgate, EC2 7588 1200 9–2D
14 Trinity Sq, EC3 7480 5500 9–3D
1 Watling St, EC4 7213 0540 9–2B
"Oh dear!"; as steakhouses become ever more popular,
this "uninspiring" steak/frites chain goes from bad to worse –
it incites rather too many reports of food that's "not very nice",
and service that's "a joke". / www.chezgerard.co.uk; 10 pm-11.30 pm;
City branches closed all or part of weekend; some booking restrictions apply.

Chez Liline N4 £44 ❶❷⑤
101 Stroud Green Rd 7263 6550 8–1D
"London's best-kept fish secret!" – Sylvain Hong's "deliciously-sauced"
Mauritian seafood is "sensational", and service is "lovely" too, at this
Finsbury Park stalwart; shame about the "awful" location and "dead"
ambience – "in a better bit of town, it would be famous".
/ ww.chezliline.co.uk; 11 pm; closed Mon.

Chez Lindsay TW10 £42 ④❸④
11 Hill Rise 8948 7473 1–4A
"Pancakes galore", "good seafood plates" and "delicious ciders" too –
all attractions of this "busy" bistro of long standing, near Richmond
Bridge; even fans, though, can find the cooking "inconsistent".
/ www.chezlindsay.co.uk; 11 pm; no Amex; set weekday L £22 (FP).

Chez Marcelle W14 £28 ❶⑤⑤
34 Blythe Rd 7603 3241 7–1D
"Marcelle has delegated more, but you can still expect a lengthy
wait", at her "eccentric" café, behind Olympia; at least your meal –
"wonderful, home-cooked Lebanese dishes", at very "restrained"
prices – will be "worth waiting for". / 10 pm; closed Mon, Tue-Thu D only,
Fri-Sun open L & D; no credit cards.

Chez Patrick W8 £45 ❸❷❸
7 Stratford Rd 7937 6388 5–2A
"Patrick is a complete Gallic charmer", and – for a small but devoted
fan club – his presence helps make it worth seeking out this old-
fashioned fish restaurant, in a quiet Kensington backwater, where the
"well executed" cuisine is "very similar to what you'd find at parallel
establishments in France". / www.chezpatrickinlondon.co.uk; 10.45 pm;
closed Sun D; set weekday L £25 (FP), set dinner £29 (FP).

Chilango £13 ❶❷④
76 Chancery Ln, WC2 7430 1231 2–1D **NEW**
27 Upper St, N1 7704 2123 8–3D
142 Fleet St, EC4 7353 6761 9–2A
As "snaking queues" attest, "the best London burritos", and "quick"
service too, have made these "buzzy" Mexicans a big hit; let's hope
"creeping prices" don't spoil it all! / www.chilango.co.uk; EC4 9 pm;
N1 10 pm, Fri & Sat midnight; EC4 closed Sat & Sun; no booking.

Chilli Cool WC1 £27 ❷⑤④
15 Leigh St 7383 3135 2–1D
"Not for the faint-hearted", "the chilli-hot dishes" at this packed
Bloomsbury café are hailed by fans as "the best Sichuan food this
side of Chongqing"; no-one seems too phased by the "shockingly bad"
service. / www.chillicool.com; 10.15 pm.

China Tang
Dorchester Hotel W1   £75   ④④❸
53 Park Ln   7629 9988   3–3A
"The best Peking duck" is a highlight, at Sir David Tang's surprisingly
"old-school" Mayfair basement Chinese, which feels "like a neat and
tidy opium den… but without the opium!"; given the prices, however,
critics feel the food is "nothing special at all" – don't, however,
miss the glamorous cocktail bar. / www.thedorchesterhotel.com; 11.30 pm;
set weekday L £41 (FP).

Chinese Cricket Club EC4   £38   ❸④⑤
19 New Bridge St   7438 8051   9–3A
It may feel "like an airport departure lounge", but this room in a
"bland hotel" can seem like "an absolute find" – "in the desert
around Blackfriars", anywhere serving "delicious" Chinese cooking
is well worth knowing about! / www.chinesecricketclub.com; 10 pm; closed
Sun; no Amex.

Chipotle WC2   £19   ❸④④
114-116 Charing Cross Rd   7836 8491   4–1A
Much-ballyhooed when it opened, a year or so ago, this Mexican
import (which has 1000 US branches) inspired remarkably little
survey feedback this year; such reports as there were on the initial,
fringe-of-Covent-Garden branch are weakly positive, however,
and further openings are seemingly planned. / www.chipotle.com; 11 pm,
Sun 10 pm; no bookings.

Chisou W1   £43   ❷❸④
4 Princes St   7629 3931   3–1C
"Fantastic" sushi and "a good range of izakaya-style dishes done very
well" inspire enthusiastic reports on this "proper" Japanese café,
near Oxford Circus; there's a "wide selection of sakes" too –
"the owner is happy to talk you through them". / www.chisou.co.uk;
10.30 pm; closed Sun.

Chiswell Street Dining Rooms EC1 NEW £53   ❸❷❸
56 Chiswell St   07872 456 090   12–2A
The latest addition to the empire of the Martin brothers (of 'Gun' and
so on fame), this comfortable, if quite loud, newcomer was already
doing impressive City-lunching business on our early-days visit; service
was notably good. / Rated on Editors' visit.

Chiswick House Cafe W4   £24   ④⑤❸
Burlington Ln   8995 6356   10–1A
"You love or hate the new building" (a symphony in concrete), but this
year-old park café undoubtedly occupies "such an idyllic spot";
"why didn't an independent get it", though? – the menu's
"very limited", and service "breaks down" at peak times.
/ www.chiswickhousecafe.com; 5 pm; L only; no Amex.

Cho-San SW15   £40   ❷❸④
292 Upper Richmond Rd   8788 9626   10–2A
"An authentic slice of Japan"; this Putney veteran may seem a little
worn nowadays, but compensates with "lovely, family service" and
"utterly dependable" fare, including some "great sushi". / 10.30 pm;
closed Mon.

Chop'd £12 ❸❸④
52 Curzon St, W1 7495 1014 3–3B
St Pancras International, NW1 7837 1603 8–3C
Unit 1 34 The North Colonnade, E14 3229 0087 11–1C
2 Horner Sq, Old Spitalfields Mkt, E1 7247 8757 12–2B
1 Leadenhall Mkt, EC3 7626 3706 9–2D
*"Choose from pre-made or pick-your-own", at this "efficient" chain,
which serves a "huge variety of fresh and healthy salads",
and "with a smile" too; "they're a bit pricey for every day, though".
/ www.chopd.co.uk; most branches 4 pm, NW1 9 pm; most branches
Sat & Sun; no Amex.*

Chor Bizarre W1 £43 ④④❷
16 Albemarle St 7629 9802 3–3C
*"Kitsch" but "comfortable", this Mayfair Indian is "crammed" with
bric-a-brac; fans say it's "an excellent venue for business or pleasure",
but service can be "brusque" or "dippy", and its "good-but-not-
outstanding" food comes "at a price". / www.chorbizarre.com; 11.30 pm,
Sun 10.30 pm.*

Choys SW3 £38 ④④④
172 King's Rd 7352 9085 5–3C
*The "fairly standard" menu is never going to set the world on fire,
but this "well-established" (1952!) Chelsea Chinese is a "friendly"
place that "rarely surprises or disappoints". / 11 pm.*

Christopher's WC2 £64 ④❸❸
18 Wellington St 7240 4222 4–3D
*It's still sometimes hailed as a top brunch or business venue, but this
grand surf 'n' turf American, in a gorgeous Covent Garden townhouse,
has had a lot of "bad days" of late, with its pricey fare seeming
"very unimaginative" – "the bar menu may be the best option".
/ www.christophersgrill.com; 11.30 pm, Sun 10.30 pm; booking: max 12;
set pre theatre £36 (FP).*

Chuen Cheng Ku W1 £33 ❸④④
17 Wardour St 7437 1398 4–3A
*"Trolleys of steaming dim sum" weaving around the "busy" dining
rooms are a trademark of this Chinatown landmark – a "fun", "fast"
and "reasonably-priced" experience ("brilliant with young kids,
as there's no hanging about"). / www.chuenchengku.co.uk; 11.45 pm.*

Churchill Arms W8 £26 ❷❸❷
119 Kensington Church St 7792 1246 6–2B
*"Always busy, always fun, always good value!" – this "bustling" but
"lovely" pub-annex, near Notting Hill Gate, is "an institution" of over
20 years' standing, serving "incredibly cheap" Thai scoff that's "tasty
well beyond its price". / 10 pm, 9.30 pm.*

Chutney SW18 £29 ❷❷❸
11 Alma Rd 8870 4588 10–2B
*Food that's "full of fresh flavours" helps make this "always-busy"
Wandsworth local "much better than your average curry house".
/ www.chutneyrestaurant.co.uk; 11.30 pm; D only.*

Chutney Mary SW10 £55 ❷❷❷
535 King's Rd 7351 3113 5–4B
*An "upmarket" World's End Indian of over 20 years' standing that
still "consistently delivers" an excellent all-round experience; service
is "wonderful" and the "interesting" cooking "subtly aromatic" too –
"not just spicy". / www.realindianfood.com; 11.30 pm, Sun 10.30 pm; closed
weekday L; booking: max 10.*

Chutneys NW1 £29 ❸❸❸
124 Drummond St 7388 0604 8–4C
The "tasty" all-you-can-eat buffet (lunch and all-day Sunday) is the
main draw to this long-serving south Indian veggie, near Euston
station – it's "incredible value". / www.chutneyseuston.co.uk; 11 pm;
no Amex; need 5+ to book.

Ciao Bella WC1 £41 ④❷❷
86-90 Lamb's Conduit St 7242 4119 2–1D
"You are always greeted like a long-lost relative", at this "noisy and
bustling" Bloomsbury veteran; the food's main virtue is arguably that
it's "cheap", but fans like its "reliability", and in any case a visit
is usually "great fun". / www.ciaobellarestaurant.co.uk; 11.30 pm,
Sun 10.30 pm.

Cibo W14 £44 ❸❸④
3 Russell Gdns 7371 6271 7–1D
Fans proclaim "exciting" food and "wonderful" wines at this once-
famous Italian, in the backwoods of Olympia; given that no one has
a bad word to say about the place, it's a bit of a mystery why
it incites so few reports. / www.ciborestaurant.net; 11 pm; closed Sun D.

Cicada EC1 £40 ❷❷❸
132-136 St John St 7608 1550 9–1B
Will Ricker's early-wave pan-Asian fusion hang-out, in Shoreditch, still
manages to be "trendy and eclectic"; hey, after all these years the
food – with "extra heat and zing" – has even "got better of late" too!
/ www.rickerrestaurants.com; 11 pm; closed Sat L & Sun; set always available
£25 (FP).

Cigala WC1 £48 ❸❸④
54 Lamb's Conduit St 7405 1717 2–1D
"Humming and popular", this Bloomsbury corner spot is of note for
its "real" ("if not entirely consistent") Spanish cooking and some
"exciting" wines to go with it; service is "friendly" too, if sometimes
"over-stretched". / www.cigala.co.uk; 10.45 pm, Sun 9.30 pm.

Le Cigalon WC2 NEW £50 ❷❷❷
115 Chancery Ln 7242 8373 2–2D
In a "light and airy" room, this new Provençal addition to the Club
Gascon stable "fills a real gap in Midtown", especially as a place
to wine and dine legal types – the lunch menu is particularly
"good value"; downstairs, in the bar, check out the pétanque court!
/ www.cigalon.co.uk/; 10 pm; closed Sat & Sun.

THE CINNAMON CLUB SW1 £67 ❷❸❷
Old Westminster Library, Great Smith St 7222 2555 2–4C
"Full of MPs, union leaders and spin-doctors... otherwise excellent!";
this "beautiful" former library, near Westminster Abbey, is renowned
as one of London's foremost subcontinentals thanks to the "exquisite"
twists it puts on Indian cuisine; prices are "hefty", though – look out
for lunch and early-evening deals. / www.cinnamonclub.com; 10.45 pm;
closed Sun; no trainers.

Cinnamon Kitchen EC2 £56 ❷❸④
9 Devonshire Sq 7626 5000 9–2D
After a cracking debut, this "slick" two-year-old sibling
to Westminster's famous Cinnamon Club ("hidden-away near
Liverpool Street") is losing some ground – the "very clever" cooking
is still "fabulous", but the style seems ever more "corporate".
/ www.cinnamon-kitchen.com; 11 pm; closed Sat L & Sun; set weekday L
£34 (FP).

Circus WC2 £58 ④④❷
27-29 Endell St 7420 9300 4–2C
You watch circus acts while you eat – often right in front of your nose – at this year-old Covent Garden burlesque-joint; the few reports it attracts suggest it's a "vibrant" experience, from which the cooking does not positively detract. / www.circus-london.co.uk; midnight, Fri & Sat 2 am; closed Sun; no Amex; set pre theatre £38 (FP).

City Café
Mint Westminster SW1 £46 ④❸④
30 John Islip St 7932 4600 2–4C
"Great-value buffets" – on Sunday and for breakfast – are the highlights at this "spacious and comfortable", if "atmosphere-free", dining room, near Tate Britain. / www.citycafe.co.uk; 10.30pm, Sun 10 pm.

City Miyama EC4 £52 ❷④⑤
17 Godliman St 7489 1937 9–3B
"The space is so dull, but the food is always good", at this "authentic" Japanese basement, in the City; "superb sushi" at the upstairs bar is a highlight. / www.miyama.co.uk; 9.30 pm; closed Sat D & Sun; set weekday L £31 (FP).

Clarke's W8 £62 ❷❷❸
124 Kensington Church St 7221 9225 6–2B
Sally Clarke's once-"pioneering" California-inspired veteran, near Notting Hill Gate, remains for most reporters a "fantastic" spot, with "elegant" decor and "refined" cuisine; a disgruntled minority, though, fear it's becoming "tired", and "trading on its reputation". / www.sallyclarke.com; 10 pm; closed Sun D; booking: max 14.

Clifton E1 £26 ❸❸❸
1 Whitechapel Rd 7377 5533 9–2D
One of the better-known Brick Lane Indians – it doesn't inspire 'raves' from reporters, but it is consistently well-rated. / www.cliftonrestaurant.com; midnight.

The Clissold Arms N2 £44 ④④④
Fortis Grn 8444 4224 1–1C
"Some food shows real flair", at this popular Muswell Hill gastropub, which benefits from a "beautiful" outside area; it's "expensive" though, and not everyone likes the reintroduction of the "garish" Kinks memorabilia to pep up the "uninspiring" modern interior. / 10 pm, Sun 9 pm.

CLOS MAGGIORE WC2 £54 ❷❶❶
33 King St 7379 9696 4–3C
"Like an enchanted garden", the "breathtaking" conservatory of this Covent Garden "oasis" is the survey's newly-crowned 'top spot for romance'; that's not its only attraction, though – reports consistently praise its "delicious" cooking and "unbeatable" service, not to mention a wine list of over 2000 bins. / www.closmaggiore.com; Mon-Sat 11 pm, Sun 10 pm.

Club Gascon EC1 £75 ❷❷❸
57 West Smithfield 7796 0600 9–2B
"Unforgettable" foie-gras, and "small plates" of other "very rich" and "crazily good" Gascon delicacies – complemented by "amazing" SW France wines – make this "elegant" and "romantic", if "tightly-packed", Smithfield favourite "an experience to savour". / www.clubgascon.com; 10 pm, Fri-Sat 10.30 pm; closed Sat L & Sun.

Coach & Horses EC1   £40   ❷❷❸
26-28 Ray St   7278 8990   9–1A
*"Tucked-away in Clerkenwell", a "reliable" and "unfussy"
gastroboozer, offering "a short menu full of seasonal food that sounds
lovely and tastes better". / www.thecoachandhorses.com; 10 pm; closed
Sat L & Sun D.*

Cochin Brasserie SW15   £30   ❷❹❹
193 Lower Richmond Rd   8785 6004   10–1A
*"Eclectic" south Indian dishes are "beautifully prepared" – and some
are "absolutely exceptional" – at this low-key Putney curry house;
"the kitchen can be slow, but waiting staff are as helpful as can be".
/ www.cochinbrasserie.com; 11 pm; D only.*

Cochonnet W9   £43   ❸❷❸
1 Lauderdale Pde   7289 0393   1–2B
*"A great little local", in Maida Vale, "which is busy every night of the
week", thanks to its "good, standard Italian fare",
not least "the best pizza". / www.cochonnet.co.uk; 10.30 pm.*

Cock Tavern EC1   £29   ❸❹❹
Smithfield Mkt   7236 4923   9–2A
*"The butchers eat here, which says it all!" – this café-like pub,
actually under Smithfield market, offers "superb full English
breakfasts", with meat "straight from the market"; Guinness on tap
too. / www.thecocktavern.com; 7.30pm; L only, closed Sat & Sun.*

Cocorino   £15   ❶❶❸
18 Chilton St, W1   7935 0860   2–1A **NEW**
18 Thayer St, W1   7935 0810   3–1A
*"A tiny hole in the wall", off Marylebone High Street, serving "world-
beating ice creams" and "delicious" focaccia-based snacks,
from breakfast onwards; there's now a nearby 'espresso room' too.
/ Thayer Street 8 pm; Chilton Street Mon-Sat 6 pm, Sun 5 pm; no Amex;
no bookings.*

Cocotte NW3 **NEW**   £43   ❹❹❸
85b Fleet Rd   7433 3317   8–2A
*Owners who are "friendly, relaxed and utterly charming" add much
to the mood at this "lovely" Gallic newcomer, by South End Green,
which serves up "fairly-priced traditional bistro fare". / 11 pm; closed
Mon, Tue L, Wed L, Thu L & Sun D; set weekday L £24 (FP).*

Cocum SW20   £30   ❸❸❸
9 Approach Rd   8540 3250   10–2B
*A Raynes Park Keralan that's "improved" in recent times, and of note
for the "consistent, well-balanced flavours" of its cuisine.
/ www.cocumrestaurant.co.uk; 10.30 pm, Sun 10 pm; no Amex.*

La Collina NW1   £47
17 Princess Rd   7483 0192   8–3B
*New owners took over this Primrose Hill Italian (which has a lovely
garden for the summer) just as our survey for the year was
concluding; let's hope the first (and so far only) report – of "delicious"
cooking and "great value for money" – is the start of a trend! / 11 pm.*

Le Colombier SW3   £58   ❸❷❷
145 Dovehouse St   7351 1155   5–2C
*"Very genteel and Parisian", Didier Garnier's "discreet" Chelsea
brasserie remains "very popular with the locals"; the food, though,
is an attraction rather incidental to the "professional" service,
the "very good and reasonably-priced wines", and the exceptional
terrace. / www.le-colombier-restaurant.co.uk; 10.30 pm, Sun 10 pm.*

Colony W1 £54 ❸④⑤

7-9 Paddington St 7935 3353 2–1A

Star chef Atul Kochar is no longer involved in this low-lit Indian yearling, in Marylebone, which is based around a tapas-style concept that's yet to catch fire; fans applaud its "exquisite" dishes, but to critics the small plates here are just "a good example of how not to do it!" / www.colonybarandgrill.com; 10.45 pm, Sun 10.30 pm; set weekday L £30 (FP).

Como Lario SW1 £47 ⑤④❸

18-22 Holbein Pl 7730 2954 5–2D

Diehard fans say "it always has a happy atmosphere", but this trattoria "classic", off Sloane Square, is badly on the slide – the food's "gone downhill fast", and service has sometimes been notably "off-hand" of late. / www.comolario.uk.com; 11.30 pm, Sun 10 pm; set Sun L £30 (FP).

The Compass N1 £38 ❸④❸

58 Penton St 7837 3891 8–3D

"A little Chapel Market gem", this "cheerful" gastropub has a "cosy" interior, and offers "accurate" cooking too. / thecompassn1.co.uk; 9.45 pm, Sun 7.45 pm; closed Mon L & Tue L; no Amex.

Comptoir Gascon EC1 £47 ❷❸❷

63 Charterhouse St 7608 0851 9–1A

"Duck and gamey delights abound", on the "hearty" and "wonderfully simple" menu of SW French fare on offer at at this "lovely" Smithfield bistro; it's "well priced" too. / www.comptoirgascon.com; 10 pm, Thu & Fri 11 pm; closed Mon & Sun.

Comptoir Libanais £18 ④⑤④

65 Wigmore St, W1 7935 1110 3–1A

Westfield, The Balcony, W12 8811 2222 7–1C

Fans still tout these "fun"-looking Middle Easterners as a decent "cheap 'n' cheerful" experience; too many reporters, however, now talk of food that's "tasteless", and service that's "unacceptably slow". / www.lecomptoir.co.uk; W12 9 pm, Thu & Fri 10 pm, Sun 6 pm; W1 9.30 pm; W12 closed Sun D; no Amex; no bookings.

Constancia SE1 £42 ❷❶❷

52 Tanner St 7234 0676 9–4D

"Everyone needs a local steakhouse like this", say fans of this "very authentic" Argentinian, just south of Tower Bridge; highlights of the "relatively short" menu include "fabulous" meat (of course) and "tasty" puddings. / www.constancia.co.uk; 10.30 pm; D only; no Amex.

Il Convivio SW1 £56 ❸❸④

143 Ebury St 7730 4099 2–4A

"Why don't more people know about this wonderful restaurant?", wonder fans of this swish Belgravia Italian; critics, though, see the glass as half-empty – they cite "nothing special on the food front", "slow service", and an interior that feels "like a rehash of a typical '90s trattoria". / www.etruscarestaurants.com; 10.45 pm; closed Sun.

Coq d'Argent EC2 £66 ④⑤④

1 Poultry 7395 5000 9–2C

"Formulaic" food, "unhelpful" service and a "lifeless" dining room, all at "sky-high prices" – no once could say a visit to this 6th-floor D&D group venue is without its pitfalls; it remains popular for City entertaining, though, thanks not least to its "memorable" rooftop gardens (for drinks). / www.coqdargent.co.uk; 9.45 pm; closed Sat L & Sun D.

Cork & Bottle WC2 £42 ⑤④❷
44-46 Cranbourn St 7734 7807 4–3B
"You don't come for the food" (not even the 'famous' cheese 'n' ham pie!) to this "secret" but "handy" hide-away, by a Leicester Square sex shop – it's the "fantastic" wine which is the real draw; "don't delay your trip, as Don, the owner, is going to retire at some point". / www.corkandbottle.net; 11.30 pm, Sun 10.30 pm; no booking after 6.30 pm.

Corner Room E2 NEW £37
Patriot Sq 7871 0461 1–2D
Don't fancy the outré fare on offer at Bethnal Green's ambitious Viajante? – try this adjacent mid-2011 newcomer, where Nuno Mendes offers a much simpler and more accessible cuisine; we sadly didn't have the opportunity to visit before this guide went to press. / www.viajante.co.uk.

Corrigan's Mayfair W1 £70 ❸❸❸
28 Upper Grosvenor St 7499 9943 3–3A
"Fish and game done to perfection" head up the list of attractions, at this Irish chef's "luxurious" Mayfair dining room; its performance "dropped off" notably this year, however, with a number of "disastrous" reports, exacerbated by "wince-making" prices. / www.corrigansmayfair.com; 11 pm, Sun 9 pm; closed Sat L; booking: max 8; set always available £44 (FP).

Costa's Grill W8 £25 ④❸④
12-14 Hillgate St 7229 3794 6–2B
An "unpretentious" and inexpensive taverna of aeons standing, just off Notting Hill Gate, with a "charming garden"; "it may be average, but I'd still happily eat here every day!" / www.costasgrill.com; 10.30 pm; closed Sun.

Côte £38 ④❸❷
124-126 Wardour St, W1 7287 9280 3–1D
17-21 Tavistock St, WC2 7379 9991 4–3D
98 Westbourne Grove, W2 7792 3298 6–1B NEW
50-54 Turnham Green Ter, W4 8747 6788 7–2A NEW
47 Kensington Ct, W8 7938 4147 5–1A
Hays Galleria, Tooley St, SE1 7234 0800 9–4D
8 High St, SW19 8947 7100 10–2B
45-47 Parsons Green Ln, SW6 7736 8444 10–1B
26 Ludgate Hill, EC4 7236 4399 9–2A NEW
"What Café Rouge used to aspire to be"; Richard Caring's burgeoning group of Gallic bistros may seem increasingly "formulaic", but it can still offer some "pleasant surprises" on the food front, and "by high street chain standards, service and atmosphere are excellent too". / www.cote-restaurants.co.uk; 11 pm.

The Courtauld Gallery Café
The Courtauld Gallery WC2 £27 ④❸❸
Somerset Hs, Strand 7848 2527 2–2D
Off a sunken courtyard, just a few feet from the Strand, a "convenient" café serving "a good choice of good-value dishes" – it's especially worth seeking out on a sunny day, when the al fresco tables offer one of London's nicest surprises. / 3 pm; no Amex.

The Cow W2 £49 ❸④❷
89 Westbourne Park Rd 7221 0021 6–1B
Tom Conran's "busy and buzzy" faux-Irish boozer, in Bayswater, continues to pack in a hip crowd with its "consistently good" realisation of simple seafood dishes – "no reservations, expect to wait"; upstairs, the formula is more formal. / www.thecowlondon.co.uk; 11 pm, Sun 10.30 pm; no Amex.

F S A

Crazy Bear W1 — £53 — ❸❸❶
26-28 Whitfield St 7631 0088 2–1C
Kick off with a cocktail in the "fun" and "vibey" basement bar, if you visit this glamorously opulent Fitzrovia venue; there's a "great range" of pan-Asian food too, but it's "expensive" and "rather overshadowed by the decor". / www.crazybeargroup.co.uk; 10.30 pm; no shorts.

Crazy Homies W2 — £42 — ❸❹❶
125 Westbourne Park Rd 7727 6771 6–1B
Tom Conran's "fun and buzzy" – read "loud" and "squashed" – Bayswater cantina is "mostly about the vibe"; but while "good Mexican food is hard to find in London", this place "makes a decent stab at it". / www.crazyhomieslondon.co.uk; 11 pm; closed weekday L; no Amex.

Criterion W1 — £66 — ❹❹❷
224 Piccadilly 7930 0488 3–3D
"Opulent" and "very spacious", this neo-Byzantine chamber, right on Piccadilly Circus, is a "stunning" space; its ambience can still seem surprisingly "low-key", though, not helped by iffy service and food that "at the price, should be better". / www.criterionrestaurant.com; 11.30 pm, Sun 9 pm; set weekday L & pre-theatre £39 (FP).

Crussh — £14 — ❸❷❹
Branches throughout London
"Healthy alternatives to your usual sandwiches" – including "great salads and soups" – win universal praise for this "innovative" small chain; "fresh juices and smoothies too", of course. / www.crussh.com; 4.30 pm-8 pm,; many branches closed all or part of weekend; no credit cards in many branches.

Cumberland Arms W14 — £41 — ❸❸❸
29 North End Rd 7371 6806 7–2D
"Unpretentious" and "mellow", this Olympia spot ticks all of the obvious boxes for a congenial local gastropub. / www.thecumberlandarmspub.co.uk; 10 pm, Sun 9.30 pm.

Curve / Manhattan Grill
London Marriott W' India Quay E14
22 Hertsmere Rd 7517 2808 11–1C
As this guide goes to press, this large waterside dining room by Canary Wharf is to be reformatted from a fish restaurant, into a steak house. / www.marriothotel.co.uk; 10.30 pm, Sun 10 pm; closed Sat L & Sun L; set always available £37 (FP).

Cut
45 Park Lane W1 NEW
45 Park Ln 7493 4545 3–4A
Opening in late-2011, this grand surf 'n' turf specialist, in a new Mayfair hotel, will be the first European venture of eminent Austrian/Californian restaurateur Wolfgang Puck. / www.45parklane.com.

Cyprus Mangal SW1 — £29 — ❷❸❹
45 Warwick Way 7828 5940 2–4B
A "cramped" Pimlico dive, where the neighbouring parking bays are "clogged with black cabs", attracted by "big plates of shish kebab" at "cheap" prices. / Sun-Thu midnight, Fri & Sat 1 am.

Da Mario SW7 £39 ④❷❸
15 Gloucester Rd   7584 9078   5–1B
*Proximity to the Albert Hall and a "buzzing" atmosphere are prime
selling points of this long-established and family-friendly Italian;
its pizza 'n' pasta fare is "reliable, but not outstanding in any way".
/ www.damario.co.uk; 11.30 pm.*

Da Mario WC2 £39 ④❷❷
63 Endell St   7240 3632   4–1C
*In touristy Covent Garden, it's "a joy", say fans, to stumble upon this
"tiny", age-old, family-run trattoria – a "genuine Italian" serving
"speedy pre-performance meals" in a "cramped" interior with
"real buzz".*

da Polpo WC2 NEW £30 ❸❷④
6 Maiden Ln   7836 8448   4–3D
*The fourth member of Russell Norman's quickly-created Venetian
tapas empire makes a handy addition to Covent Garden's improving
dining-out scene; by the group's vibey standards, though, the interior
is bare and rather lacking in character. / Rated on Editors' visit.*

Dalchini SW19 £36 ❸❸④
147 Arthur Rd   8947 5966   10–2B
*"A great cross-over of Indian and Chinese cuisine" – the 'Hakka'
dishes at this "different" local, opposite Wimbledon Park tube,
are "really interesting", and "super value" too. / www.dalchini.co.uk;
10.30 pm, Fri & Sat 11 pm; no Amex.*

Dans le Noir EC1 £70 ⑤④❶
29 Clerkenwell Grn   7253 1100   9–1A
*"If you're looking for something different", try a meal in the pitch
black, at this crackpot Farringdon theme-restaurant, where "you eat
as if you were blind" (as the staff actually are); "the novelty wears off
quickly", though – the food is "diabolical" and "overpriced", and the
staff can be "grumpy" too! / www.danslenoir.com; 9.30 pm; D only.*

Daphne NW1 £34 ❸❶❶
83 Bayham St   7267 7322   8–3C
*"Without question, the friendliest Greek in London!" – fans aren't shy
in their praise for this veteran Camden Town taverna, where the
"tasty" cuisine includes some "interesting specials"; pleasant roof
terrace. / 11.30 pm; closed Sun; no Amex.*

Daphne's SW3 £57 ❸❷❷
112 Draycott Ave   7589 4257   5–2C
*This "timeless Italian", near Brompton Cross, remains a "must-visit"
for many reporters, thanks to its "lovely", "romantic" style and its
"warm" and "professional" service; prices are "not for the faint-
hearted", but the food – "while not trail-blazing" – is "amazingly
consistent". / www.daphnes-restaurant.co.uk; 11.30 pm; set weekday L &
pre-theatre £36 (FP).*

The Dartmouth Arms SE23 £36 ❸❸❷
7 Dartmouth Rd   8488 3117   1–4D
*"Still the best for miles around" – a "gem" of a Forest Hill
gastroboozer, which wins quite a following with its "deliciously
consistent" cuisine. / www.thedartmoutharms.com; 10 pm, Sun 9 pm;
no Amex.*

FSA

Daylesford Organic £40 ④⑤④
44b Pimlico Rd, SW1 7881 8060 5–2D
208-212 Westbourne Grove, W11 7313 8050 6–1B
These "smart" deli/cafés are often "full of yummy mummies and their adorable children"; fans plug breakfasts as being of "top-quality simplicity", and say the other fare is "delicious" too – critics are more inclined to note "truly absurd" prices, and "the worst ever" service. / www.daylesfordorganic.com; 5 pm-8 pm, Sun 4 pm-6 pm; W11 no booking L.

Dean Street Townhouse W1 £58 ④❸❷
69-71 Dean St 7434 1775 4–2A
"Slightly Manhattanite, but very British", this panelled Soho dining room (part of the trendy Soho House group) is "the place to go for people-watching and general glamour"; the food – "homely" or "plain and unimaginative", according to your viewpoint – is rather incidental. / www.deanstreettownhouse.com; midnight; set pre theatre £36 (FP).

Defune W1 £46 ❷0④
34 George St 7935 8311 3–1A
A long-established Marylebone Japanese where the story never changes – the sushi is "excellent", but you pay "silly prices" to endure sitting in either a "dreary basement", or on the "characterless first floor". / 10.30 pm.

Dehesa W1 £41 00❷
25 Ganton St 7494 4170 3–2C
"Superbly moreish" Italian/Spanish tapas, "perceptive" staff and a "lively" atmosphere make this small bar/café, off Carnaby Street, a "wonderful" all-rounder (now eclipsing its elder sibling, Salt Yard); seating is limited (and "cramped" too), so "booking is essential". / www.dehesa.co.uk; 11 pm; closed Sun D.

Del'Aziz £41 ④⑤❷
24-32 Vanston Pl, SW6 7386 0086 5–4A
Westfield, Ariel Way, W12 8740 0666 7–1C
Swiss Cottage Leis' C', Adelaide Rd, NW3 7586 3338 8–2A
11 Bermondsey Sq, SE1 7407 2991 9–4D
5 Canvey St, SE1 7633 0033 9–3B
Fans really take to the "trendy" and "vibrant" style of this Moroccan-inspired chain, whose culinary attractions include an "unusual brunch", "a great mezze selection", and cakes and coffee; "awful" service, though, can take the edge off the experience, and critics find the grub "very average" too. / www.delaziz.co.uk; SW6 10.30 pm; NW3 9.30 pm; SE1 11 pm; W12 10.45 pm, Sun 9.45 pm; SE1 11 pm; NW3 D sat, sun.

Delfina SE1 £47 ❸❸❸
50 Bermondsey St 7357 0244 9–4D
"Vast and starkly white", this Bermondsey gallery creates a "fantastically airy and uncluttered space" for a meal; the cooking doesn't hit the heights it once did, but most reports still praise it as "thoughtful". / www.thedelfina.co.uk; 10 pm; closed Sun-Thu D, Fri open L & D, closed Sat.

Delfino W1 £43 ❷④④
121 Mount St 7499 1256 3–3B
"The thin-crust pizzas are historic!", at this "utilitarian" Mayfair basement-Italian – a particularly "handy" stand-by in a "stratospherically expensive part of town". / www.finos.co.uk; 11 pm; closed Sun.

La Delizia £34 ❸❸❸
63-65 Chelsea Manor St, SW3 7376 4111 5–3C
314 Trinity Rd, SW18 88759 595 10–2C NEW
It may be "cramped", but this "small, very Italian-feeling local", in a
Chelsea back street, "has been making authentic, wood-oven pizzas
since long before it was the fancy thing to do, and still turns out some
of the best"; it now has an offshoot in Wandsworth too. / 11 pm,
Sun 10.30; no Amex.

The Depot SW14 £40 ❸❷❶
Tideway Yd, Mortlake High St 8878 9462 10–1A
"Radically improved" service of late and better-rated cooking too
make this local favourite, near Barnes Bridge, more than
just an "atmosphere" recommendation nowadays – you still shouldn't
forget, though, to "ask for a window table overlooking the Thames".
/ www.depotbrasserie.co.uk; 10 pm, Sun 9.30 pm.

LES DEUX SALONS WC2 £54 ❸❹❸
40-42 William IV St 7420 2050 4–4C
"It could be Paris!"; handily located near Charing Cross, Will Smith
and Anthony Demetre's hugely popular new brasserie – a sibling
to Arbutus – is, say fans, "a brilliant addition to London"; critics,
though, "don't think the food's that exciting", and find the survey's
most-mentioned newcomer "massively overhyped".
/ www.lesdeuxsalons.co.uk; 11 pm; set weekday L & pre-theatre £28 (FP).

Le Deuxième WC2 £55 ❹❸❺
65a Long Acre 7379 0033 4–2D
"A reliable stand-by, near the Royal Opera House"; it may have
"no decor at all", but it's an "efficient" operation, offering "solid
bistro-cooking". / www.ledeuxieme.com; midnight, Sun 11 pm; set weekday
L & pre-theatre £31 (FP).

dim T £31 ❺❹❸
56-62 Wilton Rd, SW1 7834 0507 2–4B
32 Charlotte St, W1 7637 1122 2–1C
1 Hampstead Ln, N6 8340 8800 8–1B
3 Heath St, NW3 7435 0024 8–2A
Tooley St, SE1 7403 7000 9–4D
"After a bright start, quality has fallen off a cliff", at this budget pan-
Asian chain; positives include stylish interiors (and "great views"
in SE1), but the downsides can include "tasteless" food and
amateurish service. / www.dimt.co.uk; most branches 11 pm, Sun 10.30pm.

Diner £31 ❺❺❸
18 Ganton St, W1 7287 8962 3–2C
21 Essex Rd, N1 7226 4533 8–3D
64-66 Chamberlayne Rd, NW10 8968 9033 1–2B
2 Jamestown Rd, NW1 7485 5223 8–3B
128 Curtain Rd, EC2 7729 4452 12–1B
Such a shame these "lively" American diners – with the possible
exception of the Shoreditch original – so often fail to live up to the
dream; on a bad day, the food is "like cardboard", and the service
"can be pretty trying too". / www.thedinershoreditch.com; midnight; W1 &
NW1 Sun 11.30 pm; EC2 Sun & Mon 10.30 pm; booking: max 10.

Dinings W1 £42 ❶❷❺
22 Harcourt St 7723 0666 8–4A
"OK, it's in a bunker", but Tomonari Chiba's "brutalist" Japanese
basement, "tucked-away" in Marylebone, is nonetheless
an "overwhelmingly excellent" place, offering sushi and sashimi that
are "cutting-edge" creative, and "super, super, super fresh" too.
/ www.dinings.co.uk; 10.30 pm; closed Sat L & Sun.

DINNER
MANDARIN ORIENTAL SW1   £94   ❷❷❷
66 Knightsbridge   7201 3833   5–1D
"Surprisingly it lives up to the hype!"; Heston B's *"modern Olde English food"* – *"beautifully executed with a dash of showmanship"* – has made his Knightsbridge newcomer the hit of the year; prices are *"remarkable"* too, though, and the room is a bit *"hotel-like"* (even if some lucky lunchers do get *"amazing"* park-views).
/ www.dinnerbyheston.com; 10.45 pm; set weekday L £56 (FP).

Dishoom WC2   £35   ❸❸❶
12 Upper St Martins Ln   7420 9320   4–3B
"Just like Bombay in the 1950s!" – the *"delightfully elegant"* interior of this Covent Garden chain-prototype has a suitably *"energetic"* atmosphere; its *"spicy"* street food is generally *"very flavoursome"*, and hailed as *"quite authentic"* too. / www.dishoom.com; 11 pm, Fri & Sat midnight, Sun 10 pm; booking 6+ D.

Diwana Bhel-Poori House NW1   £28   ❸⑤⑤
121-123 Drummond St   7387 5556   8–4C
"A lunchtime buffet worth travelling for" is still the top tip at this *"absurdly cheap"*, '60s-survivor, veggie canteen, in the Little India near Euston; it's *"not as marvellous as it was a few years ago"* though, and still gets *"no prizes for decor"*; BYO.
/ diwanabhelpoori.co.uk; 11.45 pm, Sun 11 pm; need 10+ to book.

The Dock Kitchen
Portobello Dock W10   £49   ❸❸❶
344 Ladbroke Grove   8962 1610   1–2B
Steve Parle's *"funky"* café, by the canal in North Kensington, offers *"thoughtful"* food from an *"eclectic"* and ever-changing set menu; it's *"gone downhill"* since it opened, though – results can be *"patchy depending on the night"*, and *"amateurish"* service increasingly *"seems to believe its own PR"*. / www.dockkitchen.co.uk; 10 pm; closed Sun D.

Dockmaster's House E14   £50   ④④❸
1 Hertsmere Rd   7345 0345   11–1C
An *"out-of-the-way"* nouvelle Indian, near Canary Wharf, praised by fans for its *"inventive"* cuisine, and its *"relaxed"* setting in a lovely Georgian house; service is increasingly *"erratic"*, though, and *"some dishes work better than others"*.
/ www.dockmastershouse.com; 11 pm; closed Sat L & Sun.

Dolada W1   £51   ❸❸④
13 Albermarle St   7409 1011   3–3C
Fans of this Mayfair basement venture applaud its *"proper"* Italian cooking, *"stylish"* decor and *"discreet yet friendly"* staff... or, to put it another way, it's *"a pretty dull place, with OK food, and suited to business lunches"*. / www.dolada.co.uk; 10.30 pm; closed Sat L & Sun.

$ EC1   £42   ④④❸
2 Exmouth Mkt   7278 0077   9–1A
Dwindling feedback supports those who say this attractive Clerkenwell haunt has *"gone massively downhill"* – *"it used to do the best burger around"*, but now *"it's a place for cocktails rather than food"*. / www.dollargrills.com; 11.30 pm, Tue & Wed 11 pm, Sun & Mon 10 pm.

The Don EC4   £58   ❸❷❸
20 St Swithin's Ln   7626 2606   9–3C
*The Square Mile's "best business option" – in "characterful" premises
near Bank – has a "top-quality" restaurant on the ground floor, and a
"convivial" bistro below ("in the old port cellar"); overall, it's a very
"professional" operation, but the "outstanding" wines and sherries
are a greater draw than the "competent" cuisine.*
/ www.thedonrestaurant.com; 10 pm; closed Sat & Sun; no trainers.

don Fernando's TW9   £42   ❸❷❸
27f The Quadrant   8948 6447   1–4A
*This large family-run "Spanish tapas restaurant", by the railway
station, "has served Richmond incredibly well over the years" – it's a
"fun" place, with "responsive" service and "ever-reliable" food.*
/ www.donfernando.co.uk; 11 pm; no Amex; no booking.

Don Pepe NW8   £34   ❸❷❸
99 Frampton St   7262 3834   8–4A
*A stalwart St John's Wood tapas bar where "everything looks so tasty,
the only problem is choosing"; "revisiting after 20 years, I found
just the same waiters – they seemed a little older, but were still
just as friendly". / 11.30 pm; closed Sun; no Amex.*

Donna Margherita SW11   £41   ❷❸❷
183 Lavender Hill   7228 2660   10–2C
*"Antipasto and pizza just like they serve back in Naples" make this
"jolly" and "easy-going" Battersea spot very popular; it helps that it's
"very reasonably priced" too. / www.donna-margherita.com; 10.30 pm,
Fri-Sat 11 pm; closed weekday L.*

Dorchester Grill
Dorchester Hotel W1   £89   ❹❸❹
53 Park Ln   7629 8888   3–3A
*"Hideous" tartan decor aside, this "opulent" Mayfair grill room has
attracted (somewhat) more praise of late for its straightforward
cuisine, and its often "excellent" service – prices, though, still tend
to "exorbitant". / www.thedorchester.com; 10.45 pm, Sun 10.15 pm;
no trainers; set weekday L £52 (FP).*

Dose EC1   £76   ❷❶❹
70 Long Ln   7600 0382   9–1B
*"The best of London's Antipodean coffee shops" now occupies larger
premises next door to its original site; it's "a great place to grab and
go" at any time, with "super breakfasts" a highlight.*
/ www.dose-espresso.com; L only; no Amex.

Dotori N4   £26   ❷❸❸
3 Stroud Green Rd   7263 3562   8–1D
*"Book early, and expect to wait for a table even so", at this
"minuscule" Finsbury Park outfit, where "charming" (if "harried")
staff serve up some "super-fresh" and "authentic" Korean and
Japanese fare. / 10.30 pm; closed Mon; no Amex.*

Doukan SW18   £37   ❸❷❷
350 Old York Rd   8870 8280   10–2B
*"Tasty and varied" Moroccan grub is part of the all-round formula
that makes this friendly and atmospheric Wandsworth spot a very
superior local. / www.doukan.co.uk; Tue-Thu 10 pm, Fri-Sat 10.30 pm,
Sun 5 pm; closed Mon & Sun D; no Amex.*

Dragon Castle SE17   £35   ❷④④
100 Walworth Rd   7277 3388   1–3C
In unlovely Elephant & Castle, this "huge" Chinese "oasis" has carved out quite a name, especially for dim sum that's "hard to beat"; its ratings slid this year, though, with service sometimes seeming "overbearing" of late. / www.dragoncastle.eu; 11 pm.

Dragoncello W2 NEW   £51   ④❷❸
104a, Chepstow Rd   7221 1821   6–1B
"A tiny little Notting Hill gem" which gives an impression rather like "being served in your own front room"; the Italian fare shows "potential", but critics find prices "astronomical". / 10.30 pm, Sat & Sun 11 pm; closed Mon, Tue-Fri L.

The Drapers Arms N1   £43   ④④❸
44 Barnsbury St   7619 0348   8–3D
"I was rather hoping they'd have revamped the revamp by now!" – this elegant, well-known Islington gastropub (with garden) is still on many accounts a "lovely local", yet it too often falls short nowadays; despite the "steep" prices, the service can be "appalling", and the food is regularly "wide of the mark". / www.thedrapersarms.com; 10.30 pm; no Amex.

The Duke of Cambridge N1   £48   ④④❸
30 St Peter's St   7359 3066   1–2C
"All-organic, low food-miles, low carbon..." – "every right-on requirement you can think of" is catered for at this "buzzy" gastropub; even by trendy-Islington standards, though, service can seem a bit "casual", and cynics say the "outrageously expensive" menu "isn't actually that good". / www.dukeorganic.co.uk; 10.30 pm, Sun 10 pm; no Amex.

Duke of Sussex W4   £41   ❸❷❷
75 South Pde   8742 8801   7–1A
A "gorgeous" interior (and "great outdoor space") adds to the appeal of this "lively" tavern on the Chiswick/Acton borders; it "stands apart from the usual gastropub suspects", thanks not least to a Spanish-influenced cuisine, which is often realised to a "high" standard. / 10.30 pm, Sun 9.30 pm; closed Mon L; no Amex.

The Duke of Wellington W1   £44   ❸④❸
94a, Crawford St   7723 2790   2–1A
A "lovely little gastropub", in the heart of Marylebone, offering food that's "a notch up from the average". / www.thedukew1.co.uk; 10 pm, Sun 9 pm; no Amex.

E&O W11   £52   ❷❸❷
14 Blenheim Cr   7229 5454   6–1A
"Still buzzing!" – Will Ricker's "cool and clubby" Notting Hill hang-out still delivers up "delectable" Asian-fusion dishes in a "trendy" setting whose vibe is buoyed by a "busy" bar; "the clientele is a bit west London-Boho, but then you can't have everything". / www.rickerrestaurants.com; 11 pm, Sun 10.30 pm; booking: max 6.

E11even Park Walk SW10 NEW   £56   ❸④④
11 Park Wk   7352 3449   5–3B
Gordon Ramsay initially found fame at this Chelsea site, which continued to trade as Aubergine (RIP) until recently; in its new guise, it's a comfortable spot of place, but the Italian cuisine seems to have no aspirations much beyond "competence", and the service can be "very slow". / Rated on Editors' visit; www.atozrestaurants.com/11parkwalk; midnight.

The Eagle EC1 £27 ❸❹❶
159 Farringdon Rd 7837 1353 9–1A
The "no-frills" Clerkenwell "origin of the gastropub movement" is "still the best", say fans, and still "crazy-busy at times"; its Mediterranean cooking is "not as good as it once was", but still "surprisingly hearty and enjoyable". / 10.30 pm; closed Sun D; no Amex; no booking.

Eagle Bar Diner W1 £37 ❸❸❷
3-5 Rathbone Pl 7637 1418 4–1A
"From the quality and flavour of the beef, to the superlative side-dishes", this trendy boothed hang-out, just off Oxford Street, is worth seeking out for its "brilliant" burgers; they do a mean cocktail too. / www.eaglebardiner.com; 11 pm, Thu-Sat 1 am; closed Sun; need 6+ to book.

Ealing Park Tavern W5 £44 ❸❸❹
222 South Ealing Rd 8758 1879 1–3A
"Ealing is severely lacking in the quality restaurant department", so this "cavernous" gastropub – with its "well-cooked and well-presented dishes" – certainly stands out. / www.ealingparktavern.com; 10 pm, Sun 9 pm.

Earl Spencer SW18 £41 ❸❸❸
260-262 Merton Rd 8870 9244 10–2B
"Easy-going and spacious", this Southfields gastropub "gem" delights the locals with its "foodie" menu and its "friendly" staff; the secret, though, is well and truly out – "get there by noon at weekends or you won't get a table!" / www.theearlspencer.co.uk; 10 pm, Sun 9.30 pm; no booking Sun.

The East Hill SW18 £39 ❸❸❷
21 Alma Rd 8874 1833 10–2B
It's "the perfect local boozer", say fans of this "fun" Wandsworth hostelry, which continues to go down well with the denizens of the Nappy Valley. / www.geronimo-inns.co.uk; 10 pm, Thu-Sat 10.30 pm, Sun 9 pm.

The Easton WC1 £41 ❷❷❸
22 Easton St 7278 7608 9–1A
"A little gem off Easton Street, opposite the better-known Exmouth Market" – this "great gastropub" is "run by chef/proprietors who know what they're doing", and who serve up some "delicious" fare. / 10 pm, Sun 9.30 pm.

Eat £12 ❹❸❹
Branches throughout London
"Tasty" and "healthy" soups (in particular) and "invariably fresh" sandwiches lead fans to hail these "reliable lunch stops" as "better than Pret"; in the survey as a whole, however, their rivals just pip 'em to the post on all counts. / www.eat.co.uk; 4 pm-8 pm; most City branches closed all or part of weekend; no credit cards; no booking.

The Ebury SW1 £47 ❹❹❸
11 Pimlico Rd 7730 6784 5–2D
"A lovely atmosphere" helps make this large Pimlico bar/brasserie a "super place to hang out"; the food, though, is no more than "fine", and it's "pricey" too. / www.theebury.co.uk; 10.30 pm, Sun 10 pm.

Ebury Wine Bar SW1 £46 ❹❸❸
139 Ebury St 7730 5447 2–4A
This age-old Belgravia haunt remains an "agreeable" sort of place; not everyone is convinced by the "average" food, though – "it's more somewhere you go for the wine". / www.eburywinebar.co.uk; 10.15 pm.

Eco SW4
£36 ❸❹❸

162 Clapham High St   7978 1108   10–2D

"Still the best pizza", say fans, but this once-trendy Clapham hang-out can seem a little long-in-the-tooth nowadays, and inspires only middling levels of satisfaction overall. / www.ecorestaurants.com; 11 pm, Fri & Sat 11.30 pm.

Ed's Easy Diner
£27 ❹❸❷

12 Moor St, W1   7434 4439   4–2A
Trocadero, 19 Rupert St, W1   7287 1951   3–3D
Sedley Pl, 14 Woodstock St, W1   7493 9916   3–2B **NEW**

These "glorious", "hyper-retro" diners serve "good burgers and cheesy fries, plus milkshakes to die for" – "OK, it's not the most gourmet burger, but the place can't be beaten for fun!" / www.edseasydiner.co.uk; Rupert St 11 pm, Fri & Sat midnight; Moor St midnight, Sun 10 pm, Sedley place 9 pm; no Amex; Moor St no booking.

Edera W11
£61 ❷❶❸

148 Holland Park Ave   7221 6090   6–2A

In chichi Holland Park, this "classy local Italian", serves food that's "more upmarket than most"; particularly "charming" service contributes to an all-round performance that can only be characterised as "excellent". / www.atozrestaurants.com/edera/; 11 pm, Sun 10 pm.

Edokko WC1
£46 ❷❶❸

50 Red Lion St   7242 3490   2–1D

"No one's heard of the place", yet fans say the "beautifully executed" sushi and other "delicious" and "authentic" fare on offer at this cosy and "traditional" ("dingy") Japanese, off Holborn, are among the best in town; "the only drawback is two sittings at lunchtime". / 10 pm; closed Sat & Sun.

Eight Over Eight SW3
£52 ❷❸❷

392 King's Rd   7349 9934   5–3B

"Back in its stride" after the fire (well, almost), this "buzzy" Chelsea pan-Asian is again a "fabulous sibling to E&O", serving "imaginative", "fusion/Asian" fare; "delicious" cocktails help fuel a "fantastic vibe" – is that why everyone seems "so good-looking"? / www.rickerrestaurants.com; 11 pm, Sun 10.30 pm; closed Sun L.

Eighty-Six SW3 **NEW**
£47 ❹❺❸

86 Fulham Rd   7052 9620   5–2C

The site of Chelsea's long-established Cactus Blue (RIP) has been attractively revamped to create a bar for the local jeunesse dôrée – judged as a restaurant, though, reporters (small in number, admittedly) find the new incarnation "truly dreadful". / www.86restaurant.co.uk; 10 pm; D only, closed Sun.

Electric Brasserie W11
£49 ❹❹❷

191 Portobello Rd   7908 9696   6–1A

"Always buzzing with locals, families and Notting Hillbillies" – this "vibrant", "heart-of-Portobello" hang-out offers "top people-watching possibilites", especially at weekends; "very good" breakfasts aside, however, the food is "distinctly average". / www.electricbrasserie.com; 11 pm, Sun 10 pm; Max 8; set weekday L £28 (FP).

Elena's L'Etoile W1   £51   ⑤④④
30 Charlotte St   7636 7189   2–1C
"Sadly Elena is no longer in attendance", at this "faded" and
"elegant" Fitzrovia old-timer, and the place is in "sad decline" –
the "basic" brasserie fare is "very ordinary", with "subdued and not
particularly helpful staff" contributing to an ambience that's rather
"flat". / www.elenasletoile.co.uk; 10.30 pm; closed Sat L & Sun.

Elephant Royale
Locke's Wharf E14   £44   ④❸❸
Westferry Rd   7987 7999   11–2C
"Perfect on a summer evening", when you can enjoy the "great views"
towards Greenwich – this rather glitzy Isle of Dogs venue may not
astonish with the quality of its Thai food, but it rarely disappoints.
/ www.elephantroyale.com; 11.30 pm, Fri & Sat midnight, Sun 11 pm;
set Sun L £28 (FP).

Élysée W1   £49   ④❸❷
13 Percy St   7636 4804   2–1C
Potentially a real hidden gem, this recently-relaunched Greek
restaurant, in Fitzrovia, has a truly "beautiful" period-townhouse
interior and an "exceptional" roof garden too; so why has no one ever
heard of it? – the "mundane" cooking can't help. / Rated on Editors'
visit; www.elyseerestaurant.com; 2 am; closed Sun.

Emile's SW15   £40   ❷❶❸
96-98 Felsham Rd   8789 3323   10–2B
"Emile is the perfect host", say fans of this "intimate" Putney "gem"
– a stalwart establishment that's currently going "from strength
to strength"; "superb beef Wellington" is a long-standing highlight
on a menu that's "in a good way, rather old-fashioned".
/ www.emilesrestaurant.co.uk; 11 pm; D only, closed Sun; no Amex.

The Empress of India E9   £45   ❸❸❷
130 Lauriston Rd   8533 5123   1–2D
Nothing Indian except the name, about this popular and "good-
value" gastropub, near Victoria Park. / www.theempressofindia.com;
10 pm; closed Sun D.

Empress of Sichuan WC2   £43   ❸❸④
6 Lisle St   7734 8128   4–3A
With its "robust" Sichuanese cuisine, this "plush" spot offers "a spicy
alternative to your standard Chinatown Cantonese"; this year,
however, a minority of reporters encountered "below par" food.
/ 11 pm.

The Engineer NW1   £45   ④④❷
65 Gloucester Ave   7722 0950   8–3B
"On a sunny day, the garden comes into its own", at this once-
celebrated – and still "atmospheric" – Primrose Hill gastropub; while
the food's still "fine", though, "prices have gone crazy", and service
"could do with smartening up". / www.the-engineer.com; 10.30 pm,
Sun 10 pm; no Amex.

The English Pig EC1 NEW   £43   ❷❷④
171-176 Aldersgate St   7600 9707   9–2B
"A crazy and charismatic chef/host" helps breath life into this
"not very promising" venue – a "barn-like" site (formerly a Slug
& Lettuce) "on a roundabout at the end of London Wall";
it's generally a "convivial" enough place, though, offering
"wholesome" cuisine realised to a "high standard". / theenglishpig.co.uk;
Mon-Fri 9.30 pm, Sat 10 pm; closed Sat L & Sun.

Enoteca Turi SW15   £50   ❶❶❸
28 Putney High St   8785 4449   10–2B
"Passionate owners", Giuseppe and Pamela Turi, run this "hidden
gem", near Putney Bridge; "the best Italian wine list outside Italy"
is "cleverly matched" with "expertly prepared" dishes in a "lovely",
if low key, setting. / www.enotecaturi.com; 10.30 pm, Fri-Sat 11 pm;
closed Sun.

The Enterprise SW3   £50   ❸❸❷
35 Walton St   7584 3148   5–2C
"Shame you can't book", at this "busy" but "cosy" and perennially
fashionable Knightsbridge corner hang-out – "the food is always
good". / www.theenterprise.co.uk; 10 pm, Sat 10.30 pm; no booking, except
weekday L.

Entrée SW11 NEW   £46   ❸❹❸
2 Battersea Rise   7223 5147   10–2C
"A great addition to Battersea Rise"; it may occupy a "difficult site",
but the locals are rooting for this "unlikely" outfit, which encompasses
a "speakeasy-style" bar (below), and a restaurant above, serving
"well-executed modern European fare". / www.entreebattersea.co.uk/;
10.30 pm; closed weekday L.

Eriki NW3   £38   ❷❶❸
4-6 Northways Pde, Finchley Rd   7722 0606   8–2A
"Not to be expected on such an ugly road", this "gem among the
Swiss Cottage dross" offers notably "imaginative" Indian cooking
(in 'nouvelle' style) and "sparkling and smiley" service. / www.eriki.co.uk;
10.45 pm; closed Sat L.

Esarn Kheaw W12   £30   ❶❸④
314 Uxbridge Rd   8743 8930   7–1B
"Unexpectedly terrific" cooking – with "superb Northern Thai
specialities you won't find elsewhere" – provide ample reason
to truffle out this "treasure" of a café, in spite of its location in a tatty
corner of Shepherd's Bush. / www.esarnkheaw.co.uk; 11 pm; closed
Sat L & Sun L; no Amex.

L'Escargot W1   £54   ❸❷❷
48 Greek St   7437 2679   4–2A
This "romantic", art-filled Soho stalwart keeps a low-profile nowadays,
but it's still a "reliable" and professional operation, offering
"accomplished" Gallic cuisine; lunch and pre-theatre menus are
"very good value". / www.whitestarline.org.uk; 11.15 pm; closed Sat L & Sun;
set pre theatre £34 (FP).

Essenza W11   £53   ❸❸④
210 Kensington Park Rd   7792 1066   6–1A
"Great and honest", or "surprisingly unoriginal and ordinary"? –
the former view predominates, but the puzzlingly few reports on this
Notting Hill Italian are notably mixed; "very good fish dishes", though,
do seem to be a highlight. / www.essenza.co.uk; 11.30 pm; set weekday L
£33 (FP).

L'Etranger SW7   £64   ❸❷❸
36 Gloucester Rd   7584 1118   5–1B
"Superb wine, with hidden treasures from across the globe"
is matched up with "unusual and interesting French/Japanese fusion
cuisine", at this South Kensington venture; for critics, though,
"ridiculous" prices can rather take the edge off the experience.
/ www.etranger.co.uk; 11 pm, Sun 10 pm.

Euphorium Bakery N1 £9 ❸④❸
26a Chapel Mkt   7837 7010   8–3D
A place to "chill out with a book" on "one of the comfy sofas", this high-quality Islington café/bakery serves up "lovely, if expensive", sarnies, cakes and pastries. / www.euphoriumbakery.com; 6 pm; no Amex.

Everest Inn SE3 £33 ❷❸❷
41 Montpelier Vale   8852 7872   1–4D
"A super Blackheath curry option" – the "varied" menu of this "refined", "friendly" and "welcoming" Nepalese establishment is notable for the "clean" and "fresh" flavours it offers. / www.everestinn.co.uk; midnight, Sun 11 pm.

Eyre Brothers EC2 £55 ❸❸❸
70 Leonard St   7613 5346   12–1B
"Fine Iberian cooking" – well-matched with some "wonderful" wines – justifies the toppish prices at this "modern yet welcoming" Shoreditch bar/restaurant; lunches attract a business crowd, but evenings are "more relaxed". / www.eyrebrothers.co.uk; 10.30 pm; closed Sat L & Sun.

Faanoos £25 ❸❸❸
472 Chiswick High Rd, W4   8994 4217   7–2A
481 Richmond Road, SW14   8878 5738   1–4A
"Succulent kebabs", "gorgeous home-made bread" and fresh dips (served in "large portions" and at "good prices") win praise for these "very cheerful" Persians, in Sheen and more recently Chiswick; BYO (£4 corkage). / SW14 11 pm; W4 Fri & Sat midnight.

Fabrizio EC1 £41 ❷④④
30 Saint Cross St   7430 1503   9–1A
"Fabrizio is a star", and his "great-value" Italian, in the "Diamond District", is making a name for its "warm hospitality and delicious food"; the interior is "a bit shabby" though – "only go with business associates you know pretty well!" / www.fabriziorestaurant.co.uk; 10 pm; closed Sat L & Sun.

Fairuz W1 £44 ❸❸④
3 Blandford St   7486 8108   2–1A
"The quality of the mezze" is the particular reason to seek out this "friendly" Marylebone Lebanese – "stick to them, and you'll easily fill up". / www.fairuz.uk.com; 11.30 pm, Sun 10.30 pm; set weekday L £16 (FP).

Fakhreldine W1 £55 ④④④
85 Piccadilly   7493 3424   3–4C
Only modest feedback on this glitzy Lebanese, where lunchers get impressive Green Park views; reports, better than last year, are still a little up-and-down, but most reporters find the food at least "well-executed". / www.fakhreldine.co.uk; midnight, Sun 11 pm.

Falconiere SW7 £42 ④❸⑤
84 Old Brompton Rd   7589 2401   5–2B
Even fans can find the food "average", but this "friendly" Italian stalwart, near South Kensington tube, still has its plus points – notably the "terrific-value" set lunch. / www.ilfalconiere.co.uk; 11.15 pm; closed Sun.

La Famiglia SW10 £50 ❸❸❸
7 Langton St   7351 0761   5–3B
Fans (some of 40 years' standing) still love this ancient Chelsea trattoria, its "relaxed, Italian-style romance", its "delightful" garden, and its food which, if "hardly cutting-edge", is generally "enjoyable"; an impression of drift, though, is unavoidable. / www.lafamiglia.co.uk; 11.45 pm.

The Farm Collective EC1   £8   ❷❸❸
91 Cowcross St   7253 2142   9–1A
"You can tell they use good ingredients" – this Farringdon café/bistro
attracts positive reports overall, but it's the *"great-tasting food"* which
really stands out. / www.farmcollective.com; L only, closed Sat & Sun.

Fat Boy's   £33   ❸❹❸
10a-10b Edensor Rd, W4   8742 0249   10–1A
33 Haven Grn, W5   8998 5868   1–2A
201 Upper Richmond Rd, SW14   8876 0644   1–4A
431-433 Richmond Rd, TW1   8892 7657   1–4A
68 High St, TW8   8569 8481   1–3A
With their *"freshly-cooked"* and *"reliable"* Thai (and Chinese) fare,
these simple joints in west London generally hit the spot, even if the
service *"can be a bit hit-and-miss"*. / www.fatboysthai.co.uk; 11 pm.

Faulkner's E8   £29   ❷❷❸
424-426 Kingsland Rd   7254 6152   1–1D
"Fantastic fish at prices you could barely buy it uncooked!",
and *"a very wide selection"* too, help ensure this comfy, if dated,
Dalston chippy practically *"never disappoints"*. / 10 pm; no Amex;
need 8+ to book.

The Fellow N1   £43   ❹❹❹
24 York Way   7833 4395   8–3C
"Very handy for travellers passing through King's Cross",
this *"bustling"* gastropub is probably the top all-purpose choice
immediately around the station – no wonder it is *"usually crammed"*.
/ www.thefellow.co.uk; 10 pm; closed Sun D.

The Fentiman Arms SW8   £39   ❸❸❷
64 Fentiman Rd   7793 9796   10–1D
A *"worthy"* Vauxhall gastropub, with *"open fires in winter and
an amazing terrace for the summer"*; reports (limited) suggest the
food *"has upped its game"* of late. / www.geronimo-inns.co.uk; 10 pm,
Sun 9 pm.

Fernandez & Wells   £30   ❷❷❷
16a, St Anne's Ct, W1   7494 4242   3–1D
43 Lexington St, W1   7734 1546   3–2D
73 Beak St, W1   7287 8124   3–2D
"Small, and full of trendies", these *"rustic"* Soho pit stops offer
"mouth-watering" sarnies, tapas and nibbles, plus – in Lexington
Street – *"excellent"* Spanish wines; in St Anne's Court, it's all about
"beautiful" coffee and *"outstanding"* cakes.
/ www.fernandezandwells.com; Lexington St 10 pm; Beak St 5 pm; St Anne's
Court closed Sun.

Ffiona's W8   £47   ❹❷❶
51 Kensington Church St   7937 4152   5–1A
"Eccentric" owner Ffiona offers *"a personal and idiosyncratic
welcome to all"*, at her *"candlelit, small and intimate"* Kensington
bistro; the *"homely"* English cuisine may be *"average"*, but fans say
the experience is second to none; weekend brunch is a *"welcome
innovation"*. / www.ffionas.com; 11 pm, Sun 10 pm; D only, closed Mon;
no Amex.

Fifteen Dining Room N1   £75   ⑤⑤⑤
15 Westland Pl   3375 1515   12–1A
"Simply dreadful", *"you must warn people away!"*;
this *"extraordinarily overpriced"* Hoxton basement (in part staffed
by disadvantaged trainees) offers up *"diabolical"* Italian food and
notably *"careless"* service – if it couldn't *"live off Jamie Oliver's
name"*, it wouldn't last a week! / www.fifteen.net; 10 pm; booking: max 12.

FSA

Fifteen Trattoria N1 £51 ④⑤④
15 Westland Pl 3375 1515 12–1A
Fans are "pleasantly surprised" by the "really relaxed" vibe on the
cheaper ground floor of Jamie's Hoxton training-venture, and say the
food is "fabulous" too; doubters, however, may "admire the concept"
but still say the reality is "no better than most local Italians",
just much more expensive. / www.fifteen.net; 10.45 pm; booking: max 16.

The Fifth Floor Restaurant
Harvey Nichols SW1 £65 ④❸④
109-125 Knightsbridge 7235 5250 5–1D
From "outstanding" to "really disappointing" – reports on this stark
'90s dining room are not only mixed, but also amazingly
modest in number nowadays; an "excellent" wine list is the only
undisputed attraction. / www.harveynichols.com; 10.45 pm; closed Sun D.

54 Farringdon Road EC1 £43 ❸❸④
54 Farringdon Rd 7336 0603 9–1A
"Good and original Malay cuisine" is one of the features making this
rather oddly-decorated spot a very useful Farringdon stand-by.
/ www.54farringdon.com; 10.30 pm; closed Sun-Mon, Tue & Wed L, Sat L;
set weekday L £17 (FP), set pre-theatre £28 (FP).

Fig N1 £46 ❶❷❷
169 Hemingford Rd 7609 3009 8–3D
"How do they produce such good meals in such a tiny space?"; for a
"leisurely romantic meal", this "neighbourhood gem" is just the job –
it hasn't suffered at all from its "simpler" approach since the owner
shifted his main focus to 'North Road'. / www.fig-restaurant.co.uk; 10 pm;
D only, open Sun L only; no Amex.

La Figa E14 £36 ❸❷❸
45 Narrow St 7790 0077 11–1B
This "cheery and bustling", pizza 'n' pasta joint, in Wapping,
continues to impress all who comment on it, not least with its
"huge portions" of "freshly-cooked" fare – "you might not cross
London for it, but you'd cross the East End!" / www.lafigarestaurant.co.uk;
11 pm, Sun 10.30 pm.

Fine Burger Company £33 ④④④
330 Upper St, N1 7359 3026 8–3D
St Pancras International, Pancras Rd, NW1 7278 8056 8–3C
O2 Centre, Finchley Rd, NW3 7433 0700 8–2A
An "average-to-good" chain, whose "good thick burgers" get the
thumbs-up from most reporters. / www.fineburger.co.uk; 10 pm-11 pm,
NW1 1am, Fri-Sat midnight.

Fino W1 £52 ❷❷❷
33 Charlotte St 7813 8010 2–1C
"A real eye-opener" when it comes to "authentically Spanish" cuisine
– the Hart Brothers' "understated" yet "spectacularly good" all-
rounder, in a Fitzrovia basement, offers "tremendous" tapas,
"personable" service, "super" wines, and a list of sherries that's
simply "an education". / www.finorestaurant.com; 10.30 pm; closed
Sat L & Sun; booking: max 12.

Fire & Stone £35 ④❸❸
31-32 Maiden Ln, WC2 08443 712550 4–3D
Westfield, Ariel Way, W12 0844 371 2550 7–1C
4 Horner Sq, E1 0844 371 2550 12–2B
*"Weird and wonderful" pizzas (a "nice change from PizzaExpress!")
please fans of this small chain (whose "cavernous" and very concrete
Covent Garden branch is the most interesting); for some reporters,
though, the "novelty" is wearing thin – its "bizarre" creations,
they say, are "really gross". / www.fireandstone.com; WC2 11 pm;
W12 11 pm, Sat & Sun 11.30 pm; E1 11pm, Sun 8 pm.*

The Fire Stables SW19 £50 ④④❷
27-29 Church Rd 8946 3197 10–2B
*In the heart of ultra-cute but under-served Wimbledon Village,
a buzzy Young's gastropub worth knowing about for decent food
at "sensible prices". / www.firestableswimbledon.co.uk; 10.30 pm,
Sun 10 pm.*

Firezza £31 ❷❸④
116 Finborough Rd, SW10 7370 2255 5–3A
12 All Saints Rd, W11 7221 0020 6–1B
48 Chiswick High Rd, W4 8994 9494 7–2B
276 St Paul's Rd, N1 7359 7400 8–2D
40 Lavender Hill, SW11 7223 5535 10–1C
205 Garrett Ln, SW18 8870 7070 10–2B
*"The best take-away pizzas, bar none", thanks to their "wonderful,
crisp, thin bases" and "yummy" toppings; in some outlets you could
eat in... but "don't bother!" / www.firezza.com; 11 pm, Fri & Sat midnight;
N1 closed Sun; no Amex.*

First Floor W11 £42 ❸❸❶
186 Portobello Rd 7243 0072 6–1A
*"Shabby-chic" styling doesn't come more "romantic" than at this high-
ceilinged and candlelit Portobello Market dining room, and the food,
if a touch "hit-and-miss", is pretty good too; NB: upstairs, there's one
of London's nicer private rooms. / www.firstfloorportobello.co.uk; 11 pm;
closed Sun D.*

Fish Central EC1 £28 ❷❷❸
149-155 Central St 7253 4970 12–1A
*"The name says it all" about this "informal and friendly" East End
venture – all you get is "extremely fresh fish, cooked to perfection".
/ www.fishcentral.co.uk; 10.30 pm, Fri & Sat 11 pm; closed Sun.*

Fish Club £35 ❷❷④
189 St John's Hill, SW11 7978 7115 10–2C
57 Clapham High St, SW4 7720 5853 10–2D
*"Nothing's fancy, but everything's extremely tasty", at these "basic"
south London refectories (with wet fish counters attached); their "top-
notch", "upmarket" fish 'n' chips offer "a good twist on the traditional
formula". / www.thefishclub.com; 10 pm, Sun 9 pm; SW4 & SW11 closed
Mon L; no bookings.*

Fish in a Tie SW11 £30 ④❷❶
105 Falcon Rd 7924 1913 10–1C
*"Hidden-away in a non-glamorous road behind Clapham Junction",
this "great little Italian" makes a good "cheap 'n' cheerful" choice –
"it could charge double", say fans, "and still be as busy!"
/ www.fishinatie.co.uk; midnight; no Amex; set weekday L £18 (FP), set always
available £19 (FP).*

Fish Place SW11 NEW £51 ❷❷⑤

Vicentia Ct, Bridges Ct 7095 0410 10–1C

"A real discovery", this hidden-away Battersea newcomer – a "small glass-fronted" spot, with "amazing Thames views" – is well worth seeking out for its "interesting" menu (which includes the "lovely" fish dishes you'd hope for); it's not yet found the following it deserves, though, and atmosphere can be elusive. / www.thefishplace.co.uk; 10.30 pm; closed Mon; set weekday L £33 (FP).

fish! SE1 £48 ④⑤⑤

Cathedral St 7407 3803 9–4C

Would this glass-and-steel shed survive, were it not for its prominent Borough Market location? – the setting is clattery, the service "poor", prices "steep", and the fish "very average" – "avoid!" / www.fishkitchen.com; 10.45 pm, Sun 10.30 pm.

Fishworks £47 ❸❸④

7-9 Swallow St, W1 7734 5813 3–3D
89 Marylebone High St, W1 7935 9796 2–1A

"Good-quality fish, correctly prepared" is helping this café/fishmonger group stage something of a 'comeback' – it also benefits from an ambience "less chain-like than some of its rivals", and service that's more "efficient" too. / www.fishworks.co.uk; 10.30pm.

Fitou's Thai Restaurant W10 £24 ❷❸④

1 Dalgarno Gdns 8968 0558 6–1A

"There's no way you'd just stumble upon this bizarrely hidden-away BYO Thai" – formerly called Number One Café – opposite Little Wormwood Scrubs ; if you do, you'll find "cracking food at ridiculously cheap prices". / www.numberonethaicafe.co.uk; 10.30 pm; closed Sun L.

Five Hot Chillies HA0 £27 ❷④⑤

875 Harrow Rd 8908 5900 1–1A

Prices at this grungy café, on a busy Sudbury highway, are "hard to beat"; its very authentic Indian fare can be "excellent" too, "especially the grills"; BYO. / www.fivehotchillies.co.uk; midnight; no Amex.

500 N19 £38 ❶❶❷

782 Holloway Rd 7272 3406 8–1C

"The real biz!" – this "terrific" trattoria, "tucked-away" in an "unlikely" Archway location, is a "crowded" but really "charming" place, where a "small but original" Sicilian menu is realised "with flair"; star turn: "sublime" pasta. / www.500restaurant.co.uk; 10 pm; closed Mon & Sun L.

5 Pollen Street W1 £75 ④❸❸

5 Pollen St 7629 1555 3–2C

Opposite Pollen Street Social, and already rather eclipsed by it, this stylish Mayfair newcomer is a pleasant sort of place in a rather old-fashioned and comfortable sort of way; most aspects of the operation though seem to have struck early-days reporters (and ourselves) as rather lacking 'oomph'. / www.pollenst.com; 10.30 pm; closed Sun.

The Flask N6 £41 ❸❸❷

77 Highgate West Hill 8348 7346 1–1C

It's the "nice location and lovely beer garden" ("very busy on warm days") that make this historic Highgate coaching inn of particular note; fans insist, however, that its cooking is "above average" too. / www.theflaskhighgate.com; 10 pm, Sun 9 pm.

Flat White W1 £10 ❷❷❸
17 Berwick St 7734 0370 3–2D
You get "the most amazing coffee, plus a large dollop of chilled-out
Antipodean charm", at this "hipsters' paradise" Soho coffee shop;
"nice cakes" too. / www.flat-white.co.uk; L only; no credit cards.

Florence SE24 £38 ❹❸❸
131-133 Dulwich Rd 7326 4987 10–2D
Down Brockwell Park way, an attractive pub which – in addition
to some decent food – boasts "a wide selection of beers",
a "nice little garden", and an "enormous playroom" for the kids.
/ www.capitalpubcompany.com/the-florence/florence; 10 pm, Sun 9.30 pm;
no Amex.

Floridita W1 £61 ❹❹❹
100 Wardour St 7314 4000 3–2D
OK, "you can't hear yourself think", but this cavernous Cuban-themed
Soho joint generally gets the thumbs-up for its "vibrant" ambience;
the food, though, is "average" and "overpriced".
/ www.floriditalondon.com; 3 am, Tue & Wed 2 am; D only, closed Mon & Sun.

Food for Thought WC2 £19 ❷❹❺
31 Neal St 7836 0239 4–2C
It's "invariably crowded", but this battered Covent Garden basement
remains a "wonderful gem" thanks to its "nourishing, tasty veggie
fare in large portions", and at "rock-bottom prices" too; beware
queues; BYO. / www.foodforthought-london.co.uk; 8 pm, Sun 5 pm; no credit
cards; no booking.

The Forge WC2 £50 ❹❹❹
14 Garrick St 7379 1531 4–3C
Fans of this traditional Gallic fixture, in Covent Garden, accept it's
"nothing spectacular", but say it's a "solid performer" that's "perfect"
pre- or post-theatre; its ratings dipped this year, though,
with numerous gripes about "disappointingly average" food and
"uncaring" service. / www.theforgerestaurant.co.uk; midnight, Sun 11 pm;
set weekday L & pre-theatre £31 (FP).

Forman's E3 £52 ❷❷❹
Stour Rd, Fish Island 8525 2365 1–1D
A "great view of the Olympic Stadium" is destined to provide a major
draw, during 2012, to the dining room of this East End, canal-side,
smoked salmon factory; service is "attentive" and the "limited" menu
of "simple" fish and seafood is typically realised to an "excellent"
standard. / www.formans.co.uk; 11 pm; Closed Mon-Wed, Thu & Fri D only,
Sat open L & D, closed Sun D.

Formosa Dining Room
The Prince Alfred W9 £45 ❸❹❸
5a Formosa St 7286 3287 6–1C
A huge Victorian tavern in Maida Vale, with some "simply amazing"
architecture; its dining annex is quite a simple, modern affair,
however, offering "good, solid British food". / www.theprincealfred.co.uk;
10 pm, Fri & Sat 11 pm, Sun 9 pm; no Amex; set dinner £29 (FP).

(The Fountain)
Fortnum & Mason W1 £62 ❹❸❸
181 Piccadilly 7734 8040 3–3D
"Incredibly under-rated" as a breakfast destination, the "genteel"
buttery of this posh St James's institution is also worth seeking out for
its "scrumptious" afternoon tea, or a spot of Welsh rarebit at any
time of day; NB "very good lunchtime deals" – see also 1707.
/ www.fortnumandmason.com; 10.45 pm; closed Sun D.

Fortune Cookie W2 £28 ②④⑤
1 Queensway   7727 7260   6–2C
"Authentic Cantonese food", at "good-value" prices, wins praise for this grungy Bayswater veteran. / 11 pm; no Amex.

Four O Nine SW9 £55 ③②②
409 Clapham Rd   7737 0722   10–1D
This "quirky, concealed room", above a pub near Clapham North, "really feels like a find" – with its "sexy" decor, "flickering candles", "delicious" cocktails, and "beautifully-presented" food, it has "all the ingredients for romance". / www.fouronine.co.uk; 10.30 pm; closed weekday L.

Four Regions TW9 £41 ③②④
102-104 Kew Rd   8940 9044   1–4A
"Reliable and down-to-earth", this Chinese restaurant, on the Kew/Richmond border, is quite a "neighbourhood favourite", thanks not least to its "friendly" style and its "fair prices". / 11.30 pm, Sun 11 pm.

The Four Seasons £27 ②④⑤
12 Gerrard St, W1   7494 0870   4–3A
23 Wardour St, W1   7287 9995   4–3A NEW
84 Queensway, W2   7229 4320   6–2C
Service may be off-hand and the setting scruffy, but "the best roast duck ever" still makes quite a name for this "bustling" Bayswater Chinese – beware the "inevitable queue"; its lesser-known Chinatown siblings are "well worth a special visit too". / www.ukfourseasons.com; Queensway and Gerrard St 1 am, Sun 11 pm, Wardour St 3.30 am.

The Fox EC2 £39 ③④③
28 Paul St   7729 5708   12–2B
"Handy for both the City and trendy Shoreditch" – a traditional-looking boozer where the Mediterranean cuisine can be "really good"… even if the service is sometimes "all over the show"; the panelled upstairs dining room is a better option than the bar below. / www.thefoxpublichouse.com; 10 pm; closed Sat L & Sun D.

Fox & Grapes SW19 NEW £48 ③④③
9 Camp Rd   8619 1300   10–2A
"It's a relief finally to have something half-decent in Wimbledon", so Claude ('Hibiscus') Bosi's "uncluttered" make-over of this picturesque inn near the Common has been a "welcome" arrival; not everyone is wowed though – it's "expensive for what it is", and suffers from an "identity crisis": "is it a restaurant or a pub?" / foxandgrapeswimbledon.co.uk; 9.30pm; no Amex.

The Fox & Hounds SW11 £40 ②②②
66 Latchmere Rd   7924 5483   10–1C
"It isn't trying to be anything other than a great pub!" – this "fabulous" Battersea boozer may be just that, but its "continuously-updated" cuisine is "ever-reliable" nonetheless. / www.thefoxandhoundspub.co.uk; 10 pm; Mon-Thu D only, Fri-Sun open L & D.

The Fox and Anchor EC1 £42 ③②❶
115 Charterhouse St   7250 1300   9–1B
"Everything a pub should be" – this "cosy and beautiful" Victorian gem, tucked-away in Smithfield, serves "very British" food, executed "with a rarely found lightness of touch", and "delivered with a smile" too. / www.foxandanchor.co.uk; 9.30 pm; closed Sun D.

Foxtrot Oscar SW3 £50 ④❸④
79 Royal Hospital Rd 7352 4448 5–3D
"Nothing hits the right note", say critics of Gordon Ramsay's tenure
of this long-established Chelsea bistro; it would be fair to say, though,
that it "was never really known as a destination for amazing food",
and that the cooking – while still "entirely unmemorable" –
has improved somewhat of late. / www.gordonramsay.com/foxtrotoscar/;
10 pm, Sun 9 pm.

Franco Manca £20 ❶❸❸
144 Chiswick High Rd, W4 8747 4822 7–2A
Unit 4 Market Row, SW9 7738 3021 10–2D
"The best pizza outside Italy" – using "amazing" Neapolitan
sourdough bases – again wins raves for this teeny and "stupidly
cheap" Brixton Market pizzeria, and its Chiswick offshoot ("a big hit
with local yummy mummies") is almost as good; expansion to Covent
Garden, Brick Lane and Westfield coming soon – can quality survive?
/ www.francomanca.com; SW9 5 pm; W4 11 pm; sw9 no bookings.

Franco's SW1 £64 ④④④
61 Jermyn St 7499 2211 3–3C
A "plush" modern trattoria, in St James's, that can fit the bill if you're
looking for "a good solid option for a business lunch"; critics feel its
"rich" cuisine is "not the most inspiring", though, and fear prices
verge on "ridiculous". / www.francoslondon.com; 11 pm; closed Sun; set pre
theatre £36 (FP).

Frankie's Italian Bar & Grill £45 ⑤⑤④
3 Yeomans Row, SW3 7590 9999 5–2C
Stamford Bridge, Fulham Rd, SW6 7957 8298 5–4A NEW
Given its "pedestrian cooking" and "unwarranted prices", it's hard
to see the appeal – expect possibly with kids in tow – of MPW and
Franco Dettori's pizza chain, "bizarrely decorated" in Vegas-bling
style; the former Chiswick branch now trades under different
management – but with very similar branding – as Bardolino.
/ www.frankiesitalianbarandgrill.com; 11 pm; W4 closed Mon-Fri L.

Franklins SE22 £46 ❸④❸
157 Lordship Ln 8299 9598 1–4D
A "wonderful local bistro", in East Dulwich – a "friendly" sort
of place, it offers a "marvellously tasty" menu, on which "meaty"
dishes are a speciality. / www.franklinsrestaurant.com; 10.30 pm;
set weekday L £29 (FP).

Frantoio SW10 £50 ④❸❸
397 King's Rd 7352 4146 5–3B
A "retro" menu is served "with gusto", at this "always-cheerful" and
"noisy" Italian, near World's End; critics, though find it "all-round
mediocre" – "what do regulars see we don't?" / www.frantoio.com;
11.15 pm, Sun 10.15 pm; set weekday L £32 (FP).

Fratelli la Bufala NW3 £41 ❸④④
45a South End Rd 7435 7814 8–2A
"Part of a global chain, but you'd think it was run by some local
Italians!" – this "indispensable" Hampstead fixture serves some
"amazing" wood-fired pizza (plus a whole range of dishes featuring
buffalo mozzarella). / 11 pm; closed Mon L & Tue L; no Amex;
set weekday L £26 (FP).

Frederick's N1 £56 ④④❷
106 Islington High St 7359 2888 8–3D
"The conservatory is lovely", at this "spacious, light and airy" Islington "staple", whose "formal" but "sociable" style suits a special occasion; fans insist its cooking is "top-notch" too, but the overall view is that it's merely "acceptable". / www.fredericks.co.uk; 11 pm; closed Sun; set weekday L & pre-theatre £35 (FP).

Freemasons Arms NW3 £41 ⑤④❷
32 Downshire Hill 7433 6811 8–2A
"On the edge of Hampstead Heath", a popular pub – with a "cosy" interior, a "lovely" conservatory and "excellent garden tables" – that's "consistently packed with local families"; performance, however, is "schizophrenic", and when things go wrong the food can be "atrocious". / www.freemasonsarms.co.uk; 10 pm.

Fresco W2 £20 ❸❷❸
25 Westbourne Grove 7221 2355 6–1C
"A great variety of fresh juices", plus "amazing" Lebanese wraps – all at bargain prices – make this "modest-looking" pit stop a handy Bayswater stand-by. / www.frescojuices.co.uk; 10.30 pm.

Frizzante at City Farm
Hackney City Farm E2 £28 ❸❸❷
1a Goldsmiths Row 7729 6381 12–1D
A "busy" but "really relaxed" Italian café, on the East End's "weekend trail" between Columbia Road and Broadway Market; its "freshly-made" fare includes some good cakes and breakfasts – "don't forget to take the kids to look at the animals". / www.frizzanteltd.co.uk; D only, closed Mon; no Amex.

Frizzante Cafe
Surrey Docks Farm SE16 £23 ❸④❸
South Whf, Rotherhithe St 7231 1010 11–2B
In deepest Rotherhithe, the sweet café of a Thames-side working farm, which serves "fresh, tasty Italian-based food", plus "good coffee and lovely cakes" – "watch out for wandering chickens!" / www.frizzanteltd.co.uk; 4.30 pm; closed Mon & Tue, Wed-Sun D.

La Fromagerie Café W1 £38 ❷❸❷
2-6 Moxon St 7935 0341 3–1A
"Delectable cheeses and other gourmet delights" – including "fresh salads", "good charcuterie" and "great wine" – are on offer at the "glorious" café attached to the famous Marylebone shop; "yummy breakfasts" too. / www.lafromagerie.co.uk; 7 pm, Sat 6.30 pm, Sun 5.30 pm; L only; no booking.

The Frontline Club W2 £48 ❸❷❷
13 Norfolk Pl 7479 8960 6–1D
All the more notable "in the Paddington restaurant desert", a "leading media club" (dining room open to all) whose menu "showcases the best of British" (much of it from the owner's farm), accompanied by a "delightful" wine list ; war-reporting is the house speciality – "the photos on the wall certainly make an impression". / www.frontlineclub.com; 11 pm; closed Sun D.

Fryer's Delight WC1 £10 ❸④④
19 Theobald's Rd 7405 4114 2–1D
Views on this "cramped", "no-frills" Holborn chippy are becoming more mixed – supporters still vaunt its "classic" style, but critics are adamant that "Londoners (and tourists) have much better choices for their fish 'n' chips"; BYO. / 11 pm; closed Sun; no credit cards; no booking.

Fujiyama SW9 £28 ❸❸④
5-7 Vining St 7737 2369 10–2D
A "cheap 'n' cheerful" Brixton Japanese, popular for "steaming bowls of noodle soup", and "fresh sushi" too. / www.newfujiyama.com; 11 pm.

Fulham Wine Rooms SW6 NEW £46 ④❸❸
871-873 Fulham Rd 7042 9440 10–1B
The food can "miss", but "full marks for effort", at this Fulham newcomer, which – like its Kensington sibling – offers "a fun way to sample an extensive choice of wine" (served by the glass from an Enomatic machine). / www.greatwinesbytheglass.com; 11 pm.

Furnace N1 £36 ❸❸❸
I Rufus St 7613 0598 12–1B
A "reliable" hang-out for Hoxton trendies – a "cheerful" and "welcoming" pizzeria, just off the Square. / www.hoxtonfurnace.com; 11 pm; closed Sun L; no Amex.

Fuzzy's Grub £13 ④④④
6 Crown Pas, SW1 7925 2791 3–4D
10 Well Ct, EC4 7236 8400 9–2B
62 Fleet St, EC4 7583 6060 9–2A
"The 'roast-dinner-in-a-bap' is a king amongst sandwiches", and – along with "fab, high-quality breakfasts" – helps make this British diner/take-out chain a "pretty good-value" choice; in its own lunchtime, though, it was a legend, and some old fans feel it's "gone rapidly downhill" in recent years. / www.fuzzysgrub.com; 3 pm; no Amex; no booking.

Gaby's WC2 £28 ❸④⑤
30 Charing Cross Rd 7836 4233 4–3B
It certainly offers "no frills", but this "excellent refuelling spot", right by Leicester Square tube, is worth seeking out for its "top falafels", "great salt beef sarnies" and "super prices"; fans go further – "it's not at all as grotty as you suggest", they claim, and "its reputation for surly service is undeserved!" / midnight, Sun 10 pm; no Amex.

Gail's Bread £25 ❸❸④
138 Portobello Rd, W11 7460 0766 6–1B
282 Chiswick High Rd, W4 8995 2266 7–2A NEW
64 Hampstead High St, NW3 7794 5700 8–1A
5 Circus Rd, NW8 7722 0983 8–3A
64 Northcote Rd, SW11 7924 6330 10–2C
33-35 Exmouth Mkt, EC1 7713 6550 9–1A NEW
"First-rate coffee", "yummy cakes" and "interesting sarnies" (using "lovely" bread) help make these attractive and "bustling" café/bakeries worth seeking out, even if their prices are rather "high". / www.gailsbread.co.uk; W11 7 pm; NW3 & NW6 8 pm; no booking.

Galicia W10 £34 ❸④❸
323 Portobello Rd 8969 3539 6–1A
"An unassuming treat"; this "no-frills" North Ke sington veteran may look "shabby" from the street, but it's a "warm and buzzing" neighbourhood spot, offering competent tapas at "cheap" prices. / 11.15 pm; closed Mon; set weekday L £17 (FP).

The Gallery
Westbury Hotel W1 NEW £65 **❷0④**
Old Bond St 7629 7755 3–2C
*Ignore (if you can!) the operatic-bling styling of this large and
comfortable Mayfair newcomer (and the elevator music which goes
with it) – this is a mega-professional operation, dispensing 'hotel food'
of a very high quality; our early-days visit was for a top-value set
lunch – perfect for Bond Street shoppers. / Rated on Editors' visit;
www.westburymayfair.com.*

Gallery Mess
Saatchi Gallery SW3 £50 **④④④**
Duke of Yorks HQ, Kings Rd 7730 8135 5–2D
*A fabulous Chelsea location, with an attractive terrace overlooking
a large leafy square, adds appeal to this big and "buzzing" gallery-
café – "not bad" overall, then, even if service can "struggle", and the
straightforward food is "decent" but "uninspiring" (and a bit
"overpriced" too). / www.saatchi-gallery.co.uk; Mon-Sat 9.30 pm, Sun 6 pm.*

Gallipoli
£32 **❸④❸**
102 Upper St, N1 7359 0630 8–3D
107 Upper St, N1 7226 5333 8–3D
120 Upper St, N1 7226 8099 8–3D
*"Great as a cheap and cheerful stand-by with friends" – these
"vibrant" ("rammed-in") Turkish bistros, in the heart of Islington,
may be "rough and ready", but they "always have a good buzz",
and their food is "reliable" too. / www.cafegallipoli.com; 11 pm, Fri & Sat
midnight.*

Galoupet SW3 NEW £50 **0❷❸**
13 Beauchamp Pl 7036 3600 5–1C
*Galoupet, a vineyard from SW France, launched this Knightsbridge
restaurant in the summer of 2011, but don't assume the food is an
afterthought – on the evidence of our own early-days visit, the petits-
plats here (from an ex-Zuma chef) are spectacular. / Rated on Editors'
visit; www.galoupet.co.uk; Sun-Thu 10:30 pm, Fri-Sat 11:30 pm.*

Galvin at Windows
Park Lane London Hilton Hotel W1 £83 **❸❷❷**
22 Park Ln 7208 4021 3–4A
*It's not just the "terrific" views that make this 28th-floor Mayfair eyrie
"a wonderful place for a special occasion"; the food is "surprisingly
good" too, and "to seal the deal" – be it of a business or romantic
nature – the overall package is hard to beat. / www.galvinatwindows.com;
Mon-Wed 10.30 pm, Thu-Sat 11 pm; closed Sat L & Sun D; no Maestro;
no shorts; set weekday L £43 (FP), set pre-theatre £54 (FP).*

GALVIN BISTROT DE LUXE W1 £59 **❷0❷**
66 Baker St 7935 4007 2–1A
*"A little slice of Paris... minus the waiters!"; the Galvin brothers'
"magnificent" Marylebone "all-rounder" remains "a benchmark
of bistro-style cuisine" – "beautifully judged", and "professionally
served", in a "smart" but "convivial" setting.
/ www.galvinrestaurants.com; Mon-Wed 10.30 pm, Thu-Sat 10.45 pm,
Sun 9.30 pm.*

GALVIN LA CHAPELLE E1 £62 **❷00**
35 Spital Sq 7299 0400 12–2B
*"Your first thought is: 'wow!'", and the Galvin brothers' "spectacular"
and "luxurious" Spitalfields yearling doesn't let you down thereafter –
their "beautifully sympathetic" conversion of a high-vaulted Victorian
school hall offers "impeccable" brasserie fare that's "inventive" but
"unfussy". / www.galvinrestaurants.com; Mon-Sat 10.30 pm, Sun 9.30 pm.*

Ganapati SE15 £33 ❶❶❷

38 Holly Grove 7277 2928 1–4C

"Peckham's finest!" – this very small communal diner, where "table-sharing is de rigueur", continues to impress and amaze with its "personable" service, and with "exciting" cooking that "compares well with what you actually get in south India".
/ www.ganapatirestaurant.com; 10.30 pm, Sun 10 pm; closed Mon; no Amex; set weekday L £21 (FP).

Gandhi's SE11 £29 ❸❷❸

347 Kennington Rd 7735 9015 1–3C

It can seem "ordinary" – and lives somewhat in the shadow of the nearby Kennington Tandoori – but this "friendly" Indian is generally tipped for its "high-quality curry selection". / www.gandhis.co.uk; 11.30 pm.

Garrison SE1 £44 ❸❸❶

99-101 Bermondsey St 7089 9355 9–4D

"Cramped" but "vibey", this "stalwart" early-wave Bermondsey gastropub, near the Antiques Market, still "manages to hold its own"; "buzzy" brunches a speciality. / www.thegarrison.co.uk; 10 pm, Sun 9.30 pm.

Garufa N5 £42 ❸❹❸

104 Highbury Pk 7226 0070 8–1D

"Satisfying steaks" – the raison d'être of this "charming" Argentinian outfit, in Highbury, where the food is "sound", if "nothing exceptional". / www.garufa.co.uk; 10.30 pm; no Amex.

Gastro SW4 £44 ❹❺❸

67 Venn St 7627 0222 10–2D

"Très français" and romantic, this shabby-chic café/bistro, by the Clapham Picture House, is often tipped as a breakfast destination; overall, however, feedback has become rather mixed. / midnight; no Amex; set weekday L £27 (FP).

The Gate W6 £44 ❷❸④

51 Queen Caroline St 8748 6932 7–2C

"Surprising" dishes – "enjoyable even to dedicated carnivores" – have made a big name for this church-hall-style veggie, near the Hammersmith Odeon (and it has a "lovely courtyard" for the summer too); ratings slid this year, though, reflecting dissatisfaction with "OK but overpriced" food, and a "clinical" ambience. / www.thegate.tv; 10.30 pm, Sat 11 pm; closed Sat L & Sun.

Gaucho £59 ❸❹❸

25 Swallow St, W1 7734 4040 3–3D
60 Charlotte St, W1 7580 6252 2–1C
125 Chancery Ln, WC2 7242 7727 2–2D
89 Sloane Ave, SW3 7584 9901 5–2C
64 Heath St, NW3 7431 8222 8–1A
02 Centre, Peninsular Sq, SE10 8858 7711 11–2D
Tooley St, SE1 7407 5222 9–4D
Tow Path, TW10 8948 4030 1–4A
29 Westferry Circus, E14 7987 9494 11–1B
93a Charterhouse St, EC1 7490 1676 9–1B
5 Finsbury Ave, Broadgate, EC2 7256 6877 12–2B
1 Bell Inn Yd, EC3 7626 5180 9–2C

"Decent steak" wins many admirers for these "darkly-decorated" and "dependable" Argentinian-themed outfits, not least "for business lunching"; "crazy" prices put off quite a few reporters, though, and – on off-days – service can be "painfully bad".
/ www.gauchorestaurants.co.uk; 11 pm, Fri & Sat 11.30 pm, SE10, Piccadilly midnight, Sun 11 pm; EC3 & EC2 closed Sat & Sun; WC2 7 EC1 closed Sun.

Gauthier Soho W1   £65   ❶❷❸
21 Romilly St   7494 3111   4–3A
"A Theatreland show-stopper!"; with its "warm" welcome and
"memorable" Gallic cuisine, Alexis Gauthier's "intimate" yearling
"makes better use of this Soho townhouse than its illustrious
predecessor" (Richard Corrigan's Lindsay House, RIP);
the atmosphere of the "cramped" interior, however, can sometimes
seem rather "muted". / www.gauthiersoho.co.uk; 10.30 pm; closed Sun.

LE GAVROCHE W1   £115   ❶❶❷
43 Upper Brook St   7408 0881   3–2A
"Still cutting it after all these years", Michel Roux's "remarkable"
Mayfair basement (established by father Albert in 1967) stands out
for its "sheer professionalism", and its "peerless" realisation
of "classic" Gallic cuisine; it's "astronomically expensive", of course,
making "the best-value set lunch in town" all the more of a
"bargain". / www.le-gavroche.co.uk; 11 pm; closed Sat L & Sun; jacket
required; set weekday L £51 (FP).

Gay Hussar W1   £46   ⑤❸❷
2 Greek St   7437 0973   4–2A
It still has its fans – especially as a venue for a "sustaining" winter
lunch – but this "once-great" Soho townhouse-institution is "living
on its former reputation"; "I hope Hungarians eat better than this!"
/ www.gayhussar.co.uk; 10.45 pm; closed Sun.

Gaylord W1   £42   ❸④④
79-81 Mortimer St   7580 3615   2–1B
A "venerable" and rather "grand" Indian, just off Regent Street,
serving "good, traditional anglicised food"; even some fans, though,
rail at its "highfalutin" prices and sometimes iffy service.
/ www.gaylordlondon.com; 11.30 pm, Sun 11 pm.

Gazette   £38   ④④❷
79 Riverside Plaza, Chatfield Rd, SW11   7223 0999   10–1C
100 Balham High St, SW12   8772 1232   10–2C
Especially "as a Saturday morning retreat, with coffee, eggs and the
papers", these sarf London bistros win support with their "authentic"
scoff and "reasonable" prices; service is "erratic" though, and critics
find the food simply "pseudo". / www.gazettebrasserie.co.uk; 11 pm;
set always available £25 (FP).

Geales   £49   ❸❸④
1 Cale St, SW3   7965 0555   5–2C **NEW**
2 Farmer St, W8   7727 7528   6–2B
Tucked-away off Notting Hill Gate, this rejuvenated grand chippy
is "not what it was" in the old days, but a "reliable" option
nonetheless; fans are "impressed" by its "appallingly cramped"
Chelsea Green sibling (on the site of Tom's Place, RIP) too, but others
(with whom we tend to agree) find it "nothing to write home about".
/ www.geales.com; 10.30, Sun 9.30-10 pm; Mon L.

Geeta NW6   £18   ❸❶⑤
57-59 Willesden Ln   7624 1713   1–1B
"You'll double-take when you see how small the bill is!" – no wonder
this ultra-grungy Kilburn café still has quite a following for its "really
authentic" South Indian cuisine; not everyone, however, is convinced
that standards are being maintained; BYO. / 10.30 pm, Fri-Sat 11 pm;
no Amex.

Gelupo W1 £9 ❷❷④
7 Archer St 7287 5555 3–2D
"MMMMMmmmmmm!"; this "cool" new Soho ice cream parlour –
sorry, 'Gelateria' – from the team at Bocca di Lupo (opposite) offers
"an amazing array" of ices, sorbets and granitas, which many
reporters tip as "the best in London". / www.gelupo.com; Sun-Wed
11 pm, Thu-Sat 1 am.

Gem N1 £24 ❷0❷
265 Upper St 7359 0405 8–2D
"Incredibly fresh and tasty mezze at ridiculously low prices" make
it worth seeking out this Kurdish "staple", in Islington; the recent
renovation "has really lifted the interior". / www.gem-restaurant.co.uk;
11 pm, Fri & Sat midnight, Sun 10.30 pm.

La Genova W1 £63 ❸❷❸
32 North Audley St 7629 5916 3–2A
"You're made to feel part of the family", say fans of this "old-style"
Mayfair trattoria; it's "hugely expensive", though, and the odd former
fan fears it's losing its edge. / www.lagenovarestaurant.com; 11 pm;
closed Sun.

George & Vulture EC3 £43 ⑤④❷
3 Castle Ct 7626 9710 9–3C
"A splendidly Dickensian location" wins hearts for this historic tavern,
"tucked-away" in the City; its comfort food menu, however, ranges
from "barely adequate… to far worse". / www.georgeandvulture.com;
2.45 pm; L only, closed Sat & Sun.

Gessler at Daquise SW7 £39 ④❷❸
20 Thurloe St 7589 6117 5–2C
"This old friend has had quite a facelift", but not everyone loves the
new régime at this WWII-era Polish émigrés' café in South
Kensington; some reporters do praise its "honest and different" fare,
but critics find the approach "fussy", and say that results overall are
only "OK". / gesslerlondon.com; 11 pm; no Amex; set weekday L £24 (FP).

The Giaconda Dining Room WC2 £41 ❷❷④
9 Denmark St 7240 3334 4–1A
"Behind an unprepossessing façade", near Centre Point,
this "cramped" and "entirely unpretentious" café is an absolute
"knock-out" – the "friendly" service is incredibly "professional",
and the "tiny kitchen" turns out "probably the best-value bistro-
cooking in central London". / www.giacondadining.com; 9.15 pm; closed
Mon, Sat D & Sun.

Giant Robot EC1 £39 ❸④❷
45 Clerkenwell Rd 7065 6810 9–1A
A "very cool" Clerkenwell haunt, where "superb meatballs" are the
highlight of "a menu suited to sharing"; service, though, can be "a bit
random". / www.gntrbt.com; midnight.

Gifto's Lahore Karahi UB1 £24 ❷❸④
162-164 The Broadway 8813 8669 1–3A
"Rushed at weekends, when there are queues out the door" –
this large and "buzzy" Southall diner offers "great Punjabi" food
at "the best prices". / www.gifto.com; 11.30 pm, Sat & Sun midnight.

Gilbert Scott
St Pancras Renaissance NW1 NEW   £67   ④❷❷
Euston Rd   7278 3888   8–3C
*It may occupy an "amazing" room in a "spectacular" Victorian
building, but Marcus Wareing's much-hyped British brasserie "hasn't
yet found its stride"; service is "personable", but the "semi-historical"
menu "promises much" but is "rather less exciting on the plate".*
/ www.thegilbertscott.co.uk; 10.30 pm.

Gilgamesh NW1   £62   ❸④❷
The Stables, Camden Mkt, Chalk Farm Rd   7428 4922   8–3B
*It's not just the giant scale that makes it an "OTT" experience to visit
this "opulent" venue, over Camden Market… the bill's super-sized
too; that said, the pan-Asian food is sometimes surprisingly "great".*
/ www.gilgameshbar.com; midnight; no trainers.

Ginger & White NW3   £8   ❸❷❷
4a-5a, Perrins Ct   7431 9098   8–2A
*"Small", "cosy" and "sociable", this Hampstead café is "thriving" –
breakfasts are a highlight, but it's the coffee which really gets fans
revved up. / www.gingerandwhite.com; L only; no Mastercard.*

Giraffe   £40   ⑤④④
120 Wilton Rd, SW1   7233 8303   2–4B
6-8 Blandford St, W1   7935 2333   2–1A
19-21 The Brunswick Centre, WC1   7812 1336   8–4C
120 Holland Park Ave, W11   7229 8567   6–2A
270 Chiswick High Rd, W4   8995 2100   7–2A
7 Kensington High St, W8   7938 1221   5–1A
29-31 Essex Rd, N1   7359 5999   8–3D
196-198 Haverstock Hill, NW3   7431 3812   8–2A
46 Rosslyn Hill, NW3   7435 0343   8–2A
Royal Festival Hall, Riverside, SE1   7928 2004   2–3D
27 Battersea Rise, SW11   7223 0933   10–2C
1 Crispin Pl, E1   3116 2000   12–2B
*"Even the messiest toddler is welcomed", at this "accommodating"
and very "family-focussed" chain of 'World Food' cafés; it's also worth
seeking out for a "great brunch" but, more generally, "the accent
is on quantity not quality". / www.giraffe.net; 10.45 pm, Sun 10.30pm;
no booking, Sat & Sun 9am-5pm; set weekday L £21 (FP).*

La Giralda HA5   £27   ❸❷❸
66-68 Pinner Grn   8868 3429   1–1A
*"Waiters who've been there for decades" add to the "loud and fun"
style of this stalwart tapas bar, in a Pinner shop parade.*
/ www.lagiralda.co.uk; 10 pm; closed Mon & Sun D.

The Glasshouse TW9   £57   ❶❶❸
14 Station Pde   8940 6777   1–3A
*"Living in the shadow of sibling Chez Bruce, but holding its own!";
this "discreet" spot, by Kew Gardens, transcends its "airy" but slightly
"anodyne" interior, thanks to its "exceptional" service and its
"consistently outstanding" cuisine (to which "bright" Asian notes add
interest). / www.glasshouserestaurant.co.uk; 10.30 pm, Sun 10 pm.*

Golden Dragon W1   £30   ❸❸❸
28-29 Gerrard St   7734 2763   4–3A
*"A large and busy Chinese" in the "heart of Chinatown" where
"the classics are done very well"; top tip: "steaming hot" dim sum.*
/ 11 pm, Fri & Sat 11.30 pm, Sun 10.20 pm.

FSA

Golden Hind W1   £21   **❶❷❸**
73 Marylebone Ln   7486 3644   2–1A
The owner Mr Christou "welcomes you back like family" to this
"irresistible" Marylebone chippy, which offers some of the West End's
best "cheap 'n' cheerful" scoff; fortunately, "recent expansion hasn't
dented the warmth of the place"; BYO. / 10 pm; closed Sat L & Sun.

Goldfish   £45   **❷❸④**
82 Hampstead High St, NW3   7794 6666   8–2A
46 Gresham St, EC2   7726 0308   9–2B
"Extremely innovative" cuisine has won quite a fan club for this stylish
Chinese duo, although the "dinky" Hampstead original outlet remains
better-known than its City offshoot; conditions are "overcrowded",
though, and staff sometimes "pushy". / 10.30 pm, NW3 Sat & Sun
11 pm; EC2V closed Sat & Sun.

Good Earth   £52   **❸❸⑤**
233 Brompton Rd, SW3   7584 3658   5–2C
143-145 The Broadway, NW7   8959 7011   1–1B
"A cut above" – this smart Chinese mini-chain "has maintained high
standards for many years"; unfortunately, however, its prices
"have got a little out of hand" of late, especially as both the
Knightsbridge and Mill Hill branches look "in need of a revamp".
/ www.goodearthgroup.co.uk; 11 pm, Sun 10.30 pm.

Goodman   £60   **❷❷❸**
26 Maddox St, W1   7499 3776   3–2C
11 Old Jewry, EC2   7600 8220   9–2C
"Brilliant steaks" – London's best, for many reporters – plus "out-of-
this-world burgers", and "a wine list of full-bodied reds" win legions
of rave reviews (especially from business types) for these "New York-
style power steakhouses". / 11 pm; W1 Sun, EC2 Sat & Sun; set weekday L
£36 (FP).

Gopal's of Soho W1   £31   **❸❸❸**
12 Bateman St   7434 1621   4–2A
Just the job when you're in need of a "classic" curry house – one of
the few traditional West End joints where you can be reasonably sure
of getting some "great Indian food". / www.gopalsofsoho.co.uk; 11.30 pm.

GORDON RAMSAY SW3   £121   **④❸④**
68-69 Royal Hospital Rd   7352 4441   5–3D
Fans insist the cooking "maintains top marks", but Gordon Ramsay's
worldwide HQ, in Chelsea, can seem a "very formulaic" operation
nowadays, as well as an "eye-wateringly expensive" one; when,
we wonder, will Michelin finally feel obliged to notice that its poster
boy's flagship barely deserves two stars on current form, never mind
three? / www.gordonramsay.com; 11 pm; closed Sat & Sun; no jeans
or trainers; booking: max 8; set weekday L £61 (FP).

Gordon Ramsay at Claridge's
Claridge's Hotel W1   £100   **⑤④⑤**
55 Brook St   7499 0099   3–2B
This grand Mayfair dining room is so clearly "living on its reputation"
that you do have to wonder why its parent hotel recently extended
the lease; the potentially wonderful Deco chamber feels "about
as exciting as a post office" nowadays, and the food is too often
"shockingly bad". / www.gordonramsay.com; 11 pm, Sun 10 pm; no jeans
or trainers; booking: max 8; set weekday L £52 (FP).

Gordon's Wine Bar WC2 £27 ⑤④❶
47 Villiers St   7930 1408   4–4D
"Magical old arches" add much to the romance of this "insanely busy" wine bar, near Embankment, which also benefits from one of central London's biggest terraces; its barbecue, deli platters and cheeses are "incidental" – "it's all about quaffing the wines". / www.gordonswinebar.com; 11 pm, Sun 10 pm; no booking.

The Goring Hotel SW1 £78 ❸❶❶
15 Beeston Pl   7396 9000   2–4B
"Hopefully Royal Wedding fame won't change it!" – the "properly old-fashioned" dining room of this "quiet and refined" family-owned hotel, near Victoria, offers a "well-spaced" environment, "Rolls-Royce" service and "splendid" cooking (including a tremendous breakfast) in "traditional" style. / www.thegoring.com; 10 pm; closed Sat L; no jeans or trainers; table of 8 max; set brunch £49 (FP).

Gourmet Burger Kitchen £27 ❸④④
Branches throughout London
For its (dwindling) army of fans, this once path-breaking Kiwi-inspired chain remains a "failsafe" option for a "proper" burger (with "a good range of toppings" too); it's hard to disagree, though, with those who feel "the formula looks a bit worn, especially versus newcomers, such as Byron". / www.gbkinfo.com; 10.45 pm; EC4 10 pm; SW19 11 pm, Sun 10 pm; no booking.

Gourmet Pizza Company £31 ❸❸❸
Gabriels Wharf, 56 Upper Ground, SE1   7928 3188   9–3A
18-20 Mackenzie Walk, E14   7345 9192   11–1C
"Well-made pizza with interesting toppings" – plus "smiling" and "efficient" staff – again win praise for these superior pizza-stops; the outside tables at the SE1 branch enjoy great views of the City and St Paul's. / www.gourmetpizzacompany.co.uk; E14 10.30 pm; SE1 10.45 pm, Fri, Sat 11.15; E14 closed Sun; booking: min 7.

Gourmet San E2 £21 ❷④⑤
261 Bethnal Green Rd   7729 8388   12–1D
Ignore the "grim-looking exterior in a grim location" – it's the "deliciously spicy" and "fiery" Sichuan cooking that makes this "no-frills" East End dive so "startlingly good"; it's "cheap as chips" too. / www.oldplace.co.uk; 11 pm; D only.

Govinda's W1 £13 ❸④④
9 Soho St   7437 4928   4–1A
"Especially for a cheap lunch" near Oxford Street, the no-frills café of the Radha-Krishna Temple, just north of Soho Square, makes a great bet, thanks to its good-quality, "authentically Indian" veggie fare. / www.iskcon-london.org; 8 pm; closed Sun; no Amex.

Gow's EC2 £49 ④❸❸
81 Old Broad St   7920 9645   9–2C
"Undemanding", but "reliable for a business lunch" – this "unreconstructed City fish place", near Liverpool Street, continues to exert its rather "club-like" charm. / www.ballsbrothers.co.uk; 9.30 pm; closed Sat & Sun.

The Gowlett SE15 £35 ❷④❷
62 Gowlett Rd   7635 7048   1–4C
"Amazing pizza" – with "Rizla-thin crusts" – is the highlight at this "neighbourhood gem", in Peckham; "and you get a great array of real ales" too – "what's not to like?" / www.thegowlett.com; 10.30 pm, Sun 9 pm.

Goya SW1 £40 ④④④
34 Lupus St 7976 5309 2–4C
*"Reliable" tapas help make this "laid-back" Pimlico bar a "busy" local
rendezvous; it may also help that there's precious little else
hereabouts... / www.goyarestaurant.co.uk; 11.30 pm.*

Gran Paradiso SW1 £46 ④❸④
52 Wilton Rd 7828 5818 2–4B
*"The menu hasn't changed much in 30 years", at this Pimlico
trattoria; everyone says the food's "thoroughly reliable" though,
and this remains a "much-loved local", even if service has seemed
a little "weary" of late. / 10.45 pm; closed Sat L & Sun.*

The Grand Imperial
Guoman Grosvenor Hotel SW1 NEW £49 ④❸④
101 Buckingham Palace Rd 7821 8898 2–4B
*The scale of this grand new Chinese restaurant – in a Victorian hotel
by Victoria Station – can make it feel a bit like a "mausoleum";
service tries hard, though, and strengths include lots of space for
business meetings, and good-value lunchtime dim sum.
/ www.grandimperiallondon.com; 10 pm; no trainers.*

The Grapes E14 £44 ❸❸❷
76 Narrow St 7987 4396 11–1B
*"A Dickensian interior and great Thames views" make this "intimate"
Docklands inn "a big hit with visitors from abroad"; upstairs there's
a "small but perfectly formed restaurant", serving simple, fishy fare –
"if you can, get a window seat". / 9.30 pm; closed Sat L & Sun D.*

Grazing Goat W1 NEW £55 ❸❷❷
6 New Quebec St 7724 7243 2–2A
*"Beautifully refurbished" (by the 'Thomas Cubitt' group), this new
Marylebone gastropub is – say fans – "a breath of fresh air" locally;
critics, however, find the "uncomplicated" cuisine "overpriced",
and say it comes in "minuscule portions" too.
/ www.thegrazinggoat.co.uk; 10 pm; .*

Great Eastern Dining Room EC2 £42 ❷❸❷
54-56 Great Eastern St 7613 4545 12–1B
*Will Ricker must be proud of this ever-"trendy" Shoreditch hang-out –
thanks to its "creative" pan-Asian tapas that are "every bit as good
as the vibe", and "brilliant cocktails" too, it really has stood the
test of time. / www.rickerrestaurants.com; 10.45 pm; closed Sat L & Sun.*

Great Nepalese NW1 £28 ❸❷⑤
48 Eversholt St 7388 6737 8–3C
*"Specialities not found in your average Indian" add interest to this
"always reliable" and "very welcoming" Nepalese stalwart, in the
grim shadow of Euston Station. / www.great-nepalese.co.uk; 11.30 pm,
Sun 10 pm.*

Great Queen Street WC2 £44 ❷❸❸
32 Great Queen St 7242 0622 4–1D
*"Showcasing the best of British food!" – this "deceptively simple"
(or perhaps "self-consciously basic") Covent Garden pub-conversion
gives its famous sibling the Anchor & Hope a good run for its money,
and its "lively" ("noisy") interior is more atmospheric too. / 10.15 pm;
closed Sun D; no Amex.*

The Greedy Buddha SW6   £33   ❸❷❸
144 Wandsworth Bridge Rd   7751 3311   10–1B
"Delicious, freshly-made food" – and *"staff who work hard"* too –
win strong local praise for this *"good-value"* Fulham Nepalese.
/ www.thegreedybuddha.com; 10.30 pm, Fri & Sat 11.30 pm; closed
weekday L; no Amex.

Green & Blue SE22   £34   ❹❷❷
38 Lordship Ln   8693 9250   1–4D
"Wine heaven!" – in fact, no one bothers to mention the deli scoff
on offer at this *"chilled"* East Dulwich wine store at all; indeed, for a
small per capita charge, you can even BYO – the food, that is! –
to accompany your choice of bottle (sold, earlier in the week, at retail
prices). / www.greenandbluewines.com; Thu 11 pm, Fri & Sat midnight,
Sun 8 pm; no Amex.

Green Cottage NW3   £28   ❷❹⑤
9 New College Pde   7722 5305   8–2A
Ignore the *"dingy"* setting and the *"slightly supercilious"* service –
it's the *"great no-frills Chinese food"*, at *"reasonably prices"* too,
that makes it worth visiting this busy stalwart, near Swiss Cottage.
/ 11 pm, Sun 10 pm; no Amex.

Green Papaya E8   £30   ❷❷❷
191 Mare St   8985 5486   1–1D
An *"authentic"* Hackney Vietnamese, where *"food of a surprisingly
high standard"* is just part of a package that enthuses its (small) fan
club. / www.green-papaya.com; 11 pm; Closed L, Mon; no Amex.

Green's   £62   ❷❷❷
36 Duke St, SW1   7930 4566   3–3D
14 Cornhill, EC3   7220 6300   9–2C
Simon Parker Bowles's *"old-fashioned"* St James's bastion has traded
less on its *"clubby"* credentials of late, and more on the attractions
of some *"first-class"* fish and seafood; its offshoot – in an
"impressive" banking hall by Bank – offers *"one of the most civilised
settings for a City lunch"*. / www.greens.org.uk; SW1 11 pm; SW1 closed
Sun (May-Sep), EC3 Sat & Sun.

The Greenhouse W1   £98   ❸❷❷
27a Hays Mews   7499 3331   3–3B
An *"astonishing"* cellar (*"the wine list is two heavy tomes"*),
"faultless" cuisine, and overall *"attention to detail"* win high praise –
especially from expense accounters – for Marlon Abela's *"well-
spaced"* and *"discreet"* venture, *"in a lovely Mayfair mews"*.
/ www.greenhouserestaurant.co.uk; 11 pm; closed Sat L & Sun; booking:
max 12; set weekday L £47 (FP).

Grumbles SW1   £42   ⑤❹❹
35 Churton St   7834 0149   2–4B
Diehard fans see this *"cramped"* Pimlico local as *"a delightful
harking-back to the bistros of the '60s and '70s"*; harsher critics,
however, fear it has merely *"lost its way"*.
/ www.grumblesrestaurant.co.uk; 10.45 pm; set weekday L & pre-theatre
£27 (FP).

Guerilla Burgers W1   £30   ❸❷❷
35 James St   7486 1511   3–1A
"Che Guevara would be a fan", say those whose praise the
"humorous" decor of this funky spot near Selfridges; it offers burgers
which are decent enough, but arguably not up to the other *"excellent,
fresh-Mex"* fare. / www.guerillaburgers.com; 11 pm, Sun 10.30 pm.

The Guinea Grill W1 £63 ❷❸❸
30 Bruton Pl 7499 1210 3–3B
A "meat-lover's haven"; this "old-school" pub, "hidden-away" in a
Mayfair mews, serves up some "excellent" and "very traditional"
steaks and pies, in a "cramped" and "atmospheric" dining room
which "harks back to Edwardian days"; even fans, however, can find
it "expensive". / www.theguinea.co.uk; 10.30 pm; closed Sat L & Sun;
booking: max 8.

The Gun E14 £50 ❷❹❷
27 Coldharbour 7515 5222 11–1C
With its "lovely views" ("across the Thames to the O2 dome"),
this "beautifully-located" riverside pub is a hugely popular refuge from
nearby Canary Wharf; its "upmarket British gastropub fare" is "top-
quality" too, although it's "expensive", and service can be "slow".
/ www.thegundocklands.com; 10.30 pm, Sun 9.30 pm.

Gung-Ho NW6 £36 ❸❷❸
328-332 West End Ln 7794 1444 1–1B
"It does have its off days", but this "always-buzzing"
West Hampstead Chinese veteran is "still above-average for a local",
and "when it's good, it's very good". / www.stir-fry.co.uk; 11.30 pm;
no Amex.

Haandi SW3 £47 ❷❷❹
7 Cheval Pl 7823 7373 5–1C
Oddly 'hidden-away' in a mews opposite Harrods, this long-
established Indian offers some "terrific" Punjabi cooking that's well
worth seeking out. / www.haandi-restaurants.com; 11 pm.

Haché £35 ❸❸❸
329-331 Fulham Rd, SW10 7823 3515 5–3B
24 Inverness St, NW1 7485 9100 8–3B
"Better than Byron!" – these "cool" but "friendly" Camden Town and
Chelsea bistros have acquired a massive following by dint of their
"huge selection" of "fantastically juicy" and "well-seasoned" burgers,
that are amongst "the best in town". / www.hacheburgers.com; 10.30 pm,
Fri-Sat 11 pm, Sun 10 pm.

HAKKASAN £82 ❷❹❷
17 Bruton St, W1 7907 1888 3–2C
8 Hanway Pl, W1 7927 7000 4–1A
For a "sexy night out", these "slick", "noisy" and "über-expensive"
Chinese hotspots "still rock", not least for those in search
of "London's most finely executed dim sum"; the "très flash" new
branch in Mayfair "raises the bar even higher than the original"
(near Tottenham Court Road). / www.hakkasan.com; midnight, Sun 11 pm.

Halepi W2 £44 ❸❶❸
18 Leinster Ter 7262 1070 6–2C
"You just feel as if you are on a charming Greek island" – well,
you do need a bit of imagination – when you visit this veteran
Bayswater taverna; its diehard fan club love the hearty fare, and the
staff who "greet you like family". / www.halepi.co.uk; midnight.

Haozhan W1 £39 ❸❹❺
8 Gerrard St 7434 3838 4–3A
Is this "mould-breaking" Chinatown three-year-old beginning
to "slack"? – fans still say its "original" modern Asian cooking is "in a
different league" from its competitors, enabling it to transcend its
"drab", IKEA-esque decor; sceptics say it's on the verge of becoming
"bog-standard". / www.haozhan.co.uk; 11.30 pm, Fri & Sat midnight,
Sun 11 pm.

Harbour City W1 £30 ❷④④
46 Gerrard St 7439 7859 4–3B
"Still Gerrard Street's best for dim sum" – this Chinatown fixture offers "amazing value" at lunchtime, and its "other traditional dishes" are "reliable" too. / 11.30 pm, Fri-Sat midnight, Sun 10 pm.

Hard Rock Café W1 £47 ④❷❷
150 Old Park Ln 7629 0382 3–4B
"Still grooving after all these years", the "fun" Mayfair original branch of this global chain still pleases kids of all ages; its "basic" food is cooked only "reasonably well", but "it's the rock 'n' roll you go for". / www.hardrock.com; midnight; need 10+ to book.

Hardy's Brasserie W1 £44 ④④❸
53 Dorset St 7935 5929 2–1A
"Nicely tucked-away in a side street", this "old-fashioned" wine bar is strong on atmosphere; it offers "OK" food too, and some "diverse" wines to go with it. / www.hardysbrasserie.co.uk; 10.30 pm; closed Sat & Sun.

Hare & Tortoise £28 ❸❸❸
11-13 The Brunswick, WC1 7278 9799 2–1D
373 Kensington High St, W14 7603 8887 7–1D
38 Haven Grn, W5 8810 7066 1–2A
296-298 Upper Richmond Rd, SW15 8394 7666 10–2B
90 New Bridge St, EC4 7651 0266 9–2A
"Always busy", these pan-Asian canteens are great "for a quick exotic meal"; they serve "great-value sushi", but it's the "fine noodles" that are the "real bargain" – "go early to avoid the queues". / www.hareandtortoise-restaurants.co.uk; 10.45 pm, Fri & Sat 11.15 pm; EC4 10 pm; EC4 Sun; W14 no bookings.

Harrison's SW12 £47 ④④❸
15-19 Bedford Hill 8675 6900 10–2C
It's "buzzy and consistent", but you don't go to Sam Harrison's "neighbourhood" hang-out (formerly Balham Bar & Grill) for memorable cuisine – it's at its best as "a venue for a lazy Sunday". / www.harrisonsbalham.co.uk; 10.30 pm, Sun 10 pm; set weekday L £30 (FP).

(Georgian Restaurant) Harrods SW1 £68 ❸❸❸
87-135 Brompton Rd 7225 6800 5–1D
Of the many eating options at the Knightsbridge department store, the "quiet" and elegant top-floor main dining room is probably the best – once you're there, the enormous buffet is worth serious consideration. / www.harrods.com; 5 pm; L only.

Harry Morgan's NW8 £37 ❷❸❸
31 St John's Wood High St 7722 1869 8–3A
Back on top form post-refurbishment – this "buzzing" kosher institution, in St John's Wood, is "your classic deli", and rightly praised for its "famous chicken soup" and "the best salt beef in town!" / www.harryms.co.uk; 10 pm.

Harwood Arms SW6 £49 ❷❷❷
Walham Grove 7386 1847 5–3A
"A REAL gastropub!"; the "superb" British cooking – including "magnificent" game and "the best Scotch eggs" – has made a huge name for this Fulham backstreet boozer; it's a "laid-back" kind of place too, with staff who are "so welcoming". / www.harwoodarms.com; 9.30 pm, Sun 9 pm; closed Mon L

The Havelock Tavern W14 £43 ❷④❷
57 Masbro Rd   7603 5374   7–1C
"Back, after a rocky patch", this "genuine" gastropub, in an Olympia back street, is "always humming"; the food can be "outstanding" – service is still "slow", though, but at least "it's not surly, like it used to be". / www.thehavelocktavern.co.uk; 10 pm, Sun 9.30 pm; no booking.

The Haven N20 £47 ④④④
1363 High Rd   8445 7419   1–1B
Views on "Whetstone's finest joint" have become very mixed; for fans, this is still a "great" and "boisterous" neighbourhood place – for quite a few critics, though, it's "very mediocre" nowadays. / www.haven-bistro.co.uk; 11 pm; no Amex.

Hawksmoor £59 ❷❷❷
11 Langley St, WC2   7856 2154   4–2C
157 Commercial St, E1   7247 7392   12–2B
10-12 Basinghall St, EC2   awaiting tel   9–2C NEW
"Terrific steaks" ("mind you, you pay for 'em"), "crazy-good triple-cooked chips" and "the best cocktails" – three potent ingredients that are carving a formidable and growing reputation for these Spitalfields, Covent Garden and (from late-2011) City steakhouses. / www.thehawksmoor.com; 10.30 pm; both Sun D; no Amex.

Haz £36 ❸❸❷
9 Cutler St, E1   7929 7923   9–2D
34 Foster Ln, EC2   7600 4172   9–2B
112 Hounsditch, EC3   7623 8180   9–2D
6 Mincing Ln, EC3   7929 3173   9–3D
"Fresh" and "good-value" mezze and kebabs and "brisk" service have won a big City following for these "cramped" but "efficient" Turkish operations – thanks to their "ever-reliable" charms, they're always "buzzing". / www.hazrestaurant.co.uk; 11.30 pm; EC3 Sun.

Hazev E14 £30 ④④④
2 South Quay Sq, Discovery Dock West   7515 9467   11–1C
"Nothing special, but it's nice to have more variety in Canary Wharf" – this large and "noisy" Turkish water-sider, near South Quay DLR, "draws in the crowds" with its "tasty mezze and other dishes". / www.hazev.com; 11.30 pm, Wed-Sat 11 pm.

Hazuki WC2 £35 ❷❷④
43 Chandos Pl   7240 2530   4–4C
An "unassuming" café, near Charing Cross, that's well worth knowing about if you're looking for "interesting" Japanese food at "reasonable prices"; its interior "isn't that great", but "the grub makes up". / www.hazukilondon.co.uk; 10.30 pm, Sun 9.30 pm; closed Sat L & Sun L.

Hedone W4 NEW £79 ❷④④
301 Chiswick High Rd   8747 0377   7–2A
Foodie cognoscenti are enraptured by this ambitious, ingredient-led Chiswick newcomer, which opened in summer 2011; Mikael Jonsson's cooking undoubtedly shows huge promise, but – on our very early-days visit – all aspects of the operation needed more polish, yet prices were already sky high. / Rated on Editors' visit.

Hélène Darroze
The Connaught Hotel W1   £105   ❸❹❸
Carlos Pl   3147 7200   3–3B
"Elaborate" cuisine and "elegant" surroundings win fans for this Mayfair outpost of the acclaimed Parisienne chef; service "veers from friendly to stuffy", though, and quite a few reporters still yearn for the "good old days" (before celebrity nonsense took hold), when this was one of the classiest and most consistent destinations in town. / www.the-connaught.co.uk; 10.30 pm; closed Mon & Sun; jacket & tie; set weekday L £63 (FP).

Hellenic W1   £43   ❹❷❸
30 Thayer St   7935 1257   2–1A
In Fitzrovia, an "old-fashioned" Greek restaurant – straight from Central Casting – whose "authentic" charms still win it a small fan club. / 10.45 pm; closed Sun; no Amex.

The Henry Root SW10 NEW   £46   ❹❷❸
9 Park Walk   7352 7040   5–3B
With a feel a bit like "an upmarket gastropub", this heart-of-Chelsea newcomer is heartily praised for its "cosy and welcoming" interior, its "very attentive" staff and its "great selection of tasty dishes"; detractors, though, just find the whole show rather too "average". / www.thehenryroot.com; 11 pm.

Hereford Road W2   £42   ❷❷❹
3 Hereford Rd   7727 1144   6–1B
"No-nonsense, robust British dishes" – from "good-quality ingredients", including "good offal and game" – have won a huge fan club for Tom Pemberton's Bayswater bistro; best place to sit: the "booths-à-deux", at the front. / www.herefordroad.org; 10.30 pm, Sun 10 pm.

Hibiscus W1   £110   ❸❹❹
29 Maddox St   7629 2999   3–2C
"Brilliant" cuisine that "thinks outside the box" wins "10/10" ratings from fans of Claude Bosi's "calm" Mayfair HQ; not everyone is persuaded, though, and critics perennially complain of "ridiculous" prices for food that's "nothing special", and an ambience like a "funeral parlour" (albeit a rather comfortable one). / www.hibiscusrestaurant.co.uk; 9.45 pm; closed Mon L & Sun; set weekday L £53 (FP).

High Road Brasserie W4   £48   ❹❹❷
162-166 Chiswick High Rd   8742 7474   7–2A
A "fantastic" (and "family-friendly") brunch is a highlight at this "atmospheric" and "very popular" hang-out, on Chiswick's main drag; critics find its approach a bit too "strenuously trendy", though, especially as the "very expensive" food is "nothing special at all". / www.sohohouse.co.uk; 10.30 pm, Fri & Sat 11.30 pm, Sun 9.30 pm.

High Timber EC4   £59   ❸❷❸
8 High Timber   7248 1777   9–3B
"Wonderful South African wines" – you choose by "nipping down to the cellar" – are the highlight of this City spot, hidden-away near the wobbly bridge, and it enjoys "fine" Thames views; in comparison, the food – "excellent" steaks apart – can seem "a tasty sideline". / www.hightimber.com; 10 pm; closed Sat & Sun; set weekday L £38 (FP).

Hilliard EC4 £27 ❷❷❸
26a Tudor St 7353 8150 9–3A
"A foodie haven, just off chain-infested Fleet Street" – this "absolute joy" of a pit stop is packed with lawyers getting their daily fix of "gourmet sarnies", "imaginative salads" and "yummy coffee and cakes"; oh, and "interesting wines" too. / www.hilliardfood.co.uk; 6 pm; L only, closed Sat & Sun; no booking.

Hix W1 £61 ❸❹❸
66-70 Brewer St 7292 3518 3–2D
"Adopted by the entire Soho media class", this "buzzing" yearling is extolled for its "sophisticatedly simple" British cuisine and its "outstanding" basement bar too – no denying, though, that there are still refuseniks who find the whole experience "very average". / www.hixsoho.co.uk; 10.15 pm.

Hix Oyster & Chop House EC1 £60 ❷❸❸
36-37 Greenhill Rents, Cowcross St 7017 1930 9–1A
Mark Hix's sparsely-furnished Smithfield operation is at last establishing itself as "a seriously good place to eat"; service has "improved", as has the cooking, which majors in the "great treatment of quality ingredients", including "the freshest oysters", and "a fantastic selection of chops and steaks". / www.restaurantsetcltd.com; 10.45 pm; closed Sat L; set always available, weekday L & pre-theatre £26 (FP).

Hole in the Wall W4 £40 ❸❹❸
12 Sutton Lane North 8742 7185 7–2A
Tucked-away in Gunnersbury, an "unpretentious" gastroboozer, almost invariably hailed by locals for its "restaurant-quality" food; super garden too. / 9.45 pm, Sun 9.15 pm; closed Mon L & Tue L; no Amex.

Holly Bush NW3 £44 ❸❸❶
22 Holly Mount 7435 2892 8–1A
"Snuggle up in a nook", at this "old and atmospheric" boozer, which benefits from a gorgeous Hampstead location; the "simple, comfort food menu" goes nicely "with a pint of ale". / 10 pm, Sun 9 pm.

Homa N16 NEW £48 ❸❸❸
71-73 Stoke Newington Church St 7254 2072 1–1C
"At last, a decent European restaurant to add to Stokey's inner-city mix!" – its "stylish" and "friendly" charms have already won quite a following (...to the extent there's already the occasional fear it's 'coasting'). / www.homalondon.co.uk; 11.30 pm; closed Mon.

The Horseshoe NW3 £47 ❹❸❸
28 Heath St 7431 7206 8–2A
"Wholesome, hearty fare" and "friendly" service make this "pleasant" gastropub a handy heart-of-Hampstead stand-by; increasingly, though, "it's merging into the culinary averageness of NW3". / www.thehorseshoehampstead.com; 10pm, Fri & Sat 11 pm.

Hot Stuff SW8 £20 ❷❶❷
23 Wilcox Rd 7720 1480 10–1D
"Unless you want swanky decor", this BYO Indian in deepest Vauxhall is "brilliant", thanks to its super-"welcoming" owner, and food that's "so zingy", and "really cheap"; it's now two doors down from the original, so there's "more room now" too. / www.eathotstuff.com; 9.30 pm; no Amex.

Hoxton Apprentice N1   £45   ❸❹❷
16 Hoxton Sq   7749 2828   12–1B
The ethos – a training project for the disadvantaged – "is part of the attraction" of this Hoxton hang-out, which benefits from a pleasant terrace, and quite a stylish interior; even fans, though, can find the food "expensive for what it is". / www.hoxtonapprentice.com; 11 pm.

The Hoxton Grill EC2   £46   ❸❸❷
81 Great Eastern St   7739 9111   12–1B
The Soho House group is making quite a go of the bar/restaurant at this hip Shoreditch-fringe hotel; "great steak and chips" ("especially cheap at lunchtimes") are a highlight, and breakfasts can be "excellent" too. / www.hoxtongrill.com; 11.45 pm; set weekday L £29 (FP).

Hudsons SW15   £35   ❹❹❸
113 Lower Richmond Rd   8785 4522   10–1A
A "reliable" Putney bistro, that "continues to deliver the goods, year after year"; breakfasts – which come in "rower-sized portions" – are "a must". / www.hudsonsrestaurant.co.uk; 10 pm, Sun 9.30 pm.

Hummus Bros   £17   ❷❷❹
88 Wardour St, W1   7734 1311   3–2D
36-67 Southampton Row, WC1   7404 7079   2–1D
128 Cheapside, EC2   7726 8011   9–2B
"I had no idea the humble chickpea could be lifted to such heights!" – this hummus-mad chain is perfect for a snack that's "quick, cheap, tasty, satisfying and healthy". / www.hbros.co.uk; W1 10 pm, Thu-Sat 11 pm; WC1 9 pm; WC1, EC2 closed Sat & Sun; no booking.

Hunan SW1   £50   ❶❷❹
51 Pimlico Rd   7730 5712   5–2D
"Simply the best Chinese food in London!" – leave it to the chef to choose, and the "spectacular", "tapas-style" courses "just never stop coming", at the Peng family's "bizarre" (and decidedly unspectacular-looking) Pimlico legend; even the wine list is – in a good way – "full of unusual surprises". / www.hunanlondon.com; 11 pm; closed Sun.

Huong-Viet
An Viet House N1   £26   ❹❺❺
12-14 Englefield Rd   7249 0877   1–1C
"Full of Dalston hip kids", this "fun" BYO Vietnamese, in a De Beauvoir Town community-centre, has long been known as "an absolute bargain"; "the food's not as good as it once was", though, and "service and decor have never been strong points". / www.huongviet.co.uk; 11 pm; closed Sun; no Amex.

Hush W1   £55   ❺❺❹
8 Lancashire Ct   7659 1500   3–2B
"Trading on its prime location", just off Bond Street – and with a "hidden courtyard" too – this trendy bar/brasserie remains a "hit with the Sotheby's set"; rather worryingly, that crowd doesn't seem to mind that the food is "mediocre" and prices "absurd". / www.hush.co.uk; 11 pm; closed Sun; booking: max 12.

Ibérica   £43   ❸❸❸
195 Great Portland St, W1   7636 8650   2–1B
10 Cabot Sq, E14   awaiting tel   11–1C **NEW**
"Sophisticated but authentic dishes", and "enthusiastic" service inspire fans of this "smart" and "buzzy" tapas bar, near Great Portland Street tube; it can seem "a bit pricey" for what it is, though, and critics find the setting a tad "soulless"; a Canary Wharf offshoot opens in late-2011. / 11 pm; W1 closed Sun D.

Ida W10 £38 ❸❷❷
167 Fifth Ave 8969 9853 1–2B
*A "cheap 'n' cheerful" North Kensington café, hailed by fans as a
"fantastic local", where the Italian menu offers "incredible value".
/ www.idarestaurant.co.uk; 11 pm; closed Sat L & Sun; no Amex.*

Ikeda W1 £85 ❷❷❺
30 Brook St 7629 2730 3–2B
*"Dismal" decor ("like a cheap motel lounge") and "chronic" prices
do not quite succeed in discouraging fans of this veteran Mayfair
Japanese, where the sushi in particular is often "excellent".
/ 10.20 pm; closed Sat L & Sun.*

Ilia SW3 NEW £67 ❸❹❹
96 Draycott Ave 7225 2555 5–2C
*Most of the (surprisingly few) early-days reports on this new Chelsea
Italian (on the ex-Papillon, RIP, site) share our repeated experience
that it's a "friendly" place, offering "fresh" food in a "smart" and
"lively" setting; there's also a small band of critics, though,
who just find it "average" across the board. / www.ilia-london.com;
10.30 pm, Fri-Sat 11 pm; closed Mon L.*

Imli W1 £36 ❹❸❹
167-169 Wardour St 7287 4243 3–1D
*"For a novel and light approach" to Indian cooking, fans tip this
"buzzy" Soho canteen, and its "inventive" tapas formula; critics think
the idea is great too, but complain that the food is descending
to "chain-like" standards. / www.imli.co.uk; 11 pm, Sun 10 pm.*

Imperial China WC2 £42 ❸❸❹
25a Lisle St 7734 3388 4–3B
*"Beyond a little bridge, over an ornamental pond", you enter this
large operation in a Chinatown side street; fans say it's "better than
the places on the main drag", thanks to its civilised style, and its
"presentable" cuisine. / www.imperial-china.co.uk; midnight, Sun 10.30 pm.*

Imperial City EC3 £46 ❹❸❸
Royal Exchange, Cornhill 7626 3437 9–2C
*"In the atmospheric vaults of the Royal Exchange", this "classy"-
looking Cantonese continues to dish up "consistently good" cooking;
"it would get higher ratings, were it not for its typical high-end City
pricing". / www.orientalrestaurantgroup.co.uk; 10.30 pm; closed Sat & Sun.*

Inaho W2 £43 ❶❺❺
4 Hereford Rd 7221 8495 6–1B
*Thanks not least to its "irreproachable" sushi, this "tiny" and
"homely" Bayswater shack is hailed by fans as "the best Japanese
restaurant on the planet"; service, though, has only two speeds –
"slow" or "rushed". / 11 pm; closed Sat L & Sun; no Amex or Maestro.*

Inamo £43 ❹❹❷
4-12 Regent St, SW1 7499 8558 3–3D NEW
134-136 Wardour St, W1 7851 7051 3–1D
*Kids of all ages love the gimmick – your touch-sensitive table-top
takes orders, changes pattern, plays games and so on – at these
"fun" West End diners; the pan-Asian fare is "uninspiring and pricey"
or "perfectly good", to taste. / 10.45 pm, SW1 12 am.*

Incognico WC2 £56 ❹❹❹
117 Shaftesbury Ave 7836 8866 4–2B
*"Go for the set menus", say regulars, if you visit this heart-of-
Theatreland brasserie – if you choose its "decent, old-fashioned Gallic
fare" à la carte, you may come to the view that it is "hugely
overpriced". / www.incognico.com; 11 pm; closed Sun.*

FSA

Indali Lounge W1   £34   ❸❸❸
50 Baker St   7224 2232   2–1A
*With its "much lighter" (no-ghee) cooking, and contemporary styling,
this large Marylebone two-year-old is "an Indian unlike any other";
critics find the food "bland" and the place "lacking buzz", but the
attractions of the "excellent-value prix-fixe lunch" are undoubted.*
/ www.indalilounge.com; midnight, Sun 11 pm; closed Sat L.

India Club
Strand Continental Hotel WC2   £25   ④④④
143 Strand   7836 0650   2–2D
*"Pretend you're in India!", when you visit this "old-style-colonial"
canteen, near the High Commission – a "rather extraordinary" throw-
back, where the food is not only basic, but also "dirt cheap"; BYO.*
/ www.strand-continental.co.uk; 10.50 pm; no credit cards; booking: max 6.

Indian Moment SW11   £34   ❸❸④
44 Northcote Rd   7223 6575   10–2C
*"An extremely busy and packed-in" Battersea curry house, which
locals say is "a real cut above average"; it "doesn't break the bank"
either.*

Indian Ocean SW17   £25   ❷❸❸
216 Trinity Rd   8672 7740   10–2C
*"Around for years, but consistently of a high standard" –
this Wandsworth curry house continues to go down well with its local
fan club. / 11.30 pm.*

Indian Rasoi N2   £34   ❶❷❷
7 Denmark Ter   8883 9093   1–1B
*"Lovely, fresh, spicy flavours" are a hallmark of the "wonderful" and
"unusual" cuisine at this Muswell Hill Indian; "it's always packed,
so make sure you book". / www.indian-rasoi.co.uk; 11 pm.*

Indian Zilla SW13 NEW   £43   ❷❶❸
2-3 Rocks Ln   8878 3989   10–1A
*Indian Zing's new offshoot may occupy (formerly) "jinxed" Barnes
premises, but most reporters are confident that its "exotic" and
"heavenly" Indian cuisine will see it through; perhaps inevitably,
though, one or two critics perceive "slightly less zing" than at the
original. / www.indianzilla.co.uk; 11 pm, Sun 10.30 pm.*

Indian Zing W6   £43   ❶❷❸
236 King St   8748 5959   7–2B
*"Knocking many so-called top Indians out of the water!" – Manoj
Vasaikar's "terrific" outfit, near Ravenscourt Park, "pleases even
Michael Winner" with its "light" and "punchy" cooking, and its
"civilised", if rather "cramped", setting. / www.indianzing.co.uk; 11 pm,
Sun 10.30 pm.*

Indigo
One Aldwych WC2   £63   ④❷❸
1 Aldwych   7300 0400   2–2D
*With its view of the cocktail bar below, this "comfortable" mezzanine
makes a "pleasant" Covent Garden venue for a "business lunch" or a
"pre-theatre meal"; the food was also once quite an attraction,
but nowadays seems a little "uninspired". / www.onealdwych.com;
11.15 pm; set pre theatre £41 (FP).*

Inn the Park SW1 £48 ④⑤❸
St James's Pk 7451 9999 2–3C
"You can't beat St James's Park for a backdrop", and this striking modern café, with its many outside tables, has huge potential; sadly, though, this is true "tourist hell", offering "pricy" and "inconsistent" food, and "inexplicably poor" service. / www.innthepark.com; 9 pm; no Amex.

Inside SE10 £43 ❷❷④
19 Greenwich South St 8265 5060 1–3D
"For years, the best food in Greenwich" – it may be "cramped", "noisy" and "uncomfortably minimalist", but this "friendly" and "professional" local is adored in SE10 as a rare source of "astonishingly dependable" cooking. / www.insiderestaurant.co.uk; 10.30 pm, Fri & Sat 11 pm; closed Mon & Sun D.

Isarn N1 £43 ❷❶❸
119 Upper St 7424 5153 8–3D
An "out-of-this-world" fish curry is a culinary highlight at this Islington fixture, which is a real "cut above" the standards of your usual "local Thai"; the "speedy" service is "immensely friendly" too, but the "corridor-like" setting can feel "oddly squeezed". / www.isarn.co.uk; 11 pm; no Amex.

Ishbilia SW1 £50 ❷④⑤
9 William St 7235 7788 5–1D
Near Harvey Nics, an authentic Lebanese café with good outside seating and offering "very good mezze"; the interior, though, could do with "a bit of a refurb". / www.ishbilia.com; 11 pm.

Ishtar W1 £39 ❸❷❸
10-12 Crawford St 7224 2446 2–1A
What this "cheap 'n' cheerful" Marylebone Turk may lack in fireworks it makes up for with impressive consistency – it's especially worth seeking out for the prix-fixe lunch, which is "an amazing bargain". / www.ishtarrestaurant.com; 11 pm, Sun 10.30 pm.

Isola del Sole SW15 £46 ❸❶❷
16 Lacy Rd 8785 9962 10–2B
What's not to like about this "so welcoming" and "cosy" Italian, off Putney High Street, especially when its "traditional Sardinian cuisine" is "tasty", and rather "unusual" too? / www.isoladelsole.co.uk; 10.30 pm; closed Sun.

Itsu £31 ④④④
118 Draycott Ave, SW3 7590 2400 5–2C
100 Notting Hill Gate, W11 7229 4016 6–2B
Level 2, Cabot Place East, E14 7512 5790 11–1C
"For a healthful, rapid lunch", at "cheap" prices, most reports still say this "slick"-looking sushi, soup and salad chain is a "boon"; its ratings are still sliding, though – "what was once innovative, is now indifferent, and not that tasty". / www.itsu.co.uk; 11 pm; E14 10 pm; some are closed Sat & Sun; no booking.

THE IVY WC2 £65 ④❷❷
1-5 West St 7836 4751 4–3B
It's still "magical" for its army of fans, but this cosy, panelled Theatreland legend often seems a "shadow of its former self" nowadays, and its comfort food, in particular, has "really gone downhill" – those in the know say the (private) Ivy Club, adjacent, "is much better". / www.the-ivy.co.uk; midnight, Sun 11 pm; no shorts; booking: max 6.

Izgara N3 £33 ❸❷❸
11 Hendon Lane   8371 8282   1–1B
"Very popular and so it should be" – a Turkish café-take-away,
in North Finchley, where the basic dishes are *"very good, for a
'local'"*. / www.izgararestaurant.net; midnight.

Jai Krishna N4 £20 ❸❷❸
161 Stroud Green Rd   7272 1680   8–1D
*"It's evolved from its previous canteen setting to a more comfortable
experience"*, but this *"inexpensive"* Stroud Green favourite still has
"no pretentions", and its Indian veggie dishes are still *"brilliant"*.
/ 10.30 pm; closed Sun; no credit cards.

The Jam Tree £44 ❹❷❸
58 Milson Rd, W14   7371 3999   7–1C
541 King's Rd, SW6   3397 3739   5–4B **NEW**
"Tucked-away in Olympia", a *"lovely little gastropub"*, praised
by locals for its *"decent"* cooking and its *"sweet"* staff; it has a new
sibling at the Fulham end of the King's Road. / W14 11 pm,
Sun 10.30 pm; SW6 Mon-Thu 11 pm, Fri-Sat 2 am, Sun 10.30 pm.

Jamie's Italian £41 ❹❸❹
10-12 Upper St Martin's Ln, WC2   3326 6390   4–3B
Westfield, Ariel Way, W12   8090 9070   7–1C
2 Churchill Pl, E14   3002 5252   11–1C
Jamie Oliver's chain of *"buzzy"* and *"fun"* Italians started off as the
best restaurant venture he'd ever been associated with by far; as the
group grows, however, gravity is re-asserting itself, and gripes about
"overpriced" and *"average"* food are gaining momentum.
/ www.jamiesitalian.com; 11.30 pm, Sun 10.30 pm; over 6.

Jenny Lo's Tea House SW1 £33 ❸❶❹
14 Eccleston St   7259 0399   2–4B
The chow is *"always fresh and exciting"*, at this *"excellent, cheap,
and no-frills"* noodle house – a *"canteen-style"* veteran, near Victoria.
/ www.jennylo.co.uk; 9.55 pm; closed Sat & Sun; no credit cards; no booking.

Jin Kichi NW3 £41 ❶❷❹
73 Heath St   7794 6158   8–1A
"As good as eating in Tokyo" – London's *"homeliest and
most delicious Japanese"* may occupy *"tiny"* Hampstead premises,
but it continues to thrill its disproportionately large fan club with
"fabulous sushi and yakitori". / www.jinkichi.com; 11 pm, Sun 10 pm;
closed Mon, Tue-Fri D only, Sat & Sun open L & D.

Joanna's SE19 £44 ❸❷❷
56 Westow Hill   8670 4052   1–4D
"Stick to the basics and you won't go wrong", at this *"cramped"* but
"pleasant and welcoming" Crystal Palace favourite; its home cooking
"is a little variable", but it *"can be lovely"*. / www.joannas.uk.com; 11 pm,
Sun 10.30 pm.

Joe Allen WC2 £51 ❹❹❷
13 Exeter St   7836 0651   4–3D
Still *"vaguely glamorous"*, this *"fun"* Theatreland basement serves
*"pretty much the same menu as when it was cloned from the NYC
original in the '70s"* – the food's *"nothing special"*, except for
a burger (*"famously not on the menu"*) that's
amongst *"the best in town"*. / www.joeallen.co.uk; 12.45 am,
Sun 11.45 pm; booking: max 10 Fri & Sat.

Joe's Brasserie SW6 £41 ❸❸❸
130 Wandsworth Bridge Rd 7731 7835 10–1B
John Brinkley's long-established deepest-Fulham stalwart was "always fun"; as this guide goes to press, however, it is undergoing repairs after a fire. / www.brinkleys.com; 11 pm, Sat 11.30 pm, Sun 10.30 pm.

Jom Makan £27 ④⑤⑤
5-7 Pall Mall East, SW1 7925 2402 2–2C
South Terrace Westfields, W12 8735 5870 7–1C
This "canteen-y and rather pricey" Malaysian chain is perfectly at home in Westfield; in Trafalgar Square – with Chinatown two minutes' walk away – its raison d'être is harder to discern. / www.jommakan.co.uk; SW1 11 pm, W12 10 pm.

José SE1 NEW £45
104 Bermondsey St 7403 4902 9–4D
Brindisa's restaurant empire was built with the help of chef José Pizarro, who has now struck out on his own at these cute Bermondsey corner premises; we had yet to visit when this guide went to press, but he's doing so well, he's already on to his next opening: Pizarro.

Joy King Lau WC2 £31 ❸④④
3 Leicester St 7437 1132 4–3A
"Better than average for Chinatown"; this "buzzy" veteran, just off Leicester Square, is "not the smartest" place, but, for supporters, it remains a "regular bolt-hole", thanks to its "excellent-value dim sum" and other "tasty" fare. / 11.30 pm, Sun 10.30 pm.

Julie's W11 £58 ④④❶
135 Portland Rd 7229 8331 6–2A
"Little booths and dark corners" add charm to the "magical" setting of this "gorgeous" and "labyrinthine" Holland Park stalwart; you need to hope, though, that "the best dish is the one sat opposite you" – the cooking can be "woeful", and it comes at "criminal" prices too. / www.juliesrestaurant.com; 11 pm; closed Sun L.

The Junction Tavern NW5 £39 ❸❷❷
101 Fortess Rd 7485 9400 8–2B
A "lovely" garden, "dependable" food and notably "friendly" staff too – no wonder this "large and comfortable" Kentish town pub is always pretty "busy". / www.junctiontavern.co.uk; 10.30 pm, Sun 9.30 pm; no Amex.

Juniper Dining N5 £39 ❷❸❸
100 Highbury Pk 7288 8716 8–1D
A chef who's "a genuine enthusiast" adds style to this café-style Highbury yearling; locals rave over its keen young staff and "superb-value" bistro fare – "I'd certainly travel, if I didn't live nearby!" / www.juniperdining.co.uk; 10.30 pm; closed Mon & Sun D.

JW Steakhouse
Grosvenor House Hotel W1 £66 ④④④
86 Park Ln 7399 8460 3–3A
"Not disappointing, but nothing special" – this "large and airy" American steakhouse, right on Park Lane, does win praise for its USDA-certified steaks and "BIG" portions; it seems too "expensive" for what it is, though, to gain a widespread following among reporters. / www.jwsteakhouse.co.uk; 10.30 pm, Fri & Sat 11 pm.

K10 EC2 £37 ❸❸④
20 Copthall Ave 7562 8510 9–2C
"Perfect for a quick lunch"; with its good sushi and other "fresh" dishes, this reliable City conveyor-café is "worth the (inevitable) queue". / www.k10.net; L only, closed Sat & Sun; no booking.

F S A

Kaffeine W1 £10 ❷⓿⓿
66 Great Titchfield St 7580 6755 3–1C
*"The top place for Noho's caffeine-addict creatives", this "über-small"
and "super-friendly" café is winning a big name for its "superb
Antipodean coffee", "interesting cakes", and "brilliant, and classy
sandwiches, served Sydney-style". / www.kaffeine.co.uk; 6 pm; L only,
closed Sun; no Amex; no bookings.*

Kai Mayfair W1 £100 ❸❸④
65 South Audley St 7493 8988 3–3A
*"Stunning" Chinese food – "off the scale for simplicity and subtlety" –
inspires rave reviews for this swanky Mayfair joint; prices, however,
are equally mind-numbing, and the "glamorous" interior can seem
"somewhat lacking on the atmosphere front". / www.kaimayfair.com;
10.45 pm, Sun 10.15 pm; set weekday L £51 (FP).*

Kaifeng NW4 £61 ❷❷④
51 Church Rd 8203 7888 1–1B
*"Expensive, but worth it", this "excellent kosher Chinese", in Hendon,
attracts impressively positive reports. / www.kaifeng.co.uk; 10.30 pm;
closed Fri & Sat.*

kare kare SW5 £41 ❸❸④
152 Old Brompton Rd 7373 0024 5–2B
*Fated always to be eclipsed by the neighbouring 'Star', this South
Kensington Indian nonetheless offers some "reliable" and
"imaginative" dishes, and "good value" too. / www.karekare.co.uk;
11 pm; D only.*

Karma W14 £38 ❷⓿④
44 Blythe Rd 7602 9333 7–1D
*"Different and creative" Indian cooking – "with interesting regional
dishes" – rewards the discovery of this "contemporary"-style
operation, whose "friendly" and "efficient" style helps overcome its
"quiet" backstreet location, in Olympia. / www.k-a-r-m-a.co.uk; 11 pm;
no Amex.*

Kateh W9 NEW £39 ❸❷❸
5 Warwick Pl 7289 3393 8–4A
*"A super little Persian", newly opened in the cute, if cramped, Little
Venice site that was once Green Olive (RIP), where zesty dishes are
brought by "enthusiastic" staff. / www.kateh.co.uk; 10.45 pm,
Sun 9.30 pm; closed Mon, Tue L, Wed L & Thu L.*

Kazan £41 ❷❷❸
77 Wilton Rd, SW1 7233 8298 2–4B NEW
93-94 Wilton Rd, SW1 7233 7100 2–4B
*"Sumptuously-decorated" and "noisy", these "heaving" but "friendly"
Turkish bistros, in Pimlico, offer "reasonably-priced kebabs" that are
"a feast for both eyes and palate". / www.kazan-restaurant.com; 10 pm.*

Ken Lo's Memories SW1 £56 ❷❸❸
65-69 Ebury St 7730 7734 2–4B
*It's sometimes said to be "fading", but this "steadfast" and
"comfortable" Chinese veteran, in Belgravia, is still a favourite choice
for many reporters; it's the food – "classy and at its best truly
outstanding" – which is the prime attraction.
/ www.londonfinedininggroup.com; 11 pm, Sun 10.30 pm.*

Ken Lo's Memories of China W8 £46 ❶❷❸
353 Kensington High St 7603 6951 7–1D
"Absolutely sensational-tasting food" and *"very helpful"* service win
the highest praise for this Chinese operation, on the
Olympia/Kensington borders – an even better destination, nowadays,
than the still-excellent Belgravia original. / www.memories-of-china.co.uk;
11 pm, Sun 10 pm.

Kennington Tandoori SE11 £36 ❸❷❷
313 Kennington Rd 7735 9247 1–3C
"Popular with the neighbourhood yuppies" (and the politicos too) –
this *"stalwart curry house"* emerged from a *"refreshing"* refit
a couple of years ago, with a *"charming"* interior, *"super-polite"*
service and cooking that's *"a cut above"*.
/ www.kenningtontandoori.co.uk; midnight; no Amex.

Kensington Place W8 £50 ❸❸④
201-209 Kensington Church St 7727 3184 6–2B
It may nowadays lack its former 'buzz', but this once trail-blazing
modern British 'goldfish bowl', off Notting Hill Gate, bounced back
this year – reports are still a bit mixed, but the *"classic, well-prepared
dishes"* (especially fish) have often been *"very enjoyable"* of late.
/ www.kensingtonplace-restaurant.com; 10.30 pm, Sun 10 pm.

Kensington Square Kitchen W8 £33 ❸❷❸
9 Kensington Sq 7938 2598 5–1A
"The best brunch for miles around" – the main reason to seek out
this sweet little café, nicely hidden-away from the mêlée which
is Kensington High Street. / www.kensingtonsquarekitchen.co.uk; 5 pm,
Sun 4 pm; L only.

The Kensington Wine Rooms W8 £47 ④❷❷
127-129 Kensington Church St 7727 8142 6–2B
"Does exactly what it says on the – smart – tin"; this *"cracking"*
(if *"noisy"*) haunt, near Notting Hill Gate tube, offers *"stunning"*
wines, with 40 options by the glass (from an 'Enomatic' machine);
it also does a *"nice line in tapas"*, but *"food isn't the main event"*.
/ www.greatwinesbytheglass.com; 10.45 pm.

Kentish Canteen NW5 NEW £38 ❸❷❸
300 Kentish Town Rd 7485 7331 8–2C
A *"buzzy"* Kentish Town newcomer that lives up to its name;
it's *"not trying to do too much"*, but it's *"a very safe option"* that
"pitches good food at affordable prices". / www.kentishcanteen.co.uk;
10.30 pm.

(Brew House)
Kenwood House NW3 £28 ④④❷
Hampstead Heath 8341 5384 8–1A
*"On a bright day, nothing is better than sitting out in the peaceful
garden"* – that's the star attraction of this *"refined"* self-service café,
at the top of Hampstead Heath; *"the food isn't bad, but isn't really
the point"*. / www.companyofcooks.com; 6 pm (summer), 4 pm (winter);
no Amex.

Kenza EC2 £52 ④④❸
10 Devonshire Sq 7929 5533 9–2D
For *"a fun and lively dining experience"* – *"like being in Beirut!"* –
this *"entertaining"* cellar-Lebanese, near Liverpool Street, can be quite
a *"find"*; the belly-dancing music can be *"ear-splitting"*, though,
and not all reporters are impressed by the food.
/ www.kenza-restaurant.com; 10 pm; closed Sun.

Kerbisher & Malt W6 NEW   £13   ❷❸④
164 Shepherd's Bush Rd   3556 0228   7–1C
At last! – Brook Green finally has a good chippy, in the shape of this stylish but Spartan new café/take-away, on the former site of Snows on the Green (RIP); the fish is very good if not generous-portioned – top tip is the home made curry sauce! / Rated on Editors' visit; www.kerbisher.co.uk; 10 pm; closed Mon.

Kettners W1   £47   ④❸❸
29 Romilly St   7734 6112   4–2A
"Eat down the road first!" – it's for the champagne bar (with its "amazing list at reasonable prices") that this rambling and historic Soho "time warp" is worth seeking out; as a place to eat, it "needs serious work". / www.kettners.com; Mon-Thu 11 pm, Fri & Sat 11.30 pm, Sun 9.30 pm.

Kew Grill TW9   £53   ❸❷④
10b Kew Grn   8948 4433   1–3A
Antony Worral Thompson's small grill-restaurant, on Kew Green, put in a better showing this year, attracting general (if not quite universal) praise for its "juicy" steaks, and "attentive" service. / www.awtrestaurants.com; 10.30 pm, Fri-Sat 11 pm, Sun 10 pm; closed Mon L.

Khan's W2   £21   ❸④❸
13-15 Westbourne Grove   7727 5420   6–1C
"Unchanging standards" of "always-delicious" food make this "chaotic" and cavernous – but "fun" and "really good value" – Indian an ongoing Bayswater institution; no alcohol! / www.khansrestaurant.com; 11.30 pm, Sat-Sun midnight.

Khan's of Kensington SW7   £39   ❸❸❸
3 Harrington Rd   7584 4114   5–2B
"A reliable and well-established curry house", very handily located by South Kensington tube; it may rarely excite, but it rarely disappoints either. / www.khansofkensington.co.uk; 11.30 pm.

Khoai   £31   ❸❸④
362 Ballards Ln, N12   8445 2039   1–1B
6 Topsfield Pde, N8   8341 2120   1–1C
A duo of "basic" Vietnamese cafés – in Crouch End and North Finchley – consistently praised by reporters for their "tasty" and "good-value" fare. / 11.30 pm; N12 closed Mon; no booking Fri & Sat after 7.30 pm.

Kiasu W2   £29   ❸④④
48 Queensway   7727 8810   6–2C
A decent "cheap 'n' cheerful" Bayswater pan-Asian stand-by; it seemingly offers a "lengthy" menu, but "quite a few of the popular dishes aren't always available". / www.kiasu.co.uk; 11 pm; no Amex.

Kiku W1   £60   ❷❷④
17 Half Moon St   7499 4208   3–4B
"A genuine Tokyo experience, all the way down to the bad lighting"; this little-known heart-of-Mayfair spot offers "expertly-prepared sushi and sashimi", and at "great-value" prices too. / www.kikurestaurant.co.uk; 10.15 pm; closed Sun L; set weekday L £33 (FP).

Kimchee WC1 NEW   £31   ❸❸❸
71 High Holborn   7430 0956   2–1D
"Bringing a taste of Korea to London" – this "airy", "sleek" and "buzzing" newcomer is "in a similar mould to Ping Pong, Busaba and Wagamama", and serves food that's "fresh and extremely tasty, if a little spicy". / www.kimchee.uk.com; 10.20 pm.

Kings Road Steakhouse & Grill SW3   £56   ④④④
386 King's Rd   7351 9997   5–3B
*"An expensive dinner which failed to excite…", "never been
somewhere with such rude staff…" – ah yes, Marco Pierre White
has quickly put his inimitable stamp on this year-old Chelsea
steakhouse. / www.kingsroadsteakhouseandgrill.com; 11 pm, Sun 10 pm.*

Kipferl N1   £30   ❸❷❷
20 Camden Pas   77041 555   9–1B
*This Austrian operation, now re-located to Islington, still has "lovely
staff" and "delicious coffee and cakes", but it now also offers a "well-
prepared, if limited, menu" of more ambitious fare, plus Austrian
wines and beers. / www.kipferl.co.uk; 7.30 pm, Sat 9.30 pm, Tue and Sun
5.30 pm; closed Tue D & Sun D; no Amex.*

Kiraku W5   £33   ❶❷❸
8 Station Pde   8992 2848   1–3A
*"Always busy and full of Japanese people", this unassuming café,
near Ealing Common tube, offers "meltingly delicious" cooking
(not least "amazing sushi") at "outstanding-value" prices; ambience
is "slightly lacking", but this is somewhat offset by the "lovely and
helpful" service. / www.kiraku.co.uk; 10 pm; closed Mon; no Amex.*

Kitchen W8 W8   £59   ❶❷❷
11-13 Abingdon Road   7937 0120   5–1A
*"Who could want a better local restaurant than this?"; the interior
is admittedly "a bit John Lewis", but – when it comes to offering
"exceptional, seasonal food" at "superb-value" prices – this "smart
but informal" Kensington outfit, just off the High Street, is never
knowingly undersold; "it has improved greatly since launch".
/ www.kitchenw8.com; 10.15 pm, Sun 9.15 pm; set weekday L £35 (FP).*

Koba W1   £40   ❸❸④
11 Rathbone St   7580 8825   2–1C
*Fans say you get "the best Korean food in London" – and in
a "handy" location too – at this "bustling" table-BBQ, in Fitzrovia;
not everyone is quite so wowed, but even sceptics say the scoff
is "serviceable". / 10.30 pm; closed Sun L.*

Koffmann's
The Berkeley SW1   £75   ❷❷④
The Berkeley, Wilton Pl   7235 1010   5–1D
*"Classic Gallic bistro cooking" (including "magnificent stuffed pig's
trotter") is executed "with aplomb" at Pierre K's "elegant" (if "hotel-
ish") Knightsbridge basement yearling; those who remember him
from La Tante Claire (London's best restaurant of its day), however,
may still find the new operation a little underwhelming.
/ www.the-berkeley.co.uk; set always available £45 (FP).*

Kolossi Grill EC1   £29   ④❷❷
56-60 Rosebery Ave   7278 5758   9–1A
*A survivor from the '60s, this Farringdon Greek/Cypriot is somewhere
between rough 'n' ready and cheap 'n' cheerful – "I have been eating
here for over 40 years", says one reporter, and "just love the fact it's
so unpretentious!" / www.kolossigrill.com; 11 pm; closed Sat L & Sun;
set weekday L £16 (FP).*

Konditor & Cook £24 ❷❸❸
Curzon Soho, 99 Shaftesbury Ave, W1 7292 1684 4–3A
46 Gray's Inn Rd, WC1 7404 6300 9–1A
10 Stoney St, SE1 7407 5100 9–4C
22 Cornwall Road, SE1 7261 0456 9–4A
63 Stamford St, SE1 7921 9200 9–4A
30 St Mary Axe, EC3 0845 262 3030 9–2D
"Truly irresistible cakes", "first-class coffee" and "interesting" savouries certainly make these café/take-aways a tempting option; even fans can find them "expensive" though, or feel their service is rather "variable". / www.konditorandcook.com; 6 pm – W1 11 pm; WC1 & EC3 closed Sat & Sun; SE1 branches closed Sun; no booking.

Kopapa WC2 NEW £48 ❸❸④
32-34 Monmouth St 7240 6076 4–2B
"Inventive and tasty" small plates – with some "zingy" Pacific Rim "fusion-combinations" – have made Peter Gordon's café-style newcomer a useful addition to Covent Garden; it's "pricey", though, service can be "disjointed", and the hard-surfaced interior can be "deafening". / www.kopapa.co.uk; 10.45 pm, Fri & Sat 11.15 pm.

Kovalam NW6 £25 ❷④⑤
12 Willesden Ln 7625 4761 1–2B
"Hidden-away in a side street, but a great find" – this Kilburn Indian may occupy "a standard curry house setting", but it dishes up some "fantastic" Keralan cuisine; the bill comes as "a happy surprise" too. / www.kovalamrestaurant.co.uk; 11 pm, Fri & Sat midnight; no Amex.

Koya W1 £24 ❷❷❸
49 Frith St 7434 4463 4–2A
You get "the best udon noodles in London" (with "authentic broths" too), say fans of this popular and "bustling" Soho yearling; "expect to queue, eat and go". / www.koya.co.uk; 10.30 pm; closed Sun; no booking.

Kulu Kulu £29 ④④⑤
76 Brewer St, W1 7734 7316 3–2D
51-53 Shelton St, WC2 7240 5687 4–2C
39 Thurloe Pl, SW7 7589 2225 5–2C
They're "nothing innovative" nowadays – and they look "scruffy" – but these "no-frills" conveyor-canteens still get the thumbs-up from most reporter for their "cheap" and "relatively authentic" sushi. / 10 pm; SW7 10.30 pm; closed Sun; no Amex; no booking.

Kurumaya EC4 £37 ❷❷④
76-77 Watling St 7236 0236 9–2B
Thanks to "some of the City's best sushi" (as well as "good" hot dishes) and "smiling" service too, this "pleasant" Japanese is always "packed", both in its street-level bar and downstairs restaurant. / www.kurumaya.co.uk; 9.30 pm; closed Sat & Sun.

Kyashii WC2 £55 ④④❸
4a Upper St Martin's Ln 7836 5211 4–3B
This "futuristic" Japanese yearling ("love the fish tanks") is hailed by fans as "a welcome addition to Covent Garden"; perhaps because it's so "expensive", though, it's yet to generate much buzz, and critics see it simply as a "massive disappointment". / www.kyashii.co.uk; 10.30 pm; no shorts.

The Ladbroke Arms W11 £44 ❷❸❷
54 Ladbroke Rd 7727 6648 6–2B
This "lovely" and "upmarket" boozer, near Ladbroke Grove, serves "more than pub food" – it's always "busy" and, on a sunny day, you'll find it "hard to get a table in the garden". / www.capitalpubcompany.com; 9.30 pm; no booking after 8 pm.

Ladurée £70 ④④❸
Harrods, 87-135 Brompton Rd, SW1 7730 1234 5–1D
71-72 Burlington Arc, Piccadilly, W1 7491 9155 3–3C
1 Covent Garden Mkt, WC2 7240 0706 4–3D **NEW**
With its "delicate pâtisserie and 'macarons'", this OTT Knightsbridge grand café is a worthy outpost of the famed Parisian fixture – no great surprise that it's a tad "overpriced"; also in Covent Garden (new) and Piccadilly (mainly retail). / www.laduree.com; SW1 8.45 pm, Sun 5.45 pm; W1 6.30 pm, Sun 5 pm; W1 no booking, SW1 no booking 3 pm-6 pm; set always available £44 (FP).

Lahore Karahi SW17 £17 ❶④④
1 Tooting Hill, London 8767 2477 10–2C
This "bustling" BYO canteen, in Tooting, is known for its "tremendous" Pakistani cuisine – "expect no luxury, but the food is genuine and the place is mobbed". / www.lahorekarahi.co.uk; midnight; no Amex.

Lahore Kebab House £22 ❶⑤④
668 Streatham High Rd, SW16 8765 0771 10–2D **NEW**
2-10 Umberston St, E1 7488 2551 11–1A
"The king-pin of East End curry houses"; this "warehouse"-like "legend" is often "as busy as a Pakistani street", thanks to its "unbelievably good" scoff at dirt-cheap prices – with "fabulous" lamb chops a highlight; now also in Streatham (and, coming soon, other branches); BYO. / midnight.

Lamberts SW12 £48 ❶❶❷
2 Station Pde 8675 2233 10–2C
"Second only to Chez Bruce… and not that far behind!" – this Balham "beacon" remains a "good-value" and "professional" destination, where the "sure-footed" cuisine uses "carefully-sourced" ingredients to "great effect", and the service is "attentive, personal and jolly". / www.lambertsrestaurant.com; 10.30 pm, Sun 5 pm; closed Mon, Tue-Fri L & Sun D; no Amex.

(Winter Garden)
The Landmark NW1 £79 ④❸❷
222 Marylebone Rd 7631 8000 8–4A
"Three hours of non-stop champagne and buffet" in a "spectacular" covered atrium – the makings of the "fabulous Sunday jazz brunch" at this Marylebone hotel, which is also tipped for afternoon tea; otherwise, though, it's "expensive for what it is". / www.landmarklondon.co.uk; 10.30 pm; no trainers; booking: max 12.

Langan's Bistro W1 £44 ❸❷❷
26 Devonshire St 7935 4531 2–1A
Despite the odd hiccup, it seems to have been a good year for this "beautiful" and "cosy" pint-sized Marylebone veteran; the bistro fare may not be the main point, but it rarely disappoints. / www.langansrestaurants.co.uk; 11 pm; closed Sat L & Sun.

Langan's Brasserie W1 £61 ④④❷
Stratton St 7491 8822 3–3C
"So yesterday!"; although there's still "a real buzz" about this Mayfair old-timer, and fans do still say it's "always enjoyable", the "tasteless" food and "can't-be-bothered" service really aren't funny any more – can someone please hurry up and buy it! / www.langansrestaurants.co.uk; 11 pm, Fri & Sat 11.30 pm, Sun 4pm.

FSA

The Lansdowne NW1 £43 ❸❸❷
90 Gloucester Ave 7483 0409 8–3B
You get a taste of "Primrose Hill, without the snobbery", at this "true gastropub", which serves "hearty, but well-executed food in a bustling setting"; top tip: "top-notch" pizza.
/ www.thelansdownepub.co.uk; 10 pm, Sun 9.30 pm; no Amex.

Lantana Cafe W1 £30 ❸❸❸
13-14 Charlotte Pl 7323 6601 2–1C
"Great Aussie coffee" attracts "hordes" of caffeine-fiends to this "busy" but "relaxed" Fitzrovia joint, where brunch (a speciality) is done "with aplomb". / www.lantanacafe.co.uk; 9.30 pm; closed Mon D & Tue D; no Amex; no booking.

La Lanterna SE1 £39 ❸❶❸
6-8 Mill St 7252 2420 11–2A
"Portions are massive, and the staff always friendly and helpful", at this good-value Italian, just over Tower Bridge; pizza is the best bet. / www.pizzerialalanterna.co.uk; 11 pm, Sun 10.30 pm; closed Sat L.

The Larder EC1 £46 ❹❸❹
91-93 St John St 7608 1558 9–1A
"Bustling at lunchtime" ("fairly quiet" at night) – this Clerkenwell bar/bakery/take-away/restaurant is regularly tipped "for a business meal near the City", thanks not least to its "reliable" cuisine, served in "brasserie style". / www.thelarderrestaurant.com; 10.30 pm; closed Sat L & Sun.

Latium W1 £48 ❷❶❸
21 Berners St 7323 9123 3–1D
Maurizio Morelli's very "civilised" Italian, north of Oxford Street, is an "authentic and honest" sort of place, with notably "charming and well-informed" service; signature dish: "ravioli to die for". / www.latiumrestaurant.com; 10.30 pm, Sat 11 pm; closed Sat L & Sun.

Launceston Place W8 £72 ❷❷❷
1a Launceston Pl 7937 6912 5–1B
A "very intimate" townhouse, "on the corner of a beautiful Kensington street", where "everything is polished and understated"; staff are "extremely charming", and Tristan Welch's highly "original" food is "incredibly fresh" and "perfectly executed" – can this really be a member of the D&D group? / www.danddlondon.com; 10.30 pm; closed Mon L; set Sun L £46 (FP).

THE LEDBURY W11 £90 ❶❶❷
127 Ledbury Rd 7792 9090 6–1B
"It just gets better!"; Brett Graham's "genius" cuisine – the highest-rated in London this year – is beginning to secure international recognition for this Notting Hill pub-conversion, where "marvellous" and "unstuffy" service tops off a "staggeringly good all-round experience". / www.theledbury.com; 10.30 pm, Sun 10 pm; closed Mon L.

Lemonia NW1 £40 ⑤❷❷
89 Regent's Park Rd 7586 7454 8–3B
"It's hard to criticise, what with it always being full", but – although this "stalwart" Primrose Hill "mega-taverna" does indeed remain "fantastically buzzy" – the food it offers can seem very "jaded" nowadays. / www.lemonia.co.uk; 11.30 pm; closed Sat L & Sun D; no Amex.

Leon £22 ❸❸❸

275 Regent St, W1   7495 1514   3–1C
35-36 Gt Marlborough St, W1   7437 5280   3–2C
36-38 Old Compton St, W1   7434 1200   4–2A **NEW**
73-76 The Strand, WC2   7240 3070   4–4D
7 Canvey St, SE1   7620 0035   9–4B
Cabot Place West, E14   7719 6200   11–1C
3 Crispin Pl, E1   7247 4369   12–2B
12 Ludgate Circus, EC4   7489 1580   9–2A
86 Cannon St, EC4   7623 9699   9–3C

"The most convincing effort to re-invent fast food!" – these *"cheerful"* retro-styled cafés are *"brilliant for a quick, cheap and healthy bite on the move"*. / www.leonrestaurants.co.uk; 10 pm; W1 8.45 pm; E14 8 pm; EC4 closed Sun; W1 closed Sat & Sun; no booking L.

Leong's Legends £33 ❹❹❸

4 Macclesfield St, W1   7287 0288   4–3A
82 Queensway, W2   7221 2280   6–2C

"A slightly more unusual Taiwanese take on the typical Chinatown offering"; this *"tacky, but oddly-endearing"* place has quite a following among reporters, not least for its *"sublime"* dumplings; there's also an offshoot in Bayswater. / www.leongslegend.com; 11 pm, Sat 11.30 pm; no bookings.

Levant W1 £54 ❸❸❶

Jason Ct, 76 Wigmore St   7224 1111   3–1A

"Be transported from London to the Middle East!" – this *"darkly-lit"* Marylebone basement offers a *"superb"* atmosphere for those with a party (or romance) in mind, plus, for nourishment, *"a great selection of mezze"*. / www.levant.co.uk; 11 pm, Sat 11.30 pm.

The Light House SW19 £46 ❸❸❸

75-77 Ridgway   8944 6338   10–2B

"Off the beaten track", near Wimbledon Village, this modern bistro has long been a top option locally; the minimalist styling creates *"bad acoustics"*, though, and critics find the *"eclectic"* cuisine almost *"too imaginative"*! / www.lighthousewimbledon.com; 10.30 pm; closed Sun D.

The Lighthouse SW11 £38 ❸❷❷

441 Battersea Park Rd   7223 7721   10–1C

A Battersea gastropub which attracts most praise for its *"fabulous atmosphere"*; the *"hearty"* fare is *"sometimes very good"* too, but *"lacks a little in consistency"*. / www.thelighthousebattersea.com; 11 pm, Sun 10.30 pm Fri-Sat midnight.

Lisboa Pâtisserie W10 £8 ❷❸❹

57 Golborne Rd   8968 5242   6–1A

"Unrivalled custard tarts" and *"the best latte in the world"*! – no wonder this *"no-nonsense"* Portuguese café/pâtisserie in North Kensington is always heaving. / 7.30 pm; L & early evening only; no booking.

Little Bay £30 ❹❷❶

228 Belsize Rd, NW6   7372 4699   1–2B
228 York Rd, SW11   7223 4080   10–2B
171 Farringdon Rd, EC1   7278 1234   9–1A

"Wild", *"boudoir-esque"* decor and *"smiling"* staff set a *"celebratory"* tone at these *"quirky and fun"* budget bistros; as for the *"tasty"* fodder – *"how do they do it"* for the *"stupidly cheap"* prices? / www.little-bay.co.uk; 11.30 pm, sun 11 pm; no Amex, NW6 no credit cards.

F S A

Little Georgia Café E2 £26 ❸❸❸
87 Goldsmiths Row 7739 8154 1–2D
This "tiny" Bethnal Green café is "a lovely local", serving an "interesting" Georgian menu (on which the mezze and cheeseboard star); "BYO is a bonus". / 9.30 pm.

Little Italy W1 £66 ④④❸
21 Frith St 7734 4737 4–2A
Fans of this "pricey" late-night Soho Italian bar/restaurant/club say it's "great", even if "the food's rather beside the point", because "the dancing is the draw"; for critics, though, it's just "shockingly bad in every respect". / www.littleitalysoho.co.uk; 4 am, Sun 11.30 pm; set weekday L & pre-theatre £36 (FP).

Livebait £48 ④④⑤
21 Wellington St, WC2 7836 7161 4–3D
43 The Cut, SE1 7928 7211 9–4A
"A whiff of the production line" hangs over this "predictable" and "formulaic" fish chain; its "latrine"-like decor is no great attraction either. / www.santeonline.co.uk; 11 pm; SE1 Sun 9 pm; WC2 Sun 7.30 pm; set always available £28 (FP).

LMNT E8 £35 ❸❷❶
316 Queensbridge Rd 7249 6727 1–2D
Bonkers, pharaoh-kitsch decor and "very romantic booths" boost the vibe at this "cheap 'n' cheerful" Dalston destination – always "an enjoyable evening out". / www.lmnt.co.uk; 10.45 pm; no Amex.

Lobster Pot SE11 £56 ❸❸❸
3 Kennington Ln 7582 5556 1–3C
"Seagulls piped through the stereo" have long added to the "seaside atmosphere", at this "fantastically Gallic" Kennington stalwart, run by Hervé et sa famille; it's a "fun" place with "warm" service and sometimes "excellent" seafood, but ratings overall are not quite what they once were. / www.lobsterpotrestaurant.co.uk; 10.30 pm; closed Mon & Sun; booking: max 8.

Locanda Locatelli Hyatt Regency W1 £72 ❸❸❸
8 Seymour St 7935 9088 2–2A
Giorgio Locatelli's "chic and buzzy" Marylebone Italian still wows most reporters with its "deceptively simple" dishes, "cooked to perfection", and some "superb" wines too; "extreme" prices are beginning to take the edge off the experience, however, as are incidents of "I'm-doing-you-a-favour" service. / www.locandalocatelli.com; 11 pm, Fri & Sat 11.30 pm, Sun 10.15 pm; booking: max 8.

Locanda Ottomezzo W8 £69 ④❷❸
2-4 Thackeray St 7937 2200 5–1B
The "best breakfast menu ever", the "best coffee around" and some "delicious" Italian dishes at lunch and dinner too… – so why isn't this "cramped" Kensington café/bistro more popular?; "I'd be there daily", says one reporter, "if it wasn't so expensive!" / www.locandaottoemezzo.co.uk; 10.30 pm, Fri & Sat 10.45 pm; closed Sat L & Sun.

Loch Fyne £40 ④④④
2-4 Catherine St, WC2   7240 4999   2–2D
77-78 Gracechurch St, EC3   7929 8380   9–3C
*"Always a good stand-by"; "you know what you're going to get",
at this "straightforward" fish and seafood chain, which sets
"consistently high" standards – even critics tend not to find anything
actively wrong with it, they just gripe that it's too "unexciting"!*
*/ www.lochfyne-restaurants.com; 10 pm; WC2 10.30 pm; set always available
£24 (FP).*

Lola & Simón W6 £49 ❸❷❸
278 King St   8563 0300   7–2B
*A "very friendly" Hammersmith café that makes a handy haunt for
a "fabulous" brunch, or "fantastic" coffee and cakes; its main, quasi-
Argentinian menu is good too, if rather "unchanging" and "pricey",
and there are "gorgeous" wines to go with it. / www.lolaandsimon.co.uk;
10 pm; no Amex.*

Lola Rojo £39 ❷❸❷
140 Wandsworth Bridge Rd, SW6   7371 8396   10–1B
78 Northcote Rd, SW11   7350 2262   10–2C
*"Very creative" tapas and "lovely" wines too have won quite
a following for this "pretty, if cramped", Battersea spot; its lesser-
known Fulham outpost, gets good reports too. / www.lolarojo.net;
SW11 11 pm; SW6 11 pm; SW6 Mon-Fri D only; no Amex.*

London Wall Bar & Kitchen EC2 £35 ④④❸
150 London Wall   7600 7340   9–2B
*Thanks to its "interesting" ("foolhardy") location – "a podium of the
Barbican, near the Museum of London" – this year-old Benugo-group
brasserie can be quiet; it's undoubtedly "useful" in a thin area though,
and its menu of staples is realised to a "pretty good" standard.
/ www.londonwallbarandkitchen.com; 9 pm; closed Sat & Sun.*

Lots Road SW10 £45 ❸❷④
114 Lots Rd   7352 6645   5–4B
*The "best burger" is the foodie highlight at this pub by the entrance
to Chelsea Harbour; "very helpful" staff help pep up a rather low-key
atmosphere. / www.lotsroadpub.com; 10 pm, Sun 9.30 pm; set weekday
L £28 (FP), set Sun L £29 (FP).*

Lotus Chinese Floating Restaurant E14 £38 ④④❸
5 Baltimore Walk   7515 6445   11–2C
*Floating placidly near Canary Wharf, this large Asian barge lives up to
its name; "excellent" dim sum is the highlight of a "solid" menu
selection, which includes a buffet. / www.lotusfloating.co.uk; 10.30 pm.*

Luc's Brasserie EC3 £46 ④❸❷
17-22 Leadenhall Mkt   7621 0666   9–2D
*"Get a window seat to look down on Leadenhall Market", if you visit
this "genuine"-feeling Gallic bistro, whose "classic" cuisine is praised
by most, if not quite all, reporters. / www.lucsbrasserie.com; 9 pm; closed
Mon D, Fri D, Sat & Sun.*

Lucio SW3 £60 ❸❸❸
257 Fulham Rd   7823 3007   5–3B
*"Lucio and his family are so welcoming", and fans of this "jam-
packed" Chelsea Italian say it's a "class act" that "never fails
to deliver"; it's "cramped" however, and a small band of critics finds
the whole performance "pricey" and "dull". / 10.45 pm; set weekday L
£36 (FP).*

Lucky Seven W2   £44   ❸❸❷

127 Westbourne Park Rd   7727 6771   6–1B

Tom Conran's "funky" homage to the US diner has wonderful, retro-styling, and it "takes some beating for great burgers and shakes" too – it's a tiny place, though, so "be prepared to share a booth", and note it's "not easy to get a seat at peak times". / www.tomconranrestaurants.com; 10.15 pm, Sun 10 pm; no Amex; no booking.

Lupita WC2 NEW   £36   ④④④

13-15 Villiers St   7930 5355   4–4D

Divergent views on this 'Mexico City' street-food newcomer, on a slightly tatty strip near Charing Cross; a slight majority hail food that's "fresh", "flavourful" and "cheap", but doubters dismiss this "strangely laid-out" place as a "poor Wahaca rip-off", with "uncomfy" seating. / www.lupita.co.uk; 11 pm, Sun 8 pm.

Lutyens EC4   £62   ❸❸④

85 Fleet St   7583 8385   9–2A

Though much-touted as a "safe" haven for an "obviously businessy" lunch, Sir Terence Conran's "austere" City-fringe brasserie is "somehow less than the sum of its parts" – the interior's "pleasant, but functional", the food's "good, but formulaic", and the service "prompt, but without personality". / www.lutyens-restaurant.com; 9.45 pm; closed Sat & Sun.

The Luxe E1   £48   ⑤⑤④

109 Commercial St   7101 1751   12–2B

"He'd get kicked off the show for food like this!" – ex-Masterchef judge John Torode wins poor ratings for his Smithfield yearling; fans do praise the "good choice of breakfasts" and other British fare, but critics say "he should be ashamed" of the "woeful" cooking and "shambolic" service. / www.theluxe.co.uk; 10.30 pm; closed Sun D; booking: max 10.

Ma Cuisine TW9   £44   ④❸④

9 Station Approach   8332 1923   1–3A

"In a pretty parade of shops", by Kew Gardens station, an archetypal bistro where "all the classic French dishes are served"; it's "always humming", but reporters have a feeling that while "not bad, it could do so much better". / www.macuisinekew.co.uk; 10 pm, Fri & Sat 10.30 pm; no Amex.

Ma Goa SW15   £37   ❷①❸

242-244 Upper Richmond Rd   8780 1767   10–2B

"Wonderful and original Goan home cooking" – at a "very reasonable price" and served by "outstanding" staff – wins continuing rave reviews for this "charming" family-run Putney fixture. / www.ma-goa.com; 11 pm, Sun 10 pm; closed Mon L & Sat L.

Made In Camden
Roundhouse NW1 NEW   £31   ❸❸④

Chalk Farm Rd   7424 8495   8–2B

"A great excuse to go to a gig at the Roundhouse" – this "stripped-down" canteen is proving a "neat newcomer", thanks to its "unexpectedly good" food at "reasonable prices". / www.madeincamden.com; 10.30 pm.

Made in China SW1 £45 ④④④
37 Monck St   7222 2218   2–4C
"Fresh" Chinese cooking – some of "the only decent, affordable food in Westminster" – wins fans for this potentially "attractive" yearling, near the Home Office; the occasional reporter, however, has found declining standards of late. / www.madeinchinarestaurant.co.uk; 10.15 pm; closed Sun; no Amex.

Made in Italy SW3 £39 ❷❸❷
249 King's Rd   7352 1880   5–3C
"Divine" thin-crust pizzas (by the metre) make this "crowded" and "fun" Chelsea spot – now with spin-offs in Soho and near Selfridges – a popular destination for all the family; in warm weather, seek out the first-floor terrace. / www.madeinitalygroup.co.uk; 11.30 pm, Sun 10.30 pm; Mon-Thu D only, Fri-Sun open L & D; no Amex.

Madhu's UB1 £35 ❷❸❸
39 South Rd   8574 1897   1–3A
The quality of this superior Southall Indian has helped spawn a major outside catering empire; here at HQ, fans approve the "proper" cooking – "lovely dishes" that "don't leave you feeling over-stuffed". / www.madhusonline.com; 11.30 pm; closed Tue, Sat L & Sun L.

Madsen SW7 £47 ④④④
20 Old Brompton Rd   7225 2772   5–2B
If Copenhagen is currently the centre of the culinary world, there's no sign of it at this "pleasant" Danish two-year-old in South Kensington, which serves "simple", "home-style" fare – it has its fans, but quite a few reporters find its offering all-embracingly "pale". / www.madsenrestaurant.com; 10 pm, Fri & Sat 10.45 pm; closed Sun D; no Amex.

Magdalen SE1 £51 ❶❷❷
152 Tooley St   7403 1342   9–4D
"Inspired and interesting" British cooking ("very much in the style of St John, with an abundance of offal"), draws fans – especially from the City – to this "unassuming" and "relaxed" establishment, "hidden-away" near City Hall. / www.magdalenrestaurant.co.uk; 10 pm; closed Sat L & Sun.

Maggie Jones's W8 £60 ⑤④❶
6 Old Court Pl   7937 6462   5–1A
This "very '70s" bistro, hidden-away near Kensington Gardens, is a "lovely cosy hide-away", often tipped for romance; the cooking really is stuck in a "time warp", though, and critics find it plain "dull". / www.maggie-jones.co.uk; 11 pm, Sun 10.30 pm.

Magic Wok W2 £32 ❸❸⑤
100 Queensway   7792 9767   6–1C
"Doing the staples well, and with some great speciality dishes" – the cooking at this Queensway Chinese is "always reliable", so its "lacklustre" setting may be worth putting up with. / 11 pm.

Maison Bertaux W1 £14 ❷❸❶
28 Greek St   7437 6007   4–2A
For a "richly Bohemian" setting, you won't beat this "wildly idiosyncratic!" Soho pâtisserie (est 1871) – a "jammed-in" place, with "super-charming" service and "cakes to die for" ("and with enough calories that you probably will…"). / www.maisonbertaux.com; 10.30 pm, Sun 8 pm.

Malabar W8 £45 ❷❷❸
27 Uxbridge St   7727 8800   6–2B
This "old-faithful" Indian, hidden-away off Notting Hill Gate, "always delivers"; despite the increasing sophistication of its rivals, it still, after all these years, manages – thanks to its "muted" decor, and food that's "inventive, fresh and perfectly seasoned" – to feel "just a bit different from the run-of-the-mill". / www.malabar-restaurant.co.uk; 11.15 pm, Sun 10.30 pm.

Malabar Junction WC1 £41 ❸❸❸
107 Gt Russell St   7580 5230   2–1C
This "Tardis-like" Bloomsbury veteran has a surprisingly large and pleasant conservatory interior; its "very varied" South Indian menu – including "many veggie options" – is "well executed", and "reasonably priced" too. / www.malabarjunction.com; 11 pm.

The Mall Tavern W8 £42 ❸❸❷
71-73 Palace Gardens Ter   7229 3374   6–2B
Despite its "awkward location", just off Notting Hill Gate, this "little neighbourhood pub" has a "relaxed" and "intimate" interior (and a "pretty, small courtyard" too); its menu includes some "nice examples of modernised British staples". / www.themalltavern.com; 10 pm.

Malmaison Brasserie EC1 £52 ④❸❸
18-21 Charterhouse St   7012 3700   9–1B
A useful City-fringe business option – an attractively-located and "discreet" hotel dining room, where "you can hear yourself think". / www.malmaison.com; 10.15 pm.

La Mancha SW15 £40 ❸❷❸
32 Putney High St   8780 1022   10–2B
A "no-nonsense" Putney veteran, known for a "reliable and jolly tapas experience"; "you can't have a conversation without screaming", but that's all part of the fun. / www.lamancha.co.uk; 11 pm; need 6+ to book.

Mandalay W2 £25 ❸❸⑤
444 Edgware Rd   7258 3696   8–4A
"Still a favourite", this long-established café, near Edgware Road tube, offers "a good introduction to Burmese food", and "one of the cheapest lunches in London" too; fair to say, though, that the scoff isn't a patch on what it used to be, and the decor is, as ever, "nothing to write home about" either. / www.mandalayway.com; 10.30 pm; closed Sun.

Mandarin Kitchen W2 £37 ❷④⑤
14-16 Queensway   7727 9012   6–2C
"The best lobster noodles in London" justify braving the "curt" service and the "crammed" and "very shabby" dining room of this Bayswater "stalwart"; while it's still often tipped as "THE place for Chinese seafood", however, its food rating is not quite what it once was. / 11.30 pm.

Mangal 1 E8 £28 ❶❷❸
10 Arcola St   7275 8981   1–1C
"Incredibly good value!" – yes, that's the very worst comment anyone made this year on this "fun, no-frills Turkish BBQ", in Dalson, which serves "the juiciest kebabs ever"; "the atmosphere is best if you can sit near the hot coals"; BYO. / www.mangal1.com; midnight, Sat-Sun 1 am; no credit cards.

FSA

Mangal II N16 £39 ❸❸④
4 Stoke Newington Rd   7254 7888   1–1C
"Check if Gilbert & George are on the next table" ("they're regulars"), at this "utterly reliable" Turkish ockabasi restaurant in Dalston; "the Mangal around the corner gets all the plaudits, but this is better", fans insist. / www.mangal2.com; 1 am; no Amex or Maestro.

Mango & Silk SW14 £36 ④④❸
199 Upper Richmond Rd   8876 6220   1–4A
"Blinding" cooking and "smiling" service win acclaim from fans of Udit Sarkhel's East Sheen Indian; sadly, however, there are almost as many critics who find it a disappointment, especially in comparison to his days in Southfields. / www.mangoandsilk.co.uk; 10 pm, Fri & Sat 10.30 pm; closed weekday L.

Mango Room NW1 £41 ❸❷❷
10-12 Kentish Town Rd   7482 5065   8–3B
It's not just the "wonderful" cocktails and "always-buzzing" style that wins fans for this "unpressurised" Camden Town haunt; "it's just the place for some good West Indian food", mixing dishes both "modern and traditional". / www.mangoroom.co.uk; 11 pm.

Mango Tree SW1 £53 ❸④④
46 Grosvenor Pl   7823 1888   2–4B
Look out for "frequent offers", if you're thinking of visiting this "barn" of a place, on the edge of Belgravia – if you pay full whack, the prices for its "very tasty" Thai fare can seem rather "steep", and you may be more prone to notice the rather "soulless" and "conveyor-belt-esque" ambience too. / www.mangotree.org.uk; 11 pm, Thu-Sat 11.30 pm, Sun 10.30 pm.

Mango Tree SE1 £48 ❷❸④
5-6 Cromwell Buildings, Red Cross Way   7407 0333   9–4C
Thanks to its "interesting" and "value-for-money" cooking – and in spite of its rather "uninspiring" contemporary decor – this hidden-away Indian, near Borough Market, is always "packed". / www.justmangotree.co.uk; 11 pm.

Manicomio £56 ❸④❸
85 Duke of York Sq, SW3   7730 3366   5–2D
6 Gutter Ln, EC2   7726 5010   9–2B
Some of "the best al fresco eating in town" is to be had on the terraces of these "stylish" Italians – in Chelsea and, more implausibly, the City; their "seasonal" cuisine is "fresh"-tasting too, if on the "expensive" side for what it is. / www.manicomio.co.uk; SW3 10.30 pm, Sun 10 pm; EC2 10 pm; EC2 closed Sat & Sun.

Manna NW3 £51 ⑤④④
4 Erskine Rd   7722 8028   8–3B
This well-worn Primrose Hill veggie – the UK's oldest (1968) – needs to buck up its act; even some fans say the food is "less enticing than it was", and for critics it's just a "bitter disappointment" – "I've been veggie for 20 years, but its tasteless offerings made me want to go home and have a fry-up!" / www.mannav.com; 10.30 pm; closed Mon, Tue-Fri D only, Sat & Sun open L & D.

Manson SW6 £50 ❶④❸
676 Fulham Rd   7384 9559   10–1B
"It's an absolute treasure", say fans of Fulham's "brilliant local"; note, however, that the chef changed as our survey for the year was coming to an end - let's hope new boy Alan Stewart is keeping up the good work! / www.mansonrestaurant.co.uk; 10.30 pm, Sun 6 pm.

132

Mao Tai SW6   £60   ❸❹❸
58 New King's Rd   7731 2520   10–1B
*A Parson's Green oriental that was trendy long before the idea of a
'trendy-oriental' became commonplace; fans insist that it's a "sound
old favourite", but the cuisine of late has been rather "hit-and-miss".
/ www.maotai.co.uk; 11.30 pm; D only, ex Sun open L & D.*

Mar I Terra   £29   ❸❷❸
17 Air St, W1   7734 1992   3–3D **NEW**
14 Gambia St, SE1   7928 7628   9–4A
*"Tucked-away in railway arches near Southwark tube", this "fairly
ordinary-looking" ex-pub offers "authentic" tapas in a "relaxing"
setting; the Soho branch – not nearly as well-known – can also
be "useful". / SE1 10.30 pm; W1 11 pm; SE1 closed Sat L, Sun; W1 closed
Sun-Mon & Tue-Sat L.*

Marco
Stamford Bridge SW6   £59   ④⑤⑤
Fulham Rd   7915 2929   5–4A
*The little feedback inspired by this ambitious Gallic two-year-old,
by Stamford Bridge, suggests it's a soulless and overpriced sort
of place – we presume it survives solely by virtue of its backer,
MPW's 'celebrity' status… on which he has primarily traded for over
a decade! / www.marcorestaurant.co.uk; 10.30 pm; D only, closed
Mon & Sun.*

Marco Pierre White Steakhouse & Grill
East India House E1   £52   ④④⑤
109-117 Middlesex St   7247 5050   9–2D
*A "very underwhelming" City-fringe basement where (as usual) MPW-
branding portends nothing particularly positive – indeed, with its
"bistro food at restaurant prices" some reporters think the place
is just a plain "rip-off". / www.mpwsteakandalehouse.org; 10 pm;
closed Sun.*

MARCUS WAREING
THE BERKELEY SW1   £115   ❷❷❷
Wilton Pl   7235 1200   5–1D
*Marcus Wareing's "sensational" cuisine again won his "luxurious",
if "formal" Knightsbridge HQ the most survey nominations
as 'London's No. 1 dining room'; this year, however, a small but vocal
minority also found it "hyped" and "unjustifiably pricey" – perhaps
a blip due to losing Alyn Williams and/or launching the Gilbert Scott?
/ www.marcus-wareing.com; 10.30 pm; closed Sat L & Sun; no jeans
or trainers; booking: max 8; set weekday L £60 (FP).*

Marine Ices NW3   £35   ❸❷❷
8 Haverstock Hill   7482 9003   8–2B
*"There's no better ice cream in London", say fans of this Camden
Town "institution", run by the Manzi family "since forever…"
(the 1920s); it's a "dependable" pizza 'n' pasta stop too,
and "always buzzing with all the generations mixing happily
together". / www.marineices.co.uk; Sun 10 pm; closed Mon; no Amex.*

Market NW1   £46   ❸❸④
43 Parkway   7267 9700   8–3B
*"Normally full to the brim", this "simple" and "buzzy" Camden Town
bistro has made quite a name with its "hearty" British fare; it's "a bit
expensive", though, for a place that's so "very noisy" and "cramped".
/ www.marketrestaurant.co.uk; 10.30 pm; closed Sun D; set weekday L
£29 (FP).*

Maroush £45 ❷④④
I) 21 Edgware Rd, W2   7723 0773   6–1D
II) 38 Beauchamp Pl, SW3   7581 5434   5–1C
IV) 68 Edgware Rd, W2   7224 9339   6–1D
V) 3-4 Vere St, W1   7493 5050   3–1B
'Garden') 1 Connaught St, W2   7262 0222   6–1D
*"A fun place to visit, even at 2am!"; London's longest-established
"posh" Lebanese chain offers a range of culinary possibilities,
of which the best are arguably the handy café/take-aways (at I, II and
V); expect "zingy" mezze, "lovely light flat breads", and kebabs and
grills that are "sooooo tasty". / www.maroush.com; 12.30 am-5 am.*

The Marquess Tavern N1 £40 ❸❸❸
32 Canonbury St   7354 2975   8–2D
*In leafy Canonbury, an "elegant" gastroboozer, on an impressive
scale; the food is "consistently good" (in particular the "superb
Sunday lunch"). / www.marquesstavern.com; 10 pm; closed weekday L.*

Masala Zone £30 ❸❸❸
9 Marshall St, W1   7287 9966   3–2D
48 Floral St, WC2   7379 0101   4–2D
147 Earl's Court Rd, SW5   7373 0220   5–2A
583 Fulham Rd, SW6   7386 5500   5–4A
71-75 Bishop's Bridge Rd, W2   7221 0055   6–1C
80 Upper St, N1   7359 3399   8–3D
25 Parkway, NW1   7267 4422   8–3B
*"Big yummy thalis", composed of "interesting" and "different" Indian
dishes, maintain a large and enthusiastic following for this "smarter-
than-average" chain – "yes, it's a production line, but for value and
flavour it's solidly reliable". / www.realindianfood.com; 11 pm,
Sun 10.30 pm; no Amex; booking: min 10.*

Massimo
Corinthia Hotel SW1 [NEW] £77 ④❷❷
10 Northumberland Ave   7930 8181   2–3D
*This stupendously grand 5-star newcomer, near Embankment tube,
makes a splendid venue to impress, especially on business; Roman
chef, Massimo Riccioli's fish-heavy menu is dextrously realised too –
shame that, unless you go for the 'steal' of a set lunch menu,
it's really very overpriced. / Rated on Editors' visit;
www.massimorestaurant.co.uk; 10.45 pm; closed Sun; set pre theatre £50 (FP).*

Masters Super Fish SE1 £28 ❷④⑤
191 Waterloo Rd   7928 6924   9–4A
*A "very busy" chippy near the Old Vic, where you can hope to find
"some of the best fish 'n' chips of your life", served "in large portions,
and with all the extras"; "you certainly don't come for the terrible
ambience", however. / 10.30 pm; closed Sun, Mon L; no Amex; no booking
Fri D.*

Matsuba TW9 £43 ❷❸④
10 Red Lion St   8605 3513   1–4A
*This low-key, family-run Japanese café, in Richmond, is worth seeking
out for its "delicious", if "pricey", selection of dishes, notably some
"outstanding" sashimi and sushi. / 10.30 pm; closed Sun.*

Matsuri SW1 £84 ❷❷⑤
15 Bury St   7839 1101   3–3D
*The "excellent teppan-yaki" helps "make for a fun and different
experience", at this "very reliable" St James's Japanese; "shame
about the dreary subterranean space", though.
/ www.matsuri-restaurant.com; 10.30 pm, Sun 10 pm.*

Maxim W13   £33   ③④④
153-155 Northfield Ave   8567 1719   1–3A
"A decent Chinese in a neighbourhood without much decent Chinese food" – this Ealing stalwart is "always busy", although "dishes range from great to lacklustre". / 11.30 pm, Sun 11 pm.

maze W1   £78   ④④④
10-13 Grosvenor Sq   7107 0000   3–2A
"Little plates/big prices"; since Jason Atherton's departure, the "inventive" Mayfair tapas-restaurant he set up for Gordon Ramsay "seems to have lost its dynamism" – the ratio of supporters ("stunning", "slick") to critics ("ridiculous money", "zero ambience") is moving rapidly the wrong way. / www.gordonramsay.com/maze; 10.30 pm; set weekday L £51 (FP).

maze Grill W1   £82   ④④④
10-13 Grosvenor Sq   7495 2211   3–2A
It's always been "unatmospheric" and "pricey", but this Ramsay-group Mayfair steakhouse inspires ever more erratic feedback in all respects – for every reporter who finds the steak "fabulous" there's another who speaks in terms of "huge disappointment". / www.gordonramsay.com; 10.30 pm; no shorts; set weekday L & pre-theatre £50 (FP).

**The Meat & Wine Co
Westfield W12**   £58   ④❶④
Unit 1026 Ariel Way   8749 5914   7–1C
This "meatilicious" operation, by the entrance to Westfield, has its fans, though it leaves many reporters "full but dissatisfied" – prices are "very high", and the "flashy" interior contributes to an overall impression which is "formulaic" and "soulless". / www.themeatandwineco.com; 11.30 pm, Sun 10.30 pm; no Maestro; set weekday L £31 (FP).

Mediterraneo W11   £53   ❸❸❸
37 Kensington Park Rd   7792 3131   6–1A
A "reliable" Notting Hill "stalwart", this "lively" corner Italian – sibling to nearby Osteria Basilico – is a "cosy" sort of place, where the cooking is generally "really solid". / www.mediterraneo-restaurant.co.uk; 11.30 pm, Sun 10.30 pm; booking: max 10.

Medlar SW10 𝗡𝗘𝗪   £57   ❶❷❸
438 King's Rd   7349 1900   5–3B
"First and foremost, the food is incredible", at this "fantastic newcomer" – a plainish but comfortable dining room near World's End, created by a team that's broken away from Chez Bruce and The Square; "the atmosphere will doubtless improve as Chelsea locals find and love it". / 10.30 pm; closed Mon & Sun D.

Mekong SW1   £32   ❸❷④
46 Churton St   7630 9568   2–4B
"Great fun and excellent value" are to be had at this "tiny" Pimlico veteran, where "helpful" staff serve up "strongly-flavoured" Vietnamese food in "generous portions"; claustrophobes should avoid the basement. / 11.30 pm.

Mela WC2   £38   ❸❸❸
152-156 Shaftesbury Avenue   7836 8635   4–2B
A large but "friendly" curry house, just north of Cambridge Circus, that offers "good value" by West End standards; even long-term fans, however, may find that the cuisine is "reasonable, but no longer outstanding". / www.melarestaurant.co.uk; 11.30 pm, Sun 10.30 am.

Melati W1 £35 ④❸⑤
21 Gt Windmill St   7437 2745   3–2D
A "simple" canteen, off Piccadilly Circus, which serves "authentic
SE Asian food", and has long been "a great cheap eat in the heart
of London"; it also has a nearby namesake – unrelated! – at 30-31
Peter Street, which "overcomes a tatty first impression to deliver fine
Indonesian classics". / www.melati.co.uk; 11 pm, Sat-Sun 11.30 pm.

Mem & Laz N1 £28 ④❷❷
8 Theberton St   7704 9089   8–3D
"Cheap, fun and certainly entertaining", this "buzzy" joint,
near Angel, serves a "huge menu" which mixes Turkish and
Mediterranean dishes, all cooked to a "reliable" standard; lunch is a
particular "bargain". / www.memlaz.com; 11.30 pm, Fri & Sat midnight;
no Amex.

Memories of India SW7 £33 ❸④④
18 Gloucester Rd   7581 3734   5–1B
"It's not got the most attractive exterior (or interior!)", but this South
Kensington curry house has long been a local favourite, thanks to its
"surprisingly good" food. / www.memoriesofindia.com; 11.30 pm.

Memsaheb on Thames E14 £30 ④❷❸
65-67 Amsterdam Rd   7538 3008   11–2D
"Nothing is too much trouble" for staff at this Isle of Dogs Indian,
which benefits from "good views" of the river; the food can
be "patchy", but it mostly gets the thumbs-up. / www.memsaheb.net;
11 pm; closed Sat L; no Amex.

Menier Chocolate Factory SE1 £44 ⑤④❷
51-53 Southwark St   7407 4411   9–4B
"A meal here before a show is a special experience", say fans of this
Bohemian Southwark playhouse; viewed as a culinary performance,
however, it's most definitely "not worth crossing town for".
/ www.menierchocolatefactory.com; 11 pm; closed Mon & Sun D; set pre
theatre £29 (FP).

Mennula W1 £52 ❷❸④
10 Charlotte St   7636 2833   2–1C
"Creative" and "accomplished" cooking – from an "engaging" chef
and "sincere" staff – win high praise for this "homely" Sicilian
yearling, in Fitzrovia; service can be "erratic", though, and conditions
are "squashed". / www.mennula.com; 11 pm, Sun 9.30 pm; closed Sat L.

The Mercer EC2 £53 ❸❷❸
34 Threadneedle St   7628 0001   9–2C
"Comfortable", "elegant" and "welcoming", this former banking hall
has carved out a big reputation as a "favourite" City rendezvous,
thanks to its "unobtrusive and efficient service", and its "well-
executed" and "straightforward" cooking. / www.themercer.co.uk;
9.30 pm; closed Sat & Sun.

Le Mercury N1 £27 ④❸❷
140a Upper St   7354 4088   8–2D
"Unbeatable for romance on a budget" – this "remarkable survivor",
by Islington's Almeida Theatre, is a "cosy and candlelit spot", offering
"consistently good food" at prices that seem "unchanged since the
last century". / www.lemercury.co.uk; 1 am, Sun 11.30 pm.

Meson don Felipe SE1 £38 ④④❷
53 The Cut 7928 3237 9–4A
"Affordable" tapas and "gluggable Sangria" – plus an infamous guitarist – have long made this "fun" bar a "bustling" South Bank "bolt hole"; admittedly, it's "not a patch on the Barrafinas of the world", but that's not really the point. / www.mesondonfelipe.com; 11 pm; closed Sun; no Amex; no booking after 8 pm.

Mestizo NW1 £40 ❷❷④
103 Hampstead Rd 7387 4064 8–4C
"An unassuming eatery that tries (and often succeeds) in bringing Londoners a taste of true Mexican food" (and a "wide variety of Tequilas" to go with it); only its obscure location – a short walk north of Warren Street tube – prevents it from being better known. / www.mestizomx.com; 10.45 pm.

Mews of Mayfair W1 £56 ④❸❸
10 Lancashire Ct, New Bond St 7518 9388 3–2B
The location (just off Bond Street) and the "metro-casual" vibe make this "quirky" and hidden-away joint a natural for ladies-who-lunch, especially as the midday set menus offer "particularly good value"; dinner à la carte is a less compelling proposition. / www.mewsofmayfair.com; 11 pm; closed Sun D.

Mezzanine
Royal National Theatre SE1 £41 ④❸④
Royal National Theatre, Belvedere Rd 7452 3600 2–3D
The RNT's in-house restaurant "could be better", but by and large "does what it says on the tin"; puddings (which you can take during the interval) are "the best bit". / www.nationaltheatre.org.uk; 11 pm; closed Mon L, Fri L & Sun D.

Michael Nadra W4 £48 ❶❸④
6-8 Elliott Rd 8742 0766 7–2A
M. Nadra's cuisine "improves with every menu", and his Chiswick yearling is starting to give the nearby La Trompette (where he used to be head chef) a good "run for its money"; ambience-wise, though, overcoming the constraints of these "cramped" premises is always going to be a challenge. / www.restaurant-michaelnadra.co.uk; 10 pm, Fri & Sat 10.30 pm.

Mien Tay £23 ❶④④
180 Lavender Hill, SW11 7350 0721 10–1C
122 Kingsland Rd, E2 7729 3074 12–1B
"Genius" Vietnamese cooking – at "unbelievably low prices for the quality" – inspire nothing but adulation for these "bustling", if slightly "tacky", BYO cafés in Battersea and, now, Shoreditch. / 11 pm, Fri & Sat 11.30 pm, sun 10.30 pm; cash only.

Mildreds W1 £40 ❷④④
45 Lexington St 7494 1634 3–2D
"Almost worth giving up bacon sarnies for!" – the veggie cuisine at this buzzing Soho diner is so "innovative and exciting" (and "affordable" too) it would "please the most ardent meat eater"; staff, though, "operate on the principle that you need to win them over, not vice versa…" / www.mildreds.co.uk; 11 pm; closed Sun; no Amex; no booking.

Mill Lane Bistro NW6 NEW   £41   ❸②④
77 Mill Ln   7794 5577   1–1B
"A decent addition to the impoverished West Hampstead scene";
this Gallic yearling may have an "unprepossessing location", but it
offers "good French bistro grub" and "drinkable wines", all at
"affordable" prices. / www.milllanebistro.com; 10 pm, Fri & Sat 10.30 pm,
Sun 9 pm; closed Mon, Tue-Fri D only; no Amex.

Min Jiang
The Royal Garden Hotel W8   £68   ❶②❶
2-24 Kensington High St   7361 1988   5–1A
"Legendary Peking duck", "excellent dim sum", and "one of London's
best panoramic views" (of Kensington Gardens and beyond) are
amongst the many attractions of this "superbly sophisticated" eighth-
floor restaurant; remember to book the bird well ahead.
/ www.minjiang.co.uk; 10 pm.

Mint Leaf   £63   ❸④❸
Suffolk Pl, Haymarket, SW1   7930 9020   2–2C
Angel Ct, Lothbury, EC2   7600 0992   9–2C
"Solid cocktails" and "fresh modern cuisine" give these clubby
subcontinentals – in a Theatreland basement, and near Bank –
all the makings of "an enjoyable night out"; "extortionate" prices can
take the edge off the experience, though, making the "good-value"
prix-fixe lunch (WC2) especially worth looking out for.
/ www.mintleafrestaurant.com; SW1 10.30 pm, Sun 10 pm; EC2 10.30 pm;
SW1 closed Sat & Sun L; EC2 closed Sat & Sun; set always available £36 (FP).

Miran Masala W14   £18   ❷②⑤
3 Hammersmith Rd   7602 4555   7–1D
"Very good grilled meats and breads" – "the lamb chops are special"
– win rave reviews for this little Pakistani café, by Olympia;
its "friendly" service compensates for an interior that decidedly
"nothing special". / www.miranmasala.co.uk; midnight; D only; no Amex.

Mirch Masala   £23   ❷④④
171-173 The Broadway, UB1   8867 9222   1–3A
1416 London Rd, SW16   8679 1828   10–2C
213 Upper Tooting Rd, SW17   8767 8638   10–2D
111 Commercial Rd, E1   7247 9992   12–2D
"So cheap, and absolutely brilliant!" – these "busy and bustling"
Pakistani canteens offer "no frills", just "amazing-tasting" grills, naans
and curries; BYO. / www.mirchmasalarestaurant.co.uk; midnight;
set weekday L £10 (FP).

Misato W1   £32   ④④⑤
11 Wardour St   7734 0808   4–3A
"It runs by numbers nowadays", but this "cheap 'n' cheerful" Soho
Japanese still offers "very fast and filling" fodder, and "the queue's
just as long as it ever was". / 10.30 pm; no credit cards.

Mitsukoshi SW1   £55   ❷②⑤
Dorland Hs, 14-20 Lower Regent St   7930 0317   3–3D
"Dated, functional and really in need of a make-over" – no change,
then, at this Japanese department store basement, near Piccadilly
Circus; the food, though, "remains very good", especially if you visit
what's arguably "the best sushi bar in the West End".
/ www.mitsukoshi-restaurant.co.uk; 10 pm; set weekday L £35 (FP).

Miyama W1   £60   ❷④⑤
38 Clarges St   7499 2443   3–4B
"Top-quality sushi and sashimi", but "less-than-average decor" –
the trade-off at this "quiet" Mayfair veteran Japanese is just the same
as ever. / www.miyama-restaurant.co.uk; 10.15 pm; closed Sat L & Sun L.

The Modern Pantry EC1 £48 ❸❸❸
47-48 St Johns Sq 7553 9210 9–1A
Anna Hansen's "very light and airy" and "laid-back" Clerkenwell
venture is set in "a lovely peaceful courtyard"; the "innovative" cuisine
can be "brilliant", but critics find it "inconsistent" – there's no doubt,
though, that brunch is "outstanding". / www.themodernpantry.co.uk;
Mon-Sat 11 pm, Sun 10 pm.

Mogul SE10 £33 ❸❷❸
10 Greenwich Church St 8858 1500 1–3D
A "good Greenwich Indian" whose "very reliable" all-round charms
include a "wonderful selection of curries, perfectly cooked"; "for the
best atmosphere, book a table downstairs". / www.mogulindian.co.uk;
11.30 pm; set weekday L £21 (FP).

Mohsen W14 £27 ❷❸❺
152 Warwick Rd 7602 9888 7–1D
"Fresh and filling" Persian dishes (accompanied by "amazing bread")
make up for the "lacklustre" decor of this Kensington outfit;
its location – opposite Homebase – isn't much to write home about
either; BYO. / midnight; no credit cards.

Momo W1 £65 ❹❺❸
25 Heddon St 7434 4040 3–2C
"With all its nooks, crannies and dancers", Mourad Mazouz's "fun"
and "buzzy" Moroccan, off Regent Street, is "perfect for a date" or a
party; the "hit-and-miss" cuisine is rather beside the point
(and service may not win any prizes either...) / www.momoresto.com;
11.30 pm, Sun 11 pm; closed Sun L; set weekday L £35 (FP).

Mon Plaisir WC2 £54 ❹❹❸
19-21 Monmouth St 7836 7243 4–2B
This rambling and "very French" Covent Garden veteran (est. 1945)
"still delivers the goods" for most reporters, who love its "romantic"
style and "traditional" fare (especially the "well-priced theatre
menu"); ratings aren't a patch on a few years ago, however,
and sceptics feel that "as prices have gone up, quality has gone
down". / www.monplaisir.co.uk; 11.15 pm; closed Sun; set pre-theatre £33
(FP), set weekday L £35 (FP).

Mona Lisa SW10 £27 ❹❷❷
417 King's Rd 7376 5447 5–3B
"A great mixed clientele" ("from local Chelsea ladies to footie fans")
adds to the charm of this family-run Italian "greasy spoon",
near World's End, where "marvellous cheap food is served with
a smile". / 11 pm, Sun 5.30 pm; closed Sun D; no Amex; set weekday L
£17 (FP).

Monmouth Coffee Company £11 ❷❷❷
27 Monmouth St, WC2 7379 3516 4–2B
2 Park St, SE1 7940 9960 9–4C
34 Maltby St, SE1 7232 3010 9–4D
"Go, drink, buzz"; rivals are legion, but these "packed" Covent
Garden and Borough Market cafés are "London's reigning coffee
champions" – with their "perfect croissants and cakes", they are also
"cult" Saturday destinations, so beware the queues!
/ www.monmouthcoffee.co.uk; 6 pm-6.30 pm; SE1 2 pm; closed Sun,
Maltby St SE1 open Sat only; no Amex; no booking.

Montpeliano SW7 £62 ④④④
13 Montpelier St 7589 0032 5–1C
*"Stuck in the '80s", it may be, but this Knightsbridge trattoria is still,
for its fans, a "reliable" and "lively" classic; for critics, however, there's
"just one word for it" – "terrible!" / www.montpelianorestaurant.com;
11.45 pm, Sun 11.30 pm; set weekday L £36 (FP).*

Monty's £32 ❸❸④
692 Fulham Rd, SW6 0872 148 1291 10–1B
54 Northfield Ave, W13 8567 6281 1–2A
1 The Mall, W5 8567 8122 1–2A
*"Always-reliable" local curry houses, mainly located in Ealing; opinions
differ on which is best – ownership varies – but all offer well-rated
Nepalese fare. / 11 pm.*

Mooli's W1 £12 ❷❷④
50 Frith St 7494 9075 4–2A
*"Zingy" Indian rotis ("go for the goat", it's "sublime") and "colourful"
salads at "staggeringly low" prices make this "inventive" Soho yearling
a hot spot for a "really distinctive" bite; ratings have dipped since
opening, though, with sceptics fearing it's becoming "overhyped".
/ www.moolis.com; Mon-Wed 10 pm, Thu-Sat 11.30 pm; closed Sun.*

The Morgan Arms E3 £44 ❸❷❷
43 Morgan St 8980 6389 1–2D
*"Less and less like a pub", this "good, local East End joint" has
a strong local following, thanks not least to its "consistent" culinary
standards. / www.capitalpubcompany.com/The-Morgan-Arms; 10 pm,
Sun 9 pm.*

Morgan M N7 £64 ❶❶❸
489 Liverpool Rd 7609 3560 8–2D
*Almost "Alice-in-Wonderlandish" in its improbability, Morgan
Meunier's "phenomenal" conversion of a "dull"-looking Holloway pub
is "one of London's best French restaurants" – "if it was in Soho,
you'd need to book months ahead!" / www.morganm.com; 9 pm; closed
Mon, Tue L, Sat L & Sun D; no Amex; booking: max 8.*

Morito EC1 NEW £24 ❷❷❷
32 Exmouth Mkt 7278 7007 9–1A
*Thanks to its "divine" dishes, this new "Moro-lite" operation –
a "cramped" and "very authentic tapas bar" – has been "rammed"
since the day it opened: "arrive early!" / www.morito.co.uk; 11 pm; closed
Sun; no booking for D.*

MORO EC1 £48 ❷❷❸
34-36 Exmouth Mkt 7833 8336 9–1A
*"Superb, simple food, with zero pretentiousness" and an "always
stimulating" (if "hellishly noisy") vibe have won a legendary following
for this "inspiring" Spanish/Moorish favourite in Exmouth Market;
its ratings dipped a bit this year, however – is it becoming
"less focussed"? / www.moro.co.uk; 10.30 pm; closed Sun.*

Mosaica
The Chocolate Factory N22 £46 ❸❷❸
Unit C005, Clarendon Rd 8889 2400 1–1C
*The industrial-estate location couldn't be more "unpromising",
but this "eccentric" Wood Green venue rewards the adventurous with
its "exotic" interior and "first-class" service; the food is usually "well-
executed" too, but this year did see the occasional "grim" report.
/ www.mosaicarestaurants.com; 9.30 pm, Sat 10 pm; closed Mon,
Sat L & Sun D.*

Motcombs SW1 £58 ④④❸
26 Motcomb St 7235 6382 5–1D
On an ever-trendier corner, a welcoming establishment of long standing, comprising a "casual" upstairs bar (with al fresco tables) and a "country house"-style dining room downstairs; "the food's not really up with the prices, but this is Belgravia". / www.motcombs.co.uk; 11 pm; closed Sun D.

Moti Mahal WC2 £52 ❷❸④
45 Gt Queen St 7240 9329 4–2D
"Is this the most under-rated curry house in London?" – this increasingly well-known Covent Garden outpost of a Delhi-based group offers "exquisite" dishes which are "up with the best in India itself"; prices, however, are "decidedly high" and the interior is "not the most exciting". / www.motimahal-uk.com; 11 pm; closed Sat L & Sun.

Mount Street Deli W1 £20 ④④④
100 Mount St 7499 6843 3–3A
"Mayfair prices" somewhat colour views of this Caprice group deli/café yearling, but fans say that "limited seating is the only drawback" of a place that's "great for a quick bite" (and there aren't many of those round here…) / www.themountstreetdeli.co.uk; 6 pm, Sat 5 pm; closed Sun; no bookings.

Mr Chow SW1 £74 ④④④
151 Knightsbridge 7589 7347 5–1D
Once a glamorous Knightsbridge linchpin, this Chinese restaurant can seem "a little passé" nowadays, but it still turns out "decent" chow in a "civilised" setting, say fans; critics, though, find the whole experience "so overpriced, you're left wondering whether the food was nice after all". / www.mrchow.com; 11.45 pm.

Mr Kong WC2 £32 ❸❸④
21 Lisle St 7437 7341 4–3A
"One of the safer bets in Chinatown", this "hustling and bustling" veteran benefits from a "charming" manager and a very "dependable" standard of cooking – "avoid the obvious menu choices, and go for the specials". / www.mrkongrestaurant.com; 2.45 am, Sun 1.45 am.

Mr Wing SW5 £45 ❸④❷
242-244 Old Brompton Rd 7370 4450 5–2A
"Dark alcoves" and "novel" décor (lots of fish tanks and plants) have long made this Earl's Court Chinese a "fun" option for a party – especially when jazz is playing – or romance; "with the old manager gone", however, there are several concerns about "slipping" standards, particularly on the service front. / www.mrwing.com; 11.30 pm.

Mrs Marengos W1 £18 ❶❸④
53 Lexington St 7287 2544 3–2D
"Great breakfasts, tasty lunches and amazing cakes" are on offer at this "cute" Soho spot; it's not as well known as its big sister, Mildred's, but – as it's so small – that's perhaps a blessing. / www.mrsmarengos.co.uk; L only, closed Sun; no Amex; no booking.

Mugen EC4 £40 ❸❷❸
26 King William St 7929 7879 9–3C
"Pleasantly bustling", "extremely reliable" and with "brilliant" service, this Japanese restaurant, near Monument, is "ideal for a quick lunch". / 10.30 pm; closed Sat & Sun.

Murano W1 £90 ❸②❸
20-22 Queen St   7495 1127   3–3B
*Maybe it is "now free of the Ramsay empire", but since Angela
Hartnett's October 2010 buy-out, the ratings of this "classy",
if slightly "impersonal", Mayfair dining room, have drifted; her cuisine
is still often acclaimed as "first-rate", but those who find it "nothing
special" are becoming more vociferous. / www.angela-hartnett.com;
10.15 pm; closed Sun; set weekday L £50 (FP).*

My Old Place E1 £34 ❷⑤④
88-90 Middlesex St   7247 2200   9–2D
*Overlook the "grotty" setting and the "reluctant" service – "cheap
and fiery Sichuan cooking" makes this "authentic" spot,
near Liverpool Street, a "jewel". / www.myoldplace.co.uk; 11 pm; no Amex.*

Nahm
Halkin Hotel SW1 £80 ❸❸⑤
5 Halkin St   7333 1234   2–3A
*Shame that a "weird" ambience and "exorbitant" prices continue
to handicap David Thompson's renowned Thai dining room,
in Belgravia – the food may strike its critics as merely "pleasant
enough", but most reporters reckon it's "phenomenal".
/ www.nahm.como.bz; 10.30 pm; closed Sat L & Sun L.*

Namo E9 £30 ❸❸❸
178 Victoria Park Rd   8533 0639   1–2D
*"Authentic pho" is one of the "good range of options" on offer at this
Vietnamese local, in Hackney; "the back terrace is best in summer".
/ www.namo.co.uk; 11 pm; no Amex.*

Nando's £28 ④④④
Branches throughout London
*"Basic, simple, quick… and OK-quality for a cheap meal";
this "reliable" peri-peri chicken chain "is hardly a destination for
a night out", but its "fuss-free" charms make it "a good alternative
to a pizza", in particular for those with families in tow.
/ www.nandos.co.uk; 11.30 pm, Sun 10.30 pm; no Amex; no booking.*

Napket £20 ④④❸
5 Vigo St, W1   7734 4387   3–3D
6 Brook St, W1   7495 8562   3–2B
61 Piccadilly, W1   7493 4704   3–3C
342 King's Rd, SW3   7352 9832   5–3C
34 Royal Exchange, EC3   7621 1831   9–2C
*A growing chain of glamorous cafés, praised as "a good place for
a coffee and a sandwich", and offering "lots of bespoke options";
it's really "not cheap" though. / www.napket.com; 7 pm; W1 10 pm,
EC3 5 pm; Brook St closed Sun; EC3 closed Sat & Sun; W1 no Amex;
no bookings.*

Napulé SW6 £39 ❸④❸
585 Fulham Rd   7381 1122   5–4A
*"Still authentic, even though it's now part of a chain"; this convivial
member of the 'Made in Italy' family, by Fulham Broadway, scores
most highly for its "excellent" pizza-by-the-metre. / 11.30 pm,
Sun 10.30 pm; closed weekday L; no Amex.*

The Narrow E14 £57 ④④④
44 Narrow St   7592 7950   11–1B
*A potentially atmospheric riverside boozer in Docklands, where the
food is "uninspiring", and service too often "couldn't care less" –
in short, it's the sort of 'Kitchen Nightmare' that the proprietor,
Gordon Ramsay, is famous for fixing; so why doesn't he?
/ www.gordonramsay.com; 11 pm, Sun 10.30 pm.*

FSA

The National Dining Rooms
National Gallery WC2   £50   ⑤⑤④
Sainsbury Wing, Trafalgar Sq   7747 2525   2–2C
"Great views" reward those who bag one of the *"lovely"* window seats
in this first-floor dining room, overlooking Trafalgar Square; generally,
"the food is not so good" – the afternoon tea, though, can be
"excellent". / www.thenationaldiningrooms.co.uk; 7 pm; Sat-Thu closed
D, Fri open L & D; no Amex.

National Gallery Café
National Gallery WC2   £50   ④④④
East Wing, Trafalgar Sq   7747 5942   4–4B
*This panelled café on Trafalgar Square (no view) is ideally placed as a
central rendezvous; its wide-ranging menu – from sandwiches
to more ambitious dishes – is realised only to an "average" standard,
but it makes a handy option for a light bite or breakfast.*
/ www.thenationaldiningrooms.co.uk; 11 pm, Sun 6 pm; no Amex.

Natural Kitchen   £32   ❸❸❸
77-78 Marylebone High St, W1   3012 2123   2–1A
15-17 New Street Sq, Fetter Ln, EC4   3012 2123   9–2A
*For "casual lunches", these "friendly" and "always-packed" diners
"fill a gap" with their "interesting" salads, soups, sarnies and quiches;
who cares if purists decry the fare as "faux-Mediterranean"?* / EC4
10 pm; W1 8 pm, Sat 7 pm, Sun 5 pm; EC4 closed Sat Sun.

Nautilus NW6   £37   ❷❷④
27-29 Fortune Green Rd   7435 2532   1–1B
"North London's best fish 'n' chips" (fried in matzo meal) are,
say fans, to be found at this West Hampstead veteran; well, it's not
the *"lousy"* interior which draws the crowds! / 10 pm; closed Sun;
no Amex.

Navarro's W1   £38   ❸④❷
67 Charlotte St   7637 7713   2–1C
*An eye-catching tiled interior helps make this Fitzrovia haunt central
London's leading traditional-style tapas bar; it offers "delicious" food,
too, which comes in "surprisingly generous portions".*
/ www.navarros.co.uk; 10 pm; closed Sat L & Sun.

Nazmins SW18   £33   ❸❷④
398 Garratt Ln   8944 1463   10–2B
"Always busy", this Earlsfield Indian has a big name locally for its
"reliable and tasty" food. / www.nazmins.com; midnight.

Needoo E1   £25   ❶❸④
87 New Rd   7247 0648   12–2D
"On a par with the legendary Tayyabs, but less busy" – this *"brilliant"*
Pakistani yearling is acclaimed for its *"amazing grilled meats and
curries at low prices"*; *"staff actually smile"* too. / www.needoogrill.co.uk;
6 pm; closed Sun; no Amex.

New Culture Revolution   £31   ❸④④
305 King's Rd, SW3   7352 9281   5–3C
157-159 Notting Hill Gate, W11   7313 9688   6–2B
42 Duncan St, N1   7833 9083   8–3D
"Totally reliable and good-quality", this small and basic chain
impresses almost all reporters with its *"tasty noodles, soups and
dumplings".* / www.newculturerevolution.co.uk; 10.30 pm.

New Mayflower W1   £30   ❷❸④
68-70 Shaftesbury Ave   7734 9207   4–3A
*Consistently one of Chinatown's best performers – and traditionally
one of London's best places to eat post-midnight too –
this nondescript-looking Cantonese serves up "excellent" food;
service, though, is "businesslike, rather than friendly". / 4 am; D only;
no Amex.*

New Tayyabs E1   £27   ❶④❸
83 Fieldgate St   7247 9543   9–2D
*The "horrific" queues at this "hectic" East End Pakistani classic are
legendary, and no wonder – its "awesome" but "absurdly cheap"
lamb chops and curries offer "one of London's great eating
experiences"; "thank God they now take bookings!"; BYO.
/ www.tayyabs.co.uk; 11.30 pm.*

New World W1   £33   ④④❸
1 Gerrard Pl   7734 0396   4–3A
*"Easy to imagine you're in Hong Kong", when you visit this "giant"
and "noisy" Chinatown fixture; the lunchtime dim sum, served from
trolleys, is "excellent and very cheap" – "ignore everything else!"
/ 11.45 pm, Sun 11 pm; no booking, Sun L.*

1901
Andaz Hotel EC2   £62   ④❸❸
40 Liverpool St   7618 7000   12–2B
*"Very elegant" surroundings and an "impressive" wine list help qualify
this "very comfortable" dining room, by Liverpool Street, as a power-
dining haunt; fans find the food "sound" too, but critics dismiss it as
"pretentious". / www.andazdining.com; 10 pm; closed Sat L & Sun; booking:
max 12.*

19 Numara Bos Cirrik N16   £24   ❸❸④
34 Stoke Newington Rd   7249 0400   1–1C
*"Perhaps it's unhealthy, but by gosh it's good"; this "cheap" and "fun"
kebab house, by Hackney Central, serves up "enormous plates
of tasty grilled meat", and "fresh" mezze too. / midnight; no Amex.*

Nizuni W1 NEW   £37   ❷❷❸
22 Charlotte St   7580 7447   2–1C
*Surprisingly few reports on this Fitzrovia newcomer, which offers
"really good Asian-fusion food, much, much cheaper than nearby
Roka", and "very good sushi" too – perhaps it's because the interior's
a little "bland". / www.nizuni.com; 10.45 pm; closed Sun L; .*

Nobu
Metropolitan Hotel W1   £80   ❷④④
19 Old Park Ln   7447 4747   3–4A
*"Some now think it naff", but this epic Mayfair Japanese – which
back in 1997 kicked off a wave of trendy Asian high-flyers – still
delivers many "divine" sushi and fusion dishes; it's "eye-wateringly
expensive", though, and menu, service and decor are all now arguably
"in need of an update". / www.noburestaurants.com; Mon-Thu 10.15 pm,
Fri & Sat 11 pm, Sun 10 pm.*

Nobu W1   £84   ❸④❸
15 Berkeley St   7290 9222   3–3C
*"Clubbier" – and also a bit more "Footballers' Wives" – than its Park
Lane sibling, the younger of the Mayfair Nobus serves similarly
"exquisite" Japanese-fusion cuisine that's similarly "scandalously
overpriced"; the setting is "way-too-noisy", and "canteen-like",
but "fun"… if you like that sort of thing. / www.noburestaurants.com;
11 pm, Thu-Sat midnight, Sun 9 pm; closed Sat L & Sun L.*

Noor Jahan   £36   ❷❷④
2a, Bina Gdns, SW5   7373 6522   5–2B
26 Sussex Pl, W2   7402 2332   6–1D
"You will never be disappointed", says one of the many fans of the
"fresh-tasting" Indian food served at this "popular workhorse", whose
South Kensington location draws in a well-heeled crowd at odds with
its "gloomy" curry-house looks; similarly, the W2 spin-off is "definitely
a cut-above". / 11.30 pm, Sun 10.30 pm.

Nopi W1 NEW   £55   ❷❷❸
21-22 Warwick St   7494 9584   3–2D
Yotam Ottolenghi's has a "magical touch", say fans of this "beautiful
and casual" Soho newcomer, which offers "exotic" but "clean-tasting"
tapas displaying a "brilliant combination of Middle Eastern and Asian
influences"; we do have some sympathy , though, with those who find
it "way overpriced". / www.nopi-restaurant.com; 11.30 pm; closed Sun D.

Nordic Bakery   £15   ❸❸❷
14a, Golden Sq, W1   3230 1077   3–2D
37b, New Cavendish St, W1   7935 3590   2–1A NEW
"The antidote to everything to do with chains and Italio/American
coffee shops!" – this "minimalist", "relaxed" and "blissfully music-
free" Soho café offers "great coffee" and "cinnamon buns to die for";
a second outlet recently opened, north of Oxford Street. / Golden
Square 8 pm, Sat 7 pm, Sun 6 pm; Cavendish Street 7 pm, Sun 6 pm.

The Norfolk Arms WC1   £37   ④④❸
28 Leigh St   7388 3937   8–4C
A "casual" (going-on "erratic") Bloomsbury boozer whose "quirky"
menu offers "a choice of Spanish-style tapas or modern British
mains" – the former seem the better bet. / www.norfolkarms.co.uk;
10.15 pm.

North China W3   £36   ❷❷❸
305 Uxbridge Rd   8992 9183   7–1A
"By far the best food in Acton" is to be had at this "friendly" and
"high-quality" family-run Chinese – "worth a trip" for its "deeply
satisfying" cooking. / www.northchina.co.uk; 11 pm, Fri & Sat 11.30 pm.

The North London Tavern NW6   £43   ❸④❸
375 Kilburn High Rd   7625 6634   1–2B
A "beautifully restored" Kilburn boozer that's still "a real pub",
but where the cooking is of "good quality". / www.realpubs.co.uk;
10.30 pm, Sun 9.30 pm; no Amex.

North Road EC1   £54   ❷❸④
69-73 St John St   3217 0033   9–1B
"Fascinating" – that's the verdict on Christoffer Hruskova's "sterile"-
feeling Danish newcomer, in Clerkenwell; some of his "challenging"
("weird") flavours and food combos seem "misconceived", but a
striking number of reporters feel this is a "genuinely unique"
experience that "really lives up to the hype!"
/ www.northroadrestaurant.co.uk; Mon -Thu 10.30 pm, Fri-Sat 11 pm;
closed Sun.

North Sea Fish WC1   £34   ❸❸❸
7-8 Leigh St   7387 5892   8–4C
"Top-class fish 'n' chips" maintain the wide-ranging appeal of this
"old-fashioned" Bloomsbury chippy. / www.northseafishrestaurant.co.uk;
10.30 pm; closed Sun; no Amex.

FSA

Northbank EC4 £50 ❸❸❷
1 Paul's Walk   7329 9299   9–3B
*"An excellent position, just by the Millennium Bridge" – with fine
Thames views and an "unbeatable summer terrace" –
has traditionally been the highlight at this "friendly" bar/café;
the "creative" food, however, shows some signs of beginning
to "measure up". / www.northbankrestaurant.co.uk; 10.30 pm.*

The Northgate N1 £36 ❷❷❸
113 Southgate Rd   7359 7392   1–1C
*A De Beauvoir Town gastroboozer, hailed by the locals for its
"interesting" menu, its "consistently good" food and its "charming"
service. / 10.30 pm, Sun 9.30 pm; closed Mon L.*

Notting Hill Brasserie W11 £70 ❸❹❸
92 Kensington Park Rd   7229 4481   6–2B
*In spite of a recent revamp, this potentially very "special" and
"romantic" west London townhouse-restaurant (not brasserie) is still
putting in a much more erratic performance than it once did; reports
– especially on the service – are noticeably up-and-down.
/ www.nottinghillbrasserie.co.uk; 11 pm, Mon & Sun 10.30 pm; set weekday L
£36 (FP).*

Nottingdale W11 £37 ❷❹❷
11 Evesham St   7221 2223   6–2A
*Think River Café-lost-in-the-backwoods-of-Notting Hill, and you have
something of the flavour of this "interesting" canteen (which is part-
owned by Charles Dunstone of Carphone Warehouse fame);
its "simply-prepared" dishes offer "good flavours" from ingredients
of "high quality". / www.nottingdale.com; 7 pm; closed Sat & Sun.*

Noura £50 ❸❹❹
122 Jermyn St, SW1   7839 2020   3–3D
16 Hobart Pl, SW1   7235 9444   2–4B
2 William St, SW1   7235 5900   5–1D
16 Curzon St, W1   7495 1050   3–4B
*The style ("all shiny mirrors") is somewhere between "classy" and
"impersonal", but these "bustling" brasseries still win praise for their
"genuine" Lebanese cuisine. / www.noura.co.uk; 11.30 pm, sun 10 pm.*

Novikov W1 NEW
50 Berkeley St   awaiting tel   3–3C
*Breezing in from Moscow – from a restaurateur already claiming
50 spectacular establishments to his name – this major new Mayfair
venture, with dining rooms both Italian and Asian in style,
is scheduled to open in late-2011. / www.novikovrestaurant.co.uk.*

Nozomi SW3 £71 ④⑤④
14-15 Beauchamp Pl   7838 1500   5–1C
*An allegedly in-crowd Knightsbridge Japanese, of note for its
"very stylish bar scene"; the reporters who comment on its cuisine
(few) however, tend to find the whole show rather "pretentious".
/ www.nozomi.co.uk; 11.30 pm, Sun 10.30 pm; closed Mon L.*

Number Twelve WC1 £50 ❸❹❹
12 Upper Woburn Pl   7693 5425   8–4C
*A handy Bloomsbury address – this little-known hotel dining room,
near Euston, is "fairly formal", and so "good for business"; it serves
up "simple but tasty" cuisine "with an Italian bent".
/ www.numbertwelverestaurant.co.uk; 10.15 pm; closed Sat L & Sun.*

Numero Uno SW11 £48 ❸❷❸
139 Northcote Rd   7978 5837   10–2C
"The menu never changes, but that's a good thing", say the fans of this "friendly and efficient" Nappy Valley Italian – "we're lucky to have it as a local". / 11.30 pm; no Amex.

Nuovi Sapori SW6 £43 ❷0④
295 New King's Rd   7736 3363   10–1B
Staff are "particularly warm and welcoming", at this Fulham Italian, and the cooking is "well above average" too; shame "the ambience leaves something to be desired". / 11 pm; closed Sun.

Nusa Kitchen £10 ❷④④
9 Old St, EC1   7253 3135   9–1B
2 Adam's Ct, EC2   7628 1149   9–2C
"Queues out the door, even in the rain!" attest to the power of these City pit stops' addictive staple – "absolutely delicious soups, in a huge range of flavours, and with no duff choices". / www.nusakitchen.co.uk; 4 pm; Sat & Sun; no booking.

O'Zon TW1 £30 ❸④④
33-35 London Rd   8891 3611   1–4A
"A good range" of "well-cooked" oriental food at "reasonable prices" remains a winning proposition for this friendly Chinese in downtown Twickenham; it's "very popular with kids" too. / www.justchinese.co.uk; 11 pm, Fri & Sat 11.30 pm.

The Oak W2 £49 ❷❸❶
137 Westbourne Park Rd   7221 3355   6–1B
"Airy and always buzzing" – this gorgeous Bayswater pub-conversion is just the place if you're looking for a "relaxed and stylish" meal, with a menu including "some of the best – if not the cheapest – pizzas in town!" / www.theoaklondon.com; 10.30 pm, Sun 10 pm; Mon-Thu D only, Fri-Sun open L & D; no booking.

Odette's NW1 £57 ❷❷❷
130 Regent's Park Rd   7586 8569   8–3B
"Going places!"; Bryn Williams's "superb" and "beautifully presented" cuisine – "more consistent", of late – won renewed support this year for this "elegant" neighbourhood restaurant, which benefits from a "romantic" Primrose Hill setting. / www.odettesprimrosehill.com; 10.30 pm.

Odin's W1 £52 ④❷❷
27 Devonshire St   7935 7296   2–1A
"Utterly delightful, in an old-school, clubby sort of way" – this "civilised", art-filled Marylebone "time warp" is "just the place to take your aunt", and also perfect "for business"; the traditional cuisine is no more than "OK", but no one really seems to mind. / www.langansrestaurants.co.uk; 11 pm; closed Sat L & Sun; booking: max 12.

Okawari W5 £34 ❸❸④
13 Bond St   8566 0466   1–3A
An "always-reliable" little café, in central Ealing, which offers "simple, fresh and tasty" sushi (and so on), eaten at sunken tables. / www.okawari.co.uk; 11.15 pm, Sun 10.45 pm.

FSA

The Old Brewery SE10   £39   ④④❷
The Pepys Building, Old Royal Naval College   3327 1280   1–3D
It's "hard to find better beers in London", says fans of this converted
brewery within the old Naval College – "a great-looking place with big
copper vats", and "a huge sun trap terrace"; it's proving
a "very useful addition to Greenwich" even if the food – burgers aside
– is "not massively special". / www.oldbrewerygreenwich.com; Fri & Sat
10.30 pm, Sun-Thu 10 pm; D only; no Amex.

The Old Bull & Bush NW3   £38   ⑤⑤❷
North End Rd   8905 5456   8–1A
"After a trip to Hampstead Heath", this "always-busy" gastropub,
opposite Golder's Hill Park, makes an atmospheric destination; "it's a
bit of a production line" though – the food's "not so impressive",
and service "needs a major lift" too. / www.thebullandbush.co.uk;
9.30 pm, Sat 10 pm, Sun 9 pm; set weekday L £24 (FP).

Old Parr's Head W14   £23   ④④❸
120 Blythe Rd   7371 4561   7–1C
"Did the old Thai family go back to Thailand?" – "quality seems to be
falling and prices rising", in the restaurant of this Olympia boozer;
it still benefits from its "hidden beer garden", though, and fans still
find it a "great local". / www.theoldparrshead.co.uk; 10 pm, Sat & Sun
9.30 pm; no Amex.

Ye Olde Cheshire Cheese EC4   £36   ④④❶
145 Fleet St   7353 6170   9–2A
"A very scenic tourist-trap"; this famous Fleet Street inn – rebuilt after
the Great Fire, and Dr Johnson's local – is also popular with the
locals, and its pub fodder, though pretty ordinary, could be a lot
worse. / 9.30 pm; closed Sun D; no booking, Sat & Sun.

Oliveto SW1   £50   ❶❸④
49 Elizabeth St   7730 0074   2–4A
"The best pizza in Europe!" (well almost); no wonder that,
at weekends, this not-exactly-cheap Belgravia Sardinian is "teeming
with smartly-dressed tots and their glamorous parents" –
book ahead! / www.olivorestaurants.com; 11 pm, Sun 10.30 pm; booking:
max 7 at D.

Olivo SW1   £55   ❸❸⑤
21 Eccleston St   7730 2505   2–4B
"Lots of regulars, including a fair number of Italians" maintain the
"neighbourhood" style of this Belgravia fixture, which is still "going
strong", thanks to the quality of its "honest" Sardinian fare;
the "jaded" interior, though, is "crowded", "noisy" and
"uncomfortable". / www.olivorestaurants.com; 11 pm, Sun 10.30 pm; closed
Sat L & Sun L.

Olivomare SW1   £64   ❷❸④
10 Lower Belgrave St   7730 9022   2–4B
"Simple" but "heavenly" fish and seafood have won a major fan club
for this "brilliant" Belgravia Sardinian; not everyone, though, likes its
"snazzy interior design" – it's "like eating in a posh fridge!"
/ www.olivorestaurants.com; 11 pm, Sun 10.30 pm; booking: max 10.

Olley's SE24   £39   ❸❸④
65-69 Norwood Rd   8671 8259   10–2D
This eclectically-decorated Brockwell Park chippy is one of the
best in south London, and it raises our native dish to a standard
"well above the norm". / www.olleys.info; 10 pm, Sun 9.30 pm; closed Mon;
no Amex.

148

Olympus Fish N3 £28 ❷❷④
140-144 Ballards Ln 8371 8666 1–1B
You can have "expertly-prepared" fish – either classic-style or char-grilled – at this Turkish chippy, in Finchley; it maintains "high standards", and is always "very busy". / 11 pm; closed Mon.

1 Lombard Street EC3 £62 ④④④
1 Lombard St 7929 6611 9–3C
A heart-of-the-City rendezvous for expense-accounters (with a more "power lunch"-style restaurant attached); its cooking "has improved of late", but it is still "not exceptional", and the banking hall setting can – at peak times – seem "too much like a railway terminus" for some tastes. / www.1lombardstreet.com; 10 pm; closed Sat & Sun.

One-O-One
Sheraton Park Tower SW1 £90 ❶❸⑤
101 Knightsbridge 7290 7101 5–1D
"Quite simply the best fish restaurant in the UK"; Pascal Proyart's "stunning" cuisine can be enjoyed à la carte, tapas-style or – perhaps best of all for Knightsbridge shoppers – at a "bargain" set lunch; the "dead" interior, though, is an object lesson in "uninspiring" hotel-design. / www.oneoonerestaurant.com; 10 pm; booking: max 6.

The Only Running Footman W1 £46 ❸❸❸
5 Charles St 7499 2988 3–3B
"Quiet and spacious enough upstairs to have a relaxed meal", this seemingly "packed" pub is a Mayfair destination well worth knowing about, thanks not least to its "fresh" and "seasonal" cuisine. / www.therunningfootmanmayfair.com; 10 pm.

Opera Tavern WC2 NEW £40 ❷❸❸
23 Catherine St 7836 3680 4–3D
"A great addition to the options near the Royal Opera House" – this "stylish" (but "closely-packed") sibling to Salt Yard serves up some "tantalising" Mediterranean small dishes that "burst with flavour"; don't get too carried away, though – "the bills can add up". / www.operatavern.co.uk; 11.30 pm; closed Sun D.

The Orange SW1 £48 ❸❸❷
37 Pimlico Rd 7881 9844 5–2D
It may be "cheap only by Belgravia standards", but this elegantly "stripped-back" boozer is now starting to out-do its parent, the Thomas Cubitt, in the popularity stakes; the secret? – a "decent" menu of staples, and a scene that's always "buzzing". / www.theorange.co.uk; Mon-Thu 10 pm, Fri & Sat 10.30 pm, Sun 9.30 pm.

Orange Pekoe SW13 £19 ❸❷❷
3 White Hart Ln 8876 6070 10–1A
A "pretty" tea and coffee shop with a "sun trap terrace", near the river in Barnes, serving "tempting" cakes, sarnies and salads. / www.orangepekoeteas.com; L only.

The Orange Tree N20 £38 ❸❸❷
7 Totteridge Ln 8343 7031 1–1B
Being "beautifully located" and "very child-friendly/forgiving" – two particular virtues of this Totteridge inn (and garden), which was well-rated this year for its "above-average" gastropub fare. / www.theorangetreetotteridge.co.uk; 9.30 pm, Fri & Sat 10.30 pm, Sun 9 pm.

L'Oranger SW1 £86 ❸❸❷
5 St James's St   7839 3774   3–4D

A "blissful, hidden courtyard", for the summer months, bolsters the "stylish" appeal of this "smart" St James's fixture; after a sticky patch, it won renewed praise this year for cuisine that's generally "fine", and sometimes "outstanding". / www.loranger.co.uk; 11 pm; closed Sat L & Sun; no jeans or trainers.

Origin Asia TW9 £37 ❷❷❸
100 Kew Rd   8948 0509   1–4A

"Unusually light and unusually delicate" dishes have created a strong name locally for this Richmond "modern Indian"; even so, "it can lack atmosphere at times". / www.originasia.co.uk; 11 pm; no Amex; set weekday L £22 (FP).

Orrery W1 £68 ❸❷❷
55 Marylebone High St   7616 8000   2–1A

"The luxury of space between tables" adds to the "light and airy" charms – especially for business – of this first-floor room, overlooking a churchyard; service is "exemplary" (a rarity for the D&D group), and the Gallic cuisine is "delightful" too – if "less imaginative" than in previous years. / www.orreryrestaurant.co.uk; 10.30 pm, Fri & Sat 11 pm.

Orso WC2 £56 ❸❸④
27 Wellington St   7240 5269   4–3D

"Once a flagship for regional Italian cooking", this Covent Garden "old-time" basement is looking a bit "faded" nowadays; fans still find it a "very reliable" stand-by, though, especially post-theatre, thanks to its "personable" service and its "rustic" and "hearty" fare. / www.orsorestaurant.co.uk; midnight; set pre theatre £35 (FP).

Oscar
Charlotte Street Hotel W1 £60 ④❸❷
15 Charlotte St   7806 2000   2–1C

This Fitzrovia haunt is a 'happening' linchpin for local meedjah types – "it's a shame the restaurant doesn't live up to the bar", but it is sometimes tipped for breakfast, or for business, nonetheless. / www.charlottestreethotel.com; 10.45 pm, Sun 9.45 pm.

Oslo Court NW8 £57 ❷❶❷
Charlbert St, off Prince Albert Rd   7722 8795   8–3A

"The dessert trolley is pure theatre", at this "real 1970's"-style "time warp", at the foot of a Regent's Park apartment block – the preferred birthday-party venue locally for those of a certain age; its "hilarious" (but highly professional) staff serve up an "amazingly large" menu that delivers surprisingly "excellent" results – "you simply have to love it!" / 11 pm; closed Sun; no jeans or trainers.

Osteria Antica Bologna SW11 £39 ❸❸❸
23 Northcote Rd   7978 4771   10–2C

Rustic Italian bistro of long standing, a short step from Clapham Junction; for fans, it's a "really great" destination, and is certainly often a "busy" one too, but standards are still rather up-and-down. / www.osteria.co.uk; 10.30 pm, Sat & Sun 10 pm.

Osteria Appennino EC2 £44 ❷④④
8 Devonshire Sq   7247 4472   9–2D

A "cramped" family-run Italian near Liverpool Street, offering "beautifully thin" pizza, and "beautifully authentic" pasta too. / www.osteriarestaurants.co.uk; 10.15 pm; closed Sat & Sun.

Osteria Basilico W11   £56   ❸❸❷
29 Kensington Park Rd   7727 9957   6–1A
"Still a fun place", this "chaotic" neighbourhood Italian (specialising in pizza) remains a linchpin of the Notting Hill dining scene, and is "always busy"; sit on the ground-floor (or outside) if you can – the basement tables aren't nearly as nice. / www.osteriabasilico.co.uk; 11.30 pm, Sun 10.30 pm; no booking, Sat L.

Osteria Dell'Angolo SW1   £54   ❸❸⑤
47 Marsham St   3268 1077   2–4C
Not everyone likes the "formal, rarefied and businessy" style of this Westminster Italian – a shame, as its "classic Tuscan dishes" are "robust" and of "good quality", and complemented by an "enterprising" wine list. / www.osteriadellangolo.co.uk; 10.30 pm; closed Sat L & Sun.

Osteria dell'Arancio SW10   £53   ❸❸❸
383 King's Rd   7349 8111   5–3B
A "casual" World's End trattoria offering "real Italian country cooking"; it's the "amazing" wine list, though – "with many choices one rarely sees outside Italy" – that's the biggest attraction, enhanced by guidance from a "knowledgeable manager/sommelier". / www.osteriadellarancio.co.uk; 11 pm; closed Mon L & Sun D.

Otto Pizza W2 NEW   £25   ❷❷❸
6 Chepstow Rd   7792 4088   6–1B
"Filling and delicious pizzas with a difference" ("the cornmeal crust is somewhere between pizza and pie") earn applause for this small and basic Bayswater newcomer. / www.ottopizza.com; 11 pm, Sun 10 pm.

Ottolenghi   £47   ❶❸❸
13 Motcomb St, SW1   7823 2707   5–1D
63 Ledbury Rd, W11   7727 1121   6–1B
1 Holland St, W8   7937 0003   5–1A
287 Upper St, N1   7288 1454   8–2D
"OK, £10 for a few bits of aubergine is expensive… but I love it!"; Yotam Ottolenghi's "cramped" designer cafés/delis may be "shockingly pricey" (and "queueing is a bore"), but "who can resist" their "over-indulgent" cakes, "tempting" salads and amazing "upmarket tapas"; a wow for brunch too. / www.ottolenghi.co.uk; 10.15 pm; W8 & W11 8 pm, Sat 7 pm, Sun 6 pm; N1 closed Sun D; Holland St takeaway only; W11 & SW1 no booking, N1 booking for D only.

(Brasserie)
Oxo Tower SE1   £70   ⑤④❸
Barge House St   7803 3888   9–3A
It can be "romantic on a sunny summer evening" (or "perfect for out-of-town clients"), but otherwise "why would you want to go" even to the cheaper section of this South Bank landmark, where "you pay for the view"… and get little else besides? / www.harveynichols.com/restaurants/oxo-tower-london; 11 pm, Sun 10.30 pm; set always available £43 (FP).

(Restaurant)
Oxo Tower SE1   £81   ⑤⑤④
Barge House St   7803 3888   9–3A
"A criminal waste of one of London's best views"; the grander section on the sixth floor of this South Bank landmark serves up "dreadful" food and service is "below-average" too; it's also "wildly overpriced" – "only go if someone deep-pocketed wants to take you!" / www.harveynichols.com; 11 pm, Sun 10 pm.

Ozer W1 £42 ④④④
5 Langham Pl 7323 0505 3–1C
"Reliable, if unexciting" – this well-appointed Turkish restaurant,
just north of Oxford Circus, is a popular canteen for "BBC types"
(Broadcasting House being opposite), theatre-goers and shoppers.
/ www.sofra.co.uk; 11 pm; set weekday L & pre-theatre £27 (FP).

Le P'tit Normand SW18 £37 ❸②❸
185 Merton Rd 8871 0233 10–2B
"A little gem" of a Gallic bistro, "hidden-away in the depths
of Southfields"; its "charming patron" presides over an old-fashioned
experience worth seeking out for its consistent "good value".
/ www.leptitnormand.co.uk; 10 pm; closed Mon, Sat L & Sun D.

Pacific Oriental EC2 £48 ④❸❸
52 Threadneedle St 0871 704 4060 9–2C
"Assembly line" pan-Asian dishes come at "pretty astronomical"
prices, at this large-scale bar/brasserie/restaurant; but, hey, this is the
City, and the attractive conversion of a former banking hall helps
create a "relaxed and informal" atmosphere.
/ www.orientalrestaurantgroup.co.uk; 10.30 pm; closed Sat & Sun; no trainers.

The Paddyfield SW12 £25 ❷④❸
4 Bedford Hill 8772 1145 10–2C
This "closely-packed" Balham canteen has "incredibly friendly
(if erratic) service", and serves "delicious Vietnamese food for very
little money"; "BYO is a massive bonus". / www.thepaddyfield.co.uk;
11.30 pm; D only, closed Mon; no credit cards.

Il Pagliaccio SW6 £34 ④❸❶
182-184 Wandsworth Bridge Rd 7371 5253 10–1B
"Opera nights are the best", but – thanks to the "friendly singing
waiters" – the atmosphere at this "cheap and cheerful" Sands End
pizzeria is "always lively"; a visit here is "always an easy option with
kids". / www.paggs.co.uk; midnight; no Amex.

Le Pain Quotidien £34 ④④❸
Branches throughout London
"Lovely coffee in bowls", served with "yummy bread and a huge array
of spreads", helps make these "relaxed" Belgian communal-cafés
a good place to start the day, even if they are a trifle
"more expensive than they should be"; "great salads and
sandwiches" too. / www.painquotidien.com; 7 pm-10 pm; no booking
at some branches, especially at weekends.

The Painted Heron SW10 £53 ❶❷❸
112 Cheyne Walk 7351 5232 5–3B
"Unconventional", "very refined" food from "market-fresh"
ingredients puts this "hidden gem" (by Chelsea Embankment) well
up London's premier league of top subcontinentals – it's "not as
flashy" as the bigger names, but "every bit as good".
/ www.thepaintedheron.com; 11 pm, Sun 10.30 pm; D only, Sun open L & D.

The Palm SW1 £80 ④④⑤
1 Pont St 7201 0710 5–1D
Fans of this NYC-to-Knightsbridge steakhouse concede it's "pricey",
buy say it offers "the best USDA sirloin in town"; there are many
sceptics, however, for whom it's just "stupidly expensive".
/ www.thepalm.com/london; 11 pm, Sun 10 pm; closed weekday L.

The Palmerston SE22 £39 ❷❷❸
91 Lordship Ln 8693 1629 1–4D
"The secret is well and truly out" – the "seasonal" food at this "bubbly" East Dulwich gastropub is "darn good"; best place to sit is the "comforting wood-panelled back room". / www.thepalmerston.net; 10 pm, Sun 9.30 pm.

Palmyra TW9 £36 ❸❷④
277 Sandycombe Rd 8948 7019 1–3A
"The best falafels" are a highlight of the "very fresh" and "carefully cooked" dishes on offer at this "well-kept, quiet and pleasant" Lebanese local, in Kew. / www.palmyrarestaurant.co.uk; 10.30 pm; no Amex.

The Pantechnicon SW1 £53 ❸❸❷
10 Motcomb St 7730 6074 5–1D
"What a smart pub!" – this "comfy" and "convivial" Belgravia boozer could easily double as a gentleman's club; it may be "a little overpriced", but the food is "consistently good". / www.thepantechnicon.com; 10 pm downstairs/9.30 pm upstairs.

Pantry SW18 £18 ❸❸❸
342 Old York Rd 8871 0713 10–2B
"Much-loved and frequented", this Wandsworth café is ideal "for a quick salad or sandwich". / www.thepantrylondon.com; L only; no Amex.

Paolina Café WC1 £24 ❸④⑤
181 Kings Cross Rd 7278 8176 8–3D
In King's Cross, a "shabby", "order-by-numbers" Thai café where you're unlikely to spot the man from Michelin – "for those brave enough to step in, however, it's a real find". / 10 pm; closed Sat L & Sun; no credit cards.

Pappa Ciccia £34 ❸❸④
105-107 Munster Rd, SW6 7384 1884 10–1B
41 Fulham High St, SW6 7736 0900 10–1B
These "cheap 'n' cheerful" pizzerias have quite a local following; the Fulham High Street branch is perhaps the better of the two (and Putney is no more). / www.pappaciccia.com; 11 pm, Sat & Sun 11.30 pm; SW6 no credit cards.

Paradise by Way of Kensal Green W10 £38 ❷❷❶
19 Kilburn Ln 8969 0098 1–2B
"There's always a fun time to be had", at this "lovely" Kensal Green stalwart – a "sprawling" places with many rooms, terraces and a garden; the cooking's "almost too good to be called pub food" – "go early to avoid the scrum" (especially at weekends). / www.theparadise.co.uk; 10.30 pm, Sun 9 pm; no Amex.

El Parador NW1 £34 ❷❶❸
245 Eversholt St 7387 2789 8–3C
"A real find"; this "lovely little tapas bar", near Mornington Crescent, combines "shockingly good" food (including "a fantastic selection for veggies"), with an "interesting wine list"; there's even a "wonderful garden" too. / www.elparadorlondon.com; 11 pm, Fri-Sat 11.30 pm, Sun 9.30 pm; closed Sat L & Sun L; no Amex.

Paramount Centre Point WC1 £66 ④④❶
101-103 New Oxford St 7420 2900 4–1A
"You're definitely paying for the view" ("stunning"), when you visit the 32nd floor of Centre Point; the food is "distinctly average" and service "random"… "but you won't notice, as you'll be staring out of the window". / www.paramount.uk.net; 10.30 pm; set weekday L £42 (FP).

FSA

The Parlour Bar E14 £40 ⑤⑤⑤
Park Pavillion, 40 Canada Square Pk 0845 468 0100 11–1C
"Standards have dropped", at this "once-impressive" yearling, in a
Canary Wharf pavilion – service is "poor", and "the food gets more
mediocre with every visit". / www.theparlourbar.co.uk; 10 pm, Sun 6 pm.

Pasha SW7 £50 ⑤④❷
1 Gloucester Rd 7589 7969 5–1B
"Lovely, exotic decor" has long been the highlight at this low-profile
South Kensington Moroccan – just as well, as service is "not that
observant", and "some of the food looks like school dinners".
/ www.pasha-restaurant.co.uk; 10.45 pm, Sat & Sun 11.45 pm.

Patara £47 ❷❸❸
15 Greek St, W1 7437 1071 4–2A
3-7 Maddox St, W1 7499 6008 3–2C
181 Fulham Rd, SW3 7351 5692 5–2C
9 Beauchamp Pl, SW3 7581 8820 5–1C
"My Thai government pals take me here, so they must be authentic!"
– these "smart" and "bustling" Asian havens make a very "reliable"
option, thanks to their "polite" service and "wonderfully flavoursome"
cooking. / www.pataralondon.com; 10.30 pm.

Paternoster Chop House EC4 £53 ⑤⑤④
Warwick Ct, Paternoster Sq 7029 9400 9–2B
A D&D group operation, by St Paul's, whose "macho" meat-driven
approach "suits City business"; it has "perfect" al fresco tables too,
but the interior is "noisy", service "incredibly amateurish", the food
"very ordinary" and prices "ridiculous"! / www.danddlondon.com;
10.30 pm; closed Sat & Sun D.

Patio W12 £30 ❸❷❶
5 Goldhawk Rd 8743 5194 7–1C
"A chat with the owner is a 'must'", when visiting this very
"welcoming" Polish restaurant, right on Shepherd's Bush; its "solid,
honest, homely food", and range of vodkas – all at bargain prices –
help make it a great budget party venue. / www.patiolondon.com;
11.30 pm; closed Sat L & Sun L.

Pâtisserie Valerie £28 ⑤⑤④
Branches throughout London
"It looks the same, but oh dear it's lost its way!"; as it goes national,
this expanding pâtisserie chain (whose original Soho branch allegedly
introduced '30s-Britain to the croissant) still does "reliable" breakfasts
and "yummy" cakes, but in other respects is now "very ordinary".
/ www.patisserie-valerie.co.uk; 5 pm-8 pm; Old Compton St 7.30 pm, Wed-Sat
10.30 pm; Hans Cr 11.30 pm; no booking except Old Compton St Sun-Thu.

Patogh W1 £14 ❷❸④
8 Crawford Pl 7262 4015 6–1D
It looks a little "shabby" (like a "hole in the wall") but this
Marylebone Iranian really is "a joy" – its "fresh-grilled meats" and its
"home-made flat breads" all come "for an absolute pittance"; BYO.
/ 11 pm; no credit cards.

Patterson's W1 £71 ❸❸④
4 Mill St 7499 1308 3–2C
A "low-key family-run eatery" like this is a rarity in Mayfair, and many
fans seek out its "hidden-away" location (near Savile Row),
not least as a venue for business; the food has drifted a bit in recent
times, but is still often "superb". / www.pattersonsrestaurant.co.uk; 11 pm;
closed Sat L & Sun.

154

FSA

Paul   £32   ❸④❸
115 Marylebone High St, W1   7224 5615   2–1A
29-30 Bedford St, WC2   7836 3304   4–3C
"Fabulous sandwiches" (using "proper French bread"), "lovely"
pastries, and "stand-out" macaroons make it worth braving the oft-
"appalling" service of these café-outposts of France's biggest high
street bakery; "the nicest London branch is the Bedford St WC2
original". / www.paul-uk.com; 7 pm-8.30 pm; no booking.

Pearl WC1   £85   ④④❸
252 High Holborn   7829 7000   2–1D
This is "a jewel of a restaurant", say fans of this "impressive" ("rather
cavernous") and "sumptuously furnished" Holborn dining room;
but while Jun Tanaka's cuisine is "witty" and "adventurous",
"massive" bills depress reporter satisfaction to only a middling level
overall. / www.pearl-restaurant.com; 10 pm; closed Sat L & Sun; set weekday L
£46 (FP).

Pearl Liang W2   £39   ❶❷❷
8 Sheldon Sq   7289 7000   6–1C
"A great find... if you can find it!"; this "upmarket" Chinese
basement, hidden-away "in the Paddington Basin complex",
is "a revelation" that's "worth the trek" – the cuisine, in particular
the "wonderful" dim sum, is "simply exceptional".
/ www.pearlliang.co.uk; 11 pm.

The Peasant EC1   £45   ④❸❸
240 St John St   7336 7726   8–3D
All the more worth knowing about in the "no-man's-land" north
of Smithfield, a fine Victorian pub, which offers "decent" –
and sometimes "adventurous" – cooking; "the upstairs dining room
is preferable to the draughty downstairs bar". / www.thepeasant.co.uk;
10.45 pm, Sun 9.30 pm.

Pellicano SW3   £58   ❸❸④
19-21 Elystan St   7589 3718   5–2C
This backstreet Italian is, say fans, "the best local in Chelsea" –
"the sort of place where you eat two or three times a week";
even they can find its ambience a bit "bland", though, and critics say
this is "surely the establishment for which the term 'curate's egg' was
invented". / www.pellicanorestaurant.co.uk; 11 pm, Sun 9.30 pm;
set weekday L £37 (FP).

E Pellicci E2   £14   ❸❷❶
332 Bethnal Green Rd   7739 4873   12–1D
"The perfect East End Italian greasy spoon", this Art Deco gem
(the interior is listed) is "well worth a trip across town", especially for
breakfast; staff "treat you like family" and, crowd-wise, "this is where
old and new East End meet". / 4.15 pm; L only, closed Sun; no credit cards.

Peninsular
Holiday Inn Express SE10   £34   ❷④④
85 Bugsbys Way   8858 2028   1–3D
"Terrific-value dim sum" makes it worth seeking out this crushed-in
Greenwich spot – something of "a find", at the foot of a Holiday Inn
(even if the premises are as atmospheric as that description
suggests). / www.mychinesefood.co.uk/; 11.30 pm, Sun 11 pm.

155

The Pepper Tree SW4　　　£25　❸❸❸
19 Clapham Common S'side　7622 1758　10–2D
An "excellent", cheap 'n' cheerful Thai canteen, by Clapham South,
that "does exactly what it says on the tin" – "they get you in, the food
takes literally seconds to come, and it always tastes great".
/ www.thepeppertree.co.uk; 11 pm, Sun & Mon 10.30 pm; no Amex;
no booking at D.

Pescatori　　　£50　❸❷❹
11 Dover St, W1　7493 2652　3–3C
55-57 Charlotte St, W1　7580 3289　2–1C
To critics, these West End Italians are "dull" and
"too commercialised"; to their friends, though, they're an "institution",
offering "reliable" fish dishes, and "smart, helpful and attentive"
service. / www.pescatori.co.uk; 11 pm; closed Sat L & Sun.

Petek N4　　　£30　❷❷❷
94-96 Stroud Green Rd　7619 3933　8–1D
"Miles better than most Turkish restaurants in London", this "family-
friendly" Finsbury Park spot has been firing impressively on all
cylinders since its expansion, and it's still "always busy".
/ www.petekrestaurant.co.uk; 11 pm.

Petersham Hotel TW10　　　£61　❸❷❷
Nightingale Ln　8940 7471　1–4A
This "classy old-school dining room" has a "beautiful location
overlooking the Thames", and is especially known as a "scenic
Sunday lunch destination"; the occasional off-day, however, is not
unknown. / www.petershamhotel.co.uk; Mon-Sat 9.30 pm, Sun 8.30 pm.

Petersham Nurseries TW10　　　£56　❷❹❶
Church Ln, Off Petersham Rd　8605 3627　1–4A
A "rustic-chic" greenhouse provides the "beautiful" setting for Skye
Gyngell's "unique" café, where the "simple" and "seasonal" cooking
can be "unbelievably wonderful"; the "mountainous" prices seem
increasingly "silly" though – "it is, at the end of the day, in a garden
centre"! / www.petershamnurseries.com; L only, closed Mon.

La Petite Auberge N1　　　£35　❹❸❷
283 Upper St　7359 1046　8–2D
"It feels like rural France", at this "cosy" joint, near Islington's Almeida
Theatre – service is "very friendly" and the food, if rather "retro",
is "reasonably priced". / www.petiteauberge.co.uk; 11 pm, Fri & Sat
11.30 pm, Sun 10.30 pm; set weekday L £20 (FP).

La Petite Maison W1　　　£77　❷❷❷
54 Brook's Mews　7495 4774　3–2B
"Go through the heavy velvet curtain, and you're in the South
of France", at this glamorous Mayfair "oasis", where the "Provençal
small plates" are designed for sharing; OK, "prices are nuts",
but "everything on the menu is fresh and light, and always amazing".
/ www.lpmlondon.co.uk; 10.30 pm, Sun 9 pm.

Pétrus SW1　　　£85　❹❷❸
1 Kinnerton St　7592 1609　5–1D
"It's time to stop Gordon-bashing", say fans of his luxurious
Belgravian two-year-old, who see much to praise in the "phenomenal"
wine and "impeccable" service, and the "bargain set lunch" too;
sceptics say the cuisine is "competent" enough, but they find
it "without spirit" – "like in an upmarket international hotel chain".
/ www.gordonramsay.com/petrus; 10 pm; closed Sun; no trainers; set always
available £56 (FP).

FSA

Pham Sushi EC1 £32 ❶④④
159 Whitecross St 7251 6336 12–2A
It looks "lacklustre" – "a bare and charmless room" – but this
Japanese café, near the Barbican, "goes from strength to strength",
offering "some of the best sushi in town", and at "affordable" prices
too. / www.phamsushi.co.uk; 10 pm; closed Sat L & Sun.

The Phene SW3 £43 ④④❷
9 Phene St 7352 9898 5–3C
This leafily-located pub has, post-refurb, taken on "an eclectic and
relaxed look", and makes an attractive hang-out for the Chelsea
crowd; the food's OK, but – plus ça change – the star of the show
is the "fantastic garden" (given a St Tropez-style make-over in recent
times). / www.thephene.com; 10 pm.

Pho £33 ❷❸❸
163-165 Wardour St, W1 7434 3938 3–1D NEW
3 Great Titchfield St, W1 7436 0111 3–1C
Westfield, Ariel Way, W12 07824 662320 7–1C
86 St John St, EC1 7253 7624 9–1A
"Big bowls" of "cheap", "simple" and "vibrant" Vietnamese dishes –
particularly pho ('feu') to slurp – is making a major hit of these
"cramped" and "authentic" cafés, which (unusually for an expanding
chain) "just get better year-on-year". / www.phocafe.co.uk; EC1 10 pm,
Fri & Sat 10.30 pm; W1 10.30 pm; W12 9 pm, Sat 7 pm, Sun 6 pm;
EC1 closed Sat L & Sun; W1 closed Sun; no Amex; no booking.

The Phoenix SW3 £42 ④❺❸
23 Smith St 7730 9182 5–2D
A "buzzy" Chelsea gastropub, with an atmospheric dining room,
and a handy location, just off the King's Road; "no matter how empty
or full the place is", however, "the service lets it down"!
/ www.geronimo-inns.co.uk; 10 pm.

Phoenix Palace NW1 £44 ❷❸❸
5-9 Glentworth St 7486 3515 2–1A
"Close to an authentic Hong Kong experience"... "but you can
book!" – this "just-about-the-right-side-of-gaudy" Baker Street
"institution" serves "wonderful, un-Anglicised cooking, with plenty
of unusual dishes", plus some of "the finest dim sum in the UK";
"it's always full of Asian families". / www.phoenixpalace.co.uk; 11.15 pm,
Sun 10.30 pm.

Piccolino £44 ④④④
21 Heddon St, W1 7287 4029 3–2C
38 High St, SW19 8946 8019 10–2B
11 Exchange Sq, EC2 7375 2568 12–2B
The food may be "nothing out-of-the-ordinary", but this "buzzing"
Italian chain has its uses – the Heddon Street branch, for example,
is in a "peaceful pedestrianised oasis", off Regent St, with lovely
al fresco tables. / www.piccolinorestaurants.co.uk; 11 pm, Sun 10 pm;
EC2 closed Sat & Sun.

PIED À TERRE W1 £96 ❶❷❷
34 Charlotte St 7636 1178 2–1C
The former chef has recently departed, but – fingers crossed – we've
kept the survey rating of David Moore's "inspiring" Fitzrovia
townhouse – a "class act" long known for its "professional" style,
"thought-provoking" cuisine, and "incredible" wine; a downside? –
the interior can seem "cramped and oddly configured".
/ www.pied-a-terre.co.uk; 10.45 pm; closed Sat L & Sun; no Maestro; booking:
max 7; set weekday L £46 (FP), set pre-theatre £57 (FP).

157

The Pig's Ear SW3 £48 ❸❸❶
35 Old Church St 7352 2908 5–3C
"Quirky" and "wonderfully atmospheric", the upstairs dining room
is the highlight at this "beautiful" Art Nouveau-themed pub, tucked
away off the King's Road – a "friendly" spot, with "competent"
cooking. / www.thepigsear.info; 10 pm; closed Sun D.

Pinchito EC1 £31 ❹❸❶
32 Featherstone St 7490 0121 12–1A
"For a good night out", near Old Street, this "laid-back and bustling"
haunt – with its "decadent cocktails" – may be worth checking out;
decent tapas play a supporting role. / www.pinchito.co.uk; 11 pm; closed
Sat L & Sun.

ping pong £32 ❹❹❸
10 Paddington St, W1 7009 9600 2–1A
29a James St, W1 7034 3100 3–1A
45 Gt Marlborough St, W1 7851 6969 3–2C
48 Eastcastle St, W1 7079 0550 3–1C
48 Newman St, W1 7291 3080 3–1C
74-76 Westbourne Grove, W2 7313 9832 6–1B
83-84 Hampstead High St, NW3 7433 0930 8–2A
Southbank Centre, SE1 7960 4160 2–3D
3-6 Steward St, E1 7422 7650 9–2D
St Katharine Docks, E1 7680 7850 9–3D
3 Appold St, EC2 7422 0780 12–2B
Bow Bells Hs, 1 Bread St, EC4 7651 0880 9–2B
For a "fun" meal that's "quick and relatively cheap", these "slick"
dim sum (and cocktail) specialists have many fans; critics, though,
feel the menu "reads better than it tastes" – "what once seemed
an exciting new experience now just feels rather like a bland old
chain". / www.pingpongdimsum.com; 10 pm-11.30 pm; EC2 & EC4 closed
Sat & Sun; booking: min 8.

El Pirata W1 £36 ❹❷❶
5-6 Down St 7491 3810 3–4B
"Fantastic fun!"; especially "worth knowing about in a pricey area",
this "packed and buzzing" Mayfair haunt is "so friendly", and it
offers many "tasty tapas" too. / www.elpirata.co.uk; 11.30 pm; closed
Sat L & Sun; set weekday L £21 (FP).

El Pirata de Tapas W2 £30 ❸❷❷
115 Westbourne Grove 7727 5000 6–1B
"For an edgy, adventurous approach to tapas", some reporters really
rate this "narrow" and "very buzzy" Bayswater two-year-old; a few
repeat-visitors, though, feel the food's "lost a bit of its early-days
pizzaz". / www.elpiratadetapas.co.uk; 11 pm.

Pissarro W4 £47 ❹❹❸
Corney Reach Way 8994 3111 10–1A
Can't help feeling this Thames-side fixture, with an attractive
conservatory, trades on its "wonderful setting" – a quiet stretch
of towpath near Chiswick House; it does have its fans, but for
sceptics its "very unremarkable", and "expensive" too.
/ www.pissarro.co.uk; 10 pm.

Pizarro SE1 NEW
194 Bermondsey St awaiting tel 9–4D
Ex-Brindisa chef José Pizarro has barely got José open, and he's
already planning this new, more restaurant-like operation, to launch
in late-2011 on the site recently vacated by the Bermondsey Kitchen
(RIP).

Pizza East E1 £46 ❸❹❶
56 Shoreditch High St 7729 1888 12–1B
"An achingly hip hub for Shoreditch digerati" – Nick Jones's
"industrial-chic" warehouse-conversion serves *"thick-looking but crisp"*
pizza with an array of *"interesting toppings"*; *"non-beautiful people
may feel intimidated"*, however, by staff who are *"too trendy
to serve"*. / www.pizzaeast.com; Sun-Wed 11 pm, Thu midnight, Fri & Sat
1 am.

Pizza East Portobello W10 NEW £39
310 Portobello Rd 8969 4500 6–1A
*Shoreditch-chic comes to North Kensington, at this new offshoot –
on the former site of the Fat Badger, RIP – of Nick Jones's too-cool-
for-school East End pizzeria; it opened too late to figure in the survey,
but press reports suggest it's very like the original, if a touch less
'urban'.* / www.pizzaeastportobello.com.

Pizza Metro SW11 £36 ❸❸❷
64 Battersea Rise 7228 3812 10–2C
"Save on a trip to Naples!" – these *"chaotic"* (and *"bambino-
friendly"*) Italians are *"always very busy and relaxed"*, and they serve
the *"yummiest"* pizza (on metre-long trays) too; the new Notting Hill
branch is *"not as raucous"* as the Battersea original.
/ www.pizzametropizza.co.uk; 11 pm; closed weekday L; no Amex.

(Ciro's) Pizza Pomodoro SW3 £49 ❹❹❷
51 Beauchamp Pl 7589 1278 5–1C
"Fun and lively", this late-night Knightsbridge-cellar fixture is really
"all about the entertainment" – though it's *"cheap 'n' cheerful"*,
by local standards, the pizza *"could use an upgrade"*.
/ www.pomodoro.co.uk; 1 am; D only.

PizzaExpress £36 ❹❹❸
Branches throughout London
"Excellent new additions to the menu" have helped refresh the
offering of these gold-standard pizzerias – the survey's
most commented-upon chain; in other respects, however
"it's predictable in the best kind of way", including as *"a godsend with
kids"*. / www.pizzaexpress.co.uk; 11.30 pm-midnight; most City branches
closed all or part of weekend; no booking at most branches.

Pizzeria Malletti £7 ❷❸❸
26 Noel St, W1 7439 4096 3–1D
174-176 Clerkenwell Rd, EC1 7713 8665 2–1D
"Creative" pizzas draw an ardent fan club to these Soho (take-away
only) and Clerkenwell Italians; *"delicious risotto"* too. / 4.30 pm;
W1 cash only.

Pizzeria Oregano N1 £38 ❸❷❸
19 St Albans Pl 7288 1123 8–3D
Islington's best basic Italian – this *"bustling"* little café, down an
alleyway, is praised for its *"huge"* pizzas (with *"fantastic thin crusts"*)
and its *"lovely home-made pasta"*; *"energetic staff give quick service,
and a warm welcome to kids too"*. / 11 pm, Fri 11.30 pm, Sun 10.30 pm;
closed weekday L.

Pizzeria Pappagone N4 £32 ❸❷❸
131 Stroud Green Rd 7263 2114 8–1D
*"The owner makes you feel welcome, and there's a strong family
vibe"*, at this *"really buzzing"* Italian, near Crouch End, which serves
"huge portions of honest food" (in particular, *"proper pizza"*).
/ www.pizzeriapappagone.co.uk; midnight.

PJ's Bar and Grill SW3 £50 ④④❸
52 Fulham Rd 7581 0025 5–2C
*"Fun, reliable and boisterous", this US-themed South Kensington
bar/diner remains a top Euro/Sloane brunch spot; in general, though,
it can rather seem to be "relying on former glories" nowadays.
/ www.pjsbarandgrill.co.uk; 10.30 pm, Sun 10 pm.*

Plane Food TW6 £49 ④❸④
Heathrow Airport, Terminal 5 8897 4545 1–3A
*Views divide on Gordon Ramsay's airside diner; to critics it "exploits
its captive audience" with "very average" food at "inflated" prices –
for fans it's "a haven of sanity from the mayhem", and serves
"unbeatable breakfasts" (with a "perfect eggs Benedict" singled out
for praise). / www.gordonramsay.com; 9.30 pm.*

Plateau E14 £63 ⑤④④
Canada Pl 7715 7100 11–1C
*With its "huge windows overlooking Canada Square", this D&D
group operation is still – say fans – "probably Canary Wharf's
best restaurant"; critics of its "investment banker prices" and its "bog-
standard" cooking, though, say it "needs to compete better with new
arrivals hereabouts!" / www.plateaurestaurant.co.uk; 10 pm; closed
Sat L & Sun.*

Plum Valley W1 £34 ❸❷❸
20 Gerrard St 7494 4366 4–3A
*"Delicious dim sum all day" is a highlight of this dimly-lit, "cool and
contemporary" Chinatown scene; its more "nouvelle" culinary
aspirations, however, don't always come off. / 11.30 pm.*

Pod £13 ❸④④
124 High Holborn, WC1 3174 0541 2–1D
Tooley St, SE1 3174 0374 9–4D **NEW**
10 St Martin's Le Grand, EC1 3174 0399 9–2B
162-163 London Wall, EC2 7256 5506 9–2C
25 Exchange Sq, EC2 3174 0290 12–2B
Devonshire Sq, EC2 3174 0108 9–2D
5 Lloyds Ave, EC3 3174 0038 9–3D
1 Printer St, EC4 3174 0228 9–2A
75 King William St, EC4 7283 7460 9–3C **NEW**
*For "fresh and zingy" salads and snacks "on the go", this "healthy"
chain still has many fans; it's "not the cheapest", though, and its
ratings dipped a bit this year. / www.podfood.co.uk; 3 pm-4 pm; closed
Sat & Sun; no Amex.*

Poissonnerie de l'Avenue SW3 £67 ❸❸④
82 Sloane Ave 7589 2457 5–2C
*A notably "senior" clientele are drawn to this "elegant" –
but "crowded" and "expensive" – Chelsea "old-timer"; the lure? –
"simple but very palatable fresh fish and seafood".
/ www.poissonneriedelavenue.co.uk; 11.30 pm, Sun 11 pm.*

(Ognisko Polskie)
The Polish Club SW7 £49 ⑤④❸
55 Prince's Gate, Exhibition Rd 7589 4635 5–1C
*"A great dining space" – the time-warped interior of a grandly-housed
South Kensington émigrés' club – is the particular attraction of this
quirky venture; its basic Polish fodder plays a supporting role,
but most reporters have "no complaints". / www.ognisko.com; 11 pm;
no trainers; set weekday L £29 (FP).*

Pollen Street Social W1 NEW £64 ❶❶❷
8-10 Pollen St 7290 7600 3–2C
*Jason Atherton ('Mr Maze') was always one of the sharpest knives
in the Ramsay drawer, so it's no surprise that his first solo venture –
a "bright and hard-surfaced" Mayfair venue – is an instant smash hit:
dishes – not least the "amazing puds" – offer "excellent explorations
of flavour combinations". / www.pollenstreetsocial.com; 10.45 pm;
closed Sun.*

Polpetto
The French House W1 £35 ❷❷❶
49 Dean St 7734 1969 4–3A
*This "bijou" room, over a "characterful" Soho pub, has a certain
"je ne said quoi" for romantics; there's no booking at dinner (giving
ample scope for a glass of Ricard downstairs) but the Venetian tapas
– "better than at its parent, Polpo" – are "worth the wait".
/ www.polpetto.co.uk; 11 pm; closed Sun; book only at L.*

Polpo W1 £25 ❸❷❶
41 Beak St 7734 4479 3–2D
*"Always rammed" with an "interesting crowd", Russell Norman's
"very-NYC-Meatpacking-District" Soho haunt is just the job if you
want to feel "at the heart of the action"; the tapas-y food (notionally
Venetian) is "fine" too... "but the atmosphere's the thing".
/ www.polpo.co.uk; 11 pm, Sun 4 pm; closed Sun D; no bookings for D.*

Le Pont de la Tour SE1 £64 ④❸❷
36d Shad Thames 7403 8403 9–4D
*Fans "don't understand the perennially mixed reviews" this guide
gives to this "slick", "feel-good" D&D group Thames-sider, whose
"unbeatable views" of Tower Bridge help make it a 'natural' for
business or romance; there are still quite a few critics, though,
who find it "arrogant", and say it charges "high prices" for food that's
"15 years out of date!" / www.lepontdelatour.co.uk; 11 pm, Sun 10 pm;
no trainers.*

Popeseye £46 ❶❷❸
108 Blythe Rd, W14 7610 4578 7–1C
277 Upper Richmond Rd, SW15 8788 7733 10–2A
*"If you want a great steak, this is the place!" – this "quirky" duo
of west London bistros offer a "simple, meat-based formula that hits
the spot" (with "a fantastic wine list as a bonus"); the sole real
criticism? – "the decor needs improving". / www.popeseye.com;
10.30 pm; D only, closed Sun; no credit cards.*

La Porchetta Pizzeria £32 ❸❸❸
33 Boswell St, WC1 7242 2434 2–1D
141-142 Upper St, N1 7288 2488 8–2D
147 Stroud Green Rd, N4 7281 2892 8–1D
74-77 Chalk Farm Rd, NW1 7267 6822 8–2B
84-86 Rosebery Ave, EC1 7837 6060 9–1A
*Thanks to their "HUGE portions" of "fresh pizza" and other "home-
style dishes" – all "relatively cheap" – these "noisy" north London
Italians are always "very busy"; they're "very welcoming to kids" too.
/ www.laporchetta.net; last orders varies by branch; WC1 closed Sat L & Sun;
N1 closed Mon-Thu L; N4 closed weekday L; no Amex.*

Portal EC1 £61 ❷❷❷
88 St John St 7253 6950 9–1B
*"Portuguese food takes on a new dimension", at Antonio Correia's
"classy" Clerkenwell bar/restaurant, which has a "lovely"
conservatory, with an excellent terrace; there's a "phenomenal wine
list" too. / www.portalrestaurant.com; 10.15 pm; closed Sat L & Sun.*

FSA

La Porte des Indes W1 £63 ❸❹❷
32 Bryanston St   7224 0055   2–2A
"Imaginatively decorated" – *"think Rainforest Café for adults!"* –
this unexpectedly huge, subterranean joint, near Marble Arch, offers
a *"plush and exotic"* environment in which to enjoy some *"light"*
(and somewhat *"Frenchified"*) Indian cuisine. / www.laportedesindes.com;
11.30 pm, Sun 10.30 pm.

Porters English Restaurant WC2 £36 ❹❸❸
17 Henrietta St   7836 6466   4–3C
"Still perhaps mainly for tourists", but Lord Bradford's traditional-
English-styled Covent Garden eatery nonetheless provides hearty pies,
puds and other English fare at affordable prices; excellent-value set
menu. / www.porters.uk.com; 11.30 pm, Sun 10.30 pm; no Amex.

Il Portico W8 £46 ❸❶❷
277 Kensington High St   7602 6262   7–1D
It may *"really hark back to the Italians of the '60s and '70s"*,
but that's just how people like this *"basic"* – but *"warm"* and
"welcoming" – trattoria, next to the Kensington Odeon.
/ www.ilportico.co.uk; 11 pm; closed Sun.

Portobello Ristorante W11 £40 ❸❹❹
7 Ladbroke Rd   7221 1373   6–2B
"A bit chaotic" – but *"too busy to be all that atmospheric!"* –
this *"wildly popular"* Notting Hill Italian offers some good *"regional"*
cooking, including *"proper pizza"* (sold by the metre); *"the terrace
is lovely in summer"*. / www.portobellolondon.co.uk; 11 pm, Sun 10.15 pm;
set dinner £21 (FP).

The Portrait
National Portrait Gallery WC2 £48 ❹❷❶
St Martin's Pl   7312 2490   4–4B
"Flick between your lover's eyes and the views of the London skyline",
as you enjoy your meal at this top-floor venue, which enjoys
a *"stunning"* West End panorama; the food – *"nothing really
to grumble about"* – plays rather a supporting role. / www.searcys.co.uk;
Thu-Fri 8.30 pm; Sat-Wed closed D.

La Poule au Pot SW1 £56 ❸❸❶
231 Ebury St   7730 7763   5–2D
"Just the kind of place where a girl hopes to be proposed to!" –
this *"unashamedly old-fashioned"* Pimlico den is a *"higgledy piggledy"*
sprawl, with *"dark, candlelit corners"* and *"colourful"*, if somewhat
"arrogant", staff, who offer *"rustic"* Gallic scoff in *"large portions"*.
/ 11 pm, Sun 10 pm.

Pret A Manger £13 ❸❷❹
Branches throughout London
"Nowhere else quite matches up", say fans of this *"steadfast"*
London-based *"pit stop"* chain, whose empire now spans three
continents; the coffee, soup, sarnies and so on are all *"utterly
reliable"*, but the secret weapon is the same as ever –
the *"indefatigable cheeriness"* of the staff. / www.pret.com; generally
4 pm-6 pm; closed Sun (except some West End branches); City branches
closed Sat & Sun; no Amex; no booking.

Prince Albert NW1 £36 ❸❸❸
163 Royal College St   7485 0270   8–3C
"Whether in the relaxed pub, or the stylish restaurant above", this –
slightly *"erratic"* – Camden Town boozer is generally *"good value"*.
/ www.princealbertcamden.com; 11 pm, Sun 10.30 pm; no Amex.

The Prince Albert SW11   £40   ④❸❷
85 Albert Bridge Rd   7228 0923   5–4C
*"So popular you usually need to book", this "laid-back" boozer
(with good al fresco seating) goes down very well with those who live
round Battersea Park; the "unadventurous pub grub", however,
"doesn't always live up to expectations".
/ www.theprincealbertbattersea.co.uk; 10 pm, Sun 9 pm.*

The Prince Of Wales SW15   £42   ❸④❸
138 Upper Richmond Rd   8788 1552   10–2B
*"Super pub food, great beers, and the best chips" – all factors in the
success of this "upmarket gastropub" near East Putney station;
service, however, "can fluctuate". / www.princeofwalesputney.co.uk; 10 pm.*

Princess Garden W1   £59   ❷❷❸
8-10 North Audley St   7493 3223   3–2A
*"Swankily-located", this "well-spaced" and "brightly-lit" Mayfair
Chinese may be, but it is nonetheless applauded for its "friendly"
approach (including to families) and for dim sum that – remarkably –
offers "great value for money"; more substantial fare is "pricey but
worth it". / www.princessgardenofmayfair.com; 11.45 pm, Sun 10.45 pm.*

Princess of Shoreditch EC2   £45   ❷❸❸
76 Paul St   7729 9270   12–1B
*"A favourite gastropub of a very high standard", in Shoreditch; there's
a lively bar or – up the spiral staircase – a quieter mezzanine.
/ www.theprincessofshoreditch.com; 11 pm, Sun 10.30 pm.*

Princess Victoria W12   £46   ❷❷❷
217 Uxbridge Rd   8749 5886   7–1B
*"An incredible find in a shabby bit of Shepherd's Bush";
this "sympathetically restored" gin palace is a "fine local stalwart"
nowadays, offering "surprisingly excellent" food, a notably "classy"
wine list, "enthusiastic" service and "a nice vibe" too.
/ www.princessvictoria.co.uk; 10.30 pm, Sun 9.30 pm; no Amex; set weekday L
£27 (FP).*

Princi W1   £25   ❸④❷
135 Wardour St   7478 8888   3–2D
*"A younger crowd, who think the place über-cool" hangs out "at all
hours", at this "cosmopolitan" Soho café, where "brilliant" Italian
pastries (and breads) start the day, and "mouthwatering" savouries
and cakes become available later on; the downside? – expect
to stand. / www.princi.co.uk; midnight, Sun 10 pm; no booking.*

Prism EC3   £64   ④④④
147 Leadenhall St   7256 3875   9–2D
*"Convenience for business" – and a "smart" interior too –
must explain the continuing existence of this Harvey Nics-owned
restaurant in a former City banking hall; it's certainly not the prices
("not cheap") or the cuisine ("hit-and-miss"). / www.harveynichols.com;
10 pm; closed Sat & Sun.*

Prix Fixe W1   £29   ④❸❸
39 Dean St   7734 5976   4–2A
*The brasserie fare is decent enough, but it is the price which is – in a
good way – "the stand-out feature", at this "noisy" Soho bistro.
/ www.prixfixe.net; Wed-Sat 11.30 pm, Sun-Tue 11 pm.*

The Providores W1   £61   ③④④
109 Marylebone High St   7935 6175   2–1A
Peter Gordon's fusion menu is "so exciting", and it's "perfectly matched" with "punchy" wines too, say fans of the "rammed" space over the Tapa Room; critics, citing "hefty" bills and "seriously arrogant" service, are less convinced. / www.theprovidores.co.uk; 10.30 pm.

(Tapa Room)
The Providores W1   £48   ②④④
109 Marylebone High St   7935 6175   2–1A
"Peter Gordon's fusion-food makes for a terrific brunch" – the top time to visit his "very cramped" but "buzzy" bar/diner, in Marylebone; more serious dining involves "some outlandish food combos" – results can be "bizarre", but more often they are "spectacular". / www.theprovidores.co.uk; 10.30 pm, Sun 10 pm.

The Punch Tavern EC4   £29   ③④③
99 Fleet St   7353 6658   9–2A
"A great place for tourists and office-workers", this Victorian tavern, near Ludgate Circus, is "worth a visit for the architecture alone"; by pub standards, the food is generally "better than average" too. / www.punchtavern.com; 10 pm, Sun 7 pm; closed Sat D.

Putney Station SW15   £35   ④④③
94-98 Upper Richmond Rd   8780 0242   10–2B
One of John Brinkley's lesser-known ventures, this Putney stand-by is nonetheless true to his DNA – its comfort fare is "ordinary", but fans "love it" for its "extensive and reasonably-priced wine list". / www.brinkleys.com; midnight, Sun 4 pm; closed Sun D.

Quadrato
Four Seasons Hotel E14   £68   ④④⑤
Westferry Circus   7510 1857   11–1B
A grand Canary Wharf hotel where "the brunch buffet is just 'wow'", and the terrace can be "lovely" too; the interior is "very boring and corporate", though – a fact you may dwell on as the sometimes "very slow" service brings "pricey" Italian dishes that are "decent but not outstanding". / www.fourseasons.com; 10.30 pm.

Quaglino's SW1   £69   ⑤⑤⑤
16 Bury St   7930 6767   3–3D
Owned by the D&D (ex-Conran) group, this cavernous '90s basement, in St James's, offers "boring, boring, boring" brasserie fare at prices that too often seem "a complete rip-off"; it doesn't help that some reporters don't feel so much fed as "processed". / www.quaglinos.co.uk; 10.30 pm, Fri & Sat 11 pm; closed Sun; no trainers; set weekday L £44 (FP).

Quantus W4 NEW   £41   ③②③
38 Devonshire Rd   8994 0488   7–2A
Almost opposite La Trompette, this Chiswick newcomer inspires mixed views; to fans, its "warm service", "quirky" decor and "short-but-tempting" menu "scores highly in every way" – doubters, though, sensing local hype, say it "lacks flair". / www.quantus-london.com; 11 pm; closed Sat L.

Queen's Head W6   £36   ④②②
13 Brook Grn   7603 3174   7–1C
In summer, this picturesque Brook Green boozer comes into its own, thanks to its "most enormous and secluded garden" ("more like you'd expect in the 'burbs"); it serves a notably varied menu – more exotic choices are best avoided... / www.fullers.co.uk; 10 pm, Sun 9 pm.

Queen's Head & Artichoke NW1   £41   ④④❸
30-32 Albany St   7916 6206   8–4B
The "extensive" tapas menu in the bar is the best bet at this "lively"
("manic") boozer, near Regent's Park, whose "attractive" upstairs
room also offers a wide menu; it's generally a sound performer,
but this past year saw a few 'disasters' too. / www.theartichoke.net;
10.15 pm.

The Queens Arms SW1   £42   ❸❸❸
11 Warwick Way   7834 3313   2–4B
"A real 'find', in something of a culinary desert" – this Pimlico
"bistro/pub" is a "home-from-home" for regulars, who proclaim the
attractions of its "super" British dishes, and its "super-friendly" staff
too. / www.thequeensarmspimlico.co.uk; 10 pm.

Le Querce   £37   ❶❷❷
66-68 Brockley Rise, SE23   8690 3761   1–4D
17 Montpelier Vale, SE3   8852 9226   1–3D NEW
"Simply brilliant" and "adventurous" Sardinian fare inspires rave
reviews for this family-run Brockely favourite, where culinary highlights
include "delicious" pasta, "perfect pizza", and basil-, beetroot- and
garlic-flavoured... er, ice cream; early reports say its new Blackheath
sibling is "spot on" too. / SE23 10 pm, Sun 9 pm; SE3 10.30 pm,
Sun 8.30 pm; SE23 closed Mon & Tue L; SE3 closed Mon.

Quilon SW1   £56   ❶❶④
41 Buckingham Gate   7821 1899   2–4B
"As far from a standard Indian as a Rolls-Royce is from a scooter",
this "poised" Goan/Keralan operation offers "perfectly-spiced" food,
and service as "magically unobtrusive" as you'd hope to find at nearby
Buck House; such a shame, then, that – even by hotel standards –
the decor is deadly "dull". / www.quilon.co.uk; 11 pm, Sun 10.30 pm;
closed Sat L.

Quince
The May Fair Hotel W1 NEW   £73   ④❸⑤
Stratton St   7915 3892   3–3C
A bizarre, low-ceilinged Mayfair newcomer, whose garish interior's
supposedly Ottoman character feels as if it's been done 'by numbers';
there's nothing wrong with ex-Baltic chef (and esteemed cookbook-
writer) Silvena Rowe's cuisine, but is it really so much better than you
could find in Dalston, for a quarter of the price? / Rated on Editors' visit;
www.quincelondon.com; 10 pm.

Quirinale SW1   £60   ❷❶❸
North Ct, 1 Gt Peter St   7222 7080   2–4C
"Hidden-away near the Houses of Parliament", this "airy", "discreet"
and "comfortable" (if somewhat "corporate") basement "gem" is well
worth seeking out for its "interesting" and "eclectic" cucina
all'Italiana; "excellent-value" lunchtime prix-fixe. / www.quirinale.co.uk;
10.30 pm; closed Sat & Sun; set weekday L & pre theatre £36 (FP).

Quo Vadis W1   £58   ❷❷❷
26-29 Dean St   7437 9585   4–2A
"Sam and Eddie Hart run a tight ship", and their "club-like" and
"polished" Soho spot put in a "first-class" performance this year;
the British comfort-food menu is extremely "competently prepared",
if perhaps a little "safe". / www.quovadissoho.co.uk; 10.45 pm; closed Sun;
set pre theatre £37 (FP).

Racine SW3 £66 ❸❷❸
239 Brompton Rd 7584 4477 5–2C
"You are transported to Paris", when you visit Henry Harris's "old-fashioned-in-a-really-good-way" Knightsbridge bistro, which is widely acclaimed for its "intelligently-realised" cuisine; "prices are high", though, and drifting ratings tend to confirm that it's "getting a bit complacent". / www.racine-restaurant.com; 10.30 pm, Sun 10 pm; set always available £36 (FP).

Ragam W1 £27 ❶❷⑤
57 Cleveland St 7636 9098 2–1B
"Who cares about the dodgy decor?" – and that's after the recent redecoration! – at this "tiny and cramped" BYO dive, near the Telecom Tower; after more than twenty years, the Keralan dishes still "rock", and are still "tremendous value for money". / www.ragam.co.uk; 10.45 pm, Fri & Sat 11 pm, Sun 10 pm.

Randa W8 £45 ❸❸④
23 Kensington Church St 7937 5363 5–1A
An unlikely Lebanese pub-conversion, near Kensington High Street, offering "fresh" and "authentic" fare; service ebbs and flows, but it's "friendly" enough. / www.maroush.com; midnight.

Randall & Aubin W1 £44 ❸❸❷
16 Brewer St 7287 4447 3–2D
"It's great watching the world go by", sitting perched on a stool at this "fun" spot, "edgily-located" in the sleazy heart of Soho – a "loud" and "very buzzy" place, serving "superb", if "pricey", seafood; expect to queue. / www.randallandaubin.co.uk; 11 pm, Sun 10 pm; no booking.

Rani N3 £26 ❷❸④
7 Long Ln 8349 4386 1–1B
The interior may be "dull", but that does nothing to dim the "evergreen" charm of this "very good veggie Indian", whose excellent-value buffet includes "outstanding stuffed breads", plus "an excellent range of chutneys", "all made in-house". / www.raniuk.com; 10 pm; D only, ex Sun open L & D.

Ranoush £45 ❷④④
22 Brompton Rd, SW1 7235 6999 5–1D
338 King's Rd, SW3 7352 0044 5–3C
43 Edgware Rd, W2 7723 5929 6–1D
86 Kensington High St, W8 7938 2234 5–1A
"The best shawarma in town" is the special reason to seek out these Lebanese café/take-aways – especially in the early hours, they "tick all the boxes for a quick, cheap, tasty bite". / www.maroush.com; 1 am-3 am.

Ransome's Dock SW11 £50 ④❸④
35 Parkgate Rd 7223 1611 5–4C
This Battersea "old-stager" is an œnophile's dream, and its "brilliantly adventurous" wine list offers "amazing value"; perhaps the menu "could do with a shake-up", though? – the faithful may say the food "never disappoints", but critics find it ever more "lacklustre". / www.ransomesdock.co.uk; 11 pm; closed Sun D.

Raoul's Café   £39   ④⑤④
105-107 Talbot Rd, W11   7229 2400   6–1B
113-115 Hammersmith Grove, W6   8741 3692   7–1C **NEW**
13 Clifton Rd, W9   7289 7313   8–4A
*"If you can survive the weekend queues", these "cramped" hang-outs,
in Maida Vale and Notting Hill, are renowned for "a great buzz" and
"the best eggs Benedict" (with eggs imported from Italy!); the new
W6 branch, on the former Chez Kristof (RIP) site, is, however,
"awful". / www.raoulsgourmet.com; 10.15 pm, W11 6.15 pm; booking after
5 pm only.*

Rasa N16   £26   ❶❶❷
55 Stoke Newington Church St   7249 0344   1–1C
*"1,000,000 miles from a high street curry"; this "life-affirming" Stoke
Newington Keralan – the original of the chain – has long featured
amongst London's best Indians; it serves "vibrant" veggie dishes fans
find little short of "divine". / www.rasarestaurants.com; 10.45 pm, Fri & Sat
11.30 pm; closed weekday L.*

Rasa   £36   ❷❷❸
5 Charlotte St, W1   7637 0222   2–1C
6 Dering St, W1   7629 1346   3–2B
Holiday Inn Hotel, 1 Kings Cross, WC1   7833 9787   8–3D
56 Stoke Newington Church St, N16   7249 1340   1–1C
715 High Rd, E11   8859 1700   1–1D
*A "vibrant" taste of Kerala (mostly fish and veggie dishes)
at "brilliant" prices, have won huge acclaim for these spin-offs from
the N16 original; their ratings dipped a fraction this year, however –
hopefully just a blip. / www.rasarestaurants.com; 10.45 pm; variable hours
especially on weekends.*

Rasoi SW3   £93   ❸④❸
10 Lincoln St   7225 1881   5–2D
*"In a class of its own" – Vineet Bhattia's "surprising" Chelsea
townhouse is, say fans, "London's most interesting Indian", thanks
to his "immensely subtle" cuisine; it can feel "a little quiet", though,
and its ratings are undercut by a few sceptics for whom the
experience "doesn't hit the heights", and is "way overpriced" too.
/ www.rasoirestaurant.co.uk; 10.30 pm; closed Sat L; no trainers; set weekday L
£50 (FP).*

The Real Greek   £37   ⑤⑤④
56 Paddington St, W1   7486 0466   2–1A
60-62 Long Acre, WC2   7240 2292   4–2D
Westfield, Ariel Way, W12   8743 9168   7–1C
15 Hoxton Market, N1   7739 8212   12–1B
1-2 Riverside Hs, Southwark Br Rd, SE1   7620 0162   9–3B
6 Horner Sq, E1   7375 1364   12–2B
*A soulless Greek chain whose ratings remain on Skid Row –
even some fans say the food is "nothing special", and service can
be "laughable"; perhaps the new owners – as from mid-2011 –
can perk things up. / www.therealgreek.com; 10.45 pm; WC2 10.30 pm,
E1 Sun 7 pm; EC1 closed Sun; no Amex; WC2 no booking.*

Rebato's SW8   £39   ❷❶❶
169 South Lambeth Rd   7735 6388   10–1D
*A "jolly Spanish stalwart", in Stockwell, comprising a "busy" tapas bar
and "idiosyncratic" restaurant; the "lovely owner and really solicitous
staff" are the "top draw", but the cooking is seldom less than
"delicious". / www.rebatos.com; 10.45 pm; closed Sat L & Sun.*

Red Fort W1 £63 ❷❸❸
77 Dean St 7437 2525 4–2A
*"Refined" Indian cooking – for fans nothing short of "incredible" –
has long created a formidable reputation for this "high end" Soho
veteran, nowadays decorated in "calm", modern style; it can seem
"a little overpriced", even so. / www.redfort.co.uk; 11.30 pm; closed
Sat L & Sun L.*

The Red Pepper W9 £44 ❷❸④
8 Formosa St 7266 2708 8–4A
*"The most outstanding pizza" has long won raves for this "squeezed"
Maida Vale veteran – it's "too small and too busy", but then it always
has been... / theredpepper.net; Sat 11 pm, Sun 10.30 pm; closed weekday L;
no Amex.*

Redhook EC1 £46 ④④❸
89-90 Turnmill St 7065 6800 9–1A
*Benefitting from a wonderfully "funky" setting by Farringdon tube,
this "out-of-the-way" brasserie offered "OK" standards when
it opened last year; ratings have taken "a huge dive", though – there
are too many reports of "dreadful" food, and service that's "very,
very slow". / www.redhooklondon.com; midnight, Thu-Sat 1 am; closed Sun.*

Refettorio
The Crowne Plaza Hotel EC4 £52 ④④④
19 New Bridge St 7438 8052 9–3A
*A City business-hotel dining room that used to stand out from the
crowd (not least with its once-innovative Italian platters); the world
moves on, though, and the formula can now just seem "rather
ordinary". / www.refettorio.com; 10.30 pm, Fri & Sat 10 pm; closed
Sat L & Sun.*

Refuel
Soho Hotel W1 £55 ❸❸❷
4 Richmond Mews 7559 3007 3–2D
*"Great for a lost afternoon" – a buzzing bar is at the heart of this
"lively yet intimate" rendezvous in the heart of Soho; it's not really
what you could call a foodie destination, but fans insist the cooking
is "fabulous" too. / www.firmdale.com; midnight, Sun 11 pm.*

Le Relais de Venise L'Entrecôte £40 ❷❸❸
120 Marylebone Ln, W1 7486 0878 2–1A
5 Throgmorton St, EC2 7638 6325 9–2C
*"Just about the only choice is how you want it cooked!"; these Parisian
"steak/frites factories" have a "simple" but "brilliantly-executed"
formula, enhanced by a "delicious" secret-sauce (and free seconds);
queues are "inevitable", but they usually "move rapidly".
/ www.relaisdevenise.com; W1 11 pm, Sun 10.30 pm; EC2 10 pm; EC2 closed
Sat & Sun; no booking.*

Le Rendezvous du Café EC1 £49 ❸❷❷
22 Charterhouse Sq 7336 8836 9–1B
*"Splendid plats du jour" and "great steak/frites" typify the "simple"
and "well-cooked" fare on offer at this "very French" offshoot
of Smithfield's Café du Marché; be braced, though, for tables which
are "tiny" and "tightly-packed". / www.cafedumarche.co.uk; 10 pm; closed
Sat L & Sun.*

The Restaurant at St Paul's
St Paul's Cathedral EC4   £37   ❸④❸
St Paul's Churchyard   7248 2469   9–2B
Compared to the magnificence of the Wren setting, this restaurant-in-the-crypt feels a little "homespun"; for a "touristy venue", though, the British dishes can be "surprisingly good" and "interesting".
/ www.restaurantatstpauls.co.uk; L only; no Amex.

Retsina NW3   £41   ❸②❸
48-50 Belsize Ln   7431 5855   8–2A
"Tasty" Greek fare ("freshly cooked by Mama") and "very friendly" service earn strong local support for this "lively" and "good-value" taverna, in Belsize Park. / www.retsina-london.com; 11 pm; closed Mon L; no Amex.

Reubens W1   £50   ④⑤⑤
79 Baker St   7486 0035   2–1A
"It wouldn't last a minute in Manhattan!"; only by virtue of its rarity value as "the West End's only kosher option" is this stalwart Marylebone deli/restaurant of any interest − of the few reports it incites, rather too many are of the "worst-meal-ever" variety.
/ www.reubensrestaurant.co.uk; 10 pm; closed Fri D & Sat; no Amex.

Rhodes 24 EC2   £80   ❸❸❸
25 Old Broad St   7877 7703   9–2C
"Spectacular views", such as "to impress any business guest", reward visits to Gary R's 24th-floor City-lunching eyrie (and compensate for the slightly "tired" interior); many reporters "flinch" at the "very high" prices, but the "enjoyable" British cooking generally measures up.
/ www.rhodes24.co.uk; 9 pm; closed Sat & Sun; no shorts; booking essential.

Rhodes W1 Restaurant
Cumberland Hotel W1   £68   ④❸⑤
Gt Cumberland Pl   7616 5930   2–2A
"Opulent chandeliers" don't succeed in creating a particularly sparkling atmosphere at Gary R's luxurious − but "atmosphere-free" − dining room, near Marble Arch; reports divide on whether the food is "brilliant" or "underwhelming", but the most striking feature is just how little feedback, of any sort, the place inspires.
/ www.rhodesw1.com; 10.15 pm; closed Mon, Sat L & Sun; no jeans or trainers; set weekday L £41 (FP).

Rib Room
Jumeirah Carlton Tower Hotel SW1   £103
Cadogan Pl   7858 7250   5–1D
This swanky Knightsbridge grill room was closed for a major revamp as this guide went to press; long ago, it was the capital's only steakhouse of any note − can it now re-invent itself to ride London's steak revolution? / www.jumeirah.com; 10.45 pm, Sun 10.15 pm; set weekday L £60 (FP).

RIBA Café
Royal Ass'n of Brit' Architects W1   £46   ④⑤❷
66 Portland Pl   7631 0467   2–1B
"Wow!"; it's the "impressive surroundings" and the "wonderful Art Deco interior" of the architects' palatial Marylebone HQ that make it of interest − "service can be slow", and the food is "pricey" for what it is. / www.riba-venues.com; L only, closed Sat & Sun.

Riccardo's SW3 £42 ④④④
126 Fulham Rd   7370 6656   5–3B
"The formula works!", say fans of this "lively" Chelsea Italian, which has served "a menu of starters" since long before 'petits-plats' menus became fashionable; it's "rather crowded", though, and the food is more "variable" than it used to be. / www.riccardos.it; 11.30 pm, Sun 10.30 pm.

Riding House Café W1 NEW £44 ❷❷❶
43-51 Great Titchfield St   7927 0840   3–1C
A superb, snazzy interior – twinned with a "crowd-pleasing" menu of "comfort food" – is making a smash hit of this "comfy and casual" new Fitzrovia brasserie; let's hope it doesn't become too popular for its own good! / www.ridinghousecafe.co.uk; 11 pm.

El Rincón Latino SW4 £30 ④❷❷
148 Clapham Manor St   7622 0599   10–2D
"Full Spanish weekend fry-ups!" are a top tip at this good-value Clapham tapas bar; otherwise, the food's only middling nowadays, but the "wonderful" staff help create a good buzz. / www.rinconlatino.co.uk; 10.30 pm, Fri & Sat 11.30 pm; closed Mon-Fri L.

Rising Sun NW7 £38 ❷❷❸
137 Marsh Ln, Highwood Hill   8959 1357   1–1B
"A lovely, picturesque pub in leafy Mill Hill, now run by an Italian family" – "the owner makes a great host", and the food is "simple and well-presented". / 9.30 pm, Sun 8.30 pm; closed Mon.

Ristorante Semplice W1 £64 ❷❷❸
9-10 Blenheim St   7495 1509   3–2B
A "sophisticated" and "personable" Italian, off the top end of Bond Street, offering cuisine that's both "expert" and "refined"; only real problem? – the somewhat "cramped" lay-out. / www.ristorantesemplice.com; 10.30 pm; closed Sat L & Sun; booking: max 12.

(Palm Court)
The Ritz W1 £44 ④❸❷
150 Piccadilly   7493 8181   3–4C
"A once-in-a-lifetime experience everyone should have" – this St James's grand-hotel afternoon tea is so famous that it has become a touristic cliché… which is no doubt why critics find it "totally disappointing and over-rated". / www.theritzlondon.com; 10 pm; jacket & tie required.

The Ritz Restaurant
The Ritz W1 £118 ❸❷❶
150 Piccadilly   7493 8181   3–4C
"You don't ever forget a date at the Ritz!"; if you're looking for a "great place for a celebration", especially of a "romantic" nature, this "incomparable" Louis XVI chamber is a total "wow", and nowadays the food – traditionally lacklustre – almost lives up! / www.theritzlondon.com; 10 pm; jacket & tie required.

Riva SW13 £56 ❷❷④
169 Church Rd   8748 0434   10–1A
Andreas Riva's "serious" Barnes venture is one of London's most idiosyncratic stalwarts; to fans, it's "the perfect Italian", with "awesome" and "very interesting" cuisine and a "glamorous" vibe – to the uninitiated, it's an "overhyped" place, with "disdainful" service and "drab" decor. / 10.30 pm, Sun 9.30 pm; closed Sat L.

F S A

THE RIVER CAFÉ W6   £79   ❷❷❸
Thames Wharf, Rainville Rd   7386 4200   7–2C
"Quality is absolute", at Ruth Rogers's riverside Hammersmith canteen, world-famous for seasonal fare that's "the quintessence of Italian cuisine"; even for fans, however, bills are so "brutal" that the overall experience can be "bittersweet". / www.rivercafe.co.uk; 9 pm, Sat 9.15 pm; closed Sun D.

The Riverfront
BFI Southbank SE1   £37   ❷❷❸
Southbank   7928 0808   2–3D
"An excellent place for a quick and tasty meal on the South Bank" – this attractive Benugo-group café is very handily-located, and "good value" too. / www.riverfrontbarandkitchen.com; 9.30 pm.

Rivington Grill   £50   ❸④④
178 Greenwich High Rd, SE10   8293 9270   1–3D
28-30 Rivington St, EC2   7729 7053   12–1B
The "luxury burger" may be "great", and the brunches "excellent", but these Caprice-group bar/brasseries offer a "hit-and-miss" experience overall, and arguably a rather "unexciting" one too. / www.rivingtongrill.co.uk; 11 pm, Sun 10 pm; SE10 closed Mon, Tue L & Wed L.

Roast SE1   £64   ❸④❸
Stoney St   0845 034 7300   9–4C
"Good food… but about 20% overpriced!" – a pretty representative opinion on this "beautifully light" Borough dining room, which has "delightful views" over the Market, and serves a "traditional" menu (focussing on meat); this is a quintessentially British establishment, however, so "breakfast is much better than lunch!" / www.roast-restaurant.com; 10.15 pm, Sun 6 pm.

Rocca Di Papa   £30   ④❸❸
73 Old Brompton Rd, SW7   7225 3413   5–2B
75-79 Dulwich Village, SE21   8299 6333   1–4D **NEW**
A large but "friendly" South Kensington pizza spot, which – if you're looking for a "family meal" in this surprisingly thinly-provided area – makes a "good-value" choice; on thin feedback, its new Dulwich sibling (with outside tables) is off to a fair start too. / SW7 11.30 pm; SE21 11 pm.

Rochelle Canteen E2   £33   ❷⓿❷
Arnold Circus   7729 5677   12–1C
Don't leave it to the Bethnal Green trendies!; this small, unlicensed canteen – "tucked-away in a former school bicycle shed" – is "a real hidden gem", serving "simple but perfect" cuisine at "cheap" prices; "great alfresco dining" too. / www.arnoldandhenderson.com; L only, closed Sat & Sun; no Amex.

Rock & Sole Plaice WC2   £30   ❸④❸
47 Endell St   7836 3785   4–1C
A "great" old-fashioned chippy which is of particular note as one of the best places for a "cheap 'n' cheerful" group meal in Covent Garden; "eat in, take away, or eat outside on a warm day". / 11 pm, Sun 10.30 pm; no Amex; need 4+ to book.

Rock & Rose TW9   £54   ④❸⓿
106-108 Kew Rd   8948 8008   1–4A
It's the stylishly "kitsch" decor – "so OTT it's a laugh" – that makes this "romantic" Richmond destination worth seeking out; prices can seem "steep", though, and the "global" menu is realised only to a "mediocre" standard. / www.rockandroserestaurant.co.uk; 10 pm; set weekday L £33 (FP).

Rocket £43 ④④❸
4-6 Lancashire Ct, W1   7629 2889   3–2B
Churchill Pl, E14   3200 2022   11–1C
6 Adams Ct, EC2   7628 0808   9–2C

"Tucked-away", off Bond Street, this "vibrant" operation is a "simple and central" rendezvous, offering "well-priced" pizzas and salads; visits to the "industrially-styled" Canary Wharf spin-off are also "enjoyable". / 10.30 pm; W1 closed Sun; EC2 closed Sat & Sun; SW15 Mon-Wed D only.

Rodizio Rico £45 ⑤④⑤
111 Westbourne Grove, W2   7792 4035   6–1B
77-78 Upper St, N1   7354 1076   8–3D
11 Jerdan Pl, SW6   7183 6085   5–4A **NEW**

These all-you-can-eat, meat-heavy Brazilian buffets often divide opinion; fans say they're "excellent for groups, and good value for money" too, but for critics, who are more vocal this year, they're simply a "disaster" – "I still have flashbacks!" / www.rodiziorico.com; W2 & N1 midnight, Sun 11 pm; SE10 11 pm, Fri & Sat midnight; W2 & N1 closed weekday L; no Amex.

The Roebuck W4 £42 ❸②②
122 Chiswick High Rd   8995 4392   7–2A

An "unassuming" but "efficient" and "buzzy" Chiswick boozer, serving "classic dishes with an interesting twist"; it has a "lovely garden" too. / www.theroebuckchiswick.co.uk; Fri & Sat 10.30 pm, Mon-Thu, Sun 10 pm.

Roganic W1 **NEW** £78 ❶②⑤
19 Blandford St   7486 0380   2–1A

Simon Rogan (of Cumbria's L'Enclume fame) is one of the UK's most innovative chefs, and his talents are impressively demonstrated by the 6-course and 10-course set menus offered at the short-term (two-year) 'pop up' he launched in Marylebone in mid-2011; the setting though – especially the cramped rear room – is bare. / Rated on Editors' visit; www.roganic.co.uk; 9 pm; closed Mon & Sun.

Roka £76 ❶❸②
37 Charlotte St, W1   7580 6464   2–1C
Unit 4, Park Pavilion, 40 Canada Sq, E14   7636 5228   11–1C

"Stunning" cuisine – highlighting a 'robata' grill which creates "the most wonderful flavours" – takes centre stage at these "exciting" Japanese operations, whose "cool" styling helps create a "great buzz"; NB: the Fitzrovia original (which has a "must-do" basement bar) significantly outclasses the newer Canary Wharf branch. / www.rokarestaurant.com; 11.15 pm, Sun 10.30 pm; closed Sun D; booking: max 8.

Roots At N1 N1 **NEW** £46 ❷②④
115 Hemingford Rd   7697 4488   8–3D

"A fantastic addition to Barnsbury"; this stylishly-converted pub "operates far above the level of an average neighbourhood Indian". / www.rootsatn1.com; 10 pm, Sun 9 pm; D only, closed Mon; no Amex.

Rosa's £34 ❸④❸
48 Dean St, W1   7494 1638   4–3A
12 Hanbury St, E1   7247 1093   12–2C

These "fun" budget Thai canteens can be "inconsistent", but mostly win praise for their "vibrant" dishes; the "buzzy" original, near Brick Lane, now has a "cute" Soho sibling. / www.rosaslondon.com; 10.30 pm, Fri & Sat 11 pm; some booking restrictions apply.

The Rose & Crown N6 £45 ④④④
86 Highgate High St 8340 0770 1–1C
*This Highgate yearling – "not really a pub", more a restaurant
nowadays – does have its fans; it also faces some ominous criticisms
though, of "stodgy and bland" food and a "complacent" attitude.
/ www.roseandcrownhighgate.com; 10 pm; closed Mon L & Sun D; no Amex;
set weekday L £29 (FP).*

Rossopomodoro £40 ❸④④
50-52 Monmouth St, WC2 7240 9095 4–3B
214 Fulham Rd, SW10 7352 7677 5–3B
184a Kensington Park Rd, W11 7229 9007 6–1A
*Often "full of Italian-speaking families", these "very busy and noisy"
trattorias feel notably "authentic" (as you'd hope of a group
originating in Naples) – the pizza is "noticeably better than
at most chains". / www.rossopomodoro.co.uk; 11.30 pm; WC2 Sun
11.30 pm; set weekday L £26 (FP).*

The Rôtisserie £51 ④❸④
316 Uxbridge Rd, HA5 8421 2878 1–1A
1288 Whetstone High Rd, N20 8343 8585 1–1B
82 Fortune Green Rd, NW6 7435 9923 1–1B
87 Allitsen Rd, NW8 7722 7444 8–3A
*"Great steaks at fair prices" win praise for this "reliable" small chain;
there are also quite a few critics, though, who find it "pricey", and say
it's merely "OK if you can't be bothered to cook, but not what you
could really call a 'night out'". / www.therotisserie.co.uk; 10.30 pm,
Sun 9.30 pm; NW6, NW8 & NW20 closed Mon L, NW6 closed Sun;
no Amex (except HA5).*

Rôtisserie Bute Street SW7 £35 ❸④④
6-8 Bute St 7584 0600 5–2B
*"Good, cheap, hearty, simple" fast food is still the order of the day
at this basic South Kensington stand-by, where you can choose
anything… so long as it's rôtisserie chicken; BYO.
/ www.rotisseriebutestreet.com; 10.30 pm.*

Rotunda Bar & Restaurant
Kings Place N1 £48 ④❸❷
90 York Way 7014 2840 8–3C
*The large dining facility of this "buzzy" arts centre/office complex,
near King's Cross, undoubtedly makes "a good spot for a pre-concert
supper"; on a warm day, it's the canal-side tables – with their
"stunning" views – which are worth a journey in their own right.
/ www.rotundabarandrestaurant.co.uk; 10.30 pm.*

Roussillon SW1 £86 ❸❸④
16 St Barnabas St 7730 5550 5–2D
*This "sedate" (but quite "romantic") Gallic operation is still often
hailed as a Pimlico "hidden gem", but there's no doubt it has "slightly
lost its edge" since its former chef left last year; no reason for despair,
though – many reports do speak of "exquisite" dishes, and fans say
the new régime is "getting there". / www.roussillon.co.uk; 11 pm; closed
Sat L & Sun; no trainers; set weekday L £53 (FP).*

Roux At Parliament Square
RICS SW1 £80 ❸④⑤
12 Great George St 7334 3737 2–3C
*"Odd" decor and "eccentric" service are not the only peculiarities
which have made Michel Roux's "sepulchral" Westminster
outpost a "strange" débutante – reports on the cuisine range the
whole way from "best meal for many years" to "extremely
disappointing". / www.rouxatparliamentsquare.co.uk; 10 pm; closed
Sat & Sun; set weekday L £47 (FP).*

Roux At The Landau
The Langham W1   £80   ❷❷❷
1c, Portland Pl   7965 0165   2–1B
"The Landau is reborn", thanks to the Roux take-over of this
"palatial" and "truly lovely" dining room – the cuisine is "impeccably
executed" and service "seamless and unobtrusive"; the set lunch,
in particular, is "excellent value". / www.thelandau.com; 10 pm; closed
Sat L & Sun; no trainers.

Rowley's SW1   £62   ⑤⑤⑤
113 Jermyn St   7930 2707   3–3D
"The interior makes the atmosphere", say fans of this "traditional"
St James's steakhouse (whose tiled premises date from its days as the
birthplace of Wall's sausages); even supporters can find
it "disappointingly touristy" nowadays, however, and too many critics
feel it's "cramped", "average" and "way overpriced".
/ www.rowleys.co.uk; 11 pm.

Royal China   £46   ❷④④
24-26 Baker St, W1   7487 4688   2–1A
805 Fulham Rd, SW6   7731 0081   10–1B
13 Queensway, W2   7221 2535   6–2C
30 Westferry Circus, E14   7719 0888   11–1B
"After two years in the East, this is where I come to satisfy my dim
sum cravings!"; London's benchmark Chinese chain is "superbly
authentic", all the way down to its "bordello-glitz" decor,
and "brusque" service; NB: they're "always busy" – expect
"long queues" at peak times. / www.royalchinagroup.co.uk; 10.45 pm,
Fri & Sat 11.15 pm, Sun 9.45 pm; no booking Sat & Sun L.

Royal China Club W1   £55   ❷❸④
40-42 Baker St   7486 3898   2–1A
This "posher" (and "pricier") version of the Royal China formula
serves similarly "fantastic" food, with "phenomenal" dim sum and
lobster (from the tank) among the highlights; another advantage
of this Marylebone outlet? – "you can book!"
/ www.royalchinagroup.co.uk; 11 pm, Fri & Sat 11.30 pm, Sun 10.30 pm.

Royal China SW15   £43   ④④④
3 Chelverton Rd   8788 0907   10–2B
Famously a "very consistent" Putney destination, this "dim sum
favourite" shares roots (but not ownership) with the well-known chain;
ratings are down this year, though, and one long-term fan reports that
"food quality has dived" – hopefully just a blip!
/ www.royalchinaputney.co.uk; 11 pm, Fri-Sat 11.30 pm; only Amex.

The Royal Exchange Grand Café
The Royal Exchange EC3   £49   ④④❶
The Royal Exchange Bank   7618 2480   9–2C
The D&D group's café in the Royal Exchange's magnificent atrium
makes "a good City rendezvous"; with its "small" and "extremely
pricey" portions, it's ideal "for regular business-lunchers who don't
want to get too roly poly!" / www.royalexchange-grandcafe.co.uk; 10 pm;
closed Sat & Sun; no booking at L & D.

RSJ SE1   £49   ❸❷⑤
33 Coin St   7928 4554   9–4A
"Never disappointed in 25 years!"; this "useful" South Bank stalwart
offers an "unchanging" mix of "charming" service, "reliable" cooking,
and – last but not least – an "absolute joy" of a wine list (from the
Loire); the other constant, sadly, is an ambience that's "nothing
to shout about". / www.rsj.uk.com; 11 pm; closed Sat L & Sun.

Rugoletta N2 £36 ❸❸❸
59 Church Ln 8815 1743 1–1B
"Basic" but "buzzy", this BYO bistro – "tucked-away between shops",
in East Finchley – has made something of a name locally with its
"good-value" Italian cuisine; it's "very small, and you have to book!"
/ 10.30 pm; closed Sun.

Rules WC2 £74 ❹❸❷
35 Maiden Ln 7836 5314 4–3D
"Unbeatable for wowing foreigners!" – London's oldest restaurant
(1798) offers "old-world" (Edwardian) "opulence", "relaxed charm"
and "good, solid British food" too; ever more "frightening" prices,
however, risk making it a place for "rich tourists and expense-
accounters". / www.rules.co.uk; 11.30 pm, Sun 10.30 pm; no shorts; booking:
max 6.

S & M Café £32 ❹❹❹
4-6 Essex Rd, N1 7359 5361 8–3D
48 Brushfield St, E1 7247 2252 12–2B
Haute cuisine it ain't, but – "for reliable, solid nourishment" –
the Sausage 'n' Mash on offer at this chain of "'50s-style" British
caffs satisfies most of the (relatively few) reporters who comment
on it. / www.sandmcafe.co.uk; N1 11 pm; E1 10.30 pm; E1 closed Sun;
no Amex.

Sabor N1 £41 ❸❶❸
108 Essex Rd 7226 5551 8–3D
OK, it's "scruffily located", but this "vibrant" Islington cantina offers
"fantastic cocktails", "fresh" Latino fare and "a bit of buzz" too.
/ www.sabor.co.uk; 10.45 pm, Sat & Sun 11 pm; closed Mon, Tue-Fri D only,
Sat & Sun open L & D; no Amex.

Le Sacré-Coeur N1 £37 ❹❷❸
18 Theberton St 7354 2618 8–3D
Islington locals find their "very own little bit of Montmartre", at this
"crowded neighbourhood bistro" – a place that's "good for what it is",
in its "old-fashioned" sort of way. / www.lesacrecoeur.co.uk; 11 pm,
Sat 11.30 pm, Sun 10.30 pm; set weekday L £24 (FP).

Saf £47 ❷❹❹
Whole Foods, 63-97 High St Ken', W8 7368 4555 5–1A
152-154 Curtain Rd, EC2 7613 0007 12–1B
"I had no idea raw food could be so delicious!" – these vegan outfits
offer "surprisingly varied and intensely-flavoured" dishes; "indifferent"
service can grate, though, and the in-store Kensington branch has less
atmosphere than the Shoreditch original. / www.safrestaurant.co.uk;
EC2 11 pm, Sun 10; W8 10 pm, Sun 5 pm.

Sagar £30 ❷❷❹
17a, Percy St, W1 7631 3319 3–2B
31 Catherine St, WC2 7836 6377 4–3D
157 King St, W6 8741 8563 7–2C
"Subtle yet insistent" South Indian dishes – including "excellent
dosas" and "puri to die for" – again win a hymn of praise for these
"great cheap veggies"; "the ambience is nothing to speak of",
but staff are notably "cheerful". / www.gosagar.com; Sun-Thu 10.45 pm,
Fri & Sat 11.30 pm; set weekday L £19 (FP).

Saigon Saigon W6 £41 ❷❷❸
313-317 King St 8748 6887 7–2B
*"Surprisingly good" food ("astonishing", say fans) and "delightful"
service draw a large fan club to this "thoroughly enjoyable" and "ever-
popular" Hammersmith Vietnamese – "it looks as if it might be a bit
downmarket, but actually it's good value". / www.saigon-saigon.co.uk;
11 pm, Sun & Mon 10 pm, Fri & Sat 11.30 pm; no Amex.*

ST JOHN EC1 £72 ❷❸④
26 St John St 7251 0848 9–1B
*"An enticing way with unattractive animal parts" has won global fame
for Fergus Henderson's "Spartan" Smithfield offal-shrine; even fans
fear a "smug" attitude is "starting to cast a cloud", though,
and critics say: "one of the World's 50 Best? – you must be joking!"
/ www.stjohnrestaurant.com; 11 pm; closed Sat L & Sun D.*

St John Bread & Wine E1 £50 ❶❷❷
94-96 Commercial St 7251 0848 12–2C
*"Yes, it's as good as they say!"; St John's "younger and buzzier"
Spitalfields canteen spin-off is nowadays "a more reliable destination
than its parent" – staff are "competent and helpful", the "austere"
interior is "cool", and the British fare so "adventurous in its simplicity"
as to be really "exciting". / www.stjohnbreadandwine.com; 10.30 pm,
Sun 9.30 pm.*

St John Hotel WC2 £63 ❸④④
1 Leicester St 3301 8069 4–3A
*The St John team's "stark" make-over of Theatreland veteran Manzi's
(RIP) is off to a mixed start; fans say the "interesting" British fare
makes it "a joy", but detractors can just see a "crowded" place,
where food that's "good, but not that good" comes at "way OTT"
prices; handy in the early hours, though! / 1.30 am.*

St Johns N19 £40 ❷❷❷
91 Junction Rd 7272 1587 8–1C
*The "fantastic old ballroom interior" at this "5-star" tavern,
in Archway, is "quite something", but the "interesting" British menu –
"with great emphasis on provenance" – is quite an attraction in its
own right too. / 11 pm, Sun 9.30 pm; Mon-Thu D only, Fri-Sun open L & D;
booking: max 12.*

Le Saint Julien EC1 £50 ④❷④
62-63 Long Ln 7796 4550 9–1B
*The quality of the fare is at best "typique", but "sparkling" service
livens up this very Gallic bistro, overlooking Smithfield Market. / 10 pm;
closed Sat L & Sun.*

St Moritz W1 £52 ❸④❸
161 Wardour St 7734 3324 3–1D
*In "Swiss-chalet style", this "genuine" stalwart – with its "cosy",
if "rather kitsch", decor – makes a bizarre find in central Soho;
its "filling" fondues and other fare, however, offer "a real taste of the
Alps"! / www.stmoritz-restaurant.co.uk; 11.30 pm; closed Sat L & Sun.*

St Pancras Grand
St Pancras Int'l Station NW1 £51 ⑤⑤④
The Concourse 7870 9900 8–3C
*The "impressive" design of this grand brasserie, within St Pancras
station, may surprise Gallic visitors – shame the "formulaic" food and
"pot luck" service must quickly reinforce their most negative
preconceptions about England! / www.stpancrasgrand.com; 10.30 pm.*

Sake No Hana SW1 £60 ❸④④
23 St James's St 7925 8988 3–4C
*"Strange" and "soulless", this would-be trendy St James's Japanese
does not seem to have emerged from its 'emergency' early-days
revamp especially improved, but the basic problem is that prices can
still seem "ludicrous" – one has to wonder if the new owners as of
mid-2011, Hakkasan, are the people to put this right!
/ www.sakenohana.com; 11 pm, Fri-Sat 11.30 pm; closed Sat L & Sun.*

Saki EC1 £40 ❷❸④
4 West Smithfield 7489 7033 9–2A
*Shame it's in a basement that's "a bit on the gloomy side" –
this Smithfield Japanese offers some "top cooking", and particularly
some "very good set lunch deals". / www.saki-food.com; 10.30 pm; closed
Sat L & Sun.*

Sakonis HA0 £19 ❸④⑤
127-129 Ealing Rd 8903 9601 1–1A
*In the wilds of Wembley, a noisy, no-frills Indian canteen, particularly
praised for "fresh and tasty dosas", and its "excellent Bombay street
snacks"; there's a big Chinese menu too. / www.sakonis.co.uk; 9.30 pm;
no Amex.*

Sakura W1 £30 ❷④④
23 Conduit St 7629 2961 3–2C
*Now in a new, slightly more modern Mayfair location (a short walk
from the old Hanover Street basement), this "authentic" operation –
complete with "real Japanese patrons" – still offers "excellent quality
and value-for-money". / 10 pm.*

Salaam Namaste WC1 £34 ❷❸④
68 Millman St 7405 3697 2–1D
*"Everything tastes freshly-made and delicious", say fans of this
"excellent local Indian", hidden-away in Bloomsbury; it can sometimes
get "very busy". / www.salaam-namaste.co.uk; 11.30 pm, Sun 11 pm.*

Sale e Pepe SW1 £55 ④❸❸
9-15 Pavilion Rd 7235 0098 5–1D
*"What's happened?" at this "closely-packed" old-favourite trattoria,
behind Harrods? – some reporters "still love it", but its "welcoming"
and "flamboyant" service risks becoming "slapdash", and "the food
has been bland of late". / www.saleepepe.co.uk; 11.30 pm; closed Sun;
no shorts.*

Salloos SW1 £48 ❷❸④
62-64 Kinnerton St 7235 4444 5–1D
*A curious old place, hidden-away in a Belgravia mews, where the
"subtly-flavoured Punjabi dishes" – including "simply outstanding"
lamb chops – have long made it one of London's top 'Indians';
it's always been "expensive" too. / 11 pm; closed Sun.*

The Salt House NW8 £42 ❸❸❷
63 Abbey Rd 7328 6626 8–3A
*"Well-lit, with candles and muted decor", this "lovely neighbourhood
favourite" delivers "great" gastropub fare, for which fans travel even
from beyond St John's Wood; good terrace for the summer.
/ www.thesalthouse.co.uk; 10 pm, Sun 9.30 pm.*

F S A

Salt Yard W1 £38 ❸❷❷
54 Goode St 7637 0657 2–1B
*"Creative" Italian-Spanish tapas and "passionate" staff have made
a smash hit of this "super-busy" (and arguably "too cramped")
Fitzrovia haunt; quality, however, "seems to have gone downhill"
somewhat – the distraction of recent openings elsewhere?*
/ www.saltyard.co.uk; 11 pm; closed Sat L & Sun.

The Salusbury NW6 £41 ❸❸❸
50-52 Salusbury Rd 7328 3286 1–2B
*This "Queen's Park icon" – a "lazy weekend" kind of place with
"consistent" Mediterranean food – has been "re-fitted and revitalised
of late", in particular the adjoining former deli, which is now
an "atmospheric café" serving "good pizza, salads and coffee".*
/ www.thesalusbury.co.uk; 10.15 pm; closed Mon L.

Sam's Brasserie W4 £46 ❹❸❸
11 Barley Mow Pas 8987 0555 7–2A
*"With something for everyone", Sam Harrison's "casual"
bar/brasserie – a "buzzy" factory-conversion, "tucked-away off
Chiswick High Road" – is a "perfect local"; its "simple brasserie fare"
doesn't aim to set the world on fire, but it is "reliable" and "tasty".*
/ www.samsbrasserie.co.uk; 10.30 pm, Sun 9.30 pm; booking: max 26.

Samarqand W1 NEW £46 ❹❹❸
18 Thayer St 7935 9393 3–1A
*"Unique" is a term oft-used to describe this clubby Marylebone
basement newcomer, where "the vodka flows" in the "substantial
bar", and the clientele consists of "Russian oligarchs and leggy
blondes"; the food? – a bit beside the point.*
/ www.samarqand-restaurant.com; Mon-Sat 11 pm, Sun 10 pm.

San Daniele del Friuli N5 £39 ❸❸❷
72 Highbury Park 7226 1609 8–1D
*A long-established Highbury Park trattoria, where fans say the food
is "always good"; "helpful" staff contribute to a "good Italian
atmosphere" too. / 10.30 pm; closed Mon L, Tue L, Sat L & Sun; no Amex.*

San Lorenzo SW3 £65 ❹❹❹
22 Beauchamp Pl 7584 1074 5–1C
*The A-list is not so often seen nowadays at this once-legendary
Knightsbridge Italian, and it inspires little feedback; it is trying harder
("they even take credit cards"), but it's difficult to avoid the feeling
that these improvements are coming "too late". / 11 pm; closed Sun.*

San Lorenzo Fuoriporta SW19 £53 ❹❺❹
38 Wimbledon Hill Rd 8946 8463 10–2B
*This Wimbledon cousin of the once-famous Knightsbridge trattoria
looks like an upmarket PizzaExpress; it benefits for a cute garden but
that's the only undoubted attraction – too many diners report
"terrible" experiences, and ones that are "ridiculously overpriced"
too. / www.sanlorenzo.com; 10.45 pm, Sun 9.30 pm.*

The Sands End SW6 £46 ❷❸❷
135 Stephendale Rd 7731 7823 10–1B
*"A classy restaurant with a pub attached", this Sand's End "hotspot"
– a sibling to Manson – may be "quite expensive", but it offers some
"excellent" cooking (including "great bar nibbles").*
/ www.thesandsend.co.uk; 10 pm, Sun 9 pm.

Santa Lucia SW10 £41 ❸④❸
2 Hollywood Rd   7352 8484   5–3B
*"You get a real taste of Italy", at this hectic little Chelsea café –
"if you can bag a space, that is"; its "distracted" staff serve "great"
pizza, by the metre, from the wood-burning oven.*
/ www.madeinitalygroup.co.uk; 11.30 pm, Sun 10.30 pm; closed weekday L.

Santa Maria W5 £25 ❷❷❷
15 St Mary's Rd   8579 1462   1–3A
*"Fantastico!" – "brilliant" and "authentic" Neapolitan pizza has
quickly made a disproportionately big name for this "tiny" Ealing
newcomer; it's "always busy", though, and you can't book.*
/ www.santamariapizzeria.com; 10.30 pm.

Santa Maria del Sur SW8 £45 ❷④❸
129 Queenstown Rd   7622 2088   10–1C
*The "hype" that's surrounded this Argentinian 'parilla' in Battersea
since it featured on a Ramsay TV show leads some reporters
to suggest it's "over-rated"; even if it's not quite up to its Hackney
sibling (Buen Ayre), though, it's undoubtedly a "jovial" place, offering
"fantastic" steaks. / www.santamariadelsur.co.uk; 11.30 pm; closed
weekday L; no Amex.*

Santini SW1 £69 ④④④
29 Ebury St   7730 4094   2–4B
*This datedly glamorous Belgravian inspires little feedback nowadays;
it's most often tipped as a business lunch venue, but even fans can
find its "proper" Italian cooking "expensive" for what it is, and critics
just say prices are "ridiculous, even for SW1".*
/ www.santini-restaurant.com; 11 pm, Sun 10 pm; closed Sat L & Sun L.

Santore EC1 £37 ❸❷❸
59 Exmouth Mkt   7812 1488   9–1A
*"Almost as good as being in Italy"; this "trendy" and "buzzy"
Exmouth Market spot offers "no fancy nonsense", just "basic" and
"good-value" food – notably the "excellent, thin and crispy pizza",
served by "chatty" staff. / www.santorerestaurant.co.uk; 11 pm.*

Sapori WC2 £41 ④❸④
43 Drury Ln   7836 8296   4–2D
*A minute from the Royal Opera House, a "friendly" trattoria –
"run by real Italians!" – that makes a "useful stand-by" for locals and
opera-goers: NB "excellent-value set lunch". / 11.30 pm; no Amex;
set weekday L £22 (FP).*

Sarastro WC2 £42 ⑤⑤❶
126 Drury Ln   7836 0101   2–2D
*"Opera, violins, and occasional belly-dancing" – plus decor that's
as camp as a row of tents – help make this Theatreland oddity "quite
an experience"; the food, though, is "unmemorable"… if you're lucky.*
/ www.sarastro-restaurant.com; 10.30 pm, Thu-Sat 11.30 pm.

Sardo W1 £48 ❸❸④
45 Grafton Way   7387 2521   2–1B
*The menu – "with a Sardinian twist" – may seem a little "offbeat",
but fans extol many "unvarnished" but "delicious" meals at this
"genuine" Fitzrovia spot; the similarly "off-piste" wine list is likewise
"a treasure", but even supporters can find the overall experience
"very expensive for what it is". / www.sardo-restaurant.com; 11 pm; closed
Sat L & Sun.*

Sardo Canale NW1 £47 ④④④
42 Gloucester Ave   7722 2800   8–3B
It has something of a 'name', but this canal-side (no view) Primrose Hill Italian risks becoming a "former favourite" for many reporters – there was praise for some "fine" Sardinian cooking this year, but it was drowned out by boos from those who found it "lamentable". / www.sardocanale.com; 10 pm.

Sarracino NW6 £41 ❷❷④
186 Broadhurst Gdns   7372 5889   1–1B
The "authentically-prepared" Italian dishes – not least "fabulous" pizza, served by the metre – can come as "quite a surprise" at this "buzzy" West Hampstead Neapolitan. / www.sarracinorestaurant.com; 11 pm; closed weekday L.

Sartoria W1 £59 ❸❸❸
20 Savile Row   7534 7000   3–2C
As "a smart venue for business", the D&D group's "well-spaced and very comfortable" Mayfair dining room comes well recommended, not least for its "light" Italian fare; perhaps that's another way of saying: "while it's a very agreeable place, it's obviously not worth it if you're spending your own money…" / www.sartoria-restaurant.co.uk; 11 pm; closed Sun.

Satay House W2 £38 ❸❸④
13 Sale Pl   7723 6763   6–1D
Radically revamped in recent times, a Paddington backstreet Malaysian of long standing; fans applaud its "surprisingly good" food, but others find in it "nothing noteworthy". / www.satay-house.co.uk; 11 pm.

Satsuma W1 £35
56 Wardour St   7437 8338   3–2D
This heart-of-Soho site is being relaunched in late-2011, with a new concept – katsu curries; the proprietors are the Royal China people, so it would be surprising if it were not at least competent. / www.osatsuma.com; 10.30 pm, Wed & Thu 11 pm, Fri & Sat 10 pm; no booking.

Sauterelle
Royal Exchange EC3 £59 ④❸❸
Bank   7618 2483   9–2C
"Above the glamour of the Royal Exchange", this "beautiful" D&D group mezzanine dining room makes a particularly "useful business venue"; "it doesn't have quite the atmosphere it should", however, not helped by run-of-the-mill standards generally. / www.danddlondon.com; 9.30 pm; closed Sat & Sun.

Savoir Faire WC1 £37 ❸④❸
42 New Oxford St   7436 0707   4–1C
"A 'find' in the Holborn vacuum" – this "friendly" small-scale bistro serves "freshly-prepared" French food", at "value-for-money" prices. / www.savoir.co.uk; 11 pm.

(River Restaurant)
The Savoy Hotel WC2 £85 ⑤⑤❸
91 The Strand   7836 4343   4–3D
"How could they make such a special place such a turn-off?" – the window tables still have "gorgeous river views", but the relaunch of this grand-hotel-classic has proved a real damp squib – service is both "over-fussy" and "badly coordinated", and the food "just like in many other hotels"; the wine prices are terrifying too. / www.fairmont.com/savoy/; 10.30 pm.

(Savoy Grill)
The Savoy Hotel WC2 £79 ❸❷❸
Strand 7592 1600 4–3D
This Art Deco power-dining room has had a "superb" refurbishment,
and most reporters applaud the Ramsay group for its "enthusiastic"
service and "solid" menu of "retro" British "classics" – such a
repertoire can also seem "unexciting", though, and critics say the
place "doesn't yet live up to its iconic reputation".
/ www.gordonramsay.com/thesavoygrill/; 11 pm, Sun 10.30 pm; jacket required.

Scalini SW3 £65 ❹❹❸
1-3 Walton St 7225 2301 5–2C
The food "always keeps you coming back", say fans of this ever-
"packed" Knightsbridge Italian – who cares if it's "a bit expensive"?;
given the "noisy" and "cramped" interior, and staff who "rush you
through", however, others are less forgiving. / www.scalinionline.com;
11.45 pm.

Scandinavian Kitchen W1 £12 ❸❷❷
61 Great Titchfield St 7580 7161 2–1B
"Impressive brunches" and "super coffee and cakes" are highlights
at this "great, informal community café", in Fitzrovia; as you may
possibly have guessed, it celebrates all things Scandi-tastic.
/ www.scandikitchen.co.uk; L only.

Scarpetta TW11 £40 ❸❸❹
78 High St 8977 8177 1–4A
A "small and authentic" Teddington Italian that's made itself
"extremely popular" with its "imaginative" cuisine; "good pizzas" are
a highlight. / www.scarpetta.co.uk; 11 pm, Mon & Sun 10 pm; no shorts.

The Scarsdale W8 £38 ❹❸❷
23a Edwardes Sq 7937 1811 7–1D
A "gorgeous sitting area out front" is the highlight at this beautifully-
located pub – "the food's nothing special, but it's a lovely oasis away
from the hustle of Kensington High Street". / 10 pm, Sun 9.30 pm.

Scoffers SW11 £39 ❹❶❷
6 Battersea Rise 7978 5542 10–2C
A romantic-looking Battersea local – not many places have
a "magical indoor tree", after all – which has its fans, particularly
as a brunch venue; critics, though, just find it "very average".
/ www.scoffersrestaurant.co.uk; Mon 10 pm, Tue-Sat midnight, Sun 6 pm;
closed Mon & Sun D.

SCOTT'S W1 £73 ❷❶❶
20 Mount St 7495 7309 3–3A
For sheer "A-list" glamour, nowhere beats Richard Caring's
magnificent Mayfair all-rounder, with its "very classy", "old-school"
décor, "impeccable" service and "fabulous" traditional seafood
(amongst the best in town). / www.scotts-restaurant.com; 10.30 pm,
Sun 10 pm; booking: max 6.

The Sea Cow SE22 £28 ❸❸❸
37 Lordship Ln 8693 3111 1–4D
"A smart fish 'n' chip shop with bench seating", in East Dulwich,
that's long been a local favourite, thanks to its "wide selection of fish,
cooked traditional-style or grilled", and its "short but reasonably-
priced wine list". / www.theseacow.co.uk; 11 pm, Sun 10 pm; closed Mon L;
no Amex.

Sea Pebbles HA5 £27 ❸❸④
348-352 Uxbridge Rd 8428 0203 1–1A
"Superb freshly-cooked fish 'n' chips" is the draw to this "simple and
unpretentious" Hatch End chippy; your fish can be grilled, or fried
in batter or matzo meal. / 9.45 pm; closed Sun; debit cards only; need 8+
to book.

Seafresh SW1 £33 ❸④⑤
80-81 Wilton Rd 7828 0747 2–4B
"They do more than just fish 'n' chips" – "the extensive menu
includes Dover sole and lobster" – at this "no-frills" Pimlico chippy;
the style, though, is rather "dated". / www.seafresh-dining.com; 10.30 pm;
closed Sun.

Searcy's Brasserie EC2 £54 ④④❸
Level 2, Barbican Centre 7588 3008 12–2A
The name says it all, really – the Barbican's in-house brasserie
is "not memorable", but it's a "pleasant" enough room, offering "OK"
food and service to its (semi-) captive audience. / www.searcys.co.uk;
10.30 pm; closed Sat L & Sun.

The Sea Shell NW1 £40 ❸❸❸
49 Lisson Grove 7224 9000 8–4A
"Better", as a result of its post-fire refurb, this now rather "pleasant"
Marylebone legend is again cooking up "top-rate fish 'n' chips".
/ www.seashellrestaurant.co.uk; 10.30 pm; closed Sun.

Sedap EC1 £24 ❸④⑤
102 Old St 7490 0200 12–1A
"There's not much elbow room", at this "canteen-like" modern café,
in Shoreditch, but fortunately its "home-style" Nyonya (Chinese-
Malaysian) cooking is worth squeezing in for, and it comes
at "amazingly reasonable" prices. / www.sedap.co.uk; 10.30 pm; closed
Sat L & Sun L; no Amex.

Serafino W1 £57 ❸②④
8 Mount St 7629 0544 3–3B
"A good-value Italian in the heart of Mayfair" – and there aren't too
many of those! – where "they serve all the standard dishes with flair";
for maximum economy, seek out the café-style operation, hidden-
away in the basement. / www.finos.co.uk; 10.45 pm; closed Sat L & Sun.

Seven Park Place SW1 £72 ❶❶❷
7-8 Park Pl 7316 1600 3–4C
"Little-known", but worth discovering; ex-Aubergine chef William
Drabble "really knows his stuff", and cranks out "wonderfully
inventive" dishes at this "luxurious" (if oddly broken-up) dining room,
"tucked-away in a St James's side street".
/ www.stjameshotelandclub.com; 10 pm; closed Mon & Sun; set weekday L
£43 (FP).

Seven Stars WC2 £33 ④④❷
53 Carey St 7242 8521 2–2D
"Just behind the Royal Courts of Justice, and often filled with denizens
of the courts", this "tiny and ancient pub" is at its best when
"hilarious" landlady Roxy Beaujolais is in evidence; the "home-
cooking" is sometimes "slapdash", though, and the place can feel
"crammed-in" and "chaotic". / 11 pm, Sun 10.30 pm.

Seventeen W11 £41 ❷❷❸
17 Notting Hill Gate   7985 0006   6–2B
*Not helped by an unattractive location right on Notting Hill Gate,
and despite considerable investment in night-clubby decor,
this Chinese yearling has attracted little attention; the few reports
there are, however, tend to be rather positive.*
/ www.seventeen-london.co.uk; 11.30 pm.

1707
Fortnum & Mason W1 £47 ❹❸❸
181 Piccadilly   7734 8040   3–3D
*"More than 1,000 wines" – "one of London's best selections", all at
"modest mark-ups" – is the stand-out attraction at this civilised bar,
in the basement of the famously posh St James's grocers; with its
simple "deli"-style fare it makes a handy option for a "light bite".*
/ www.fortnumandmason.co.uk; 7 pm, Sun 5 pm.

Shaka Zulu NW1 £64 ❺❹❷
Stables Mkt   3376 9911   8–3B
*"They spent about a zillion pounds on the decor", at this gigantic,
"loud" Camden Town yearling, where "Las Vegas meets Africa";
shame they didn't invest as much in the service ("truly awful"), or the
cooking ("rubbish"). / www.shaka-zulu.com; 10 pm; closed weekday L.*

Shampers W1 £43 ❸❷❷
4 Kingly St   7437 1692   3–2D
*"Always humming", this "welcoming" '70s wine bar is an "unfailing"
Soho institution, serving "good honest food", and where Simon the
owner "looks after you and invariably recommends a decent bottle" –
"great fun". / www.shampers.net; 10.45 pm; closed Sun.*

Shanghai E8 £34 ❸❸❶
41 Kingsland High St   7254 2878   1–1C
*A Dalston Chinese of note for its decor ("make sure you sit in the
former pie 'n' eel shop bit, at the front"), and its sometimes
"fantastic" food ("especially the dim sum"); karaoke, however, is an
ever present risk – "where else can you enjoy top salt 'n' pepper
squid to the sound of Celine Dion being murdered next door…?"*
/ www.wengwahgroup.com; 11 pm; no Amex.

Shanghai Blues WC1 £60 ❷❹❷
193-197 High Holborn   7404 1668   4–1D
*"Dark and intriguing" decor, plus "really superb" cuisine –
not least "fabulous dim sum" – makes this "glossy" conversion of a
former library not only "the best restaurant around Holborn", but also
one of the capital's top Chinese; it's certainly no bargain, but it really
deserves wider recognition. / www.shanghaiblues.co.uk; 11.30 pm.*

J SHEEKEY WC2 £67 ❶❶❷
32-34 St Martin's Ct   7240 2565   4–3B
*"London's finest seafood restaurant"; this "special" but remarkably
"understated" Theatreland veteran remains the survey's most-
mentioned spot – its "suave" staff serve up "simple" but "superb"
dishes in a "bustling" series of "clubby" (if "cramped") chambers.*
/ www.j-sheekey.co.uk; midnight, Sun 11 pm; booking: max 6.

J Sheekey Oyster Bar WC2 £46 ❷❶❶
32-34 St Martin's Ct   7240 2565   4–3B
*"For sheer pleasure and joie-de-vivre", this "glamorous" add-on
to Theatreland's famous fish veteran really is a gem; with its "utterly
charming" staff and "to-die-for seafood", it's "fabulous for a pre-
/post- theatre bite" – if you can, bag a seat at the bar.*
/ www.j-sheekey.co.uk; midnight, Sun 11 pm; booking: max 3.

Shepherd's SW1 £50 ④❸❸
Marsham Ct, Marsham St 7834 9552 2–4C
*"For MPs, and those lunching them", this "discreet" Westminster
dining room can make a "very comfortable" and "quietly efficient"
choice, offering "straightforward" British fare of "steady" quality... or,
to put it another way: "you pay a lot for pretty average comfort food".
/ www.langansrestaurants.co.uk; 10.45 pm; closed Sat & Sun.*

Shilpa W6 £30 ❶❸⑤
206 King St 8741 3127 7–2B
*It looks totally "forgettable", but this Hammersmith Keralan is a
"gem", where "excellent" cooking comes at "amazing" prices –
well worth putting up with the "charmingly chaotic" service.
/ www.shilparestaurant.co.uk; 11 pm, Thu-Sat midnight; no Amex.*

The Ship SW18 £46 ❸❸❶
41 Jews Row 8870 9667 10–2B
*This "buzzy" and "atmospheric" boozer's special attraction is its large
Thames-side terrace, with spiffing river views and extensive al fresco
seating (so arrive early for your weekend lunch!) – "great food, and in
summer there's the added bonus of a huge BBQ". / www.theship.co.uk;
10 pm; no Amex; no booking, Sun L.*

Siam Central W1 £29 ❸④❸
14 Charlotte St 7436 7460 2–1C
*A "decent" and "reasonably-priced" Fitzrovia corner Thai, which
continues to attract praise for cooking which is "packed full
of flavour". / 10.45 pm, Sun 10.15 pm.*

Signor Sassi SW1 £62 ❸❸❷
14 Knightsbridge Grn 7584 2277 5–1D
*"A trusted favourite"; this "bustling" ("loud") Knightsbridge Italian
earns its enduring popularity with "good" ("if unspectacular") food,
and "warm" service in "traditional style". / www.signorsassi.co.uk;
11.30 pm, Sun 10.30 pm.*

Simplicity SE16 £45 ④❸❸
1 Tunnel Rd 7232 5174 11–2A
*"Hidden-away in the back streets of Rotherhithe", this "friendly" and
"intimate" spot pleases most, if not quite all, the locals, with its
"very good breakfast", and other more substantial fare too.
/ www.simplicityrestaurants.com; 10.30 pm; closed weekday L; no Amex.*

Simply Indian SE1 £25 ❸④④
25 Tabard St 7407 5005 1–3C
*"A bargain BYO Indian, conveniently close to London Bridge station" –
the food is "innovative" and "of reasonably good quality", but service
can be "iffy". / www.simplyindian.co.uk; 11.30 pm.*

Simpson's Tavern EC3 £37 ④❸❶
38 1/2 Ball Ct, Cornhill 7626 9985 9–2C
*"Still a great institution for City schoolboys" – this cramped
chophouse "classic" (1757) delivers a menu of unreformed British
stodge – don't miss the savoury speciality of 'stewed cheese';
"generally, men love it, and women don't". / www.simpsonstavern.co.uk;
3 pm; L only, closed Sat & Sun.*

Simpsons-in-the-Strand WC2 £75 ④⑤④
100 Strand 7836 9112 4–3D
*"Sadly now for (rich) tourists", this "olde-worlde" Covent Garden
classic is "just not what it's cracked up to be" nowadays – its iffy
"traditional" fare is "poorly served", and "overpriced" too; the "meaty
breakfast", however, still comes "thoroughly recommended".
/ www.simpsonsinthestrand.co.uk; 10.45 pm, Sun 9 pm; no trainers.*

Singapore Garden NW6 £45 ❷❷❸
83a Fairfax Rd   7624 8233   8–2A
"London's top Singaporean" (not a tough contest, admittedly) –
this "always-busy" Swiss Cottage veteran is "a cut above" your typical
local, and serves dishes of "consistently high quality".
/ www.singaporegarden.co.uk; 11 pm, Fri & Sat 11.30 pm.

(Gallery)
Sketch W1 £64 ⑤⑤④
9 Conduit St   7659 4500   3–2C
It's "designed to impress" (and has "the best loos in London"),
but few places achieve such dire ratings in the survey as this
"happening" – read hilariously "pretentious" and "overpriced" –
Mayfair venue, where the food is "so bad" it could only ever
be "a sideshow". / www.sketch.uk.com; 11 pm; D only, closed Sun; booking:
max 10.

(Lecture Room)
Sketch W1 £102 ⑤⑤❸
9 Conduit St   7659 4500   3–2C
This "hysterically poncy" dining room, on the first floor of an
impressive Mayfair palazzo, is overseen from afar by Parisian über-
chef Pierre Gagnaire; fans say its OTT formula is "brilliant" –
detractors just find it "shockingly bad", and insanely overpriced too.
/ www.sketch.uk.com; 10.30 pm; closed Mon, Sat L & Sun; no trainers; booking:
max 8; set weekday L £56 (FP).

(The Parlour)
Sketch W1 £45 ④④❸
9 Conduit St   7659 4533   3–2C
The "quirky" pâtisserie of this Mayfair palazzo is arguably the
most useful part – fans proclaim it "a hidden gem for afternoon tea".
/ www.sketch.uk.com; closed Sun; no Amex; no booking.

Skipjacks HA3 £38 ❶❷⑤
268-270 Streatfield Rd   8204 7554   1–1A
"Always busy, often with queues out the door" – this family-run
Harrow chippy may look "very ordinary", but the fish (grilled,
steamed or fried) is "amazing", and "great value"; fortunately the
service is "super-fast" too. / 10.30 pm; closed Sun.

Skylon
South Bank Centre SE1 £55 ④④❷
Southbank Centre, Belvedere Rd   7654 7800   2–3D
"To-die-for views" through the huge windows lend quite a "sense
of occasion" to this "light", "airy", and glamorously '50s-tastic
operation, in the Festival Hall; the food, though, too often seems
"around the standard of a company canteen", and "massively
overpriced" too. / www.skylonrestaurant.co.uk; 10.45 pm, Sun 10.30 pm;
no trainers.

Slurp £26 ❸❸⑤
104-106 Streatham High Rd, SW16   8677 7786   10–2D
138 Merton Rd, SW19   8543 4141   10–2B
"You wouldn't linger", but – for a quick, filling, delicious bowl of rice
or noodles – check out these "canteen-like" operations,
in Wimbledon and Streatham. / www.slurprestaurant.co.uk; 11 pm;
no Amex.

Smith Square SW1 [NEW]   £41
St John's, Smith Sq   7222 2779   2–4C
*The new name for the dining operation (fka the Footstool) beneath
the deconsecrated Westminster church that's now a concert hall;
it has as yet inspired no survey commentary, but we include it for its
practical attractions in a thin area.* / www.leafi.co.uk; 10 pm depends
on concert; no Amex.

Smithfield Bar & Grill EC1   £52   ④④④
2-3 West Smithfield   7246 0900   9–2A
*The "louche" and "glitzy" ("'80s-throwback") feel does the place
no favours, but this "buzzy" Smithfield spot has its fans… even
if reports on its steaks and other fare, range from "fantastic"
to "distinctly average".* / www.blackhouse.uk.com; 10.30 pm; closed
Sat L & Sun.

(Ground Floor)
Smiths of Smithfield EC1   £29   ④④❷
67-77 Charterhouse St   7251 7950   9–1A
*"Unrivalled for weekend brunch" – the ground-floor bar/diner of this
warehouse-conversion, by Smithfield Market, does "marvellous"
breakfasts, and has a "brilliant buzz most mornings"; at other times
– little commented-on – it's a place for a "fast, effective bite".*
/ www.smithsofsmithfield.co.uk; L only.

(Dining Room)
Smiths of Smithfield EC1   £50   ④④❸
67-77 Charterhouse St   7251 7950   9–1A
*A certain "infectious vibe" is the only reliable attraction of the
"buzzy" (very "loud") first floor of this Smithfield behemoth; at best,
it offers a "convenient" venue for "OK" burgers and other "simple"
fare, but service is "slow", and the food can be "unexciting".*
/ www.smithsofsmithfield.co.uk; 10.45 pm; closed Sat L & Sun; booking:
max 12.

(Top Floor)
Smiths of Smithfield EC1   £65   ④④❸
67-77 Charterhouse St   7251 7950   9–1A
*"Beautiful views of the City" and "wonderful steaks" have long made
this "bright" dining room a "solid" option for business entertaining;
perhaps that's why prices can seem "very high" – both food and
service are "very ordinary" by comparison.*
/ www.smithsofsmithfield.co.uk; 10.45 pm; closed Sat L & Sun D; booking:
max 10.

Sofra   £35   ④④④
1 St Christopher's Pl, W1   7224 4080   3–1A
18 Shepherd St, W1   7493 3320   3–4B
36 Tavistock St, WC2   7240 3773   4–3D
11 Circus Rd, NW8   7586 9889   8–3A
*"Well-prepared" mezze, in particular, still commend this long-
established Turkish bistro-chain to many reporters; they're "variable",
though – when an experience is both "formulaic" and "chaotic",
it arguably offers the worst of all possible worlds!* / www.sofra.co.uk;
11 pm-midnight.

Soho Japan W1   £40   ❸❷④
52 Wells St   7323 4661   2–1B
*It looks like the Irish pub it once was, but this "easy-going" Japanese
spot, just north of Oxford Street, is tipped for some "very good"
dishes.* / www.sohojapan.co.uk; 10.30 pm; closed Sat L & Sun; no Amex.

Solly's NW11 £42 ④⑤⑤
146-150 Golders Green Rd   8455 0004   1–1B
With its "informal" café/take-away, and grander restaurant upstairs, this busy Israeli is a linchpin of the Golder's Green strip, serving "plentiful helpings of standard kosher fare"; it can seem "rather pricey" and complacent, though, and critics fear it's simply "lost the plot". / 10.30 pm; closed Fri D & Sat L; no credit cards.

Somerstown Coffee House NW1 £36 ④❸❸
60 Chalton St   7691 9136   8–3C
Between Euston and King's Cross, a "great boozer/restaurant combo"; it remains a pretty "dependable" destination but, of late, the "previously adventurous French dishes have seemed a little more ordinary than before". / www.somerstowncoffeehouse.co.uk; 10 pm.

Sông Quê E2 £29 ❷⑤⑤
134 Kingsland Rd   7613 3222   12–1B
"OK, so it's scruffy, noisy and chaotic", but this "no-frills" Shoreditch caff still draws queues with its "amazingly fresh" Vietnamese dishes, not least "the best pho" – "and at these prices, who's complaining?" / 11 pm; no Amex.

Sonny's SW13 £48 ④❷❸
94 Church Rd   8748 0393   10–1A
As "a solid, dependable neighbourhood restaurant", this "convivial" Barnes local of (very) long standing still has much going for it; even fans, however, would concede that nowadays "its strength lies in its consistency, not its flair". / www.sonnys.co.uk; 10.30 pm Fri & Sat 11 pm; closed Sun D; set weekday L £29 (FP), set dinner £32 (FP).

La Sophia W10 NEW £46 ❷❷④
46 Golborne Road   8968 2200   6–1A
An "intimate" Mediterranean newcomer, in North Kensington, already attracting plaudits for its "good food" and its "obliging" service. / www.lasophia.co.uk; Sun 10pm, Fri & Sat 11 pm, 10.30 pm.

Sophie's Steakhouse £44 ④❸❸
29-31 Wellington St, WC2   7836 8836   4–3D
311-313 Fulham Rd, SW10   7352 0088   5–3B
As "a good place to socialise", this "always-packed" Chelsea steakhouse still has many fans for its "great buzz" and "pretty good" steaks; its ratings are waning, though, with the food at the "more impersonal" Covent Garden sibling reckoned a particular "yawn". / www.sophiessteakhouse.com; SW10 11.45 pm, Sun 11.15 pm; WC2 12.45 pm, Sun 11 pm; no booking; set weekday L £26 (FP).

Soseki EC3 £55 ❷❷❷
1f, 20 Bury St   7621 9211   9–2D
"A Japanese oasis in the heart of the City!" – this "serene" and "beautiful" spot, by the Gherkin, offers "very well-executed" cuisine, with "a rich sense of ceremonial"; it makes a "great place for a business lunch or dinner", but – if you get one of the booths – can be "very romantic" too. / www.soseki.co.uk; 10 pm; closed Sat & Sun; booking: max 12.

Sotheby's Café W1 £52 ❷❷❷
34-35 New Bond St   7293 5077   3–2C
"It's not exactly cheap", but the café off the foyer of the famous Mayfair auction house offers a simple but classy menu, realised to a "consistently excellent" standard. / www.sothebys.com; L only, closed Sat & Sun; booking: max 8.

Spaniard's Inn NW3 £40 ❸❸❶
Spaniards Rd, Hampstead Heath   8731 8406   8–1A
"Quirky" and "most atmospheric", this ancient pub, north
of Hampstead Heath, is "a great spot for those with dogs or kids",
thanks not least to its "huge beer garden"; the food is nothing special,
but that does nothing to dent the place's enormous popularity.
/ www.thespaniardshampstead.co.uk; 10 pm.

Spianata & Co £10 ❷❸④
Tooley St, SE1   8616 4662   9–4D NEW
41 Brushfield St, E1   7655 4411   12–2B
20 Holborn Viaduct, EC1   7248 5947   9–2A
17 Blomfield St, EC2   7256 9103   9–2C
29-30 Leadenhall Mkt, EC3   7929 1339   9–2D
73 Watling St, EC4   7236 3666   9–2B
"Panini heaven"; spianata, Roman-style – using "awesome own-baked
bread", with "great quality ingredients and combos" – are the
highlight at these "grab-and-go" pit stops. / www.spianata.com; 3.30 pm;
EC3 11 pm; closed Sat & Sun; E1 closed Sat; no credit cards; no booking.

Spice Market
W Hotel London W1 NEW £75 ④④④
10 Wardour St   7758 1088   4–3A
"A shambles"; top NYC chef Jean-Georges Vongerichten's much-hyped
fusion newcomer, off Leicester Square, offers "hit-and-miss" cooking,
"patchy" service and an interior that's "great... if you've never been
inside a boutique hotel before"; drinks prices can seem exorbitant
too. / www.spicemarketlondon.co.uk; Sun-Wed 11 pm, Thu-Sat 11.30 pm;
set weekday L £41 (FP), set pre-theatre £43 (FP).

The Spread Eagle SE10 £51 ④④❸
1-2 Stockwell St   8853 2333   1–3D
This "fine old building" – an olde-worlde Greenwich tavern – offers
a "very comfortable" location for a meal; it may seem rather
"overpriced", though – for critics, "the sumptuous decor only
heightens the disappointment". / www.spreadeaglerestaurant.co.uk;
10.30 pm; no Amex; set Sun L £33 (FP).

Spuntino W1 NEW £41 ❸❷❷
61 Rupert St   no tel   3–2D
With its "grimy Americana" (Lower East Side-style), its "achingly cool"
staff, and its menu of calorific "US faves", Russell Norman's "studied"
newcomer – "in the sleaziest heart of Soho" – has inspired
"evangelical fervour" amongst fashionista twenty/thirty-somethings;
doubters, though, find the whole shtick "a bit meh". / Rated on Editors'
visit; www.spuntino.co.uk; 11.30 pm, Sun 10.30 pm.

THE SQUARE W1 £106 ❷❷❸
6-10 Bruton St   7495 7100   3–2C
"Superb in every department" – the "complex" cuisine Phil Howard
offers at this acclaimed Mayfair dining room is complemented by an
"immense" wine list of "amazing" quality; the ambience can seem
"sombre", though, not helped by the place's popularity with "Identikit
men in suits". / www.squarerestaurant.com; 9.45 pm, Sat 10.15 pm,
Sun 9.30 pm; closed Sat L & Sun L; booking: max 8; set weekday L £56 (FP).

Sree Krishna SW17 £26 ❶❷❸
192-194 Tooting High St   8672 4250   10–2C
On top form at present, this "friendly" Tooting veteran dishes
up "some of the best south Indian food in London" (including
an "astonishing selection of starters"); "if you want to go off-piste,
they are very good at preparing a feast for you"; BYO.
/ www.sreekrishna.co.uk; 11 pm, Fri & Sat midnight.

Star of India SW5   £49   ❷❹❸
154 Old Brompton Rd   7373 2901   5–2B
*"An old favourite that still delivers"; perhaps surprisingly, though,
it's not the characterful ("dated") decor of this South Kensington
veteran which attracts attention, nor the "slow" and sometimes "off-
hand" service – rather, it's the "lovely, fresh and interesting" cuisine!
/ www.starofindia.eu; 11.45 pm, Sun 11.15 pm.*

Starbucks   £14   ❹❸❸
Branches throughout London
*Barristas who seem "genuinely happy to serve" and "comfy branches
for a chat" create the "welcoming" appeal of this "formulaic" mega-
chain; even those who think "the coffee is great", however, may feel
its paninis, cakes and other fare "are not". / www.starbucks.com;
6.30 pm-11 pm; most City branches closed all or part of weekend; no booking.*

Stein's TW10   £29   ❸❹❷
Towpath (Rear of 55 Petersham Rd)   8948 8189   1–4A
*For "a really fun day by the riverside" ("with the added bonus of a
gated play area for kids"), try this "lovely" German beer garden,
near Richmond Bridge – "a totally relaxed place" with a good-value,
if admittedly "rather sausage-heavy", menu. / www.stein-s.com; 9.30 pm;
no Amex.*

Stick & Bowl W8   £23   ❸❸❸
31 Kensington High St   7937 2778   5–1A
*"Unassuming, easily-overlooked and shabby", this handy Chinese
chow house, in Kensington, is a "rushed" sort of place where you eat
"squashed in on bar stools"; thanks to its "huge" and "cheap" noodle
dishes, "it's always busy, mostly with Asians". / 10.45 pm; no credit cards;
no booking.*

Sticky Fingers W8   £43   ❹❹❸
1a Phillimore Gdns   7938 5338   5–1A
*"Good big juicy burgers" and other "fattening" American fare help
make this veteran Kensington diner a popular nomination for those
with kids in tow; "if you get bored, you can look at the Rolling Stones
memorabilia on the walls". / www.stickyfingers.co.uk; 11.30 pm.*

Stock Pot   £27   ❺❹❹
40 Panton St, SW1   7839 5142   4–4A
273 King's Rd, SW3   7823 3175   5–3C
*These "die hard" '60s canteens are "oh-so-dependable" for "old-
fashioned, school-dinners scoff at great prices"; "don't linger, though
– they're for fuelling up!" / SW1 11.30 pm, Wed-Sat midnight, Sun 11 pm
SW3 10.15 pm, Sun 9.45 pm; no Amex.*

Strada   £38   ❹❹❸
Branches throughout London
*"A very good alternative to Pizza Express" (which it lags only narrowly
in all survey-categories), this popular Italian chain is "pretty reliable",
and "well geared up to cope with kids". / www.strada.co.uk;
10.30 pm-11 pm; some booking restrictions apply.*

Stringray Café   £27   ❹❹❹
36 Highbury Pk, N5   7354 9309   8–2D
Tufnell Pk, NW5   7482 4855   8–2B
109 Columbia Rd, E2   7613 1141   12–1C
*"Oversized pizza and giant pastas" come at "very cheap" prices,
at these "basic", "busy" and "cheerful" Italian stand-bys;
E2 (near Columbia Road Market) scores best, while N5 (near the
Arsenal ground) is best-known. / www.stringraycafe.co.uk; 11 pm; no Amex.*

Sufi W12 £30 ❸❷④
70 Askew Rd 8834 4888 7–1B
"A simple Persian café", in the depths of Shepherd's Bush; its "lovely" staff serve up some "excellent" grills, and the bread to go with them is "to die for". / www.sufirestaurant.com; 11 pm.

Suk Saran SW19 £42 ❸④④
29 Wimbledon Rd 8947 9199 10–2B
Looking for a "real taste of Thailand"? – the food at this high-street operation, near Wimbledon station, is "surprisingly good". / www.sukhogroup.com; 11 pm; booking: max 20; set weekday L £30 (FP).

Sukho Fine Thai Cuisine SW6 £40 ❶❷❸
855 Fulham Rd 7371 7600 10–1B
"Dishes look like works of art, and taste like masterpieces too", at this "obliging" and "reasonably-priced" Thai café; even though it's "cramped" and rather "out of the way", in deepest Fulham, "you must book". / www.sukhogroup.co.uk; 11 pm.

The Summerhouse W9 £45 ④④❶
60 Blomfield Rd 7286 6752 8–4A
"The food's nothing to shout about but, with that view of the canal, who cares?" – that's the trade-off at this summer-only 'pop-up', in Little Venice, which serves a "slightly overpriced menu, focussed on fish". / www.summerhousebythewaterway.co.uk; 10.30 pm, Sun 10 pm; Mon-Fri closed D, Sat & Sun open L & D; no Amex.

Sumosan W1 £75 ❸❸❸
26b Albemarle St 7495 5999 3–3C
"It doesn't pull in the crowds like some of its rivals", but this "high-end" Mayfair haunt still serves some "mind-blowing" sushi and other Japanese fusion fare that's on a par with the Nobus of the world – it is likewise "priced for oligarchs", of course, but the style is relatively low-key. / www.sumosan.com; 11.30 pm, Sun 10.30 pm; closed Sat L & Sun L.

supperclub W10 £62 ④④❶
12 Acklam Rd 8964 6600 6–1A
"Lounging on beds is a perfect way to spend a romantic evening with someone", say fans of this decadent North Kensington nitespot, where cabaret is a feature; "it's an interesting experience but, for the quality of the food, an outrageously expensive one". / www.supperclub.com; 10.30 pm; D only.

Le Suquet SW3 £65 ❸④④
104 Draycott Ave 7581 1785 5–2C
A "very authentic French fish restaurant", on a quiet Chelsea corner (where "sitting outdoors on a warm night evokes the Côte d'Azur"); the style may be "dated", but notably good fruits-de-mer are a highlight of the "consistent" menu. / 11.30 pm.

Sushi of Shiori NW1 £38 ❶❶④
144 Drummond St 7388 9962 8–4C
A "tiny, Tokyo-style" joint, lost "amidst the curry houses of Drummond Street", hailed by all who comment on it for "exquisite" sushi – "authentic", "beautifully presented", and with "really unusual flavours"; "best option is the Omakase – you set a price and leave the selections to the chef". / www.sushiofshiori.co.uk; 10 pm; closed Mon & Sun; no Amex; set always available £32 (FP).

Sushisamba EC2 NEW
Heron Tower, 110 Bishopsgate awaiting tel 9–2D
At the top of the City's Heron Tower – an offshoot of a trendy NYC Japanese/South American fusion specialist, scheduled to open in late-2011.

Sushi-Say NW2 £41 ❶❶❸
33b Walm Ln 8459 7512 1–1A
"The freshest sushi this side of Tokyo" and other "ethereal" Japanese dishes ("it's always worth asking about the day's specials") draw fans from far and wide to this "unlikely" – but "really outstanding" – family-run outfit, in deepest Willesden. / 10 pm, Sat 10.30 pm, Sun 9.30 pm; closed Mon, Tue-Fri D only, Sat & Sun open L & D; no Amex.

Sushinho SW3 £47 ❹❸❷
312-314 King's Rd 7349 7496 5–3C
Thanks to its "happy music" and "fantastic cocktails", this "elegant" Chelsea bar/restaurant certainly has a "good vibe"; Brazil meets Japan on its weird-looking fusion menu – there are some "delicious" outcomes, but results are "not consistent", and some of the prices are "eye-popping". / www.sushinho.com; 10 pm; closed Mon L, Tue L & Sun L.

The Swan W4 £39 ❷❸❷
119 Acton Ln 8994 8262 7–1A
"A really classy neighbourhood pub", "hidden-away" in a Chiswick backwater, and complete with "a lovely garden"; service is "charming", and the "earthy gastro-fare" offers some "first-rate value". / theswanchiswick.co.uk; 10 pm, Fri & Sat 10.30 pm, Sun 10 pm; closed weekday L.

Swan & Edgar NW1 £37 ❹❹❷
43 Linhope St 7724 6268 2–1A
"A lovely, tiny place" that's making "a useful addition to the Baker Street area"; this somewhat eccentric gastropub offers "comforting", if slightly "hit-and-miss", cooking, plus "good wines by the glass". / www.swanandedgar.co.uk; 10 pm, Sun 9 pm; D only, ex Sun open L & D.

The Swan at the Globe SE1 £48 ❹❹❷
21 New Globe Walk 7928 9444 9–3B
"Excellent views of the Thames and St Paul's" reward visitors to the first-floor dining room of the Bard's re-created South Bank theatre; the food – briefly bucked up after the arrival of Ramsay-protégé Mark Sargeant – has quickly reverted to its "unadventurous" old ways. / www.swanattheglobe.co.uk; 10.30 pm; closed Sun D.

Sweet & Spicy E1 £11 ❷❷❺
40 Brick Ln 7247 1081 12–2C
"Unbelievably cheap and authentic Indian/Pakistani food" wins praise for this "down-to-earth" caff – one of the best bets on Brick Lane; "good service" too. / www.sweetandspicylondon.co.uk; 11 pm, Fri & Sat midnight; no Amex.

Sweetings EC4 £58 ❸❸❸
39 Queen Victoria St 7248 3062 9–3B
"Still Dickensian, still unique!"; "everyone should lunch at least once", at this "marvellous" City "throwback", which serves "very good" – and "very expensive" – seafood; NB: "get there early to avoid the pinstriped throngs!" / 3.30 pm; L only, closed Sat & Sun; no booking.

Taberna Etrusca EC4 £48 ❹❹❹
9 Bow Churchyard 7248 5552 9–2C
This "traditional" and ever-popular City Italian, with its sunny al fresco tables, remains "as good as it has been for years" – the less kind would say this means it is still "no great shakes". / www.etruscarestaurants.com; closed Sat & Sun.

The Table SE1 £40 ④❸❸
83 Southwark St   7401 2760   9–4B
*A trendy communal canteen (part of an architects' practice), not far
from Southwark Bridge, where "fantastic" breakfasts are a highlight,
and which is good for lunch too; views (few) on the place's attractions
at dinner are rather mixed. / www.thetablecafe.com; 10.30 pm; closed
Mon D & Sun D.*

Taiwan Village SW6 £32 ❶❶❸
85 Lillie Rd   7381 2900   5–3A
*Given its "unpromising location" – just off the North End Road –
this sensational Chinese/Taiwanese outfit can seem like "a major
discovery"; choose the 'Leave It With Us' menu option for some
"amazing flavours", at "incredible-value" prices.
/ www.taiwanvillage.com; 11.30 pm; closed weekday L; booking: max 20.*

Tajima Tei EC1 £32 ❶❷④
9-11 Leather Ln   7404 9665   9–2A
*"Simple and unpretentious, but never failing to impress" –
this "very genuine" and "good-value" Japanese, off Hatton Garden,
is well worth seeking out for its "quality" cuisine. / www.tajima-tei.co.uk;
10 pm; closed Sat & Sun; no booking, L.*

Talad Thai SW15 £28 ❸❸⑤
320 Upper Richmond Rd   8246 5791   10–2A
*Not quite the 'rave' it once was, but this "functional" Putney Thai
retains an "authentic" quality that commends it to most reporters;
it's part 'n' parcel with the "handy oriental supermarket next door".
/ www.taladthai.co.uk; 10.30 pm, Sun 9.30 pm; no Amex.*

Tamarai WC2 £52 ④④④
167 Drury Ln   7831 9399   4–1C
*A "trendy"-looking Indian basement, in Covent Garden;
some reporters love its "darkly atmospheric" style, "clubby"
atmosphere, and "interesting" dishes – critics, however, "just do not
understand the fuss". / www.tamarai.co.uk; 11 pm; D only, closed Sun.*

Tamarind W1 £68 ❸❸④
20 Queen St   7629 3561   3–3B
*"Creative" Indian cooking and "attentive" service still win high praise
for this "sophisticated" Mayfair basement; critics fear, however,
that "the spark has gone", and the overall performance does indeed
risk becoming rather "middle-of-the-road".
/ www.tamarindrestaurant.com; 11 pm, Sun 10.30 pm; closed Sat L;
set weekday L £38 (FP).*

Tandoori Nights SE22 £35 ❸❸❸
73 Lordship Ln   8299 4077   1–4D
*The menu may be "due for an update", but this East Dulwich curry
house "continues to serve consistently tasty and freshly-spiced" North
Indian food. / www.tandoorinightsdulwich.co.uk; 11.30 pm; closed
weekday L & Sat L.*

Tangawizi TW1 £41 ❸❸④
406 Richmond Rd   8891 3737   1–4A
*"Some real hits, the odd miss" – that's what you should expect if you
visit this "very busy" Twickenham subcontinental. / www.tangawizi.co.uk;
11 pm, Sun 10.30 pm; D only.*

Tapas Brindisa £39 ❷❸❷
46 Broadwick St, W1 7534 1690 3–2D
18-20 Southwark St, SE1 7357 8880 9–4C
"Just like being in an upscale Madrid tapas place" – the *"chaotic"*
Borough original has won an enormous following for its *"gutsy"* fare,
and even if it's a tad *"pricey for what it is"*, you must *"arrive early"*;
Soho (formerly Tierra Brindisa) is now a sibling – historically it's
lagged SE1 in all areas but service. / 10.45 pm, Sun 10 pm; W1 booking:
max 10.

Taqueria W11 £34 ④④❸
139-143 Westbourne Grove 7229 4734 6–1B
"Absolutely not Tex-Mex!" – this *"casual and buzzy"* Notting Hill
Mexican actually delivers *"something akin to the real thing"*, with its
fresh tacos and *"wonderful"* drinks; even so, it's really *"not cheap"*
and a bit *"variable"* too, so *"best for a snack and a beer"*.
/ www.taqueria.co.uk; Mon-Thu 11 pm, Fri & Sat 11.30 pm, Sun 10.30 pm;
no Amex; no booking Fri-Sun.

Taro £28 ❸❸❸
10 Old Compton St, W1 7439 2275 4–2B
61 Brewer St, W1 7734 5826 3–2D
"Fast, cheerful and reliable" – these *"busy"* Japanese canteens,
in Soho, offer an *"impressively wide"* menu of *"simple"* sushi, noodle
and curry dishes, at *"cheap"* prices. / www.tarorestaurants.co.uk;
10.30 pm, Sun 9.30 pm; no Amex; Brewer St only small bookings.

Tartine SW3 £46 ❸④❸
114 Draycott Ave 7589 4981 5–2C
"A nice place after a bit of Sloaney shopping" – and *"not overpriced
by Chelsea standards"*, either – this superior Brompton Cross pit stop
serves *"high-quality"* open sandwiches (pain Poilâne), and other light
bites. / www.tartine.co.uk; Mon-Wed 11.30 pm, Thu-Sat 12pm,
Sun 10.30 pm.

Tas £32 ④❸❸
22 Bloomsbury St, WC1 7637 4555 2–1C
33 The Cut, SE1 7928 2111 9–4A
72 Borough High St, SE1 7403 7200 9–4C
76 Borough High St, SE1 7403 8557 9–4C
37 Farringdon Rd, EC1 7430 9721 9–1A
"Affordable" and pretty *"reliable"* too, these ever-*"crowded"* Turkish
restaurants are often hailed as an *"excellent stand-by"*
(not least *"for big groups"*); critics, though, do feel the food *"has gone
downhill"* in recent times. / www.tasrestaurant.com; 11.30 pm,
Sun 10.30 pm; set always available £20 (FP).

Tas Pide SE1 £30 ④❷❷
20-22 New Globe Walk 7928 3300 9–3B
A *"jolly"* Anatolian café, opposite Shakespeare's Globe, which
is named after its Turkish *'pizza'* speciality – a *"cheap"* and
"enjoyable" snack, preferable to the *"rather ordinary"* mezze also
available. / www.tasrestaurant.com/tas_pide; 11.30 pm, Sun 10.30 pm.

La Tasca £30 ⑤❸❸
Branches throughout London
*"Staff who try hard can't make up for food that's very ordinary and
tasteless"*, at these lively – but on occasion *"diabolical"* – tapas joints;
perhaps the most eloquent commentary on the London outlets is the
tiny number of reports they inspire. / www.latasca.co.uk; 11 pm;
E14 10.45 pm; booking: min 8.

(Rex Whistler)
Tate Britain SW1   £51   ❸❸❷
Millbank 7887 8825 2–4C
The "beautiful" Whistler-muralled dining room of this Westminster
gallery offers rather "old-fashioned" British food that's "always good";
even so, the scoff's "beside the point", compared to the "out-of-this-
world" wine list (which is "fairly-priced" too). / www.tate.org.uk;
L & afternoon tea only.

(Restaurant, Level 7)
Tate Modern SE1   £43   ❹❹❷
Bankside 7887 8888 9–3B
"Stunning views" – some of London's finest – are the draw to this
South Bank gallery's "buzzy" 7th-floor café; fans say the "simple"
fare is "enjoyable" too, but to critics it's just "basic" and
"very ordinary". / www.tate.org.uk; 9.30 pm; Sun-Thu closed D, Fri & Sat
open L & D.

(Café, Level 2)
Tate Modern SE1   £36   ❸❹❸
Bankside 7401 5014 9–3B
The Tate's ground-floor café is sometimes "too busy", but foodwise
it generally proves the more reliable of the two major options at this
much-visited museum of modern art; it's a strikingly-designed and kid-
friendly space, where the straightforward food usually satisfies.
/ www.tate.org.uk/modern/eatanddrink; Fri 9.30 pm; L & tea only, ex Fri open
L & D.

Tatra W12   £35   ❹❹❹
24 Goldhawk Rd 8749 8193 7–1C
On a corner near Goldhawk Road tube, this year-old venture goes
largely un-noticed, but it's a "pleasant and efficient" spot offering
"substantial portions of well-prepared Polish food".
/ www.tatrarestaurant.co.uk; 11 pm, Sun 10 pm.

Telegraph SW15   £36   ❹❹❸
Telegraph Rd 8788 2011 10–2A
"After a walk or bike ride on Wimbledon Common", this 'country pub
in London' (their words) makes a "cosy" destination; there's "ample
outdoor seating", but "it can get crowded" nonetheless.
/ www.thetelegraphputney.co.uk; 8.30 pm, Fri & Sat 9.30 pm.

Tempo W1 NEW   £58   ❸❷❸
54 Curzon St 7629 2742 3–3B
"Innovative" and "polished" cooking – from a Japanese chef! –
has helped make Henry Togna's "friendly" Italian newcomer (on the
site of Franks, RIP) a welcome addition to Mayfair; discreetly hidden-
away upstairs, there's a "fabulous" bar. / www.tempomayfair.co.uk;
10.30 pm; closed Sat L & Sun; Table max 8.

Ten Ten Tei W1   £35   ❸❸⑤
56 Brewer St 7287 1738 3–2D
"Basic Japanese fare at very competitive prices" – the lure to this
"grim"-looking Soho canteen; some regulars, though, fear that it has
"slipped" of late. / 10 pm; closed Sun; no Amex; no booking Fri & Sat.

Tendido Cero SW5   £38   ❸❸❷
174 Old Brompton Rd 7370 3685 5–2B
With its "bubbly" style and "very dependable" cuisine, "Cambio
de Tercio's fabulous, more tapas-y younger sibling" offers "a really fun
night out"; this South Kensington dining room's "ruthless" two-sittings
policy can be "annoying", though, and pricing can grate.
/ www.cambiodetercio.co.uk; 11 pm.

FSA

Tendido Cuatro SW6 £39 ❷❷❷
108-110 New King's Rd   7371 5147   10–1B
*"Interesting tapas", "wonderful paella" and "fabulous red wine"
create a more-than-local following for this Fulham outpost of the
Cambio de Tercio empire. / www.cambiodetercio.co.uk; 11 pm.*

Tentazioni SE1 £49 ❸❸❸
2 Mill St   7394 5248   11–2A
*What's happening at this "quirky" and "stylish" Italian, "hidden-away
down an alley near Tower Bridge"? – its "interesting" regional cooking
"is not of the quality it was", and service (though often "lovely") has
sometimes seemed "disinterested" of late. / www.tentazioni.co.uk;
10.45 pm; closed Sat L & Sun; set weekday L £21 (FP).*

The Terrace in the Fields WC2 £39 ❸④❷
Lincoln's Inn Fields   7430 1234   2–2D
*Leafy Lincoln's Inn Fields provides the "terrific", location ("really
coming into its own in the summer") for this "rather hidden-away"
modern shed, which serves "interesting" West Indian-influenced food.
/ www.theterrace.info; 9 pm; L only, closed Sat & Sun.*

Terranostra EC4 £45 ❸❷④
27 Old Bailey   3201 0077   9–2A
*Near the Old Bailey, a low-key spot worth seeking out for its
"comparatively simple" Sardinian food, which is often "done really
well". / www.terranostrafood.co.uk; 10 pm; closed Sat L & Sun.*

TERROIRS WC2 £46 ❷❸❸
5 William IV St   7036 0660   4–4C
*"Phenomenally innovative" ('biodynamique') wines twinned with
a petits-plats-based menu of "rich" and "earthy" fare – including
much charcuterie and cheese – have made a massive name for this
"cramped" but "deservedly busy" and "convivial" spot, near Charing
Cross. / www.terroirswinebar.com; 11 pm; closed Sun.*

Texture W1 £79 ❷❶❸
34 Portman St   7224 0028   2–2A
*A grand Marylebone dining room where Angar Sverrisson's
"fascinating" cuisine – "subtle flavours, brilliantly juxtaposed" and
with no butter or cream in the savoury dishes – comes "perfectly
combined" with business partner Xavier Rousset's wine selection;
if there's a niggle it's the setting – for some reporters it just "doesn't
work". / www.texture-restaurant.co.uk; 10.30 pm; closed Mon & Sun;
set weekday L £46 (FP).*

Thai Corner Café SE22 £23 ❸❸❸
44 North Cross Rd   8299 4041   1–4D
*"Delicious, authentic, casual, essential to book..." – this BYO
East Dulwich café remains a "very dependable" local. / 10.30 pm;
closed Mon L; no credit cards.*

Thai Garden SW11 £30 ❸④④
58 Battersea Rise   7738 0380   10–2C
*A "stalwart" Battersea Thai that "never lets you down" – the food
is "not adventurous", but it is "tasty" and "fairly-priced".
/ www.thaigarden.co.uk; 11 pm; D only.*

Thai on the River SW11 £42 ❸④❸
2 Lombard Rd   7924 6090   5–4B
*Overlooking the Thames, this Battersea Thai survives on its all-round
appeal, even if the cognoscenti may find the food a little 'safe'.
/ www.thaiontheriver.com; 10.30 pm.*

Thai Pot WC2   £36   ❸❷❸
1 Bedfordbury   7379 4580   4–4C
*"Very close to the Coliseum, and ideal for a group meal before
a show", this "lively and cheerful" stand-by is "not unduly expensive",
and it's "always popular". / www.thaipot.biz; 11.15 pm; closed Sun.*

Thai Square   £35   ❹❸❸
21-24 Cockspur St, SW1   7839 4000   2–3C
27-28 St Annes Ct, W1   7287 2000   3–1D
5 Princess St, W1   7499 3333   3–1C
148 The Strand, WC2   7497 0904   2–2D
166-170 Shaftesbury Ave, WC2   7836 7600   4–1B
229-230 Strand, WC2   7353 6980   2–2D
19 Exhibition Rd, SW7   7584 8359   5–2C
347-349 Upper St, N1   7704 2000   8–3D
2-4 Lower Richmond Rd, SW15   8780 1811   10–1A
136-138 Minories, EC3   7680 1111   9–3D
1-7 Great St Thomas Apostle, EC4   7329 0001   9–3B
*An Asian chain that's seen ratings ebb in recent years; fans still find
it a "solid" performer, but sceptics say it "trades on its name and
strong branch locations" – in particular, its striking SW15 site
(by Putney Bridge) enjoys "fantastic Thames views".
/ www.thaisquare.net; 10 pm-11.30 pm; SW1 Fri & Sat 1 am; WC2, EC3,
EC4 & St Annes Ct closed Sat & Sun.*

Thali SW5 NEW   £45   ❷❷❹
166 Old Brompton Rd   7373 2626   5–2B
*Still limited feedback on this oddly-configured (railway carriage-style)
recent addition to South Kensington's 'Indian corner'; all reporters,
however, have enjoyed the "flavoursome" cuisine. / www.thali.uk.com;
11.30 pm, Sun 10.30 pm; set weekday L £24 (FP).*

Theo Randall
InterContinental Hotel W1   £80   ❷❸❹
1 Hamilton Pl   7318 8747   3–4A
*"Beautifully-married" flavours – including some "mouthwatering
pasta"… and "even better fish!" – justify a trip to this celebrated
chef's Mayfair Italian; well, it certainly can't be the "underwhelming"
setting, or the sometimes "weak" service. / www.theorandall.com;
11.15 pm; closed Sat L & Sun; set always available £52 (FP).*

34 Grosvenor Square W1 NEW
34 Grosvenor Sq   awaiting tel   3–3A
*Watch out Duke! – of Westminster, that is – as Richard Caring's
take-over of Mayfair continues apace; the concept of the
latest outpost, set to open in late-2011, is 'the grill version of Scott's'
(itself two minutes' walk away).*

The Thomas Cubitt SW1   £61   ❸❸❷
44 Elizabeth St   7730 6060   2–4A
*"Ridiculously posh" for a pub, this "buzzy" Belgravian has become
a linchpin of the area's social scene; "the bar food is very good" –
above, there's a "terrific" dining room, where "roasts are a real
highlight". / www.thethomascubitt.co.uk; 10 pm; closed Sat L & Sun D;
booking only in restaurant.*

tibits W1   £33   ❸❹❸
12-14 Heddon St   7758 4110   3–2C
*"It's not that it's the most amazing food ever, but the whole idea
is fantastic" – this "pleasant" Swiss operation, just off Regent Street,
dishes up some "delicious and very healthy" veggie fare, charged
by weight. / www.tibits.co.uk; 11.30 pm, Sun 10 pm; no Amex; Only bookings
for 8+.*

Timo W8   £56   ❷⓪④
343 Kensington High St   7603 3888   7–1D
*"A warm and wonderful host welcomes you as if you were family",
at this somewhat anonymous-looking Kensington-fringe Italian;
"sometimes the food is very good, but at other times it's just good".
/ www.timorestaurant.net; 11 pm; closed Sun; set weekday L £32 (FP).*

Tinello SW1   £39   ❷⓪❷
87 Pimlico Rd   7730 3663   5–2D
*Fresh "from the Locatelli stable", this "lovely" and "vibrant" Pimlico
Italian has been "packed ever since it opened"; the cooking
"combines comfort food with intensely-flavoured Tuscan invention",
but it is arguably eclipsed by the "perfect" service. / www.tinello.co.uk;
10.30 pm; closed Sun.*

Toff's N10   £35   ❷❷④
38 Muswell Hill Broadway   8883 8656   1–1B
*"Everything a chippy ought to be" – this "very busy" Muswell Hill
veteran dishes up "beautifully fresh fish" and "the best chips"; service
is "terrific" too; BYO. / www.toffsfish.co.uk; 10 pm; closed Sun.*

Toku
Japan Center SW1   £35   ❸❸④
14-16 Regent St   3405 1246   3–3D
*For a "no-fuss" bite in the heart of the West End, this "authentic"
Japanese café/canteen (part of a store, formerly in a different
location nearby) makes a handy find, serving "simple" fare
at "reasonable" prices (especially "if you print out the weekly voucher
on the website"). / 9 pm, Sun 8.45 pm; no Amex; no booking Sat.*

Tokyo Diner WC2   £26   ④❷❸
2 Newport Pl   7287 8777   4–3B
*A "cosy and traditional-looking" little stalwart, mislocated
in Chinatown; some dishes "rock", other's "less so", but "at the
prices, who's complaining?" / www.tokyodiner.com; midnight; no Amex;
no booking, Fri & Sat.*

Tom Aikens SW3   £101
43 Elystan St   7584 2003   5–2C
*This celebrity chef's Chelsea HQ re-opens in late-2011, after a major
refurbishment; in the prior year, ratings slumped, and some reporters
saw the place as a "rip-off"... so there's plenty of scope for
improvement. / www.tomaikens.co.uk; 11 pm; closed Sat L & Sun; jacket
and/or tie; booking: max 8.*

Tom Ilic SW8   £46   ❷❷⑤
123 Queenstown Rd   7622 0555   10–1C
*Tom Ilic is undoubtedly "a talent", and the "very porky menu"
he offers at this "great-value" Battersea fixture is "always exciting",
and service is "very welcoming and efficient" too; shame the setting
is so very "unexciting". / www.tomilic.com; 10.30 pm; closed Mon,
Tue L & Sun D.*

Tom's Deli W11   £33   ❸④❸
226 Westbourne Grove   7221 8818   6–1B
*Tom Conran's "friendly" deli, in the trendy heart of Notting Hill,
is primarily known for its "excellent breakfast/brunch" (for which it's
usually "difficult to get a seat"). / www.tomsdeli.co.uk; 5 pm; L only;
no Amex; no booking.*

Tom's Kitchen SW3 £59 ④⑤④
27 Cale St   7349 0202   5–2C
Tom Aiken's once-oh-so-fashionable Chelsea hang-out seems ever more passé – it offers "overpriced and very average" gastropub fare, and service that's really "not great"; obvious solution? – announce a roll-out of six more branches... / www.tomskitchen.co.uk; 11 pm.

Tom's Terrace
Somerset House WC2 £52 ⑤④❸
150 Strand   7845 4646   2–2D
A spin-off of the rather ragged Tom Aikens empire, this clubby, tented Ibiza-style operation pops up on the wonderful terrace of Somerset House every summer – the little feedback it inspires suggests its location is the only undoubted plus.
/ www.tomskitchen.co.uk/somersethouse; 9.30 pm, Sun 4 pm; no booking.

The Tommyfield SE11 £46 ⑤⑤④
185 Kennington Ln   7735 1061   1–3C
Oh dear! – only a year or so in business, the relaunch of Kennington's former White Hart "has gone downhill really fast", with all-round standards too often seeming "distinctly average" nowadays.
/ www.thetommyfield.com; 10.15 pm.

Tompkins E14 £50 ⑤④④
3 Pan Peninsula Sq   8305 3080   11–2C
A "stark" modern yearling, seemingly designed for the business crowd, in a skyscraper, by South Quay; it can seems "cavernous and empty" – perhaps because the whole experience is rather "drab"?
/ www.tompkins.uk.com; 10.30 pm, Sun 8.30 pm.

Tortilla £18 ❸❸④
6 Market Place, W1   7637 2800   3–1C
6a, King St, W6   8741 7959   7–2C **NEW**
13 Islington High St, N1   7833 3103   8–3D
106 Southwark St, SE1   7620 0285   9–4B
18 North Colonnade, E14   7719 9160   11–1C
28 Leadenhall Mkt, EC3   7929 7837   9–2D **NEW**
With their "healthy, delight-giving burritos", these Cal-Mex pit stops make a "fresh and exciting" refuelling option. / www.tortilla.co.uk; W1 & N1 11 pm, Sun 9 pm, SE1 & E14 9 pm, EC3 7 pm; E14 Sun 7 pm; SE1 & EC3 closed Sat & Sun; no Amex.

Tosa W6 £34 ❸④④
332 King St   8748 0002   7–2B
A Japanese café, near Stamford Brook, that's "a bit of a squash"; its "family-friendly" charms generally win people over, though, and the menu is "good all-round", with the yakitori "the real treat".
/ www.tosauk.com; 10.30 pm.

Toto's SW1 £67 ❸❸❸
Lennox Gardens Mews   7589 0075   5–2C
This "upscale" Italian, near Harrods, has a "lovely" interior, and the food's "reliable" too; the style that strikes fans as "refreshingly untrendy", however, is now at risk of seeming simply "dated", and while "the menu probably hasn't changed since the '80s, the prices certainly have!" / 11 pm, Sun 10.30 pm.

The Trafalgar Tavern SE10 £45 ⑤④❸
28 Park Row   8858 2909   1–3D
A majestic Thames-side location sets the scene at this historic and "lovely" Greenwich tavern; shame the food's so "lazy" though, and it can "take an age to be served" too. / www.trafalgartavern.co.uk; 10 pm; closed Sun D; no Amex.

The Tree House SW13 £38 ④❸❷
73 White Hart Ln 8392 1617 10–1A

"A nice outdoor terrace for a sunny day" is a highlight of this
"welcoming" pub-conversion – nowadays more a wine bar/restaurant
– on the fringes of Barnes; the food is a bit incidental.
/ www.treehousepeople.com; 11 pm, Fri & Sat midnight, Sun 10.30 pm.

TRINITY SW4 £56 ❶❶❷
4 The Polygon 7622 1199 10–2D

"The residents of Clapham are spoilt", says one of the fans of this
dazzling neighbourhood blockbuster, where Adam Byatt's "carefully
balanced" cuisine "just gets better and better"; it's a "stylish" place
too, where "incredibly accommodating staff" contribute to the
"convivial" ambience. / www.trinityrestaurant.co.uk; 10.30 pm; closed
Mon L & Sun D.

Trishna W1 £51 ❶❷❸
15-17 Blandford St 7935 5624 2–1A

"Like going to India, but without the jet lag!"; "magical" dishes that
are "light", "vibrant" and "perfectly spiced" win rave reviews for this
Marylebone seafood-specialist – offshoot of a restaurant famous
in Mumbai. / www.trishnalondon.com; Mon-Sat 10.45 pm, Sun 9.45 pm.

Les Trois Garçons E1 £67 ❸❸❶
1 Club Row 7613 1924 12–1C

"Don't be put off by all the stuffed animals!" – they form part of the
"magical" setting you'll find at this fabulously "quirky" East End pub-
conversion; as you'd expect, the Gallic cuisine rather plays second
fiddle, but it's often been "better than expected" of late.
/ www.lestroisgarcons.com; Mon 9.30 pm, Tue-Thu 10 pm, Fri & Sat 10.30 pm;
closed Sat L & Sun D; need credit card to book £25 deposit; set weekday L
£39 (FP).

Trojka NW1 £29 ④④❸
101 Regent's Park Rd 7483 3765 8–2B

"An unusual atmosphere" adds interest to a trip to this crowded
Russian café/bistro, in Primrose Hill; the scoff is often "tasty" too,
but the entertainments – and the vodka selection – are arguably
a greater attraction. / www.trojka.co.uk; 10.30 pm; no Amex.

LA TROMPETTE W4 £63 ❶❶❷
5-7 Devonshire Rd 8747 1836 7–2A

"Why go into town when this is on my doorstep?"; this sibling to Chez
Bruce remains "the jewel in Chiswick's crown", twinning "faultless"
cuisine with an "eclectic and fascinating" wine list; it's a "chic" but
"unstuffy" place too (if a little on the "squashed" side).
/ www.latrompette.co.uk; 10.30 pm, Sun 10 pm.

Troubadour SW5 £36 ⑤❸❶
263-265 Old Brompton Rd 7370 1434 5–3A

Fans – some of decades' standing – still relish this wonderfully
Bohemian Earls's Court fixture, for breakfast, for coffee, or even for
a "romantic" bite; the food is not art, however, and prices are really
pushing it nowadays. / www.troubadour.co.uk; 11 pm.

Truc Vert W1 £52 ❸④④
42 North Audley St 7491 9988 3–2A

"No frills, but very cute", this Mayfair deli/diner is "a little piece
of France"; main meals here can sometimes seem "a bit hectic" to be
truly enjoyable, but – for a "fabulous breakfast" – this is undoubtedly
a top destination. / www.trucvert.co.uk; 10 pm; closed Sun D.

Trullo N1 £36 ❷0❷
300-302 St Paul's Rd   7226 2733   8–2D
"River Café-esque food at non-River Café prices" has instantly created
a "real buzz" around this "rustic" Islington newcomer… to the extent
that it's "often impossible to get a table"; critics may cry "hype",
but most reporters "absolutely love the place".
/ www.trullorestaurant.com; 10.30 pm; closed weekday L & Sun D.

Tsunami £48 ❶④❸
93 Charlotte St, W1   7637 0050   2–1C
5-7 Voltaire Rd, SW4   7978 1610   10–1D
"Nobu-quality" fare, including "incredible sushi and sashimi" –
"at much lower prices", and "without the hype" – wins rave reviews
for these Japanese-fusion ventures; service can be "a let-down"
though (and the "unsexy" Fitzrovia spin-off is something of a
disappointment compared to the "buzzy" Clapham original).
/ www.tsunamirestaurant.co.uk; SW4 10.30 pm, Fri & Sat 11 pm,
Sun 9.30 pm; W1 11 pm; SW4 Mon - Fri D only; W1 closed Sun, Sat D only;
no Amex.

Tsuru £28 ❸④④
201 Bishopsgate, EC2   7377 1166   12–2B
10 Queen St, EC4   7377 6367   9–2B NEW
4 Canvey St, SE1   7928 2228   9–4B
These "bustling" Japanese "fast-food" operations – on the South
Bank, and in the City – serve "authentic dishes, which go beyond
simple sushi and noodles" ("excellent katsu curries", for example),
and at "reasonable prices" too! / www.tsuru-sushi.co.uk; EC2 9 pm;
SE1 9 pm, Sat 7 pm, EC4 10; EC2 & EC4 closed Sat & Sun, SE1 closed Sun;
no booking L.

28-50 EC4 £49 ❸❷❸
140 Fetter Ln   7242 8877   9–2A
"Once you get over the inauspicious office-block-basement location",
this City-fringe yearling is "the perfect modern wine bar" –
a "packed" but "cosy" place, where a "short but well-executed"
menu complements a range of 50 or so "incredible" wines by the
glass. / www.2850.co.uk; 9.30 pm; closed Sat & Sun.

2 Amici SW1 £44 ④④④
48a Rochester Rw   7976 5660   2–4C
On most accounts, this "small and friendly" Westminster Italian is a
handy "cheap 'n' cheerful" local; it is not without critics, though,
for whom its whole approach reeks of the "lowest common
denominator". / 11 pm; closed Sat L & Sun.

Two Brothers N3 £35 ❷❸④
297-303 Regent's Park Rd   8346 0469   1–1B
You get "really excellent fish" and "chunky chips", at this "basic and
often-crowded" Finchley institution – one of the capital's top chippies.
/ www.twobrothers.co.uk; 10.15 pm; closed Mon & Sun; no booking at D.

202
Nicole Farhi W11 £50 ④❸❸
202 Westbourne Grove   7727 2722   6–1B
That quintessential "buzzy Notting Hill atmosphere" doesn't come
more concentrated than at this "hip" (and "pricey") brunch-and-lunch
spot (which is integrated into a fashion store); "reliable" food plays
rather a supporting role. / 10 pm; closed Mon D & Sun D; only D.

2 Veneti W1 £47 ❸❷④
10 Wigmore St 7637 0789 3–1B
Near Wigmore Hall, this "calm and discreet oasis" is a "useful option in a poorly-served area" – the Venetian-based cooking is "interesting" and "reliable", and service is "warm" ("especially if they know you"). / www.2veneti.com; 10.30 pm, Sat 11 pm; closed Sat L & Sun.

Uli W11 £38 ❸❶❸
16 All Saints Rd 7727 7511 6–1B
"Michael is an exceptional host", and his staff are "always smiling", say fans of this "excellent, unassuming and well-priced" pan-Asian, near Portobello Market; the food is usually "really inventive" and "yummy" (although this year did see the odd "horror" too). / www.uli-oriental.co.uk; 11 pm; D only, closed Sun; no Amex.

Umu W1 £85 ❸❸❷
14-16 Bruton Pl 7499 8881 3–2C
"Beautiful" and "understated", this small Mayfair mews spot – with its "divine sushi", and other "intricate and fabulously-presented" "Kyoto-style" dishes – is sometimes tipped as "the best Japanese in London"; for a few reporters, however, it's still a case of 'Emperor's new clothes', and at "ludicrous" prices too. / www.umurestaurant.com; 11 pm; closed Sat L & Sun; no trainers; booking: max 14.

The Union Café W1 £54 ❸④④
96 Marylebone Ln 7486 4860 3–1A
Wine at (highish) "retail" prices adds to the "buzz" at John Brinkley's "airy" neighbourhood stand-by, near trendy Marylebone High Street; food-wise, it offers an "unadventurous" but "safe" mix, with "delicious burgers" a speciality. / www.brinkleys.com; 11 pm; closed Sun D.

Union Street Café SE1 NEW
Harling Hs, Union St awaiting tel 9–4B
A 250-seater newcomer, scheduled to open near Borough Market in late-2011; most of Gordon Ramsay's 'catering for the masses' efforts so far have been pretty dismal – perhaps this place can mark a change of course?

Uno SW1 £47 ④④④
1 Denbigh St 7834 1001 2–4B
On a prime Pimlico corner, a "closely-packed" (and sometimes very noisy) neighbourhood Italian; despite its "reliable" cooking (including pizza), it never seems to rise to more than stand-by status. / www.uno1.co.uk; 10 pm, Fri & Sun 10.30 pm.

Upstairs Bar SW2 £45 ❷❶❶
89b Acre Ln (door on Branksome Rd) 7733 8855 10–2D
"Like a supper-club, only better" – Brixton's "magnificently romantic" secret "hide-away" ("ring a bell to enter") is a "small, but perfectly formed" Gallic place whose overall "professionalism" would shame many much bigger names, not least with its "outrageously good value"! / www.upstairslondon.com; Tue-Thu 9.30 pm, Fri-Sat 10.30 pm; D only, closed Mon & Sun.

Le Vacherin W4 £52 ❸❸❸
76-77 South Pde 8742 2121 7–1A
An "authentic slice of France", hidden-away "in the back of beyond" (on the Acton/Chiswick borders); it's won a large and very "faithful" clientele over the years, by offering "classic" cuisine ("good, without being memorable") at "sensible prices". / www.levacherin.co.uk; 10.30 pm, Fri & Sat 11 pm, Sun 10 pm; closed weekday L.

Valentina £39 ❸❸❸
210 Up' Richmond Rd W, SW14   8392 9127   1–4A
75 Upper Richmond Rd, SW15   8877 9906   10–2B
Upmarket deli/diners in Sheen and Putney, which offer "lovely Italian food", and have quite a "feel-good factor" too – their "straightforward" style pleases all who comment on them. / SW15 10 pm, SW14 10.30 pm.

Vanilla W1 £50 ❹❹❸
131 Great Titchfield St   3008 7763   3–1C
Declining feedback on this style-conscious Fitzrovia basement, known for its striking (but now "slightly tatty") monochrome decor, romantic booths and punchy cocktails – "definitely worth a try... but maybe only once". / www.vanillalondon.com; 10 pm; closed Mon, Tue, Wed, Thu L, Fri L & Sun; no trainers; booking: max 6.

Vanilla Black EC4 £47 ❷❷❹
17-18 Tooks Ct   7242 2622   9–2A
"Fine veggie dining is a rarity", and you find it at an unusually "imaginative" and "accomplished" level at this Chancery Lane two-year-old – pity the atmosphere doesn't have a bit more oomph. / www.vanillablack.co.uk; 10 pm; closed Sat L & Sun; Fri & Sat nights; 8 group max.

Vapiano W1 £30 ❹❹❹
19-21 Great Portland St   7268 0080   3–1C
"Removed from the tourist/shopper crowds of Oxford Street", this large self-service food court strikes many reporters as a "decent" place for a quick meal, with a hint of Continental style thrown in; on the downside, it can seem "cavernous", "brash" and "noisy". / www.vapiano.co.uk; 11 pm, Sun 10 pm.

Vasco & Piero's Pavilion W1 £52 ❷❷❸
15 Poland St   7437 8774   3–1D
This "unassuming" Soho favourite "has been around for donkeys years", and offers "a tiny haven in a mad world"; "high-quality, fresh pasta" is the highlight of the "classic" Italian food, but it's the "very welcoming" service that really makes the experience. / www.vascosfood.com; 10.30 pm; closed Sat L & Sun.

Veeraswamy W1 £68 ❸❸❸
Victory Hs, 99-101 Regent St   7734 1401   3–3D
A "classic that keeps re-inventing itself"; London's oldest Indian – "terrifically-located", near Piccadilly Circus – is an all-round "winner", thanks to its "refined", "21st century" decor and its "contemporary cuisine"; ratings dipped a bit this year, though – "have they become too relaxed?" / www.realindianfood.com; 10.30 pm, Sun 10 pm; booking: max 12.

Venosi SW3 NEW £53 ❹❷❹
87 Sloane Ave   7998 5019   5–2C
"Deserving a larger clientele", says the – sole! – reporter to comment on this new Chelsea Italian; it's certainly a "friendly" place, useful for Brompton Cross shoppers, but we couldn't on our own visit see any reason actively to seek it out. / Rated on Editors' visit; www.venosi.co.uk; 10.45 pm; closed Sun; set weekday L £25 (FP).

El Vergel SE1 £29 ❷❷❷
132 Webber St   7401 2308   9–4B
"Amazingly, it's just as good in premises five times the size!" – this "incredible" Latino is going strong on its year-old new site, serving "some of the best Hispanic food in the UK", and at "ludicrously cheap" prices too. / www.elvergel.co.uk; 9.45 pm Sat; Mon-Fri closed D, Sat open L & D, closed Sun; no Amex.

Verru W1 NEW   £51   ②③④
69 Marylebone Ln   7935 0858   2–1A
*A "cosy" Marylebone newcomer that's so tiny "it's going to be tough
to make it a success"; staff "try hard" though, and on most accounts
its "eclectic", Scandinavian-influenced cuisine is "well-executed" and
"convincing"; "excellent-value set lunch menu". / www.verru.co.uk;
set weekday L £30 (FP).*

Verta SW11 NEW   £58   ④④④
Bridges Court Rd   7978 0875   10–1C
*Aside from "good views over the Thames", the virtues of this
"charmless" dining room by Battersea's helipad (opened as part of a
Von Essen hotel, shortly before that group went bust) are quite hard
to see; unless, of course, you're really desperate to arrive
by helicopter... / www.hotelverta.com; 10.30 pm, Sun 10 pm; set weekday L
£36 (FP).*

Vertigo 42
Tower 42 EC2   £64   ④③❶
25 Old Broad St   7877 7842   9–2C
*"Amazing views" make this "well-spaced" 42nd-floor City eyrie
just the place to woo a client or lover; stick to fizz and nibbles,
though – the fare is decidedly "average". / www.vertigo42.co.uk;
10.45 pm; closed Sat L & Sun; no shorts; booking essential.*

VIAJANTE E2   £90   ②②③
Patriot Sq   7871 0461   1–2D
*"Some dishes astound... some miss by quite a way", at Nuno
Mendes's "experimental" open-kitchen yearling, in Bethnal Green;
sceptics may find the cooking occasionally "over-engineered",
but most reporters still feel it's "some of the most exciting food
currently available in London". / www.viajante.co.uk; 9.30 pm; closed
Mon L & Tue L; set weekday L £48 (FP).*

Vicino SW6   £40   ❸③③
189 New King's Rd   7736 1145   10–1B
*A "good neighbourhood Parson's Green Italian" that's a "solid
performer", and which benefits from a "a great family atmosphere
at weekends"; the menu, though, "could perhaps be a bit shorter".
/ www.vicinorestaurant.com; 11 pm; closed Sun D.*

Il Vicolo SW1   £48   ④④④
3-4 Crown Passage   7839 3960   3–4D
*Fans still say this St James's Sicilian, hidden-away down a cute alley,
is a "predictable but dependable" favourite, albeit a "cramped" and
"noisy" one; a couple of reports this year, however, suggest that
standards are not being maintained. / 10 pm; closed Sat L & Sun.*

The Victoria SW14   £41   ❸③②
10 West Temple   8876 4238   10–2A
*"In a leafy street near Richmond Park", and with a "great garden for
the kids to let off steam", Paul Merrett's large East Sheen gastropub
has a particular name as a family destination (and can sometimes
seem "overrun" at weekends); the food, though, is "consistently
good". / www.thevictoria.net; 10 pm, Sat 10 pm; closed Sun D; no Amex.*

Viet W1   £21   ❸④④
34 Greek St   7494 9888   4–3A
*"You usually have to queue, and often end up sharing a table with
strangers", at this "basic" Soho Vietnamese; no one minds, though –
"for under a tenner", you can "stuff yourself" with "a good range
of phos, and other tasty options"; BYO. / 10.30 pm, Fri 11 pm; closed
Sun; no Amex; no booking.*

Viet Garden N1 £35 ❸❸④
207 Liverpool Rd 7700 6040 8–2D
"Light and lovely" Vietnamese dishes, at *"value-for-money"* prices, have long made this *"tired"*-looking Angel veteran well worth seeking out; beware, though: *"it does get very busy"*. / www.vietgarden.co.uk; 11 pm, Sat 11.30 pm; no Amex.

Viet Grill E2 £34 ❷④❷
58 Kingsland Rd 7739 6686 12–1B
"Stunningly fresh" and *"fragrant"* food – all at *"incredibly cheap"* prices – remains the hallmark of this *"über-busy"* and *"vibrant"* Shoreditch Vietnamese; service, though, *"could be improved a lot"*. / www.vietnamesekitchen.co.uk; 11 pm, Fri & Sat 11.30 pm, Sun 10.30 pm.

Viet Hoa E2 £27 ❷④④
70-72 Kingsland Rd 7729 8293 12–1B
"Super food, very cheap" – that's the deal that's made this *"authentic"* Shoreditch Vietnamese quite a hit; *"it's gone a bit upmarket after a revamp"*, though – *"not necessarily what the place is about"*. / www.viethoarestaurant.co.uk; 11.30 pm.

Vijay NW6 £29 ❶❷④
49 Willesden Ln 7328 1087 1–1B
There's *"no 'designer' packaging"*, at this rather *"dilapidated"*-looking Kilburn veteran – just *"seriously delicious"* south Indian dishes, including *"divine dosas"*, at *"great-value"* prices. / www.vijayrestaurant.co.uk; 10.45 pm, Fri & Sat 11.45 pm.

Villa Bianca NW3 £56 ④❷❸
1 Perrins Ct 7435 3131 8–2A
Mega-cutely located in a little lane just off Hampstead High Street, this *"traditional"* Italian is a *"pricey"* sort of place, but reporters – more positive of late – see it as *"dependable for good, slightly old-fashioned cooking"*. / www.villabiancanw3.com; 11.30 pm.

Village East SE1 £46 ❸❷❷
171-173 Bermondsey St 7357 6082 9–4D
A *"laid-back"* and *"buzzy"* brasserie, with a *"very cool"* location in a row of Bermondsey railway arches; the menu has *"something for everyone"* – particularly as a weekend brunch destination, this place *"really hits the spot"*. / www.villageeast.co.uk; 10 pm, Sun 9.30 pm; closed Sat D & Sun D.

Villandry W1 £53 ④⑤④
170 Gt Portland St 7631 3131 2–1B
Smart Marylebone deli/diner that fans find a *"reliable"* stop that's *"pleasant enough for lunch"*; it's quite *"cold"* style-wise, though, and perennially *"let down"* by its *"dreadful, dreadful"* service; the offshoot 'Kitchens' were sold in mid-2011. / www.villandry.com; 10.30 pm; closed Sun.

The Vincent Rooms
Westminster Kingsway College SW1 £26 ❸④❸
76 Vincent Sq 7802 8391 2–4C
The *"great value"* of this Westminster catering-college restaurant *"makes up for any lapses"*, such as the *"inevitably patchy"* service (*"some students are really nervous"*); if you hit a good day, though, the food from the trainee chefs can be *"excellent"* too. / www.thevincentrooms.com; 9 pm; times vary; only term times; closed Mon D, Wed D, Fri D, Sat & Sun; no Amex.

Vingt-Quatre SW10   £46   ④④④
325 Fulham Rd   7376 7224   5–3B
*A 24/7 Chelsea veteran which fans say is "not just for night owls",
as it serves useful "hang-over food" and other "quick snacks" during
daylight hours too; for critics, though, it's just "one to avoid unless
you're desperate in the early hours". / www.vingtquatre.co.uk; open 24
hours; no booking.*

Vinoteca   £39   ❸❷❶
15 Seymour Pl, W1   7724 7288   2–2A **NEW**
7 St John St, EC1   7253 8786   9–1B
*"The clue is rather in the name", at this "bustling" wine bar duo
in Smithfield and now also Marylebone – yes, "there's some decent
fodder", but the main event is an "intriguing" selection of "incredible"
wines, delivered by "enthusiastic" and "professional" staff. / 10 pm,
W1 4 pm; EC1 Sun, W1 Sun D.*

Vivat Bacchus   £51   ④④⑤
4 Hay's Ln, SE1   7234 0891   9–4C
47 Farringdon St, EC4   7353 2648   9–2A
*A "treasure" of a wine list ("leaning heavily to South Africa") and
a "fabulous" cheese selection – both chosen in walk-in cellars –
are stand-out features of these City-fringe and Southwark wine bars;
the food's "nothing special", though, and no one's wild about the
ambience either. / www.vivatbacchus.co.uk; 9.30 pm; EC4 closed Sat & Sun;
SE1 closed Sat L & Sun; set always available £32 (FP).*

Vrisaki N22   £32   ④❸④
73 Middleton Rd   8889 8760   1–1C
*"Much too much food" – the main problem when visiting this "jolly"
and "good-value" Bounds Green veteran, hidden-away behind
a kebab shop; "the mezze deal is the thing to go for". / 11.30 pm,
Sun 9 pm.*

Wagamama   £33   ④❸④
8 Norris St, SW1   7321 2755   4–4A
Harvey Nichols, Knightsbridge, SW1   7201 8000   5–1D
101a Wigmore St, W1   7409 0111   3–1A
10a Lexington St, W1   7292 0990   3–2D
4a Streatham St, WC1   7323 9223   2–1C
1 Tavistock St, WC2   7836 3330   4–3D
14a Irving St, WC2   7839 2323   4–4B
26a Kensington High St, W8   7376 1717   5–1A
N1 Centre, 37 Parkfield St, N1   7226 2664   8–3D
11 Jamestown Rd, NW1   7428 0800   8–3B
Royal Festival Hall, Southbank Centre, SE1   7021 0877   2–3D
50-54 Putney High St, SW15   8785 3636   10–2B
46-48 Wimbledon Hill Rd, SW19   8879 7280   10–2B
Jubilee Place, 45 Bank St, E14   7516 9009   11–1C
1a Ropemaker St, EC2   7588 2688   12–2A
22 Old Broad St, EC2   7256 9992   9–2C
Tower Pl, EC3   7283 5897   9–3D
109 Fleet St, EC4   7583 7889   9–2A
30 Queen St, EC4   7248 5766   9–3B
*"A favourite oriental fix for a fast lunch" – this benchmark noodle-
chain still has a huge following for its "honest meals for
honest money" (and as "a great venue with kids" too); for critics,
though, the experience – perhaps inevitably – "doesn't seem as fresh
as once it did". / www.wagamama.com; no booking.*

Wahaca £29 ④❸❸
80-82 Wardour St, W1   7734 0195   3–2D
66 Chandos Pl, WC2   7240 1883   4–4C
Westfield, Ariel Way, W12   8749 4517   7–1C
Unit 4, Park Pavilion, 40 Canada Sq, E14   7516 9145   11–1C
"Wagamama a lo Mexicano"; they're "fun" and they're "festive",
and these "zoo-like" latinos still please fans with their "cheap" and
"tasty" bites; standards, though, aren't a patch on the early days.
/ www.wahaca.com; 11 pm; no booking.

The Wallace
The Wallace Collection W1 £50 ④④❶
Hertford Hs, Manchester Sq   7563 9505   3–1A
"A wonderful oasis"; this "spectacular" atrium of a Marylebone
palazzo is a "beautiful" space, where the food is "a bit pricey" for
what it is, but the service – if still sometimes "disinterested" –
has somewhat improved of late. / www.thewallacerestaurant.com; Fri & Sat
9.15 pm; Sun-Thu closed D; no Amex.

The Walmer Castle W11 £36 ❸②②
58 Ledbury Rd   7229 4620   6–1B
"Still as busy as ever"; "for tasty and good-value Thai fare",
this atmospheric Notting Hill pub remains "a destination venue".
/ www.walmercastle.co.uk; 11 pm.

Walnut NW6 £39 ❸②②
280 West End Ln   7794 7772   1–1B
"A West Hampstead gem" – this "friendly" fixture developed
"a strong environmental theme" long before it became fashionable,
and its "seasonal" dishes please all who comment on them; only real
downside? – "hard" seating. / www.walnutwalnut.com; 11 pm; D only,
closed Mon.

Wapping Food E1 £48 ❸④❶
Wapping Power Station, Wapping Wall   7680 2080   11–1A
With its "very cutting-edge" vibe, this former hydraulic power station
– now part art-space, part restaurant – provides a "fabulous,
industrial-chic" setting for weekend brunch, lunch or dinner;
the cooking is "good" too, if perhaps on the "pricey" side for what
it is. / www.thewappingproject.com; midnight; Mon-Fri D only, Sat open L & D,
closed Sun D.

The Warrington W9 £56 ⑤⑤⑤
93 Warrington Cr   7592 7960   8–4A
According to Gordon Ramsay's website, this huge Maida Vale boozer
offers an 'enchanting journey' and 'sophisticated' British cooking –
reporters, on the other hand, rate it like "a tired Torquay hotel",
where the food is "bland and incredibly expensive", and the service
simply "shocking". / www.gordonramsay.com; 10 pm, Fri & Sat 10.30 pm,
Sun 9 pm; Casual; set weekday L £36 (FP).

Watatsumi
The Club Quarters Hotel WC2 NEW £55 ④❸④
7 Northumberland Ave   7036 8520   2–3C
Handy for Trafalgar Square, a decent, if perhaps not inspired,
Japanese newcomer, housed in marbled Edwardian splendour;
its well-spaced tables are useful for business, and its set lunch menus
should also interest West End visitors generally. / Rated on Editors' visit;
www.watatsumi.co.uk; 11 pm.

The Water Margin NW11   £28   ❸②④
96 Golders Green Road   8458 5815   1–1B
The food comes "piping hot" and "bursting with flavour", at this stalwart Cantonese on Golder's Green's main drag, where "smiling" staff take the edge off a dining room that's rather "in need of a revamp". / www.the-water-margin.co.uk; 11 pm; no Amex.

Waterloo Bar & Kitchen SE1   £43   ④❸④
131 Waterloo Rd   7928 5086   9–4A
"In an area badly served for decent food", this "bustling" brasserie, near the Old Vic, makes a reliably "useful" stand-by, and out-scores its similarly-named rival, the Waterloo Brasserie. / www.barandkitchen.co.uk; 10.30 pm.

Waterloo Brasserie SE1   £47   ⑤⑤④
119 Waterloo Rd   7960 0202   9–4A
Fans find it "perfect before the Old Vic", but this brilliantly-located brasserie (right by the railway station) is a terrible missed opportunity – critics say that its "unexciting" food and "slapdash" service make it "very much a restaurant of last resort". / www.waterloobrasserie.co.uk; 11 pm; closed Sun.

The Waterway W9   £47   ④⑤❷
54 Formosa St   7266 3557   8–4A
"It's the setting you come for!"; this canal-side Maida Vale hang-out has a "delightful terrace", which makes it – just about – worth braving the "variable" food, and the sometimes "terrible" service. / www.thewaterway.co.uk; 10.30 pm, Sun 10 pm.

The Well EC1   £48   ❸④❸
180 St John St   7251 9363   9–1A
"Still a place to return to, despite the increasing competition in Clerkenwell", say fans of this long-established gastropub – they rate its cooking highly, but reports are far less numerous than once they were. / www.downthewell.com; 10.30 pm, Sun 9.30 pm.

The Wells NW3   £43   ❸❷❷
30 Well Walk   7794 3785   8–1A
"Cosseted among the leafy gardens of Hampstead", this "very characterful" pub makes "an easy choice for all the family"; with "helpful" staff and "consistently good" food, it is also "perfect after a hearty walk on the Heath". / www.thewellshampstead.co.uk; 10 pm, Sun 9.30 pm.

The Westbourne W2   £40   ❸④❷
101 Westbourne Park Villas   7221 1332   6–1B
On a sunny Sunday, the terrace of this "absolute-favourite" local "hang-out" heaves with "hip Notting Hill types, and their kids"; the cooking is on the better side of what you might expect, but the "frosty" service "certainly leaves room for improvement". / www.thewestbourne.com; 10 pm, Sun 9.30 pm; closed Mon L.

The Wet Fish Cafe NW6   £40   ❸❷❷
242 West End Ln   7443 9222   1–1B
An "excellent local café and brasserie", that's often – and especially for breakfast and brunch – "bustling" with West Hampstead types; NB: the name reflects the ex-fishmonger premises, not the menu. / www.thewetfishcafe.co.uk; 10 pm; closed Mon L; no Amex.

The Wharf TW11 £50 ④❷❷
22 Manor Rd   8977 6333   1–4A
For "a leisurely meal watching the boats go by" ("ask for a window
seat"), the attractions of this "relaxed" Thames-side bar/restaurant
near Teddington Lock are self-evident; the brasserie fare can
sometimes "fall short", but it's mostly pretty "reliable".
/ www.thewharfteddington.com; 9.45 pm.

Wheeler's SW1 £58 ⑤④⑤
72-73 St James's St   7408 1440   3–4D
"MPW should stick to making stock-cube adverts", says one of the
many critics of the celebrity-chef's "drab" and "disappointing" fish
restaurant, by St James's Palace – "simply don't bother!"
/ www.wheelersrestaurant.org; 11 pm; closed Sat L & Sun; set always available £39 (FP).

White Horse SW6 £43 ❸❸❸
1-3 Parsons Grn   7736 2115   10–1B
"The Sloaney Pony isn't as Sloaney as it used to be", but this Parson's
Green landmark still gets "exceedingly busy"; the food is "reliable",
both inside and out (there's a large terrace), and there is an
"excellent range of beers and wines" to go with it.
/ www.whitehorsesw6.com; 10.30 pm.

The White Swan EC4 £49 ❷❸④
108 Fetter Ln   7242 9696   9–2A
"Surprising to find such good food in a pub"; "first-class" British
cooking and "interesting wine" make this "professionally run" City-
fringe dining room a handy business-lunch option.
/ www.thewhiteswanlondon.com; 10 pm; closed Sat & Sun.

Whitechapel Gallery Dining Room E1 £38
77-82 Whitechapel High St   7522 7896   12–2C
This elegant but tightly-packed, East End gallery dining room offers
a handy stand-by in a thin area; owing to various changes of régime
this year, we don't think a rating appropriate.
/ www.whitechapelgallery.org/dine; 9.30 pm; closed Mon, Tue D & Sun D.

Whits W8 £46 ❸❶❸
21 Abingdon Rd   7938 1122   5–1A
"Refreshingly genuine service" adds to the "congenial" charm of this
"personal" bistro, tucked-away off Kensington High Street; fans also
hail its "serious" Gallic cuisine, but doubters find it "rather average".
/ www.whits.co.uk; 10.30 pm; D only, closed Mon & Sun.

Wild Honey W1 £53 ❸❸❸
12 St George St   7758 9160   3–2C
"Inventive cooking, and one of London's most flexible wine lists" –
all at "very fair prices" – have made a formidable name for this
"lovely wood-panelled room" (a "former gents' outfitters"), in Mayfair;
sliding ratings, however, are grist to the mill of those who discern
"an over-riding feeling of complacency". / www.wildhoneyrestaurant.co.uk;
11 pm, Fri & Sat 11.30 pm, Sun 10 pm.

William Curley £17 ❶❸❸
198 Ebury St, SW1   7730 5522   5–2D
10 Paved Ct, TW9   8332 3002   1–4A
The smart Belgravia café of "the best chocolatier in London" – worth
seeking out for its "stunning" puddings and cakes, and "luscious" hot
choc' too. / www.williamcurley.co.uk; 6.30 pm.

Wiltons SW1   £97   ④❷❷
55 Jermyn St   7629 9955   3–3C
"Quiet and dignified, as befits one's sole" (ho, ho) – this "convivial
grande dame" of "timeless" St James's dining remains a top
destination for "superb" fish, oysters and game; bills, however, are
as "brutal" as the overall experience is "refined". / www.wiltons.co.uk;
10.30 pm; closed Sat & Sun; jacket required.

The Windmill W1   £36   ❷④❸
6-8 Mill St   7491 8050   3–2C
"Pies to die for" make it well worth seeking out this very traditional
boozer, near Savile Row; it boasts a "nicely kept ale cellar" too.
/ www.windmillmayfair.co.uk; 9.30 pm, Sat 4 pm; closed Sat D & Sun; no Amex.

The Windsor Castle W8   £34   ④④❶
114 Campden Hill Rd   7243 8797   6–2B
"Like Alice in Wonderland, full of cubby holes and low doors",
this "lovely" ancient tavern, near Notting Hill Gate, also has
a gorgeous garden; its "normal pub fayre", however, tends
to "unexceptional". / www.thewindsorcastlekensington.co.uk; 10 pm,
Sun 9 pm; set always available £21 (FP).

Wine Gallery SW10   £50   ④❸❷
49 Hollywood Rd   7352 7572   5–3B
"If you're interested more in socialising than food", you "can't
go wrong" at John Brinkley's age-old Chelsea wine bar – it's the good
wine at reasonable prices, though, which is the real attractions, rather
than the "simple" cuisine. / www.brinkleys.com; 11.30 pm; closed Sun D;
booking: max 12; set weekday L £27 (FP).

The Wine Library EC3   £28   ⑤❸❶
43 Trinity Sq   7481 0415   9–3D
"A great concept for wine-lovers" – an ancient City cellar, selling
"an amazing selection" at "fantastic" prices (scarcely higher than
retail); the cheese and pâté buffet accompaniment is pretty "basic"
but, say fans, "what more do you need?" / www.winelibrary.co.uk; 8 pm,
Mon 6 pm; closed Mon D, Sat & Sun.

Wolfe's WC2   £43   ❸④④
30 Gt Queen St   7831 4442   4–1D
The '70s styling of this comfortable diner can seem distinctly passé,
but this Covent Garden stalwart still has its (generally older) fans,
who acclaim its "heavenly" burgers. / www.wolfes-grill.net; Fri & Sat
10.30 pm, Mon-Thu 10 pm, Sun 9 pm.

THE WOLSELEY W1   £57   ❸❷❶
160 Piccadilly   7499 6996   3–3C
Everyone who's anyone is to be found, throughout the day – from the
"terrific" breakfast onward – at Corbin & King's "star-studded" grand
café, by the Ritz; it can seem "crowded and noisy", though, and the
brasserie fare is "competent, rather than dazzling".
/ www.thewolseley.com; midnight, Sun 11 pm.

Wong Kei W1   £26   ④⑤④
41-43 Wardour St   7437 8408   4–3A
"Nowadays, you can even buy a T-shirt!" celebrating the "legendarily
rude" staff at this "massive" Chinatown institution; it's questionable
whether they truly live up to that billing any more, but the "fast and
furious" chow on offer is still "plentiful, cheap and edible". / 11.30 pm,
Fri & Sat 11.45 pm, Sun 10.30 pm; no credit cards; no booking.

Woodlands £35 ❸❸④
37 Panton St, SW1 7839 7258 4–4A
77 Marylebone Ln, W1 7486 3862 2–1A
102 Heath St, NW3 7794 3080 8–1A
*"An ideal place for a quick vegetarian fix" – a "consistently good"
(if "not very atmospheric") Indian mini-chain that's been around for
yonks.* / www.woodlandsrestaurant.co.uk; 10 pm; NW3 no L Mon; set L £22 (FP).

Wright Brothers £51 ❷❸❸
12-13 Kingly St, W1 7434 3611 3–2D
11 Stoney St, SE1 7403 9554 9–4C
*In "rough and ready" Borough Market – and now in more
"glamorous" and "restaurant-like" premises in Soho too – these
"bubbly" bars have won cult status for their "heavenly bivalves",
and other "awesome, fresh seafood"; the original branch is better.*
/ 10.30 pm, Sun 9 pm; booking: max 8.

XO NW3 £47 ❸④❸
29 Belsize Ln 7433 0888 8–2A
*Reports on this "trendy" Belsize Park outpost of Will ('E&O') Ricker's
empire are rather up-and-down, and even fans sometimes find its
pan-Asian tapas dishes "rather pricey" for what they are – "look out
for special offers!"* / www.rickerrestaurants.com; 10.30 pm; set weekday L £29 (FP).

Yalla Yalla £31 ❸❸❷
1 Green's Ct, W1 7287 7663 3–2D
12 Winsley St, W1 7637 4748 3–1C NEW
*"Like being in Beirut"; this "tiny" and "squished-in" Soho "hole in the
wall" has quickly made a name for "scrumptious" street food (spicy
wraps, mezze and kebabs) at "recession-busting" prices, and it's
"great fun" too; an offshoot recently opened near Oxford Circus.*
/ Green's Court 11 pm, Winsley Street 11.30 pm; Winsley Street closed Sun.

Yashin W8 NEW £65 ❷④④
1a, Argyll Rd 7938 1536 5–1A
*"A definite addition to London's dining scene" – this ambitious
Kensington newcomer serves "very creative" and exquisitely
presented sushi and sashimi, in a Manhattan-esque (and very un-
Japanese) setting; it's "too expensive" however, service is stilted,
and its dark-toned decor is a bit oppressive.* / www.yashinsushi.com; 10 pm.

Yauatcha W1 £65 ❶④❷
Broadwick Hs, 15-17 Broadwick St 7494 8888 3–2D
*"Mind-blowing", "new-wave" dim sum – "the best this side of HK" –
make a perennial hit of this "funky" Soho spot, with its "club-like"
(but "cramped") basement, and "sophisticated" (but less vibey)
ground-floor dining room; service, though, can be "supercilious".*
/ www.yauatcha.com; 11.15 pm, Sun 10.30 pm.

The Yellow House SE16 £41 ❷❷④
126 Lower Rd 7231 8777 11–2A
*The "best in SE16!" (not, admittedly, London's most hotly-contested
postcode) – this "fabulous local" is a "friendly" Surrey Quays spot,
where "slightly different" pizza and "yummy" puds are among the
culinary highlights.* / www.theyellowhouse.eu; 10.30 pm, Sun 9.30 pm; closed
Mon, Tue–Sat closed L, Sun open L & D.

Yi-Ban E16 £42 ❸④④
Regatta Centre, Dockside Rd 7473 6699 11–1D
*"It has a terrible location, is utterly impossible to get to, and hidden-
away in a concrete shed with views of London City Airport"… but,
fortunately, "superb dim sum" (and other "reliable" fare) reward
those who seek out this obscure dockside Chinese.* / www.yi-ban.co.uk;
10.45 pm.

Yming W1   £40   **❷⓿❸**
35-36 Greek St   7734 2721   4–2A
"Better than most of its neighbours in nearby Chinatown", Christine Lau's Soho Chinese remains a "long-term favourite"; the food is "really lovely", and staff – led by maître d' William – are "superbly welcoming" too. / www.yminglondon.com; 11.45 pm; set L & pre-th £21 (FP).

Yo Sushi   £27   **⑤⑤⑤**
Branches throughout London
A conveyor-chain whose "concept" has long seemed rather "stale"; "the food's at best OK, and at worst it can be vile" – "if that's sushi, I'm a Martian!". / www.yosushi.co.uk; 10.30 pm; no booking.

York & Albany NW1   £50   **④④④**
127-129 Parkway   7388 3344   8–3B
"We loved it when it opened, but it's gone off in a big way..." – as is the case in many parts of the Gordon Ramsay empire, this "grand" (and potentially "chic") Regent's Park tavern serves up some "very mediocre" fare nowadays, and service can be "appalling" too. / www.gordonramsay.com; 10.30 pm, Sun 8 pm.

Yoshino W1   £37   **❷⓿❸**
3 Piccadilly Pl   7287 6622   3–3D
"A little secret within 200 yards of Piccadilly Circus"; this minimalist Japanese café, off a small alleyway, offers "terrific" food – including "immaculate" sushi – and "very smiley" service too; it's even "reasonably priced"! / www.yoshino.net; 10.30 pm; closed Sun.

Yum Yum N16   £42   **❸❸❷**
187 Stoke Newington High St   7254 6751   1–1D
This "massive" Stoke Newington Thai really "rocks!" – it's a "well-run" and "trusty" operation, that year-in, year-out churns out "reasonably-priced" fare, and "good cocktails" too. / www.yumyum.co.uk; 11 pm, Fri & Sat midnight.

Yuzu NW6   £38   **❷④⑤**
102 Fortune Green Rd   7431 6602   1–1B
Ambience may be lacking, and the seating "too close for comfort", but this West Hampstead Japanese is, on most accounts, "an under-rated neighbourhood gem", which serves "interesting" dishes rather "in the style of Nobu"! / www.yuzu-restaurants.com; 10.30 pm; D only.

Zafferano SW1   £69   **❸④❸**
15 Lowndes St   7235 5800   5–1D
Many reporters still find the cooking at this smart Belgravian "consistently very good", but the volume of complaints about "clumsy" service and "significant overpricing" are such nowadays that the oft-repeated claims that this is 'London's best Italian' are clearly no longer sustainable. / www.zafferanorestaurant.com; 11 pm.

Zaffrani N1   £41   **❸❸❸**
47 Cross St   7226 5522   8–3D
"Still an excellent curry"; this Islington Indian wins praise for its "fresh" and "tasty" cuisine (with "a myriad of delicate flavours"); "distant" service, however, can take the edge off the experience. / www.zaffrani-islington.co.uk; 11 pm.

Zaika W8   £59   **⓿❷❸**
1 Kensington High St   7795 6533   5–1A
"Under-appreciated" but "always a winner" – this "incredible" Indian offers really "imaginative" and "beautifully realised" cuisine, in "elegant" (but perhaps slightly "unatmospheric") former banking premises, opposite Kensington Gardens. / www.zaika-restaurant.co.uk; 10.45 pm, Sun 9.45 pm; closed Mon L; set pre theatre £36 (FP).

Zayna W1 £45 ❷④④
25 New Quebec St 7723 2229 2–2A
A "quality" Pakistani curry house, hidden-away near Marble Arch;
it may be "small in size", and offer "inconsistent" service, but the
food is "great". / www.zaynarestaurant.co.uk; 11.15 pm, Fri & Sat 11.45 pm;
set weekday L £29 (FP).

Zero Degrees SE3 £37 ❸④❷
29-31 Montpelier Vale 8852 5619 1–4D
"Offbeat pizzas" and "good home brews" – that's the deal that
keeps this chrome-decorated Blackheath microbrewery very busy;
only real problem? – "it can get a bit loud when it's full".
/ www.zerodegrees.co.uk; midnight, Sun 11.30 pm.

Ziani's SW3 £52 ❸❷❷
45 Radnor Walk 7351 5297 5–3C
"You can't beat this small and hidden-away trattoria", say Chelsea
locals; OK, it's "packed", "very noisy" and "a bit pricey", but it's
"never dull", and a "lovely venue for a family treat". / www.ziani.co.uk;
11 pm, Sun 10.30 pm.

Zilli Fish W1 £69 ④④④
36-40 Brewer St 7734 8649 3–2D
For "unfancy, but fresh and well-presented" fish dishes, this TV chef's
Soho corner spot still has many fans; those who remember its glory
days, however, feel it's "looking past its prime, and needs some TLC
at all levels". / www.zillirestaurants.co.uk/fish; 11 pm; closed Sun.

Zilli Green W1 £38
41 Dean St 7734 3924 4–2A
Aldo Zilli's "pleasant" enough veggie-Italian closed its doors
just before this guide went to press; we're told that they're actively
looking for a relaunch site, ideally in Soho.
/ www.zillirestaurants.co.uk/green; 11 pm; closed Mon L, Tue L & Sun D.

Zizzi £44 ④④④
Branches throughout London
"Branches vary greatly", perhaps explaining the up-and-down nature
of reports on this "rustic"-themed Italianate chain; fans say they're
"a welcome change from PizzaExpress", but their ratings lag their
rival (and by quite a margin). / www.zizzi.co.uk; 11 pm.

Zucca SE1 £40 ❶❶❷
184 Bermondsey St 7378 6809 9–4D
"Professionalism", "friendly hospitality" and "unfussy" but "uniformly
excellent" cooking (from an open kitchen), at "sensible prices" –
all the ingredients which have made a huge hit of this "relaxed"
Bermondsey Italian yearling; "the only snag? – getting a table!"
/ www.zuccalondon.com; 10 pm; closed Mon & Sun D; no Amex.

ZUMA SW7 £77 ❶❸❷
5 Raphael St 7584 1010 5–1C
"There's no sign of any recession" ("good luck getting a table!"),
at this "buzzy, brash and glitzy" Knightsbridge scene – London's No.
1 Japanese – which is as "exciting" as it is "seriously expensive";
"if your date turns out to be dull, there are lots of beautiful people
to watch". / www.zumarestaurant.com; 10.45 pm, Sun 10.15 pm; booking:
max 8.

INDEXES

BREAKFAST
(with opening times)

Central

Abokado: *WC2 (7.30)*
Adam Street *(9)*
Amaranto *(6.30 am, Sat-Sun 7 am)*
Apsleys *(7)*
aqua nueva *(Sun brunch 12 pm)*
Asia de Cuba *(7)*
Athenaeum *(7)*
Aubaine: *W1 (8, Sat 10)*
Automat *(Mon-Fri 7)*
Baker & Spice: *SW1 (7)*
Balans: *all central branches (8)*
Bar Boulud *(6.30)*
Bar Italia *(6.30)*
Benugo: *all central branches (7.30)*
Bistro 1: *Beak St W1 (Sun 11)*
Black & Blue: *Berners St W1 (9)*
The Botanist *(8, Sat & Sun 9)*
La Bottega: *Eccleston St SW1 (8, Sat 9); Lower Sloane St SW1 (8, Sat 9, Sun 10)*
Boyd's Brasserie *(7.30, Sun 8)*
Brasserie Roux *(6.30, Sat & Sun 7)*
Browns (Albemarle) *(7, Sun 7.30)*
The English Tea Rm (Browns) *(8)*
Browns: *WC2 (9, 10 Sat & Sun)*
Café Bohème *(8, Sat & Sun 9)*
Café in the Crypt *(Mon-Sat 8)*
Café Luc *(Sat & Sun 9)*
Caffè Vergnano: *WC2 (8, Sun 11)*
Canteen: *W1 (8, Sat & Sun 9)*
Cecconi's *(7 am, Sat & Sun 8 am)*
The Chelsea Brasserie *(8)*
Chez Gérard: *Chancery Ln WC2 (8)*
Chop'd: *W1 (7)*
Christopher's *(Sat & Sun 11.30)*
The Cinnamon Club *(Mon-Fri 7.30)*
City Café *(6.30, Sat & Sun 7)*
Cocorino: *Thayer St W1 (7, Sat 8, Sun 9)*
Comptoir Libanais: *W1 (8.30)*
Côte: *W1 (8, Sat & Sun 9)*
The Courtauld Gallery Café *(10)*
Daylesford Organic: *SW1 (8, Sun 10)*
Dean Street Townhouse *(Mon-Fri 7, Sat-Sun 8)*
Diner: *W1 (10, Sat & Sun 9)*
Dishoom *(8, Sat & Sun 10)*
Dorchester Grill *(7, Sat & Sun 8)*
The Duke of Wellington *(Sat 9.30)*
Eagle Bar Diner *(Sat 10.30)*
The Ebury *(Sat & Sun 11)*
Fernandez & Wells: *Beak St W1 (7.30, sat& sun 9); Lexington St W1 (7 am); St Anne's Ct W1 (8, sat 10)*
Flat White *(8, Sat & Sun 9)*
The Fountain (Fortnum's) *(7.30, Sun 11)*
Franco's *(7.30, Sat 8)*
La Fromagerie Café *(8, Sun 9, Sun 10)*
Fuzzy's Grub: *SW1 (7)*
Gelupo *(9, Sat & Sun 12)*
Giraffe: *W1 (7.45, Sat & Sun 9)*
The Goring Hotel *(7, Sun 7.30)*
Guerilla Burgers *(11)*
Hélène Darroze *(Sat 11)*
Indigo *(6.30)*
Inn the Park *(8, Sat & Sun 9)*
Joe Allen *(8)*
JW Steakhouse *(6.30 pm, Sat & Sun 7 pm)*
Kaffeine *(7.30, Sat 9)*
Kazan (Cafe): *Wilton Rd SW1 (8 am, Sun 9 am)*
Konditor & Cook: *WC1 (9.30); W1 (9.30, Sun 10.30)*
Kopapa *(8.30, Sat & Sun 10)*
Ladurée: *W1 (9); SW1 (Mon - Sat 9, Sun noon - 1.30)*
Lantana Cafe *(8, Sat & Sun 9)*
Leon: *WC2 (7.30, Sat 9, Sun 10); Gt Marlborough St W1 (9.30, Sat & Sun 10.30)*
Maison Bertaux *(8.30, Sun 9)*
maze Grill *(6.45)*
Monmouth Coffee Company: *WC2 (8)*
Mount Street Deli *(8, Sat 9)*
Mrs Marengos *(8, Sat noon)*
Napket: *Vigo St W1, Brook St W1 (7.30); Piccadilly W1 (8)*
The National Dining Rooms *(10)*
National Gallery Café *(8, Sat & Sun10)*
Natural Kitchen: *W1 (8, Sat 9, Sun 11)*
Nopi *(8, Sat 9, Sun 10)*
Nordic Bakery: *Golden Sq W1 (Mon-Fri 8, Sat 9, Sun 11)*
Noura: *William St SW1 (8)*
Number Twelve *(7, Sat & Sun 7.30)*
The Only Running Footman *(7.30, Sat & Sun 9)*
The Orange *(8)*
Oscar *(7, Sun 12)*
Ottolenghi: *SW1 (8, Sun 9)*
Ozer *(8)*
The Pantechnicon *(Sat & Sun 8.30)*
Paramount *(8)*
Paul: *WC2 (7.30); W1 (7.30, Sat & Sun 8)*
Pearl *(6.30, Sat & Sun 7)*
The Portrait *(10)*
Princi *(7, Sun 9)*
Providores (Tapa Room) *(9, Sat & Sun 10)*
Ranoush: *SW1 (9)*
Refuel *(7, Sun 8)*
Rib Room *(7, Sun 8)*
RIBA Café *(8)*
Riding House Café *(8 am, Sat & Sun 9 am)*
Ritz (Palm Court) *(7, Sun 8)*
The Ritz Restaurant *(7, Sun 8)*
Roux At The Landau *(7)*
St John Hotel *(7)*
Savoy (River Rest') *(7 am, Sun 7.30 am)*
Scandinavian Kitchen *(8, Sat & Sun 10)*
Serafino *(7)*
Simpsons-in-the-Strand *(Mon-Fri 7.30)*
The Sketch (Parlour) *(Mon-Fri 8, Sat 10)*
Sophie's Steakhouse: *all branches (Sat & Sun 11)*
Sotheby's Café *(9.30)*
Spice Market *(7, Sat & Sun 8)*
Stock Pot: *SW1 (9.30)*
Tate Britain (Rex Whistler) *(Sat-Sun 10)*
The Terrace in the Fields *(Mon-Fri 9)*
tibits *(9, Sun 11.30)*
Tom's Terrace *(10 Sat & Sun)*
Truc Vert *(7.30, Sat & Sun 9)*
The Union Café *(Sat & Sun 11)*
The Wallace *(10)*
William Curley: *all branches (9.30, Sun 10.30)*
Wolfe's *(9)*
The Wolseley *(7, Sat & Sun 8)*
Yalla Yalla: *Green's Ct W1 (Sat-Sun 10)*

West

Adams Café *(7.30 am)*
Annie's: *W4 (Tue - Thu 10, Fri & Sat 10.30, Sun 10)*
Aubaine: *SW3 (8, Sun 9); W8 (Mon-Sat*

8 am, 9 am Sun)
Baker & Spice: all west branches (7, Sun 8)
Balans West: SW5, W4, W8 (8)
Bedlington Café (8.30)
Beirut Express: W2 (7)
Benugo: W12 (9)
Best Mangal: SW6 (10-12)
Bistro K (9)
Blakes (7)
Bluebird Café (8, Sat & Sun 10)
La Bottega: Gloucester Rd SW7 (8, Sat 9, Sun 9)
La Brasserie (8)
Bumpkin: SW7 (11 am)
The Cabin (Sat & Sun 10)
Café Laville (10, Sat & Sun 9.30)
Chelsea Bun Diner (7, Sun 9)
The Chelsea Kitchen (7, Sun 8)
Chiswick House Cafe (9)
Comptoir Libanais: W12 (9.30)
Daylesford Organic: W11 (8, Sun 11)
Del'Aziz: W12 (8); SW6 (8 am)
Electric Brasserie (8)
Fresco (8, Sun 9)
Gail's Bread: W11 (7, Sat & Sun 8)
Gallery Mess (10)
Geales Chelsea Green: SW3 (9 am Sat & Sun)
Giraffe: W4, W8 (7.45, Sat & Sun 9); W11 (8, Sat & Sun 9)
The Greedy Buddha (Sat & Sun 10)
The Henry Root (Sat - Sun 9.30 am)
High Road Brasserie (7, Sat & Sun 8)
Joe's Brasserie (Sat & Sun 11)
Julie's (9, Sun 10.30)
Kensington Square Kitchen (8.30, Sun 9.30)
Lisboa Pâtisserie (7)
Lola & Simón (8, Sat & Sun 9.30)
Lucky Seven (Mon noon, Tue-Thu 10, Fri-Sun 9)
Mona Lisa (7)
Napket: SW3 (8)
Nottingdale (Mon-Fri 7)
Ottolenghi: W11 (8, Sun 8.30)
Pappa Ciccia: Fulham High St SW6 (7.30)
Pissarro (Sat & Sun 9)
Ranoush: W8 (10); W2 (9); SW3 (noon)
Raoul's Café & Deli: W11 (8.30); W9 (8.30 am)
Sam's Brasserie (9)
Sophie's Steakhouse: all branches (Sat & Sun 11)
Stock Pot: SW3 (8)
Tartine (11)
Tom's Deli (8, Sun 9)
Tom's Kitchen (8, Sat & Sun 10)
Troubadour (9)
202 (Mon & Sun 10, Tue-Sat 8.30)
Vingt-Quatre (24 hrs)
The Waterway (10 Sat & Sun)
White Horse (9.30)

North
The Almeida ( )
Banners (9, Sat & Sun 10)
Blue Legume (9.30)
Caponata (9, Sun 10)
Chamomile (7, Sat & Sun 8)
Chop'd: NW1 (7)
Del'Aziz: NW3 (8)
Diner: N1, NW10 (sat, sun 9)
The Engineer (9)
Euphorium Bakery (7.30, Sun 9)
Fifteen Trattoria (7.30, Sun 8)
Fine Burger Company: NW1 (7 am);

N1, NW3 (midday, Sat & Sun 11 am)
Gail's Bread: NW3 (7, Sat & Sun 8)
Gallipoli: Upper St N1, Upper St N1 (10.30)
Garufa (10)
Ginger & White (7.30, Sat & Sun 8.30)
Giraffe: N1, Rosslyn Hill NW3 (7.45, Sat & Sun 9); Haverstock Hill NW3 (8, Sat & Sun 9)
Harry Morgan's (9)
Homa (9, Sun 10)
Juniper Dining (Sat & Sun 9)
Kentish Canteen (10)
Kenwood (Brew House) (9)
Kipferl (9, Sun 10)
Landmark (Winter Gdn) (7)
The Lansdowne (Sat & Sun 9.30)
Ottolenghi: N1 (8, Sun 9)
Rugoletta (9)
S & M Café: N1 (7.30)
St Pancras Grand (7, Sun 9)
Stringray Café: N5 (11); NW5 (Fri-Sun 11)
Trojka (Mon-Fri 8)
The Wet Fish Cafe (10)
York & Albany (7)

South
Annie's: SW13 (Tue-Sun 10)
Archduke Wine Bar (Sat & Sun10)
The Bingham (7, Sat-Sun 8)
The Bolingbroke (Sat & Sun 10)
Brasserie James (Sat & Sun 10 am)
Browns: SE1 (11 am)
Buenos Aires Cafe: SE10 (7.30 am)
Butcher & Grill: SW11 (8.30); SW19 (Sat & Sun 8.30)
Caffè Vergnano: SE1 (8, Sat & Sun 11)
Canteen: SE1 (8, Sat & Sun 9)
Chapters (8, Sun 9)
Le Chardon: SW4 (9); SE22 (Sat & Sun 9.30)
Del'Aziz: all south branches (8)
The Depot (Sat 9.30)
Doukan (9)
Fat Boy's: TW8 (Mon-Fri 11.30)
fish! (Thu-Fri 7, Sat 8, Sun 10)
Franklins (Sat 10)
Frizzante Cafe (10)
Garrison (8, Sat & Sun 9)
Gastro (9)
Gazette: SW12 (7); SW11 (8)
Giraffe: all south branches (7.45, Sat & Sun 9)
Green & Blue (9, Sun 11)
Harrison's (9.30, Sat & Sun 9)
Hudsons (9.30, Sat & Sun 9)
Joanna's (9)
Konditor & Cook: Cornwall Road SE1, Stoney St SE1 (7.30 am)
Lola Rojo: SW11 (Sat & Sun 11)
Monmouth Coffee Company: Park St SE1 (7.30); Maltby St SE1 (9)
Orange Pekoe (9)
Le P'tit Normand (Sun 9)
Pantry (8, Sat 8.30 & Sun 9.30)
Petersham Hotel (Mon-Fri 7, Sat & Sun 8)
Plane Food (5.30)
Putney Station (Sat & Sun 11)
El Rincón Latino (Sat & Sun 11)
The Riverfront (9.30)
Rivington Grill: SE10 (Thurs-Sun 10)
Roast (7, Sat 8)
Scoffers (10.30, Sun 9)
Sonny's (Sat & Sun 10)
The Table (7.30, Sat-Sun 9)
Tapas Brindisa: SE1 (Fri-Sat 9, Sun 11)

BUSINESS

Odin's
One-O-One
L'Oranger
Orrery
Oscar
The Palm
The Pantechnicon
Paramount
Patterson's
Pearl
Pétrus
Pied à Terre
Quilon
Quirinale
Quo Vadis
Refuel
Rhodes W1 Restaurant
Rib Room
Roka: *all branches*
Roussillon
Roux At Parliament Square
Roux At The Landau
Rules
Santini
Sartoria
Savoy Grill
Savoy (River Rest')
Scott's
J Sheekey
Shepherd's
Simpsons-in-the-Strand
The Square
Tamarind
Theo Randall
2 Veneti
Veeraswamy
Il Vicolo
The Wallace
Wheeler's
Wild Honey
Wiltons
The Wolseley
Zafferano

West
Bibendum
The Capital Restaurant
Gaucho: *SW3*
Gordon Ramsay
The Ledbury
Poissonnerie de l'Avenue
Racine
Tom Aikens
La Trompette
Zuma

North
Frederick's
Gaucho: *NW3*
Landmark (Winter Gdn)
Rotunda Bar & Restaurant
St Pancras Grand

South
Blueprint Café
Brasserie Joël
Butlers Wharf Chop House
Le Cassoulet
Chez Gérard: *all branches*
Delfina
Gaucho: *SE1, TW10*
The Glasshouse
Magdalen
Oxo Tower (Brass')
Oxo Tower (Rest')
Le Pont de la Tour

Roast
Skylon
Vivat Bacchus: *all branches*
Zucca

East
Alba
Amerigo Vespucci
L'Anima
Bevis Marks
Bleeding Heart
Boisdale of Bishopsgate
Bonds
Café du Marché
Caravaggio
Catch
Chamberlain's
The Chancery
Chez Gérard: *all branches*
Cinnamon Kitchen
City Miyama
Club Gascon
Coq d'Argent
Curve
Dockmaster's House
The Don
Eyre Brothers
Forman's
The Fox and Anchor
Galvin La Chapelle
Gaucho: *E14, EC2, EC3*
Goodman City : *all branches*
Gow's
Green's: *all branches*
High Timber
The Hoxton Grill
Imperial City
Luc's Brasserie
Lutyens
Malmaison Brasserie
The Mercer
Moro
1901
1 Lombard Street
Pacific Oriental
Paternoster Chop House
Plateau
Portal
Prism
Quadrato
Refettorio
Rhodes 24
Roka: *all branches*
The Royal Exchange Grand Café
St John
Sauterelle
Searcy's Brasserie
Smiths (Top Floor)
Smiths (Dining Rm)
Sweetings
Taberna Etrusca
Tompkins
Vertigo 42
Vivat Bacchus: *all branches*
The White Swan

BYO

(Bring your own wine at no or low – less than £3 – corkage. Note for £5-£15 per bottle, you can normally negotiate to take your own wine to many, if not most, places.)

Central

Food for Thought
Fryer's Delight
Golden Hind
India Club
Paolina Café
Patogh
Ragam
Viet

West

Adams Café
Alounak: *all branches*
Bedlington Café
Café 209
Chelsea Bun Diner
Fitou's Thai Restaurant
Five Hot Chillies
Mirch Masala: *all branches*
Mohsen
Pappa Ciccia: *Munster Rd SW6*
Rôtisserie Bute Street

North

Ali Baba
Diwana Bhel-Poori House
Geeta
Huong-Viet
Rugoletta
Toff's
Vijay

South

Amaranth
Green & Blue
Hot Stuff
Lahore Karahi
Lahore Kebab House: *all branches*
Mien Tay: *all branches*
Mirch Masala: *all branches*
The Paddyfield
Simply Indian
Sree Krishna
Thai Corner Café

East

Lahore Kebab House: *all branches*
Little Georgia Café
Mangal 1
Mien Tay: *all branches*
Mirch Masala: *all branches*
New Tayyabs

CHILDREN

*(h – high or special chairs
m – children's menu
p – children's portions
e – weekend entertainments
o – other facilities)*

Central

Abeno: *WC2 (h);WC1 (hm)*
About Thyme *(hp)*
Acorn House *(h)*
Al Duca *(hp)*

Al Hamra *(hp)*
Al Sultan *(h)*
Albannach *(hmp)*
All Star Lanes: *all branches (hm)*
Alloro *(p)*
Apsleys *(hp)*
Arbutus *(hp)*
Asadal *(hp)*
Asia de Cuba *(hp)*
L'Atelier de Joel Robuchon *(hp)*
Athenaeum *(m)*
Aubaine: *all branches (h)*
L'Autre Pied *(hp)*
Axis *(hm)*
Babbo *(hp)*
Back to Basics *(hp)*
Balans: *all central branches (hm)*
Bank Westminster *(hp)*
Bar Boulud *(hp)*
Bar Italia *(hp)*
Bar Trattoria Semplice *(hp)*
Il Baretto *(h)*
Barrica *(p)*
Bar Shu *(h)*
Beiteddine *(p)*
Belgo Centraal: *Earlham St WC2 (hm); Kingsway WC2 (m)*
Bellamy's *(h)*
Benares *(h)*
Benihana: *W1 (hm)*
Benito's Hat: *Goodge St W1 (hp)*
Benja *(h)*
Bentley's *(h)*
Bincho Yakitori *(hp)*
Bocca Di Lupo *(hp)*
Bodean's: *W1 (ehm)*
The Botanist *(h)*
Boudin Blanc *(hp)*
Boulevard *(hm)*
Boyd's Brasserie *(hp)*
Brasserie Roux *(hm)*
Browns (Albemarle) *(hmp)*
The English Tea Rm (Browns) *(h)*
Browns: *W1, WC2 (hm)*
Bumbles *(h)*
Byron: *Wellington St WC2 (hm)*
C London *(hp)*
Café Bohème *(h)*
Café des Amis *(h)*
Café Emm *(p)*
Café España *(h)*
Café in the Crypt *(hp)*
Café Luc *(hm)*
Café Pacifico *(hm)*
Caffè Caldesi *(hp)*
Caffè Vergnano: *WC2 (p)*
Cantina Laredo *(hm)*
Cape Town Fish Market *(hp)*
Le Caprice *(hp)*
Cecconi's *(hp)*
Le Cercle *(p)*
Chabrot Bistrot d'Amis *(p)*
The Chelsea Brasserie *(hm)*
Chez Gérard: *all central branches (em)*
China Tang *(h)*
Chipotle *(h)*
Chisou *(h)*
Chor Bizarre *(h)*
Christopher's *(hm)*
Chuen Cheng Ku *(h)*
Ciao Bella *(h)*
Cigala *(h)*
The Cinnamon Club *(h)*
City Café *(hm)*
Clos Maggiore *(hp)*
Colony *(hp)*
Como Lario *(hp)*

Yi-Ban *(h)*

ENTERTAINMENT
(Check times before you go)

Central
All Star Lanes: WC1
(bowling, DJ Sat)
Bentley's
(pianist, Wed-Sat)
Bincho Yakitori
(DJ, Mon; occasional live music, Wed)
Boisdale
(jazz, Mon-Sat)
The English Tea Rm (Browns)
(pianist, daily)
Café in the Crypt
(jazz, Wed night)
Le Caprice
(pianist, nightly)
Ciao Bella
(pianist, nightly)
Circus
(circus entertainment, nightly)
Criterion
(live music, Fri & Sat; jazz trio, Sun)
Eagle Bar Diner
(DJ, Thu-Sat)
Élysée
*(live music, belly dancing, smashing plates
Thurs, Fri, Sat)*
Floridita
(live Cuban music, nightly)
Hakkasan: Hanway Pl W1
(DJ, nightly)
Hard Rock Café
(regular live music)
Harrods (Georgian Rest')
(pianist till 5.30 pm)
Imperial China
(pianist; private rooms with karaoke)
Ishtar
(live music, Tue-Sat; belly dancer, Fri & Sat)
Joe Allen
(pianist, Mon-Sat)
Kettners
(pianist Tue-Sat)
Langan's Brasserie
(jazz, Fri & Sat)
Levant
(belly dancer, nightly)
Little Italy
(DJ, Mon-Sat)
Maroush: W1
(music & dancing, nightly)
Mint Leaf: SW1
(DJ, Fri D)
Momo
(live world music, Tue)
Noura: W1
(belly dancer, Fri&Sat)
L'Oranger
(pianist, Fri & Sat)
Oscar
(film club, Sun)
Pearl
(pianist, Wed-Sat)
Quaglino's
(jazz, nightly)
Red Fort
(DJ, Fri & Sat)
Refuel
(film club, Sun 3.30 pm)
The Ritz Restaurant
(live music, Fri & Sat)
Roka: W1

(DJ, Thu-Sat)
Samarqand
(Karaoke and games consoles)
Sarastro
(opera, Sun & Mon D)
Savoy Grill
(pianist, nightly)
Savoy (River Rest')
(cabaret music)
Shanghai Blues
(live jazz, Fri & Sat)
Simpsons-in-the-Strand
(pianist, nightly)
Sketch (Gallery)
(DJ, Thu-Sat)
Tamarai
(club nights, Fri & Sat)
Thai Square: SW1
(DJ, Fri & Sat)
Tom's Terrace
(DJ, Thu-Fri)
Vanilla
(DJ's, Fri & Sat)
The Windmill
(live music, Mon)

West
All Star Lanes: W2
(bowling, DJ Thu-Sat)
Babylon
*(nightclub, Fri & Sat; magician,
Sun; jazz, Tue)*
Beach Blanket Babylon: all branches
(DJ, Fri & Sat)
Belvedere
(pianist, nightly Sat & Sun all day)
Benugo: Cromwell Rd SW7
(jazz, Wed)
Big Easy
(live music, nightly)
Brompton Bar & Grill
(jazz, third Fri of the month)
Le Café Anglais
(magician, Sun L)
Chella
(live music, Sun)
Cheyne Walk Brasserie
(jazz, first Mon of month)
Del'Aziz: SW6
(belly dancer, Thu-Sat, live acoustic music);
W12
(live Jazz, Fri-Sat)
Formosa Dining Room
(quiz, Tue)
Frankie's Italian Bar & Grill: SW3
(magician, Sun)
Harwood Arms
(quiz night, Tue)
Maroush: I) 21 Edgware Rd W2
(music & dancing, nightly)
Mr Wing
(jazz, Thu-Sat)
Notting Hill Brasserie
(jazz, nightly, Sun L)
Nozomi
(DJ, every night)
Okawari
(karaoke)
Old Parr's Head
(quiz night, Mon; poker, Tue)
Il Pagliaccio
(Elvis impersonator, monthly)
Paradise by Way of Kensal Green
*(burlesque, Mon; comedy nights, Wed; DJ,
Fri-Sun)*
Pasha

(belly dancer, weekends; tarot card reader, special occasions)

(Ciro's) Pizza Pomodoro
(live music, nightly)

Rôtisserie Bute Street
(live music)

Sam's Brasserie
(live music, first and third Sun of month)

Sticky Fingers
(face painter, Sun)

supperclub
(shows, nightly)

Troubadour
(live music, most nights)

The Waterway
(live music, Thu)

North

Bull & Last
(pub quiz, Sun)

Camino
(DJ, Thu-Sat)

Caponata
(live music, Tue-Sun)

Del'Aziz: NW3
(live Jazz, Fri & Sat)

The Fellow
(DJ, Thu-Fri)

Gilgamesh
(DJ, Fri & Sat)

The Haven
(jazz, Tue-Thu)

Isarn
(live music)

Landmark (Winter Gdn)
(pianist & musicians, daily)

Mestizo
(DJ, Thu)

The North London Tavern
(jazz, Sun; quiz night, Mon; open mic, Tue; Every third Thu comedy)

Prince Albert
(quiz, Sun D)

Rotunda Bar & Restaurant
(jazz, Fri)

Shaka Zulu
(music, bi-weekly)

Thai Square: N1
(DJ, Thu-Sat)

Trojka
(Russian music, Fri & Sat)

Villa Bianca
(guitarist, Mon-Thu; pianist, Sat & Sun)

The Wet Fish Cafe
(Spanish soul, occasionally)

York & Albany
(quiz night, Mon)

South

Al Forno: SW15
(live music, Sat)

Archduke Wine Bar
(jazz, Mon-Sun)

Avalon
(DJ, Fri & Sat)

Bayee Village
(pianist, Mon-Wed)

Bengal Clipper
(pianist, Tue-Sat)

Brasserie Toulouse-Lautrec
(live music, nightly)

Cantina Vinopolis
(singer, Fri)

Del'Aziz: Canvey St SE1
(live balkan, gypsy and folk rhythms, wed live jazz, fri belly dancing); Bermondsey

Sq SE1
(live Jazz Wed & Sat; belly-dancing Fri)

Entrée
(jazz, Thu-Sat D)

The Fentiman Arms
(quiz night, Tue)

Florence
(play room)

The Gowlett
(DJ, Sun; Lucky 7s, Thu)

The Lighthouse
(live music)

The Little Bay: SW11
(opera, Thu-Sat; piano, Wed & Sun)

Meson don Felipe
(guitarist, nightly)

Oxo Tower (Brass')
(live jazz, Sat & Sun L, Sun-Mon D)

Le Pont de la Tour
(pianist, every evening; live jazz trio, Sun L)

The Prince Of Wales
(quiz night, Sun)

Roast
(jazz, Sun)

Santa Maria del Sur
(live music, Mon)

The Ship
(live music, Sun; quiz, Wed)

Tas: The Cut SE1, Borough High St SE1
(guitarist, nightly)

Tas Pide
(live music, daily D)

Thai Square: SW15
(DJ, Fri & Sat)

The Victoria
(Singer, one Wed a month)

The Wharf
(Salsa night, first Wed of month)

East

All Star Lanes: E1
(bowling)

Beach Blanket Babylon: all branches
(DJ, Fri & Sat)

Bistrotheque
(regular drag shows and cabarets, piano brunch)

Boisdale of Canary Wharf
(live music, daily)

Café du Marché
(pianist & bass, Mon-Thu, pianist, Fri & Sat)

Cinnamon Kitchen
(DJ, Wed-Fri)

Coq d'Argent
(jazz, Sun L)

Elephant Royale
(live music, Thu-Sat)

Frizzante at City Farm
(agriturismo night, Thu in summer)

Great Eastern Dining Room
(DJ, Fri & Sat)

The Hoxton Grill
(DJ, Thu-Sat)

Kenza
(belly dancers, Mon-Sat; tarot reader, Fri)

The Little Bay: EC1
(opera, Thu-Sat)

Mint Leaf: EC2
(Jazz, Fri D; DJ, weekends)

The Narrow
(quiz night, Mon; comedy, monthly; acoustic, Wed)

1901
(violinist or other live music, Wed-Thu)

Pizza East
(DJ, live music, quiz nights, Tue, Thu, Sat)

LATE

(open till midnight or later as shown; may be earlier Sunday)

Le Mercury (1 am, not Sun)
19 Numara Bos Cirrik
Pizzeria Pappagone
La Porchetta Pizzeria: N4, NW1 (Sat &
   Sun midnight); N1 (weekends midnight)
Rodizio Rico: N1
Sofra: all branches
Yum Yum (Fri & Sat midnight)

South
Archduke Wine Bar (Fri & Sat 1 am)
Basilico: all south branches
Belgo: SW4 (midnight, Thu 1 am, Fri & Sat
   2 am)
Buona Sera: all branches
Caffé Vergnano: SE1
Cah-Chi: SW18 (not Sat & Sun)
Champor-Champor
Everest Inn
Firezza: SW11 ; SW18 (Fri & Sat midnight)
Fish in a Tie
Gastro
Green & Blue (Fri & Sat midnight)
Kennington Tandoori
Lahore Karahi
Lahore Kebab House: all branches
The Lighthouse (Fri & Sat midnight)
Mirch Masala: all branches
Nazmins
Putney Station
Scoffers (Thu-Sat)
Sree Krishna (Fri & Sat midnight)
The Tree House (Fri & Sat midnight)
Tsunami: SW4 (Fri-Sun midnight)
Zero Degrees

East
Brick Lane Beigel Bake (24 hours)
Cellar Gascon
Clifton
The Diner: EC2 (not Sun & Mon)
Elephant Royale (Fri & Sat midnight)
Giant Robot
Lahore Kebab House: all branches
Mangal 1 (midnight, Sat-Sun 1 am)
Mirch Masala: all branches
Pizza East (Thu midnight, Fri & Sat 1 am)
La Porchetta Pizzeria: EC1 (Sat & Sun
   midnight)
Redhook (midnight, Thu-Sat 1 am)
Rocket: E14
Sweet & Spicy (Fri & Sat midnight)
Wapping Food

OUTSIDE TABLES
(* particularly recommended)

Central
Abokado: WC2
Al Duca
Al Hamra
Al Sultan
Amaranto
Andrew Edmunds
Antidote
aqua kyoto*
aqua nueva
Archipelago
L'Artiste Musclé
Atari-Ya: W1
Aubaine: W1
Aurora
L'Autre Pied
Back to Basics
Baker & Spice: SW1

Balans: Old Compton St W1
Bam-Bou
Bank Westminster
Bar Italia
Bar Trattoria Semplice
Barrafina
Barrica
Benito's Hat: Goodge St W1
Bentley's
Benugo: all central branches
Bincho Yakitori
Bistro 1: Frith St W1, WC2
The Botanist
La Bottega: Lower Sloane St SW1, Eccleston
   St SW1
Boudin Blanc
The Bountiful Cow
Busaba Eathai: WC1
Café Bohème
Café des Amis
Café Luc
Caffè Caldesi
Cantina Laredo
Caraffini
Cecconi's
Cha Cha Moon
Chez Gérard: all central branches
Chisou
Ciao Bella
Cigala
City Café
Cocorino: Thayer St W1
Colony
Comptoir Libanais: W1
Côte: WC2
The Courtauld Gallery Café
Da Mario
Daylesford Organic: all branches
Dean Street Townhouse
Dehesa
Delfino
dim T: W1
Diner: W1
The Duke of Wellington
The Easton
Ed's Easy Diner: Moor St W1
Élysée
Fairuz
5 Pollen Street
Franco's
Giraffe: W1
Goodman: W1
Gordon's Wine Bar
Goya
Grazing Goat
Grumbles
Guerilla Burgers
Hard Rock Café
Hardy's Brasserie
Hellenic
Hush
Indali Lounge
Inn the Park
Ishbilia
Ishtar
Jenny Lo's Tea House
Kaffeine
Kazan: all branches
Kopapa
Kyashii
Ladurée: SW1, W1
Lantana Cafe
Leon: Gt Marlborough St W1, WC2
Levant
Little Italy
Lupita
Maison Bertaux

Mennula
Momo
Mooli's
Motcombs
Mount Street Deli
Napket: *all central branches*
Nizuni
The Norfolk Arms
Olivomare
The Only Running Footman
Opera Tavern
The Orange
L'Oranger
Orrery
Oscar
Ozer
The Pantechnicon
Pescatori: *Charlotte St W1*
La Petite Maison
Piccolino: *W1**
ping pong: *Eastcastle St W1*
El Pirata
La Porchetta Pizzeria: *WC1*
La Poule au Pot
Prix Fixe
Providores (Tapa Room)
The Queens Arms
Quince
Quo Vadis
Le Relais de Venise L'Entrecôte: *all branches*
Reubens
RIBA Café*
The Ritz Restaurant
Rock & Sole Plaice
Roka: *W1*
Salaam Namaste
Salt Yard
Santini
Sardo
Savoir Faire
Scandinavian Kitchen
Scott's
Serafino
Shampers
Siam Central
Sofra: *Shepherd St W1, WC2*
Soho Japan
Tapas Brindisa Soho: *W1*
Taro: *Brewer St W1*
Tate Britain (Rex Whistler)
Tempo
The Terrace in the Fields
The Thomas Cubitt
tibits
Toku
Tom's Terrace*
Toto's
Trishna
Truc Vert
Tsunami: *W1*
Uno
Vapiano
Villandry
Vinoteca Seymour Place: *all branches*
William Curley: *all branches*
Wolfe's
Yalla Yalla: *Green's Ct W1*
Zilli Fish
Zilli Green

West
The Abingdon
L'Accento Italiano
Admiral Codrington
Al-Waha

Anarkali
Angelus
The Anglesea Arms
The Anglesea Arms
Annie's: *all branches*
The Ark
The Atlas*
Aubaine: *SW3*
Babylon
Baker & Spice: *SW3*
Balans: *W12, W4*
Beach Blanket Babylon: *W11*
Bedlington Café
Beirut Express: *SW7*
Belvedere
Benugo: *Cromwell Rd SW7*
Best Mangal: *SW6, North End Rd W14*
Bistro K
Black & Blue: *SW7, W8*
Blakes
Bluebird Café
La Bottega: *Gloucester Rd SW7*
La Bouchée
La Brasserie
Brinkley's
Bumpkin: *SW7*
Butcher's Hook
Byron: *Gloucester Rd SW7, W8*
The Cabin
Café Laville
Cambio de Tercio
Canta Napoli: *W4*
Capote Y Toros
The Carpenter's Arms
Carvosso's
Casa Brindisa
Casa Malevo
Cassis Bistro
Charlotte's Place
Charm
Chelsea Bun Diner
Chiswick House Cafe
Cibo
Cochonnet
Costa's Grill
Côte: *W8*
The Cow
Cumberland Arms
Daylesford Organic: *all branches*
Del'Aziz: *all branches*
La Delizia Limbara: *all branches*
The Dock Kitchen*
Duke of Sussex
E&O
E l l even Park Walk
Ealing Park Tavern
Edera
Electric Brasserie
The Enterprise
Essenza
Falconiere
La Famiglia*
Fat Boy's: *all west branches*
Fire & Stone: *W12*
Firezza: *W11, W4*
First Floor
Fitou's Thai Restaurant
Frantoio
Fresco
Fulham Wine Rooms
Gail's Bread: *W11*
Gallery Mess
The Gate
Geales: *W8*
Giraffe: *W4*
Haché: *all branches*
The Havelock Tavern

Queen's Head & Artichoke
Retsina
Rising Sun
Rodizio Rico: *N1*
The Rose & Crown
Rôtisserie: *HA5, NW6*
Rotunda Bar & Restaurant*
S & M Café: *all branches*
Le Sacré-Coeur
St Johns
The Salt House*
The Salusbury
Sea Pebbles
Singapore Garden
Sofra: *NW8*
Solly's
Somerstown Coffee House
Spaniard's Inn
Swan & Edgar
Trojka
Villa Bianca
Walnut
The Wells*
The Wet Fish Cafe
Yuzu

South
The Abbeville
Al Forno: *SW19*
The Anchor & Hope
Annie's: *all branches*
Antelope
Antipasto & Pasta
Applebee's Cafe
Archduke Wine Bar
Avalon*
Baltic
Bangalore Express: *SE1*
La Barca
Bayee Village
Bellevue Rendez-Vous
Bennett Oyster Bar
The Bingham
Black & Blue: *SE1*
Bodean's: *SW4*
The Bolingbroke
Brinkley's Kitchen
Brouge: *TW2*
The Brown Dog
Browns: *SE1*
Brula
Buenos Aires: *SE3*
Buona Sera: *SW11*
Butcher & Grill: *all branches*
Butlers Wharf Chop House
Cafe Strudel
Caffé Vergnano: *SE1*
Cannizaro House
Canteen: *SE1*
Cantina del Ponte
Cantinetta
Canton Arms
Chapters
Le Chardon: *all branches*
Chez Gérard: *SE1*
Chutney
Côte: *SW19*
The Dartmouth Arms
Del'Aziz: *all branches*
Delfina
La Delizia: *all branches*
The Depot
dim T: *SE1*
don Fernando's
Donna Margherita
Doukan

Earl Spencer
The East Hill
Eco
Everest Inn
Fat Boy's: *SW14,TW1*
The Fentiman Arms
Fish Place
fish!
Florence
Four Regions
The Fox & Hounds
Franco Manca: *SW9*
Franklins
Frizzante Cafe
Ganapati
Gastro
Gaucho: *TW10*
Gazette: *SW11*
Giraffe: *all south branches*
Gourmet Pizza Company: *all branches*
The Gowlett
Harrison's
Hudsons
Joanna's
La Lanterna
The Light House
The Lighthouse
Livebait: *SE1*
Lola Rojo: *SW11*
Ma Cuisine
Mango & Silk
Mar I Terra: *SE1*
Numero Uno
The Old Brewery*
Orange Pekoe
Origin Asia
Osteria Antica Bologna
Oxo Tower (Brass')
Oxo Tower (Rest')
The Palmerston
Palmyra
Pantry
The Pepper Tree
Petersham Hotel
Petersham Nurseries
Le Pont de la Tour
Popeseye: *SW15*
The Prince Albert
The Prince Of Wales
Putney Station
Le Querce: *SE23*
Ransome's Dock
Real Greek: *SE1*
The Riverfront
Rivington Grill: *SE10*
Rock & Rose
San Lorenzo Fuoriporta
Santa Maria del Sur
Scoffers
The Ship*
Simplicity
Stein's*
The Swan at the Globe
The Table
Tas: *The Cut SE1*
Tas Pide
Telegraph
Thai on the River
Thai Square: *SW15*
The Trafalgar Tavern
The Tree House
Valentina: *SW15*
El Vergel
Verta
The Victoria
Vivat Bacchus: *SE1*
Waterloo Brasserie

PRIVATE ROOMS

**(for the most comprehensive
listing of venues for functions –
from palaces to pubs – visit
www.hardens.com/party, or buy
*Harden's London Party, Event
& Conference Guide*, available
in all good bookshops)
* particularly recommended**

ROMANTIC

Central
Andrew Edmunds
Archipelago
L'Atelier de Joel Robuchon
Aurora
Bam-Bou
Boudin Blanc
Café Bohème
Le Caprice
Cecconi's
Le Cercle
Chor Bizarre
Clos Maggiore
Corrigan's Mayfair
Crazy Bear
Dean Street Townhouse
Les Deux Salons
Elena's L'Etoile
L'Escargot
Galvin at Windows
Gauthier Soho
Le Gavroche
Gay Hussar
Gordon Ramsay at Claridge's
Gordon's Wine Bar
Hakkasan: *Hanway Pl W1*
Hush
The Ivy
Kettners
Langan's Bistro
Langan's Brasserie
Levant
Locanda Locatelli
Marcus Wareing

West
Albertine
Angelus
Annie's: *W4*
The Ark
Assaggi
Babylon
Beach Blanket Babylon: *all branches*
Belvedere
Bibendum
Blakes
La Bouchée
Brinkley's
Café Laville
Charlotte's Place
Cheyne Walk Brasserie
Le Colombier
Daphne's
E&O
Eight Over Eight
La Famiglia
Ffiona's
First Floor
Julie's
Launceston Place
The Ledbury
Maggie Jones's
Mediterraneo
Mr Wing
Notting Hill Brasserie
Osteria Basilico
Paradise by Way of Kensal Green
Pasha
Patio
Pissarro
Polish Club
Portobello Ristorante
Racine
The River Café
Star of India
The Summerhouse
supperclub
Le Suquet
La Trompette
Troubadour
Le Vacherin
The Walmer Castle
Zuma

North
Anglo Asian Tandoori

ROOMS WITH A VIEW

NOTABLE WINE LISTS

CUISINES

An asterisk (*) after an entry indicates exceptional or very good cooking

AMERICAN
Central
All Star Lanes (WC1)
Automat (W1)
Bodean's (W1)
Christopher's (WC2)
Circus (WC2)
Guerilla Burgers (W1)
Hard Rock Café (W1)
Joe Allen (WC2)
Spuntino (W1)

West
All Star Lanes (W2)
Big Easy (SW3)
Bodean's (SW6)
Lucky Seven (W2)
Sticky Fingers (W8)

South
Bodean's (SW4)

East
All Star Lanes (E1)
Barbecoa (EC4)
Bodean's (EC3)
Giant Robot (EC1)
The Hoxton Grill (EC2)

AUSTRALIAN
Central
Lantana Cafe (W1)

BELGIAN
Central
Belgo Centraal (WC2)

North
Belgo Noord (NW1)

South
Belgo (SW4)
Brouge (TW2, TW9)

BRITISH, MODERN
Central
About Thyme (SW1)*
Acorn House (WC1)
Adam Street (WC2)
Alyn Williams (W1)
Andrew Edmunds (W1)
Arbutus (W1)*
Athenaeum (W1)*
Aurora (W1)
The Avenue (SW1)
Axis (WC2)
Balthazar (WC2)
Bank Westminster (SW1)
Bellamy's (W1)
Bob Bob Ricard (W1)
The Botanist (SW1)
Café Emm (W1)
Café Luc (W1)
Le Caprice (SW1)
Criterion (W1)
Daylesford Organic (SW1)
Dean Street Townhouse (W1)
Le Deuxième (WC2)
Dorchester Grill (W1)

The Duke of Wellington (W1)
The Easton (WC1)*
Ebury Wine Bar (SW1)
The Fifth Floor Restaurant (SW1)
Gordon's Wine Bar (WC2)
The Goring Hotel (SW1)
Grazing Goat (W1)
Hardy's Brasserie (W1)
Hix (W1)
Hush (W1)
Indigo (WC2)
Inn the Park (SW1)
The Ivy (WC2)
Kettners (W1)
Langan's Brasserie (W1)
Mews of Mayfair (W1)
The Norfolk Arms (WC1)
The Only Running Footman (W1)
The Orange (SW1)
Oscar (W1)
Ozer (W1)
The Pantechnicon (SW1)
Paramount (WC1)
Patterson's (W1)
Pollen Street Social (W1)*
The Portrait (WC2)
Quaglino's (SW1)
The Queens Arms (SW1)
Quo Vadis (W1)*
Refuel (W1)
Rhodes W1 Restaurant (W1)
RIBA Café (W1)
Roganic (W1)*
Roux At Parliament Square (SW1)
Roux At The Landau (W1)*
Rowley's (SW1)
Seven Park Place (SW1)*
Seven Stars (WC2)
1707 (W1)
Shampers (W1)
Smith Square (SW1)
Sotheby's Café (W1)*
Tate Britain (Rex Whistler) (SW1)
The Terrace in the Fields (WC2)
The Thomas Cubitt (SW1)
Tom's Terrace (WC2)
The Union Café (W1)
Vanilla (W1)
Villandry (W1)
The Vincent Rooms (SW1)
Vinoteca Seymour Place (W1)
Wild Honey (W1)
The Wolseley (W1)

West
The Abingdon (W8)
Admiral Codrington (SW3)
The Anglesea Arms (W6)*
The Anglesea Arms (SW7)
Babylon (W8)
Beach Blanket Babylon (W11)
Belvedere (W8)
Bluebird (SW3)
Brinkley's (SW10)
Brompton Bar & Grill (SW3)
The Builders Arms (SW3)
Butcher's Hook (SW6)
The Cadogan Arms (SW3)
The Carpenter's Arms (W6)
Clarke's (W8)*
The Cow (W2)
Daylesford Organic (W11)
The Dock Kitchen (W10)
Duke of Sussex (W4)
Ealing Park Tavern (W5)

Eighty-Six *(SW3)*
Electric Brasserie *(W11)*
The Enterprise *(SW3)*
First Floor *(W11)*
Formosa Dining Room *(W9)*
The Frontline Club *(W2)*
Harwood Arms *(SW6)**
The Havelock Tavern *(W14)**
Hedone *(W4)**
The Henry Root *(SW10)*
High Road Brasserie *(W4)*
Hole in the Wall *(W4)*
Jam Tree *(SW6,W14)*
Joe's Brasserie *(SW6)*
Julie's *(W11)*
Kensington Place *(W8)*
Kensington Square Kitchen *(W8)*
Kitchen W8 *(W8)**
The Ladbroke Arms *(W11)**
Launceston Place *(W8)*
The Ledbury *(W11)**
Lots Road *(SW10)*
The Mall Tavern *(W8)*
Manson *(SW6)**
Marco *(SW6)*
Notting Hill Brasserie *(W11)*
Paradise by Way of Kensal
  Green *(W10)**
The Phene *(SW3)*
The Phoenix *(SW3)*
Pissarro *(W4)*
Princess Victoria *(W12)**
Queen's Head *(W6)*
The Roebuck *(W4)*
Sam's Brasserie *(W4)*
The Sands End *(SW6)**
supperclub *(W10)*
Tom Aikens *(SW3)*
Tom's Deli *(W11)*
Tom's Kitchen *(SW3)*
Vingt-Quatre *(SW10)*
The Warrington *(W9)*
The Waterway *(W9)*
The Westbourne *(W2)*
White Horse *(SW6)*
Whits *(W8)*

North
The Albion *(N1)*
Bald Faced Stag *(N2)*
The Barnsbury *(N1)*
Bradley's *(NW3)*
Charles Lamb *(N1)*
The Clissold Arms *(N2)*
The Compass *(N1)*
The Drapers Arms *(N1)*
The Duke of Cambridge *(N1)*
The Engineer *(NW1)*
The Fellow *(N1)*
Frederick's *(N1)*
Freemasons Arms *(NW3)*
The Haven *(N20)*
The Horseshoe *(NW3)*
Hoxton Apprentice *(N1)*
The Junction Tavern *(NW5)*
Juniper Dining *(N5)**
Landmark (Winter Gdn) *(NW1)*
The Lansdowne *(NW1)*
Made In Camden *(NW1)*
Mango Room *(NW1)*
Market *(NW1)*
Mosaica *(N22)*
The North London Tavern *(NW6)*
The Northgate *(N1)**
Odette's *(NW1)**

The Old Bull & Bush *(NW3)*
Prince Albert *(NW1)*
Rising Sun *(NW7)**
Roots At N1 *(N1)**
The Rose & Crown *(N6)*
Rotunda Bar & Restaurant *(N1)*
St Pancras Grand *(NW1)*
Walnut *(NW6)*
The Wells *(NW3)*
The Wet Fish Cafe *(NW6)*

South
The Abbeville *(SW4)*
Alma *(SW18)*
Antelope *(SW17)**
Avalon *(SW12)*
The Bingham *(TW10)*
Blueprint Café *(SE1)*
The Bolingbroke *(SW11)*
The Brown Dog *(SW13)*
Cannizaro House *(SW19)*
Cantina Vinopolis *(SE1)*
Chapters *(SE3)*
Chez Bruce *(SW17)**
The Dartmouth Arms *(SE23)*
The Depot *(SW14)*
Earl Spencer *(SW18)*
The East Hill *(SW18)*
Emile's *(SW15)**
Entrée *(SW11)*
The Fentiman Arms *(SW8)*
The Fire Stables *(SW19)*
Florence *(SE24)*
Four O Nine *(SW9)*
Franklins *(SE22)*
Garrison *(SE1)*
The Glasshouse *(TW9)**
Harrison's *(SW12)*
Inside *(SE10)**
Lamberts *(SW12)**
The Lighthouse *(SW11)*
Magdalen *(SE1)**
Menier Chocolate Factory *(SE1)*
Mezzanine *(SE1)*
The Old Brewery *(SE10)*
Oxo Tower (Rest') *(SE1)*
The Palmerston *(SE22)**
Petersham Hotel *(TW10)*
Petersham Nurseries *(TW10)**
Plane Food *(TW6)*
Le Pont de la Tour *(SE1)*
The Prince Albert *(SW11)*
The Prince Of Wales *(SW15)*
Ransome's Dock *(SW11)*
Rivington Grill *(SE10)*
Rock & Rose *(TW9)*
RSJ *(SE1)*
Scoffers *(SW11)*
Simplicity *(SE16)*
Skylon *(SE1)*
Sonny's *(SW13)*
The Swan at the Globe *(SE1)*
The Table *(SE1)*
Tom Ilic *(SW8)**
The Tommyfield *(SE11)*
The Tree House *(SW13)*
Trinity *(SW4)**
Union Street Café *(SE1)*
Verta *(SW11)*
The Victoria *(SW14)*
Waterloo Bar & Kitchen *(SE1)*
The Wharf *(TW11)*

East
Ambassador *(EC1)*

Beach Blanket Babylon (E1)
Bevis Marks (EC3)
Bistro du Vin (EC1)
Bistrotheque (E2)
The Boundary (E2)
Bread Street Kitchen (EC4)
Café Below (EC2)
Caravan (EC1)*
The Chancery (EC4)*
Chiswell Street Dining Rms (EC1)
Coach & Horses (EC1)*
The Don (EC4)
The Empress of India (E9)
The Fox (EC2)
Gow's (EC2)
The Gun (E14)*
High Timber (EC4)
Hilliard (EC4)*
The Larder (EC1)
London Wall Bar & Kitchen (EC2)
Malmaison Brasserie (EC1)
The Mercer (EC2)
The Modern Pantry (EC1)
The Morgan Arms (E3)
The Narrow (E14)
North Road (EC1)*
Northbank (EC4)
1 Lombard Street (EC3)
The Parlour Bar (E14)
The Peasant (EC1)
Princess of Shoreditch (EC2)*
Prism (EC3)
The Restaurant at St Paul's (EC4)
Rhodes 24 (EC2)
Rivington Grill (EC2)
Rochelle Canteen (E2)*
Searcy's Brasserie (EC2)
Smithfield Bar & Grill (EC1)
Smiths (Ground Floor) (EC1)
Tompkins (E14)
Vertigo 42 (EC2)
Vinoteca (EC1)
Wapping Food (E1)
The Well (EC1)
The White Swan (EC4)*
Whitechapel Gallery (E1)

BRITISH, TRADITIONAL
Central
Boisdale (SW1)
The English Tea Rm (Browns) (W1)
Browns (Albemarle) (W1)
Canteen (W1)
Corrigan's Mayfair (W1)
Dinner (SW1)*
The Fountain (Fortnum's) (W1)
Fuzzy's Grub (SW1)
Great Queen Street (WC2)*
Green's (SW1)*
The Guinea Grill (W1)*
Hardy's Brasserie (W1)
Harrods (Georgian Rest') (SW1)
The National Dining Rooms (WC2)
Odin's (W1)
Porters English Restaurant (WC2)
Rib Room (SW1)
Rules (WC2)
St John Hotel (WC2)
Savoy Grill (WC2)
Scott's (W1)*
Shepherd's (SW1)
Simpsons-in-the-Strand (WC2)
Wiltons (SW1)
The Windmill (W1)*

West
Bumpkin (SW7,W11)
Ffiona's (W8)
Hereford Road (W2)*
Maggie Jones's (W8)

North
Bull & Last (NW5)*
Gilbert Scott (NW1)
Holly Bush (NW3)
Kentish Canteen (NW5)
The Marquess Tavern (N1)
S & M Café (N1)
St Johns (N19)*

South
The Anchor & Hope (SE1)*
Butlers Wharf Chop House (SE1)
Canteen (SE1)
Canton Arms (SW8)*
Fox & Grapes (SW19)
Roast (SE1)

East
Albion (E2)
Boisdale of Bishopsgate (EC2)
Canteen (E1, E14)
Cock Tavern (EC1)
The English Pig (EC1)*
The Farm Collective (EC1)*
The Fox and Anchor (EC1)
Fuzzy's Grub (EC4)
George & Vulture (EC3)
Green's (EC3)*
Hix Oyster & Chop House (EC1)*
Ye Olde Cheshire Cheese (EC4)
Paternoster Chop House (EC4)
E Pellicci (E2)
S & M Café (E1)
St John (EC1)*
St John Bread & Wine (E1)*
Simpson's Tavern (EC3)
Sweetings (EC4)

EAST & CENT. EUROPEAN
Central
Gay Hussar (W1)
The Wolseley (W1)

West
Tatra (W12)

North
Kipferl (N1)
Trojka (NW1)

FISH & SEAFOOD
Central
Back to Basics (W1)*
Belgo Centraal (WC2)
Bellamy's (W1)
Bentley's (W1)*
Cape Town Fish Market (W1)
Fishworks (W1)
Green's (W1)*
Livebait (WC2)
Loch Fyne (WC2)
Olivomare (SW1)*
One-O-One (SW1)*
The Pantechnicon (SW1)
Pescatori (W1)
Quaglino's (SW1)
Randall & Aubin (W1)
Rasa Samudra (W1)*

Rib Room (SW1)
Royal China Club (W1)*
Scott's (W1)*
J Sheekey (WC2)*
J Sheekey Oyster Bar (WC2)*
Wheeler's (SW1)
Wiltons (SW1)
Wright Brothers (W1)*
Zilli Fish (W1)

West
Bibendum Oyster Bar (SW3)
Big Easy (SW3)
Le Café Anglais (W2)
Chez Patrick (W8)
The Cow (W2)
Geales (W8)
Geales Chelsea Green (SW3)
Mandarin Kitchen (W2)*
Poissonnerie de l'Avenue (SW3)
The Summerhouse (W9)
Le Suquet (SW3)

North
Belgo Noord (NW1)
Bradley's (NW3)
Chez Liline (N4)*
Olympus Fish (N3)*
Sea Pebbles (HA5)
Toff's (N10)*

South
Applebee's Cafe (SE1)*
Bennett Oyster Bar (SW11)
Fish Place (SW11)*
fish! (SE1)
Gastro (SW4)
Livebait (SE1)
Lobster Pot (SE11)
Wright Brothers (SE1)*

East
Catch (EC2)
Chamberlain's (EC3)
Curve (E14)
Fish Central (EC1)*
Forman's (E3)*
Gow's (EC2)
The Grapes (E14)
Loch Fyne (EC3)
Redhook (EC1)
The Royal Exchange Grand
    Café (EC3)
Sweetings (EC4)

FRENCH
Central
Alain Ducasse (W1)
Antidote (W1)
L'Artiste Musclé (W1)
L'Atelier de Joel Robuchon (WC2)*
L'Autre Pied (W1)*
Bar Boulud (SW1)*
Bellamy's (W1)
Bistro du Vin (W1)
Boudin Blanc (W1)
Boulevard (WC2)
Brasserie Roux (SW1)
Brasserie St Jacques (SW1)
Café Bohème (W1)
Café des Amis (WC2)
Le Cercle (SW1)*
Chabrot Bistrot d'Amis (SW1)
The Chelsea Brasserie (SW1)
Chez Gérard (W1,WC2)

Le Cigalon (WC2)*
Clos Maggiore (WC2)*
Côte (W1,WC2)
Les Deux Salons (WC2)
The Ebury (SW1)
Elena's L'Etoile (W1)
Élysée (W1)
L'Escargot (W1)
The Gallery (W1)*
Galvin at Windows (W1)
Galvin Bistrot de Luxe (W1)*
Gauthier Soho (W1)*
Le Gavroche (W1)*
The Giaconda Dining Room (WC2)*
Gordon Ramsay at Claridge's (W1)
The Greenhouse (W1)
Hélène Darroze (W1)
Hibiscus (W1)
Incognico (WC2)
Koffmann's (SW1)*
Langan's Bistro (W1)
Marcus Wareing (SW1)*
maze (W1)
Mon Plaisir (WC2)
Odin's (W1)
L'Oranger (SW1)
Orrery (W1)
Pearl (WC1)
La Petite Maison (W1)*
Pétrus (SW1)
Pied à Terre (W1)*
La Poule au Pot (SW1)
Prix Fixe (W1)
Randall & Aubin (W1)
Le Relais de Venise
    L'Entrecôte (W1)*
The Ritz Restaurant (W1)
Roussillon (SW1)
Savoir Faire (WC1)
Sketch (Lecture Rm) (W1)
Sketch (Gallery) (W1)
The Square (W1)*
Terroirs (WC2)*
Verru (W1)*
Villandry (W1)
The Wallace (W1)

West
Albertine (W12)
Angelus (W2)*
L'Art du Fromage (SW10)
Belvedere (W8)
Bibendum (SW3)
Bistro K (SW7)
La Bouchée (SW7)
La Brasserie (SW3)
Le Café Anglais (W2)
The Capital Restaurant (SW3)
Cassis Bistro (SW3)
Charlotte's Bistro (W4)
Charlotte's Place (W5)
Cheyne Walk Brasserie (SW3)
Chez Patrick (W8)
Le Colombier (SW3)
Côte (SW6,W2,W4,W8)
Electric Brasserie (W11)
L'Etranger (SW7)
Galoupet (SW3)*
Gordon Ramsay (SW3)
Notting Hill Brasserie (W11)
The Pig's Ear (SW3)
Poissonnerie de l'Avenue (SW3)
Quantus (W4)
Racine (SW3)
Rôtisserie Bute Street (SW7)

La Sophia (W10)*
Le Suquet (SW3)
Tartine (SW3)
La Trompette (W4)*
Le Vacherin (W4)
Whits (W8)

North
L'Absinthe (NW1)
The Almeida (N1)
Les Associés (N8)
L'Aventure (NW8)*
Bistro Aix (N8)*
Blue Legume (N16)
Bradley's (NW3)
La Cage Imaginaire (NW3)
Charles Lamb (N1)
Cocotte (NW3)
Fig (N1)*
Le Mercury (N1)
Mill Lane Bistro (NW6)
Morgan M (N7)*
Oslo Court (NW8)*
La Petite Auberge (N1)
Le Sacré-Coeur (N1)
St Johns (N19)*
Somerstown Coffee House (NW1)
The Wells (NW3)

South
Bellevue Rendez-Vous (SW17)*
Brasserie James (SW12)
Brasserie Joël (SE1)*
Brasserie Toulouse-Lautrec (SE11)
Brula (TW1)*
La Buvette (TW9)
Le Cassoulet (CR2)
Le Chardon (SE22, SW4)
Chez Gérard (SE1)
Chez Lindsay (TW10)
Côte (SE1, SW19)
Gastro (SW4)
Gazette (SW11, SW12)
Lobster Pot (SE11)
Ma Cuisine (TW9)
Le P'tit Normand (SW18)
The Spread Eagle (SE10)
Upstairs Bar (SW2)*
Waterloo Brasserie (SE1)

East
Bistrot Bruno Loubet (EC1)*
Bleeding Heart (EC1)*
Le Bouchon Breton (E1)
Bar Battu (EC2)
Brasserie Blanc (EC2)
Brawn (E2)*
Café du Marché (EC1)*
Cellar Gascon (EC1)
Chez Gérard (EC2, EC3, EC4)
Club Gascon (EC1)*
Comptoir Gascon (EC1)*
Coq d'Argent (EC2)
Côte (EC4)
The Don (EC4)
Galvin La Chapelle (E1)*
Luc's Brasserie (EC3)
Lutyens (EC4)
1901 (EC2)
Plateau (E14)
Relais de Venise L'Entrecôte (EC2)*
Le Rendezvous du Café (EC1)
The Royal Exchange Grand
   Café (EC3)
Le Saint Julien (EC1)

Sauterelle (EC3)
Les Trois Garçons (E1)
28-50 (EC4)

FUSION
Central
Archipelago (W1)
Asia de Cuba (WC2)
Kopapa (WC2)
Providores (Tapa Room) (W1)*

West
E&O (W11)*
Eight Over Eight (SW3)*
L'Étranger (SW7)
Sushinho (SW3)

North
XO (NW3)

South
Champor-Champor (SE1)*
Tsunami (SW4)*
Village East (SE1)

East
Caravan (EC1)*
Viajante (E2)*

GAME
Central
Boisdale (SW1)
Rules (WC2)
Wiltons (SW1)

West
Harwood Arms (SW6)*

North
San Daniele del Friuli (N5)

East
Boisdale of Bishopsgate (EC2)

GERMAN
South
Stein's (TW10)

GREEK
Central
Élysée (W1)
Hellenic (W1)
Real Greek (W1, WC2)

West
Costa's Grill (W8)
Halepi (W2)
The Real Greek (W12)

North
Carob Tree (NW5)
Daphne (NW1)
Lemonia (NW1)
The Real Greek (N1)
Retsina (NW3)
Vrisaki (N22)

South
Real Greek (SE1)

East
Kolossi Grill (EC1)
Real Greek (E1)

HUNGARIAN
Central
Gay Hussar *(W1)*

South
Cafe Strudel *(SW14)*

INTERNATIONAL
Central
Balans *(W1)*
Boulevard *(WC2)*
Browns *(SW1,W1,WC2)*
Bumbles *(SW1)*
Café in the Crypt *(WC2)*
City Café *(SW1)*
Cork & Bottle *(WC2)*
The Forge *(WC2)*
Giraffe *(SW1,W1,WC1)*
Gordon's Wine Bar *(WC2)*
Govinda's *(W1)*
Grumbles *(SW1)*
Motcombs *(SW1)*
National Gallery Café *(WC2)*
Novikov *(W1)*
The Providores *(W1)*
Sarastro *(WC2)*
Savoy (River Rest') *(WC2)*
Stock Pot *(SW1)*
Terroirs *(WC2)**

West
Annie's *(W4)*
Balans West *(SW5,W12,W4,W8)*
Blakes *(SW7)*
Café Laville *(W2)*
Chelsea Bun Diner *(SW10)*
The Chelsea Kitchen *(SW10)*
Foxtrot Oscar *(SW3)*
Gallery Mess *(SW3)*
The Gate *(W6)**
Giraffe *(W11,W4,W8)*
The Kensington Wine Rooms *(W8)*
Lola & Simón *(W6)*
Medlar *(SW10)**
Michael Nadra *(W4)**
Mona Lisa *(SW10)*
The Scarsdale *(W8)*
Stock Pot *(SW3)*
202 *(W11)*
The Windsor Castle *(W8)*
Wine Gallery *(SW10)*

North
The Arches *(NW6)*
Banners *(N8)*
Browns *(N1)*
The Flask *(N6)*
Giraffe *(N1,NW3)*
The Haven *(N20)*
The Old Bull & Bush *(NW3)*
The Orange Tree *(N20)*
Petek *(N4)**
Spaniard's Inn *(NW3)*
Swan & Edgar *(NW1)*

South
Annie's *(SW13)*
Brinkley's Kitchen *(SW17)*
Browns *(SE1)*
Delfina *(SE1)*
Giraffe *(SE1,SW11)*
Green & Blue *(SE22)*
Hudsons *(SW15)*
Joanna's *(SE19)*
The Light House *(SW19)*

The Riverfront *(SE1)**
The Ship *(SW18)*
Tate Modern (Level 2) *(SE1)*
Tate Modern (Level 7) *(SE1)*
Telegraph *(SW15)*
The Trafalgar Tavern *(SE10)*
Vivat Bacchus *(SE1)*
The Wharf *(TW11)*
The Yellow House *(SE16)**

East
Browns *(E14, EC2)*
Dans le Noir *(EC1)*
$ *(EC1)*
Giraffe *(E1)*
LMNT *(E8)*
The Luxe *(E1)*
The Punch Tavern *(EC4)*
Les Trois Garçons *(E1)*
Vivat Bacchus *(EC4)*
The Wine Library *(EC3)*

IRISH
East
Lutyens *(EC4)*

ITALIAN
Central
Al Duca *(SW1)*
Alloro *(W1)*
Amaranto *(W1)*
Apsleys *(SW1)*
Babbo *(W1)*
Bar Trattoria Semplice *(W1)*
Il Baretto *(W1)**
Bertorelli *(W1)*
Bertorelli *(WC2)*
Bocca Di Lupo *(W1)**
La Bottega *(SW1)*
C London *(W1)*
Caffè Caldesi *(W1)*
Caffè Vergnano *(WC2)*
Caraffini *(SW1)*
Cecconi's *(W1)*
Ciao Bella *(WC1)*
Cocorino *(W1)**
Como Lario *(SW1)*
Il Convivio *(SW1)*
Da Mario *(WC2)*
da Polpo *(WC2)*
Dehesa *(W1)**
Delfino *(W1)**
Dolada *(W1)*
5 Pollen Street *(W1)*
Franco's *(SW1)*
La Genova *(W1)*
Gran Paradiso *(SW1)*
Incognico *(WC2)*
Jamie's Italian *(WC2)*
Latium *(W1)**
Little Italy *(W1)*
Locanda Locatelli *(W1)*
Mennula *(W1)**
Murano *(W1)*
Number Twelve *(WC1)*
Oliveto *(SW1)**
Olivo *(SW1)*
Olivomare *(SW1)**
Opera Tavern *(WC2)**
Orso *(WC2)*
Osteria Dell'Angolo *(SW1)*
Ottolenghi *(SW1)**
Pescatori *(W1)*
Piccolino *(W1)*
Polpetto *(W1)**

Polpo (W1)
La Porchetta Pizzeria (WC1)
Princi (W1)
Quirinale (SW1)*
Ristorante Semplice (W1)*
Rossopomodoro (WC2)
Sale e Pepe (SW1)
Salt Yard (W1)
Santini (SW1)
Sapori (WC2)
Sardo (W1)
Sartoria (W1)
Serafino (W1)
Signor Sassi (SW1)
Tempo (W1)
Theo Randall (W1)*
Tinello (SW1)*
Toto's (SW1)
2 Amici (SW1)
2 Veneti (W1)
Uno (SW1)
Vapiano (W1)
Vasco & Piero's Pavilion (W1)*
Il Vicolo (SW1)
Zafferano (SW1)
Zilli Fish (W1)
Zilli Green (W1)

West

L'Accento Italiano (W2)
Aglio e Olio (SW10)
The Ark (W8)
Assaggi (W2)*
La Bottega (SW7)
Buona Sera (SW3)
Canta Napoli (W4)
Carvosso's (W4)
Cavallino (SW3)
Cibo (W14)
Da Mario (SW7)
Daphne's (SW3)
La Delizia Limbara (SW3)
Dragoncello (W2)
El leven Park Walk (SW10)
Edera (W11)*
Essenza (W11)
Falconiere (SW7)
La Famiglia (SW10)
Frankie's Italian Bar & Grill (SW3, SW6)
Frantoio (SW10)
Ida (W10)
Ilia (SW3)
Jamie's Italian (W12)
Locanda Ottomezzo (W8)
Lucio (SW3)
Made in Italy (SW3)*
Manicomio (SW3)
Mediterraneo (W11)
Montpeliano (SW7)
Napulé (SW6)
Nottingdale (W11)*
Nuovi Sapori (SW6)*
The Oak (W2)*
Osteria Basilico (W11)
Osteria dell'Arancio (SW10)
Ottolenghi (W11, W8)*
Il Pagliaccio (SW6)
Pappa Ciccia (SW6)
Pellicano (SW3)
Il Portico (W8)
Portobello Ristorante (W11)
The Red Pepper (W9)*
Riccardo's (SW3)
The River Café (W6)*

Rocca Di Papa (SW7)
Rossopomodoro (SW10, W11)
San Lorenzo (SW3)
Santa Lucia (SW10)
Scalini (SW3)
Timo (W8)*
Venosi (SW3)
Vicino (SW6)
Ziani's (SW3)

North

Artigiano (NW3)
L'Artista (NW11)
Il Bacio (N16, N5)
La Brocca (NW6)
Canonbury Kitchen (N1)
Canta Napoli (N12)
Caponata (NW1)
La Collina (NW1)
Fifteen Dining Room (N1)
Fifteen Trattoria (N1)
500 (N19)*
Fratelli la Bufala (NW3)
Marine Ices (NW3)
Ottolenghi (N1)*
Pizzeria Oregano (N1)
Pizzeria Pappagone (N4)
La Porchetta Pizzeria (N1, N4, NW1)
Rugoletta (N2)
The Salt House (NW8)
The Salusbury (NW6)
San Daniele del Friuli (N5)
Sardo Canale (NW1)
Sarracino (NW6)*
Trullo (N1)*
Villa Bianca (NW3)
York & Albany (NW1)

South

A Cena (TW1)*
Al Forno (SW15, SW19)
Antipasto & Pasta (SW11)
La Barca (SE1)
Buona Sera (SW11)
Cantina del Ponte (SE1)
Cantinetta (SW15)
La Delizia (SW18)
Donna Margherita (SW11)*
Enoteca Turi (SW15)*
Frizzante Cafe (SE16)
Isola del Sole (SW15)
La Lanterna (SE1)
Numero Uno (SW11)
Osteria Antica Bologna (SW11)
Piccolino (SW19)
Pizza Metro (SW11)
Le Querce (SE23, SE3)*
Riva (SW13)*
San Lorenzo Fuoriporta (SW19)
Scarpetta (TW11)
Tentazioni (SE1)
Valentina (SW14, SW15)
Zucca (SE1)*

East

Al Volo (E1)*
Alba (EC1)
Amerigo Vespucci (E14)
Amico Bio (EC1)
L'Anima (EC2)
Bertorelli (EC3)
Il Bordello (E1)*
Caravaggio (EC3)
Fabrizio (EC1)*
La Figa (E14)

Frizzante at City Farm (E2)
Giant Robot (EC1)
Jamie's Italian (E14)
Manicomio (EC2)
Osteria Appennino (EC2)*
E Pellicci (E2)
Piccolino (EC2)
La Porchetta Pizzeria (EC1)
Quadrato (E14)
Refettorio (EC4)
Santore (EC1)
Taberna Etrusca (EC4)
Terranostra (EC4)

MEDITERRANEAN
Central
About Thyme (SW1)*
Aurelia (W1)
Bistro 1 (W1,WC2)
Hummus Bros (W1,WC1)*
Massimo (SW1)
Nopi (W1)*
The Norfolk Arms (WC1)
Quince (W1)
Riding House Café (W1)*
Rocket (W1)
Truc Vert (W1)

West
The Atlas (SW6)*
Cochonnet (W9)
Cumberland Arms (W14)
Del'Aziz (SW6,W12)
Locanda Ottomezzo (W8)
Made in Italy (SW3)*
Mediterraneo (W11)
Raoul's Café (W9)
Raoul's Café & Deli (W11,W6)
La Sophia (W10)*
The Swan (W4)*
Tom's Deli (W11)
Troubadour (SW5)

North
Camden Brasserie (NW1)
Del'Aziz (NW3)
Homa (N16)
The Little Bay (NW6)
Mem & Laz (N1)
Petek (N4)*
Queen's Head & Artichoke (NW1)
Stringray Café (N5, NW5)

South
Cantina del Ponte (SE1)
Cantina Vinopolis (SE1)
Del'Aziz (SE1)
Fish in a Tie (SW11)
The Fox & Hounds (SW11)*
The Little Bay (SW11)
Oxo Tower (Brass') (SE1)
Putney Station (SW15)
The Wharf (TW11)

East
Ambassador (EC1)
Bonds (EC2)
The Eagle (EC1)
Eyre Brothers (EC2)
Hummus Bros (EC2)*
The Little Bay (EC1)
Portal (EC1)*
Rocket (EC2)
Stringray Globe Café (E2)
Vinoteca (EC1)

ORGANIC
Central
Acorn House (WC1)
Daylesford Organic (SW1)

West
Daylesford Organic (W11)

North
The Duke of Cambridge (N1)
Holly Bush (NW3)
Walnut (NW6)

East
Saf (EC2)*
Smiths (Dining Rm) (EC1)

POLISH
West
Gessler at Daquise (SW7)
Polish Club (SW7)
Patio (W12)

South
Baltic (SE1)

PORTUGUESE
West
Lisboa Pâtisserie (W10)*

East
Corner Room (E2)
The Gun (E14)*
Portal (EC1)*

RUSSIAN
Central
Samarqand (W1)

North
Trojka (NW1)

SCANDINAVIAN
Central
Nordic Bakery (W1)
Scandinavian Kitchen (W1)
Texture (W1)*
Verru (W1)*

West
Madsen (SW7)

East
North Road (EC1)*

SCOTTISH
Central
Albannach (WC2)
Boisdale (SW1)

East
Boisdale of Bishopsgate (EC2)
Boisdale of Canary Wharf (E14)

SPANISH
Central
aqua nueva (W1)
Barrafina (W1)*
Barrica (W1)
Café España (W1)
Cigala (WC1)
Dehesa (W1)*
Fino (W1)*

Goya (SW1)
Ibérica (W1)
Mar I Terra (W1)
Navarro's (W1)
Opera Tavern (WC2)*
El Pirata (W1)
Salt Yard (W1)
Tapas Brindisa Soho (W1)*

West
Cambio de Tercio (SW5)*
Capote Y Toros (SW5)
Casa Brindisa (SW7)
Duke of Sussex (W4)
Galicia (W10)
Lola Rojo (SW6)*
El Pirata de Tapas (W2)
Tendido Cero (SW5)
Tendido Cuatro (SW6)*

North
La Bota (N8)
Café del Parc (N19)*
Camino (N1)
Don Pepe (NW8)
La Giralda (HA5)
El Parador (NW1)*

South
Angels & Gypsies (SE5)*
don Fernando's (TW9)
José (SE1)
Lola Rojo (SW11)*
La Mancha (SW15)
Mar I Terra (SE1)
Meson don Felipe (SE1)
Pizarro (SE1)
Rebato's (SW8)*
El Rincón Latino (SW4)
Tapas Brindisa (SE1)*

East
Eyre Brothers (EC2)
Ibérica (E14)
Morito (EC1)*
Moro (EC1)*
Pinchito (EC1)

STEAKS & GRILLS
Central
Black & Blue (W1)
Bodean's (W1)
The Bountiful Cow (WC1)
Boyd's Brasserie (WC2)
Chez Gérard (W1,WC2)
Christopher's (WC2)
Cut (W1)
Gaucho (W1,WC2)
Goodman (W1)*
The Guinea Grill (W1)*
Hawksmoor (WC2)*
JW Steakhouse (W1)
maze Grill (W1)
The Palm (SW1)
Rowley's (SW1)
Sophie's Steakhouse (WC2)
34 Grosvenor Square (W1)
Wolfe's (WC2)

West
Black & Blue (SW3, SW7,W8)
Bodean's (SW6)
The Cabin (W4)
Gaucho (SW3)
Haché (SW10)

Kings Road Steakhouse (SW3)
The Meat & Wine Co (W12)
PJ's Bar and Grill (SW3)
Popeseye (W14)*
Sophie's Steakhouse (SW10)

North
Camden Brasserie (NW1)
Garufa (N5)
Gaucho (NW3)
Haché (NW1)
Rôtisserie (HA5, N20, NW6, NW8)

South
Archduke Wine Bar (SE1)
Black & Blue (SE1)
Bodean's (SW4)
Buenos Aires (SE3)
Butcher & Grill (SW11, SW19)
Cattle Grid (SW11, SW12)
Chez Gérard (SE1)
Constancia (SE1)*
Gaucho (SE1, SE10,TW10)
Kew Grill (TW9)
Popeseye (SW15)*

East
A La Cruz (EC1)
Buen Ayre (E8)*
Chez Gérard (EC2, EC3, EC4)
Gaucho (E14, EC1, EC2, EC3)
Goodman City (EC2)*
Hawksmoor (E1, EC2)*
MPW Steakhouse & Grill (E1)
Redhook (EC1)
Simpson's Tavern (EC3)
Smithfield Bar & Grill (EC1)
Smiths (Top Floor) (EC1)
Smiths (Dining Rm) (EC1)
Smiths (Ground Floor) (EC1)

SWISS
Central
St Moritz (W1)

VEGETARIAN
Central
Chop'd (W1)
Food for Thought (WC2)*
Govinda's (WC2)
Hummus Bros (W1,WC1)
Malabar Junction (WC1)
Masala Zone (W1)
Mildreds (W1)*
Ragam (W1)*
Rasa (W1)*
Rasa Maricham (WC1)*
Roussillon (SW1)
Sagar (W1)*
tibits (W1)
Woodlands (SW1,W1)
Zilli Green (W1)

West
The Gate (W6)*
Masala Zone (SW5, SW6,W2)
Saf (W8)*
Sagar (W6)*

North
Chop'd (NW1)
Chutneys (NW1)
Diwana Bhel-Poori House (NW1)
Geeta (NW6)

Kovalam *(NW6)**
Manna *(NW3)*
Masala Zone *(N1)*
Rani *(N3)**
Rasa *(N16)**
Rasa Travancore *(N16)**
Sakonis *(HA0)*
Vijay *(NW6)**
Woodlands *(NW3)*

South
Ganapati *(SE15)**
Le Pont de la Tour *(SE1)*
Sree Krishna *(SW17)**

East
Amico Bio *(EC1)*
Carnevale *(EC1)*
Chop'd *(E1, E14, EC3)*
Hummus Bros *(EC2)**
Saf *(EC2)**
Vanilla Black *(EC4)**

AFTERNOON TEA
Central
Brasserie Roux *(SW1)*
The English Tea Rm (Browns) *(W1)*
The Fountain (Fortnum's) *(W1)*
La Fromagerie Café *(W1)**
Ladurée *(SW1,W1,WC2)*
Napket *(W1)*
Oscar *(W1)*
Ritz (Palm Court) *(W1)*
The Sketch (Parlour) *(W1)*
Villandry *(W1)*
William Curley *(SW1)**
The Wolseley *(W1)*
Yauatcha *(W1)**

West
Napket *(SW3)*

South
San Lorenzo Fuoriporta *(SW19)*

East
Napket *(EC3)*

BURGERS, ETC
Central
Automat *(W1)*
Black & Blue *(W1)*
Byron *(SW1,W1,WC2)*
Diner *(W1)*
Eagle Bar Diner *(W1)*
Ed's Easy Diner *(W1)*
Guerilla Burgers *(W1)*
Hard Rock Café *(W1)*
Joe Allen *(WC2)*
Wolfe's *(WC2)*

West
Big Easy *(SW3)*
Black & Blue *(SW3, SW7,W8)*
Byron *(SW3, SW5, SW7,W12,W8)*
Haché *(SW10)*
Lucky Seven *(W2)*
Sticky Fingers *(W8)*
Troubadour *(SW5)*

North
Byron *(N1)*
Diner *(N1, NW1, NW10)*
Fine Burger Company *(N1, NW1,*

NW3)
Haché *(NW1)*
Harry Morgan's *(NW8)**

South
Black & Blue *(SE1)*
Byron *(SW15)*

East
Byron *(E14, EC2)*
The Diner *(EC2)*
$ *(EC1)*
Smithfield Bar & Grill *(EC1)*
Smiths (Dining Rm) *(EC1)*

CRÊPES
South
Chez Lindsay *(TW10)*

FISH & CHIPS
Central
Fryer's Delight *(WC1)*
Golden Hind *(W1)*
North Sea Fish *(WC1)*
Rock & Sole Plaice *(WC2)*
Seafresh *(SW1)*

West
Geales *(W8)*
Kerbisher & Malt *(W6)**

North
Nautilus *(NW6)**
The Sea Shell *(NW1)*
Skipjacks *(HA3)**
Toff's *(N10)**
Two Brothers *(N3)**

South
Brady's *(SW18)*
Fish Club *(SW11, SW4)**
Masters Super Fish *(SE1)**
Olley's *(SE24)*
The Sea Cow *(SE22)*

East
Ark Fish *(E18)**
Faulkner's *(E8)**

ICE CREAM
Central
Gelupo *(W1)**

North
Marine Ices *(NW3)*

PIZZA
Central
Il Baretto *(W1)**
Delfino *(W1)**
Fire & Stone *(WC2)*
Oliveto *(SW1)**
Piccolino *(W1)*
Pizzeria Malletti *(W1)**
La Porchetta Pizzeria *(WC1)*
Rocket *(W1)*
Sapori *(WC2)*

West
Basilico *(SW6)**
Buona Sera *(SW3)*
Cochonnet *(W9)*
Da Mario *(SW7)*
La Delizia Limbara *(SW3)*

Fire & Stone (W12)
Firezza (SW10,W11,W4)*
Franco Manca (W4)*
Frankie's Italian Bar & Grill (SW3)
Made in Italy (SW3)*
The Oak (W2)*
Osteria Basilico (W11)
Otto Pizza (W2)*
Pizza East Portobello (W10)
(Ciro's) Pizza Pomodoro (SW3)
The Red Pepper (W9)*
Santa Maria (W5)*

North
Il Bacio (N16, N5)
Basilico (N1, N8, NW3)*
La Brocca (NW6)
Firezza (N1)*
Furnace (N1)
Marine Ices (NW3)
Pizzeria Oregano (N1)
La Porchetta Pizzeria (N1, N4, NW1)

South
Al Forno (SW15, SW19)
Basilico (SW11, SW14)*
Buona Sera (SW11)
Donna Margherita (SW11)*
Eco (SW4)
Firezza (SW11, SW18)*
Franco Manca (SW9)*
Gourmet Pizza Company (SE1)
The Gowlett (SE15)*
La Lanterna (SE1)
Piccolino (SW19)
Pizza Metro (SW11)
Rocca Di Papa (SE21)
Zero Degrees (SE3)

East
Il Bordello (E1)*
Fire & Stone (E1)
Gourmet Pizza Company (E14)
Piccolino (EC2)
Pizza East (E1)
Pizzeria Malletti (EC1)*
La Porchetta Pizzeria (EC1)
Rocket (E14)
Rocket (EC2)

SANDWICHES, CAKES, ETC
Central
Abokado (W1)
Aubaine (W1)
Baker & Spice (SW1)
Bar Italia (W1)
Benugo (W1)
The Courtauld Gallery Café (WC2)
Fernandez & Wells (W1)*
Flat White (W1)*
La Fromagerie Café (W1)*
Fuzzy's Grub (SW1)
Kaffeine (W1)*
Konditor & Cook (W1,WC1)*
Ladurée (SW1,W1)
Leon (W1,WC2)
Maison Bertaux (W1)*
Monmouth Coffee Company (WC2)*
Mount Street Deli (W1)
Mrs Marengos (W1)*
Napket (W1)
Natural Kitchen (W1)
Paul (W1,WC2)
Pod (WC1)
Scandinavian Kitchen (W1)

The Sketch (Parlour) (W1)

West
Aubaine (SW3, W8)
Baker & Spice (SW3, W9)
Benugo (SW7, W12)
Bluebird Café (SW3)
Chiswick House Café (W4)
Fulham Wine Rooms (SW6)
Gail's Bakery (W4)
Gail's Bread (W11)
Lisboa Pâtisserie (W10)*
Napket (SW3)
Tom's Deli (W11)
Troubadour (SW5)

North
Benugo (NW1)
Chamomile (NW3)
Euphorium Bakery (N1)
Gail's Bread (NW3, NW8)
Ginger & White (NW3)
Kenwood (Brew House) (NW3)

South
Benugo (SE1)
Caffè Vergnano (SE1)
Gail's Bread (SW11)
Konditor & Cook (SE1)*
Leon (SE1)
Monmouth Coffee Company (SE1)*
Orange Pekoe (SW13)
Pantry (SW18)
Pod (SE1)
Spianata & Co (SE1)*
William Curley (TW9)*

East
Abokado (EC1, EC4)
Benugo (EC1)
Brick Lane Beigel Bake (E1)*
Caffè Vergnano (EC4)
Dose (EC1)*
Fuzzy's Grub (EC4)
Gail's Bakery (EC1)
Konditor & Cook (EC3)*
Leon (E1, E14, EC4)
Natural Kitchen (EC4)
Nusa Kitchen (EC1, EC2)*
Pod (EC1, EC2, EC3, EC4)
Spianata & Co (E1, EC1, EC2, EC3, EC4)*

SALADS
Central
Chop'd (W1)
Kaffeine (W1)*
Natural Kitchen (W1)

West
Beirut Express (SW7, W2)*

North
Chop'd (NW1)

East
Chop'd (E1, E14, EC3)
Natural Kitchen (EC4)

ARGENTINIAN
Central
Gaucho (W1, WC2)

West
Casa Malevo (W2)

Gaucho *(SW3)*
Lola & Simón *(W6)*
Quantus *(W4)*

North
Garufa *(N5)*
Gaucho *(NW3)*

South
Buenos Aires Cafe *(SE10, SE3)*
Constancia *(SE1)*
Gaucho *(SE1,TW10)*
Santa Maria del Sur *(SW8)**

East
Buen Ayre *(E8)**
Gaucho *(E14, EC2, EC3)*

BRAZILIAN
West
Rodizio Rico *(SW6,W2)*
Sushinho *(SW3)*

North
Rodizio Rico *(N1)*

East
Sushisamba *(EC2)*

CUBAN
Central
Floridita *(W1)*

South
Angels & Gypsies *(SE5)**

MEXICAN/TEXMEX
Central
Benito's Hat *(W1,WC2)*
Café Pacifico *(WC2)*
Cantina Laredo *(WC2)*
Chilango *(WC2)**
Chipotle *(WC2)*
Lupita *(WC2)*
Tortilla *(W1)*
Wahaca *(W1,WC2)*

West
Crazy Homies *(W2)*
Taqueria *(W11)*
Tortilla *(W6)*
Wahaca *(W12)*

North
Chilango *(N1)**
Mestizo *(NW1)**
Tortilla *(N1)*

South
Tortilla *(SE1)*

East
Barbecoa *(EC4)*
Chilango *(EC4)**
Tortilla *(E14, EC3)*
Wahaca *(E14)*

PERUVIAN
East
Sushisamba *(EC2)*

SOUTH AMERICAN
West
Quantus *(W4)*

North
Sabor *(N1)*

South
El Vergel *(SE1)**

East
A La Cruz *(EC1)*

AFRO-CARIBBEAN
Central
The Terrace in the Fields *(WC2)*

North
Mango Room *(NW1)*

MOROCCAN
West
Adams Café *(W12)*
Pasha *(SW7)*

South
Doukan *(SW18)*

NORTH AFRICAN
Central
Momo *(W1)*

West
Azou *(W6)*
Del'Aziz *(SW6)*

East
Kenza *(EC2)*

SOUTH AFRICAN
North
Shaka Zulu *(NW1)*

TUNISIAN
West
Adams Café *(W12)*

EGYPTIAN
North
Ali Baba *(NW1)*

ISRAELI
Central
Gaby's *(WC2)*

North
Solly's *(NW11)*

KOSHER
Central
Reubens *(W1)*

North
Kaifeng *(NW4)**
Solly's *(NW11)*

East
Bevis Marks *(EC3)*
Brick Lane Beigel Bake *(E1)**

LEBANESE
Central
Al Hamra (W1)
Al Sultan (W1)*
Beiteddine (SW1)
Comptoir Libanais (W1)
Fairuz (W1)
Fakhreldine (W1)
Ishbilia (SW1)*
Levant (W1)
Maroush (W1)*
Noura (SW1,W1)
Ranoush (SW1)*
Yalla Yalla (W1)

West
Al-Waha (W2)*
Beirut Express (SW7,W2)*
Chez Marcelle (W14)*
Comptoir Libanais (W12)
Fresco (W2)
Maroush (SW3)*
Maroush (W2)*
Pasha (SW7)
Randa (W8)
Ranoush (SW3,W2,W8)*

South
Palmyra (TW9)

East
Kenza (EC2)

MIDDLE EASTERN
Central
Patogh (W1)*

North
Solly's (NW11)

East
Morito (EC1)*

PERSIAN
West
Alounak (W14,W2)
Chella (W4)
Faanoos (W4)
Kateh (W9)
Mohsen (W14)*
Sufi (W12)

South
Faanoos (SW14)

SYRIAN
West
Abu Zaad (W12)

TURKISH
Central
Cyprus Mangal (SW1)*
Ishtar (W1)
Kazan (SW1)*
Quince (W1)
Sofra (W1,WC2)
Tas (WC1)

West
Best Mangal (SW6,W14)

North
Beyoglu (NW3)
Gallipoli (N1)

Gem (N1)*
Izgara (N3)
Mangal II (N16)
19 Numara Bos Cirrik (N16)
Petek (N4)*
Sofra (NW8)

South
Tas (SE1)
Tas Pide (SE1)

East
Haz (E1, EC2, EC3)
Hazev (E14)
Mangal I (E8)*
Tas (EC1)

AFGHANI
North
Afghan Kitchen (N1)*

BURMESE
West
Mandalay (W2)

CHINESE
Central
Ba Shan (W1)*
Baozi Inn (WC2)*
Bar Shu (W1)*
Cha Cha Moon (W1)
Chilli Cool (WC1)*
China Tang (W1)
Chuen Cheng Ku (W1)
Empress of Sichuan (WC2)
The Four Seasons (W1)*
Golden Dragon (W1)
The Grand Imperial (SW1)
Hakkasan (W1)*
Haozhan (W1)
Harbour City (W1)*
Hunan (SW1)*
Imperial China (WC2)
Jenny Lo's Tea House (SW1)
Joy King Lau (WC2)
Kai Mayfair (W1)
Ken Lo's Memories (SW1)*
Made in China (SW1)
Mekong (SW1)
Mr Chow (SW1)
Mr Kong (WC2)
New Mayflower (W1)*
New World (W1)
Plum Valley (W1)
Princess Garden (W1)*
Royal China (W1)*
Royal China Club (W1)*
Shanghai Blues (WC1)*
Wong Kei (W1)
Yauatcha (W1)*
Yming (W1)*

West
Choys (SW3)
Fortune Cookie (W2)*
The Four Seasons (W2)*
Good Earth (SW3)
Ken Lo's Memories of China (W8)*
Magic Wok (W2)
Mandarin Kitchen (W2)*
Maxim (W13)
Min Jiang (W8)*
Mr Wing (SW5)
New Culture Revolution (SW3,W11)

North China (W3)*
Pearl Liang (W2)*
Royal China (SW6,W2)*
Seventeen (W11)*
Stick & Bowl (W8)
Taiwan Village (SW6)*

North
Alisan (HA9)*
Goldfish (NW3)*
Good Earth (NW7)
Green Cottage (NW3)*
Gung-Ho (NW6)
Kaifeng (NW4)*
New Culture Revolution (N1)
Phoenix Palace (NW1)*
Sakonis (HA0)
Singapore Garden (NW6)*
The Water Margin (NW11)

South
Bayee Village (SW19)
Dalchini (SW19)
Dragon Castle (SE17)*
Four Regions (TW9)
O'Zon (TW1)
Peninsular (SE10)*
Royal China (SW15)

East
Chinese Cricket Club (EC4)
Goldfish City (EC2)*
Gourmet San (E2)*
Imperial City (EC3)
Lotus Chinese Floating
  Restaurant (E14)
My Old Place (E1)*
Royal China (E14)*
Shanghai (E8)
Yi-Ban (E16)

CHINESE, DIM SUM
Central
Chuen Cheng Ku (W1)
dim T (W1)
Golden Dragon (W1)
Hakkasan (W1)*
Harbour City (W1)*
Imperial China (WC2)
Joy King Lau (WC2)
Leong's Legends (W1)
New World (W1)
ping pong (W1)
Princess Garden (W1)*
Royal China (W1)*
Royal China Club (W1)*
Shanghai Blues (WC1)*
Yauatcha (W1)*

West
Leong's Legends (W2)
Min Jiang (W8)*
Pearl Liang (W2)*
ping pong (W2)
Royal China (SW6,W2)*

North
Alisan (HA9)*
dim T (N6, NW3)
Phoenix Palace (NW1)*
ping pong (NW3)

South
dim T (SE1)

Dragon Castle (SE17)*
Peninsular (SE10)*
ping pong (SE1)
Royal China (SW15)

East
Lotus Chinese Floating
  Restaurant (E14)
ping pong (E1, EC2, EC4)
Royal China (E14)*
Shanghai (E8)
Yi-Ban (E16)

GEORGIAN
East
Little Georgia Café (E2)

INDIAN
Central
Amaya (SW1)*
Benares (W1)*
Chor Bizarre (W1)
The Cinnamon Club (SW1)*
Dishoom (WC2)
Gaylord (W1)
Gopal's of Soho (W1)
Imli (W1)
Indali Lounge (W1)
India Club (WC2)
Malabar Junction (WC1)
Masala Zone (W1,WC2)
Mela (WC2)
Mint Leaf (SW1)
Mooli's (W1)*
Moti Mahal (WC2)*
La Porte des Indes (W1)
Ragam (W1)*
Red Fort (W1)*
Sagar (W1,WC2)*
Salaam Namaste (WC1)*
Salloos (SW1)*
Tamarind (W1)*
Trishna (W1)*
Veeraswamy (W1)
Woodlands (SW1,W1)
Zayna (W1)*

West
Anarkali (W6)
Bombay Bicycle Club (W11)
Bombay Brasserie (SW7)
Bombay Palace (W2)*
Brilliant (UB2)*
Chutney Mary (SW10)*
Five Hot Chillies (HA0)*
Gifto's (UB1)*
The Greedy Buddha (SW6)
Haandi (SW3)*
Indian Zing (W6)*
kare kare (SW5)
Karma (W14)*
Khan's (W2)
Khan's of Kensington (SW7)
Madhu's (UB1)*
Malabar (W8)*
Masala Zone (SW5, SW6, W2)
Memories of India (SW7)
Mirch Masala (UB1,W14)*
Monty's (SW6,W13,W5)
Noor Jahan (SW5,W2)*
The Painted Heron (SW10)*
Rasoi (SW3)
Sagar (W6)*
Star of India (SW5)*
Thali (SW5)*

Zaika *(W8)**

North
Anglo Asian Tandoori *(N16)**
Chutneys *(NW1)*
Diwana Bhel-Poori House *(NW1)*
Eriki *(NW3)**
Geeta *(NW6)*
Great Nepalese *(NW1)*
Indian Rasoi *(N2)**
Jai Krishna *(N4)*
Kovalam *(NW6)**
Masala Zone *(N1, NW1)*
Rani *(N3)**
Roots At N1 *(N1)**
Sakonis *(HA0)*
Vijay *(NW6)**
Woodlands *(NW3)*
Zaffrani *(N1)*

South
Babur *(SE23)**
Bangalore Express *(SE1)*
Bengal Clipper *(SE1)*
Bombay Bicycle Club *(SW12)*
Chutney *(SW18)**
Cochin Brasserie *(SW15)**
Dalchini *(SW19)*
Everest Inn *(SE3)**
Ganapati *(SE15)**
Gandhi's *(SE11)*
Hot Stuff *(SW8)**
Indian Moment *(SW11)*
Indian Ocean *(SW17)**
Indian Zilla *(SW13)**
Kennington Tandoori *(SE11)**
Lahore Karahi *(SW17)**
Ma Goa *(SW15)**
Mango & Silk *(SW14)*
Mango Tree *(SE1)**
Mirch Masala *(SW16, SW17)**
Mogul *(SE10)*
Nazmins *(SW18)*
Origin Asia *(TW9)**
Simply Indian *(SE1)*
Sree Krishna *(SW17)**
Tandoori Nights *(SE22)*
Tangawizi *(TW1)*

East
Anokha Restaurant *(EC3, EC4)**
Bangalore Express *(EC3)*
Café Spice Namaste *(E1)**
Cinnamon Kitchen *(EC2)**
Clifton *(E1)*
Dockmaster's House *(E14)*
Lahore Kebab House *(E1)**
Memsaheb on Thames *(E14)*
Mint Leaf *(EC2)*
Mirch Masala *(E1)**
Needoo *(E1)**
New Tayyabs *(E1)**
Rasa Mudra *(E11)**
Sweet & Spicy *(E1)**

INDIAN, SOUTHERN
Central
India Club *(WC2)*
Malabar Junction *(WC1)*
Quilon *(SW1)**
Ragam *(W1)**
Rasa *(W1)**
Rasa Maricham *(WC1)**
Sagar *(W1)**
Woodlands *(SW1, W1)*

West
Sagar *(W6)**
Shilpa *(W6)**

North
Chutneys *(NW1)*
Geeta *(NW6)*
Kovalam *(NW6)**
Rani *(N3)**
Rasa *(N16)**
Rasa Travancore *(N16)**
Vijay *(NW6)**
Woodlands *(NW3)*

South
Cochin Brasserie *(SW15)**
Cocum *(SW20)*
Ganapati *(SE15)**
Sree Krishna *(SW17)**

East
Rasa Mudra *(E11)**

INDONESIAN
Central
Melati *(W1)*

West
Kiasu *(W2)*

JAPANESE
Central
Abeno *(WC1, WC2)*
Abokado *(W1, WC2)*
aqua kyoto *(W1)*
Atari-Ya *(W1)**
Benihana *(W1)*
Bincho Yakitori *(W1)*
Chisou *(W1)**
Defune *(W1)**
Dinings *(W1)**
Edokko *(WC1)**
Hazuki *(WC2)**
Ikeda *(W1)**
Inamo *(W1)*
Kiku *(W1)**
Koya *(W1)*
Kulu Kulu *(W1, WC2)*
Kyashii *(WC2)*
Matsuri *(SW1)**
Misato *(W1)*
Mitsukoshi *(SW1)**
Miyama *(W1)**
Nizuni *(W1)**
Nobu *(W1)**
Nobu *(W1)*
Roka *(W1)**
Sake No Hana *(SW1)*
Sakura *(W1)**
Satsuma *(W1)*
Soho Japan *(W1)*
Sumosan *(W1)*
Taro *(W1)*
Ten Ten Tei *(W1)*
Toku *(SW1)*
Tokyo Diner *(WC2)*
Tsunami *(W1)**
Umu *(W1)**
Wagamama *(SW1, W1, WC1, WC2)*
Watatsumi *(WC2)*
Yoshino *(W1)**

West
Atari-Ya *(W5)**

Benihana (SW3)
Inaho (W2)*
Itsu (SW3, W11)
Kiraku (W5)
Kulu Kulu (SW7)
Nozomi (SW3)
Okawari (W5)
Sushinho (SW3)
Tosa (W6)
Wagamama (W8)
Yashin (W8)*
Zuma (SW7)*

North
Asakusa (NW1)*
Atari-Ya (NW4, NW6)*
Bento Cafe (NW1)*
Café Japan (NW11)*
Dotori (N4)*
Jin Kichi (NW3)*
Sushi of Shiori (NW1)*
Sushi-Say (NW2)*
Wagamama (N1, NW1)
Yuzu (NW6)*

South
Cho-San (SW15)*
Fujiyama (SW9)
Matsuba (TW9)*
Slurp (SW16, SW19)
Tsunami (SW4)*
Tsuru (SE1)
Wagamama (SE1, SW15, SW19)

East
Abokado (EC1, EC4)
City Miyama (EC4)*
Itsu (E14)
K10 (EC2)
Kurumaya (EC4)*
Mugen (EC4)
Pham Sushi (EC1)*
Roka (E14)*
Saki (EC1)*
Soseki (EC3)*
Sushisamba (EC2)
Tajima Tei (EC1)*
Tsuru (EC2, EC4)
Wagamama (E14, EC2, EC3, EC4)

KAZAKHSTANI
Central
Samarqand (W1)

KOREAN
Central
Asadal (WC1)
Kimchee (WC1)
Koba (W1)

North
Dotori (N4)*

South
Cah-Chi (SW18, SW20)

MALAYSIAN
Central
C&R Cafe (W1)
Jom Makan (SW1)
Melati (W1)
Spice Market (W1)

West
Awana (SW3)
Jom Makan (W12)
Kiasu (W2)
Satay House (W2)

North
Singapore Garden (NW6)*

South
Champor-Champor (SE1)*

East
54 Farringdon Road (EC1)
Sedap (EC1)

PAKISTANI
Central
Salloos (SW1)*

West
Mirch Masala (UB1, W14)*

South
Lahore Karahi (SW17)*
Lahore Kebab House (SW16)*
Mirch Masala (SW16, SW17)*

East
Lahore Kebab House (E1)*
Mirch Masala (E1)*
Needoo (E1)*
New Tayyabs (E1)*

PAN-ASIAN
Central
Banana Tree Canteen (W1)
Colony (W1)
dim T (SW1, W1)
Haozhan (W1)
Hare & Tortoise (WC1)
Inamo (SW1)
Tamarai (WC2)

West
Banana Tree Canteen (W2, W9)
E&O (W11)*
Eight Over Eight (SW3)*
Hare & Tortoise (W14, W5)
Mao Tai (SW6)
Uli (W11)

North
The Banana Tree Canteen (NW6)
dim T (N6, NW3)
Gilgamesh (NW1)
XO (NW3)

South
The Banana Tree Canteen (SW11)
dim T (SE1)
Hare & Tortoise (SW15)
O'Zon (TW1)

East
Banana Tree Canteen (EC1)
Cicada (EC1)*
Great Eastern Dining Room (EC2)*
Hare & Tortoise (EC4)
Pacific Oriental (EC2)

THAI
Central
Benja (W1)*

259

CUISINES | ASIAN

Blue Jade *(SW1)*
Busaba Eathai *(SW1,W1,WC1)*
C&R Cafe *(W1)*
Crazy Bear *(W1)*
Mango Tree *(SW1)*
Mekong *(SW1)*
Nahm *(SW1)*
Paolina Café *(WC1)*
Patara *(W1)**
Rosa's Soho *(W1)*
Siam Central *(W1)*
Spice Market *(W1)*
Thai Pot *(WC2)*
Thai Square *(SW1,W1,WC2)*

West
Addie's Thai Café *(SW5)**
Bangkok *(SW7)**
Bedlington Café *(W4)*
Busaba Eathai *(W12)*
C&R Cafe *(W2)*
Café 209 *(SW6)*
Charm *(W6)*
Churchill Arms *(W8)**
Esarn Kheaw *(W12)**
Fat Boy's *(W4,W5)*
Fitou's Thai Restaurant *(W10)**
Old Parr's Head *(W14)*
Patara *(SW3)**
Sukho Fine Thai Cuisine *(SW6)**
Thai Square *(SW7)*
The Walmer Castle *(W11)*

North
Isarn *(N1)**
Thai Square *(N1)*
Yum Yum *(N16)*

South
Amaranth *(SW18)**
Fat Boy's *(SW14,TW1,TW8)**
The Paddyfield *(SW12)**
The Pepper Tree *(SW4)*
Suk Saran *(SW19)*
Talad Thai *(SW15)*
Thai Corner Café *(SE22)*
Thai Garden *(SW11)*
Thai on the River *(SW11)*
Thai Square *(SW15)*

East
Busaba Eathai *(EC1)*
Elephant Royale *(E14)*
Rosa's *(E1)*
Thai Square *(EC4)*
Thai Square City *(EC3)*

UZBEKISTANI
Central
Samarqand *(W1)*

VIETNAMESE
Central
Bam-Bou *(W1)*
Cây Tre *(W1)**
Mekong *(SW1)*
Pho *(W1)**
Spice Market *(W1)*
Viet *(W1)*

West
Kiasu *(W2)*
Pho *(W12)**
Saigon Saigon *(W6)**

North
Huong-Viet *(N1)*
Khoai *(N8)*
Khoai Cafe *(N12)*
Viet Garden *(N1)*

South
Mien Tay *(SW11)**
The Paddyfield *(SW12)**

East
Cây Tre *(EC1)**
Green Papaya *(E8)**
Mien Tay *(E2)**
Namo *(E9)*
Pho *(EC1)**
Sông Quê *(E2)**
Viet Grill *(E2)**
Viet Hoa *(E2)**

AREA OVERVIEWS

CENTRAL

Soho, Covent Garden & Bloomsbury
(Parts of W1, all WC2 and WC1)

£90+	L'Atelier de Joel Robuchon	*French*	②③②
	Asia de Cuba	*Fusion*	④⑤④
£80+	Pearl	*French*	④④③
	Savoy (River Rest')	*International*	⑤⑤③
£70+	Rules	*British, Traditional*	④③②
	Savoy Grill	"	③②③
	Simpsons-in-the-Strand	"	④⑤④
	Ladurée	*Afternoon tea*	④④③
	aqua kyoto	*Japanese*	③③①
	Spice Market	*Vietnamese*	④④④
£60+	Christopher's	*American*	④③③
	Adam Street	*British, Modern*	④④②
	Hix	"	③④③
	Indigo	"	④②③
	The Ivy	"	④②②
	Paramount	"	④④①
	St John Hotel	*British, Traditional*	③②④
	J Sheekey	*Fish & seafood*	⓪⓪②
	Zilli Fish	"	④④④
	Gauthier Soho	*French*	⓪②③
	Little Italy	*Italian*	④④③
	aqua nueva	*Spanish*	④④④
	Floridita	*Cuban*	④④④
	Shanghai Blues	*Chinese*	②④②
	Yauatcha	"	⓪④②
	Red Fort	*Indian*	②③③
£50+	Circus	*American*	④④②
	Joe Allen	"	④④②
	Arbutus	*British, Modern*	②②③
	Axis	"	④②④
	Bob Bob Ricard	"	④②②
	Dean Street Townhouse	"	④③②
	Le Deuxième	"	④③⑤
	Quo Vadis	"	②②②
	Refuel	"	③③②
	Tom's Terrace	"	⑤④③
	The National Dining Rms	*British, Traditional*	⑤⑤④
	Wright Brothers	*Fish & seafood*	②③③
	Bistro du Vin	*French*	④③④
	Café des Amis	"	④④④
	Chez Gérard	"	⑤⑤⑤
	Le Cigalon	"	②②②
	Clos Maggiore	"	②⓪⓪
	Les Deux Salons	"	③④③
	L'Escargot	"	③②②
	Incognico	"	④④④
	Mon Plaisir	"	④④③
	The Forge	*International*	④④④
	National Gallery Café	"	④④④

	Bocca Di Lupo	*Italian*	②	②	②
	Number Twelve	"	③	④	④
	Orso	"	③	③	④
	Vasco & Piero's Pavilion	"	②	②	③
	Nopi	*Mediterranean*	②	②	③
	Albannach	*Scottish*	⑤	⑤	⑤
	Gaucho	*Steaks & grills*	③	④	③
	Hawksmoor	"	②	②	②
	St Moritz	*Swiss*	③	④	③
	Moti Mahal	*Indian*	②	③	④
	Kyashii	*Japanese*	④	④	③
	Watatsumi	"	④	③	④
	Tamarai	*Pan-Asian*	④	④	④
£40+	All Star Lanes	*American*	④	⑤	③
	Bodean's	"	④	⑤	④
	Spuntino	"	③	②	②
	Acorn House	*British, Modern*	④	④	⑤
	Andrew Edmunds	"	③	②	⓿
	Aurora	"	③	③	②
	The Easton	"	②	②	③
	Kettners	"	④	③	③
	The Portrait	"	④	②	⓿
	Shampers	"	③	②	②
	Great Queen Street	*British, Traditional*	②	③	③
	Cape Town Fish Market	*Fish & seafood*	③	④	④
	Livebait	"	④	④	⑤
	Loch Fyne	"	④	④	④
	J Sheekey Oyster Bar	"	②	⓿	⓿
	Antidote	*French*	③	④	③
	Café Bohème	"	④	②	⓿
	The Giaconda	"	②	②	④
	Randall & Aubin	"	③	③	②
	Terroirs	"	②	③	③
	Kopapa	*Fusion*	③	③	④
	Gay Hussar	*Hungarian*	⑤	③	②
	Balans	*International*	④	③	③
	Browns	"	⑤	④	④
	Cork & Bottle	"	⑤	④	②
	Giraffe	"	⑤	④	④
	Sarastro	"	⑤	⑤	⓿
	Bertorelli	*Italian*	⑤	⑤	⑤
	Ciao Bella	"	④	②	②
	Dehesa	"	⓿	⓿	②
	Jamie's Italian	"	④	③	④
	Rossopomodoro	"	③	④	④
	Sapori	"	④	③	④
	Barrafina	*Spanish*	⓿	⓿	②
	Cigala	"	③	③	④
	Opera Tavern	"	②	③	③
	The Bountiful Cow	*Steaks & grills*	③	④	④
	Boyd's Brasserie	"	④	④	④
	Sophie's Steakhouse	"	④	③	③
	Mildreds	*Vegetarian*	②	④	④
	Wolfe's	*Burgers, etc*	③	④	④
	Café Pacifico	*Mexican/TexMex*	⑤	④	③
	Cantina Laredo	"	③	④	⑤
	Bar Shu	*Chinese*	②	④	③

	Empress of Sichuan	"	❸❸④
	Imperial China	"	❸❸④
	Yming	"	❷❶❸
	Malabar Junction	Indian	❸❸❸
	Edokko	Japanese	❷❶❸
	Inamo	"	④④❷
	Asadal	Korean	❸④④
	Benja	Thai	❷❷❸
	Patara	"	❷❸❸
£35+	Belgo Centraal	Belgian	④④❸
	Café Emm	British, Modern	④④❸
	The Norfolk Arms	"	④④❸
	The Terrace	"	❸④❷
	Porters	British, Traditional	④❸❸
	Côte	French	④❸❷
	Savoir Faire	"	❸④❸
	Real Greek	Greek	⑤⑤④
	Boulevard	International	⑤⑤④
	Da Mario	Italian	④❷❷
	Polpetto	"	❷❷⓪
	Zilli Green	"	– – –
	Tapas Brindisa Soho	Spanish	❷❸❷
	Fire & Stone	Pizza	④❸❸
	Lupita	Mexican/TexMex	④④④
	Sofra	Turkish	④④④
	Dishoom	Indian	❸❸⓪
	Imli	"	④❸④
	Mela	"	❸❸❸
	Rasa Maricham	Indian, Southern	❷❷❸
	Abeno	Japanese	❸❷④
	Hazuki	"	❷❷④
	Satsuma	"	– – –
	Ten Ten Tei	"	❸❸⑤
	Melati, Gt Windmill St	Malaysian	④❸⑤
	Haozhan	Pan-Asian	❸④⑤
	Busaba Eathai	Thai	❸❸❷
	Thai Pot	"	❸❷❸
	Thai Square	"	④❸❸
	Cây Tre	Vietnamese	❷④④
£30+	Seven Stars	British, Modern	④④❷
	da Polpo	Italian	❸❷④
	La Porchetta Pizzeria	"	❸❸❸
	Byron	Burgers, etc	❸❸❸
	Diner	"	⑤⑤❸
	North Sea Fish	Fish & chips	❸❸❸
	Rock & Sole Plaice	"	❸④❸
	Fernandez & Wells	Sandwiches, cakes, etc	❷❷❷
	Paul	"	❸④❸
	Yalla Yalla	Lebanese	❸❸❷
	Tas	Turkish	④❸❸
	Ba Shan	Chinese	❷④❸
	Chuen Cheng Ku	"	❸④④
	Golden Dragon	"	❸❸❸
	Harbour City	"	❷④④
	Joy King Lau	"	❸④④
	Mr Kong	"	❸❸④

New Mayflower	"		②③④
New World	"		④④③
Plum Valley	"		③②③
Leong's Legends	Chinese, Dim sum		④④③
ping pong	"		④④③
Gopal's of Soho	Indian		③③③
Masala Zone	"		③③③
Sagar	"		②②④
Salaam Namaste	"		②③④
Bincho Yakitori	Japanese		③④④
Misato	"		④④⑤
Wagamama	"		④③④
Kimchee	Korean		③③③
Banana Tree Canteen	Pan-Asian		③②③
Rosa's Soho	Thai		③④③
Pho	Vietnamese		②③③
£25+	Prix Fixe	French	④③③
	Café in the Crypt	International	④④③
	Gordon's Wine Bar	"	⑤④①
	Polpo	Italian	③②①
	Princi	"	③④②
	Café España	Spanish	③②②
	Mar I Terra	"	③②③
	Ed's Easy Diner	Burgers, etc	④③②
	Bar Italia	Sandwiches, cakes, etc	③④①
	The Courtauld (Café)	"	④③③
	Wahaca	Mexican/TexMex	④③③
	Gaby's	Israeli	③④⑤
	Cha Cha Moon	Chinese	④④③
	Chilli Cool	"	②⑤④
	The Four Seasons	"	②④⑤
	Wong Kei	"	④⑤④
	India Club	Indian	④④④
	Kulu Kulu	Japanese	④④⑤
	Taro	"	③③③
	Tokyo Diner	"	④②③
	Hare & Tortoise	Pan-Asian	③③③
£20+	Bistro 1	Mediterranean	④③④
	Konditor & Cook	Sandwiches, cakes, etc	②③③
	Leon	"	③③③
	Benito's Hat	Mexican/TexMex	③②④
	Koya	Japanese	②②③
	Paolina Café	Thai	③④⑤
	Viet	Vietnamese	③④④
£15+	Hummus Bros	Mediterranean	②②④
	Nordic Bakery	Scandinavian	③③②
	Food for Thought	Vegetarian	②④⑤
	Mrs Marengos	Sandwiches, cakes, etc	①③④
	Chipotle	Mexican/TexMex	③④④
	Baozi Inn	Chinese	②⑤④
	Abokado	Japanese	④③④
	C&R Cafe	Thai	③④⑤
£10+	Govinda's	International	③④④
	Caffè Vergnano	Italian	④③③

	Fryer's Delight	Fish & chips	③④④
	Flat White	Sandwiches, cakes, etc	②②③
	Maison Bertaux	"	②③❶
	Monmouth Coffee Co	"	②②②
	Pod	"	③④④
	Chilango	Mexican/TexMex	❶②④
	Mooli's	Indian	②②④
£5+	Gelupo	Ice cream	②②④
	Pizzeria Malletti	Pizza	②③③

Mayfair & St James's (Parts of W1 and SW1)

£110+	Alain Ducasse	French	④④④
	Le Gavroche	"	❶❶②
	Hibiscus	"	③④④
	The Ritz Restaurant	"	③②❶
£100+	G Ramsay at Claridges	French	⑤④⑤
	Hélène Darroze	"	③④③
	Sketch (Lecture Rm)	"	⑤⑤③
	The Square	"	②②③
	Kai Mayfair	Chinese	③③④
£90+	Wiltons	British, Traditional	④②②
	The Greenhouse	French	③③②
	Murano	Italian	③②③
£80+	Dorchester Grill	British, Modern	④③④
	Galvin at Windows	French	③②②
	L'Oranger	"	③③②
	C London	Italian	⑤⑤④
	Theo Randall	"	②③④
	maze Grill	Steaks & grills	④④④
	Hakkasan	Chinese	②④②
	Ikeda	Japanese	②②⑤
	Matsuri	"	②②⑤
	Nobu, Park Ln	"	②④④
	Nobu, Berkeley St	"	③④③
	Umu	"	②③②
£70+	Bellamy's	British, Modern	③②③
	Patterson's	"	③③④
	Seven Park Place	"	❶❶②
	Browns (Albemarle)	British, Traditional	③②②
	Corrigan's Mayfair	"	③③③
	Scott's	Fish & seafood	②❶❶
	maze	French	④④④
	La Petite Maison	"	②②②
	Amaranto	Italian	– – –
	Babbo	"	④④⑤
	5 Pollen Street	"	④③③
	Ladurée	Afternoon tea	④④③
	Quince	Turkish	④③⑤
	China Tang	Chinese	④④③
	Benares	Indian	②②③
	Sumosan	Japanese	③③③

£60+			
Athenaeum	British, Modern	① ② ③
Le Caprice	"	③ ① ②
Criterion	"	④ ④ ②
Langan's Brasserie	"	④ ④ ②
Pollen Street Social	"	① ① ②
Quaglino's	"	⑤ ⑤ ⑤
The Fountain (Fortnum's)	British, Traditional	④ ③ ③
Green's	"	② ② ②
Bentley's	Fish & seafood	② ③ ③
Brasserie Roux	French	③ ② ③
The Gallery	"	② ⓪ ④
Sketch (Gallery)	"	⑤ ⑤ ④
Cecconi's	Italian	③ ② ⓪
Franco's	"	④ ④ ④
La Genova	"	③ ② ③
Ristorante Semplice	"	② ② ③
Goodman	Steaks & grills	② ② ③
The Guinea Grill	"	② ③ ③
JW Steakhouse	"	④ ④ ④
Rowley's	"	⑤ ⑤ ⑤
Momo	North African	④ ⑤ ③
Mint Leaf	Indian	③ ④ ③
Tamarind	"	③ ③ ④
Veeraswamy	"	③ ③ ③
Benihana	Japanese	④ ③ ③
Kiku	"	② ② ④
Miyama	"	② ④ ⑤
Sake No Hana	"	③ ④ ④

£50+			
Automat	American	④ ④ ④
The Avenue	British, Modern	④ ③ ③
Hush	"	⑤ ⑤ ④
Mews of Mayfair	"	④ ③ ③
Sotheby's Café	"	② ② ②
Wild Honey	"	③ ③ ③
The Wolseley	"	③ ② ⓪
Pescatori	Fish & seafood	③ ② ④
Wheeler's	"	⑤ ④ ⑤
Boudin Blanc	French	③ ④ ②
Brasserie St Jacques	"	④ ③ ④
Chez Gérard	"	⑤ ⑤ ⑤
Alloro	Italian	③ ③ ③
Dolada	"	③ ③ ④
Sartoria	"	③ ③ ③
Serafino	"	③ ② ④
Tempo	"	③ ② ③
Truc Vert	Mediterranean	③ ④ ④
Gaucho	Steaks & grills	③ ④ ③
Aubaine	Sandwiches, cakes, etc	④ ④ ④
Fakhreldine	Lebanese	④ ④ ④
Noura	"	③ ④ ④
Princess Garden	Chinese	② ② ③
Mitsukoshi	Japanese	② ② ⑤

£40+			
Hard Rock Café	American	④ ② ②
Inn the Park	British, Modern	④ ⑤ ③
The Only Running Footman	"	③ ③ ③
1707	"	④ ③ ③

			Rating
	Fishworks	Fish & seafood	③③④
	Browns	International	⑤④④
	Al Duca	Italian	④④⑤
	Bar Trattoria Semplice	"	④④⑤
	Piccolino	"	④④④
	Il Vicolo	"	④④④
	Rocket	Mediterranean	④④③
	Ritz (Palm Court)	Afternoon tea	④③②
	Delfino	Pizza	②④④
	The Sketch (Parlour)	Sandwiches, cakes, etc	④④③
	Al Hamra	Lebanese	④⑤④
	Al Sultan	"	②③⑤
	Chor Bizarre	Indian	④④②
	Chisou	Japanese	②③④
	Inamo	Pan-Asian	④④②
	Patara	Thai	②③③
£35+	The Windmill	British, Traditional	②④③
	L'Artiste Musclé	French	④③③
	El Pirata	Spanish	④②⓪
	Sofra	Turkish	④④④
	Woodlands	Indian	③③④
	Rasa	Indian, Southern	②②③
	Toku	Japanese	③③④
	Yoshino	"	②⓪③
	Busaba Eathai	Thai	③③②
	Thai Square	"	④③③
£30+	tibits	Vegetarian	③④③
	Byron	Burgers, etc	③③③
	Benugo	Sandwiches, cakes, etc	④⑤③
	Sakura	Japanese	②④④
	Wagamama	"	④③④
£25+	English Tea Rm (Browns)	British, Traditional	③②⓪
	Stock Pot	International	⑤④④
	Ed's Easy Diner	Burgers, etc	④③②
	Jom Makan	Malaysian	④⑤⑤
£20+	Napket	Afternoon tea	④④③
	Mount Street Deli	Sandwiches, cakes, etc	④④④
£15+	La Bottega	Italian	③③③
£10+	Fuzzy's Grub	Sandwiches, cakes, etc	④④④
	Chop'd	Salads	③③④

Fitzrovia & Marylebone (Part of W1)

			Rating
£90+	Pied à Terre	French	⓪②②
£80+	Roux At The Landau	British, Modern	②②②
	Hakkasan	Chinese	②④②
£70+	Roganic	British, Modern	⓪②⑤
	Locanda Locatelli	Italian	③③③
	Texture	Scandinavian	②⓪③
	Roka	Japanese	⓪③②

£60+	Oscar	*British, Modern*	④③②
	Rhodes W1 Restaurant	*"*	④③⑤
	L'Autre Pied	*French*	②②③
	Orrery	*"*	③②②
	The Providores	*International*	③④④
	La Porte des Indes	*Indian*	③④②
£50+	Café Luc	*British, Modern*	④④②
	Grazing Goat	*"*	③②②
	The Union Café	*"*	③④④
	Vanilla	*"*	④④③
	Odin's	*British, Traditional*	④②②
	Pescatori	*Fish & seafood*	③②④
	Elena's L'Etoile	*French*	⑤④④
	Galvin Bistrot de Luxe	*"*	②⓪②
	Villandry	*"*	④⑤④
	The Wallace	*"*	④④⓪
	Archipelago	*Fusion*	③③⓪
	Il Baretto	*Italian*	②④④
	Caffè Caldesi	*"*	④②③
	Mennula	*"*	②③④
	Verru	*Scandinavian*	②③④
	Fino	*Spanish*	②②②
	Gaucho	*Steaks & grills*	③④③
	Reubens	*Kosher*	④⑤⑤
	Levant	*Lebanese*	③③⓪
	Royal China Club	*Chinese*	②③④
	Trishna	*Indian*	⓪②③
	Colony	*Pan-Asian*	③④⑤
	Crazy Bear	*Thai*	③③⓪
£40+	The Duke of Wellington	*British, Modern*	③④③
	Hardy's Brasserie	*"*	④④③
	Ozer	*"*	④④④
	RIBA Café	*"*	④⑤②
	Back to Basics	*Fish & seafood*	②②④
	Fishworks	*"*	③③④
	Langan's Bistro	*French*	③②②
	Le Relais de Venise	*"*	②③③
	Providores (Tapa Room)	*Fusion*	②④④
	Élysée	*Greek*	④③②
	Hellenic	*"*	④②③
	Giraffe	*International*	⑤④④
	Latium	*Italian*	②⓪③
	Sardo	*"*	③③④
	2 Veneti	*"*	③②④
	Riding House Café	*Mediterranean*	②②⓪
	Ibérica	*Spanish*	③③③
	Black & Blue	*Steaks & grills*	④④④
	Fairuz	*Lebanese*	③③④
	Maroush	*"*	②④④
	Royal China	*Chinese*	②④④
	Gaylord	*Indian*	③④④
	Zayna	*"*	②④④
	Defune	*Japanese*	②⓪④
	Dinings	*"*	⓪②⑤
	Soho Japan	*"*	③②④
	Tsunami	*"*	⓪④③

	Koba	*Korean*	③③④
	Samarqand	*Uzbekistani*	④④③
	Bam-Bou	*Vietnamese*	③③②
£35+	Vinoteca Seymour Place	*British, Modern*	③②❶
	Canteen	*British, Traditional*	④④④
	Real Greek	*Greek*	⑤⑤④
	Navarro's	*Spanish*	③④②
	Salt Yard	*"*	③②②
	Eagle Bar Diner	*Burgers, etc*	③③②
	La Fromagerie Café	*Sandwiches, cakes, etc*	②③②
	Ishtar	*Turkish*	③②③
	Sofra	*"*	④④④
	Woodlands	*Indian*	③③④
	Rasa Samudra	*Indian, Southern*	②②③
	Nizuni	*Japanese*	②②③
£30+	Guerilla Burgers	*American*	③②②
	Lantana Cafe	*Australian*	③③③
	Vapiano	*Italian*	④④④
	Barrica	*Spanish*	③③②
	Benugo	*Sandwiches, cakes, etc*	④⑤③
	Paul	*"*	③④③
	Natural Kitchen	*Salads*	③③③
	Yalla Yalla	*Lebanese*	③③②
	ping pong	*Chinese, Dim sum*	④④③
	Indali Lounge	*Indian*	③③③
	Sagar	*"*	②②④
	Wagamama	*Japanese*	④③④
	dim T	*Pan-Asian*	⑤④③
	Pho	*Vietnamese*	②③③
£25+	Ragam	*Indian*	❶②⑤
	Atari-Ya	*Japanese*	❶②④
	Siam Central	*Thai*	③④③
£20+	Golden Hind	*Fish & chips*	❶②③
	Leon	*Sandwiches, cakes, etc*	③③③
	Benito's Hat	*Mexican/TexMex*	③②④
£15+	Cocorino	*Italian*	❶❶③
	Nordic Bakery	*Scandinavian*	③③②
	Tortilla	*Mexican/TexMex*	③③④
	Comptoir Libanais	*Lebanese*	④⑤④
	Abokado	*Japanese*	④③④
£10+	Scandinavian Kitchen	*Scandinavian*	③②②
	Kaffeine	*Sandwiches, cakes, etc*	②❶❶
	Patogh	*Middle Eastern*	②③④

Belgravia, Pimlico, Victoria & Westminster (SW1, except St James's)

£110+	Marcus Wareing	French	②②②
£100+	Rib Room	British, Traditional	– – –
£90+	Dinner	British, Traditional	②②②
	One-O-One	Fish & seafood	①③⑤
	Apsleys	Italian	③②③
£80+	Roux At Parliament Square	British, Modern	③④⑤
	Pétrus	French	④②③
	Roussillon	"	③③④
	The Palm	Steaks & grills	④④⑤
	Nahm	Thai	③③⑤
£70+	The Goring Hotel	British, Modern	③①①
	Koffmann's	French	②②④
	Massimo	Mediterranean	④②②
	Ladurée	Afternoon tea	④④③
	Mr Chow	Chinese	④④④
£60+	The Fifth Floor Restaurant	British, Modern	④③④
	The Thomas Cubitt	"	③③②
	Harrods (Georgian Rest')	British, Traditional	③③③
	Olivomare	Fish & seafood	②③④
	Quirinale	Italian	②①③
	Santini	"	④④④
	Signor Sassi	"	③③②
	Toto's	"	③③③
	Zafferano	"	③④③
	Boisdale	Scottish	④④②
	Amaya	Indian	①②②
	The Cinnamon Club	"	②③②
£50+	Bank Westminster	British, Modern	④③④
	The Botanist	"	⑤⑤⑤
	The Pantechnicon	"	③③②
	Tate Britain (Rex Whistler)	"	③③②
	Shepherd's	British, Traditional	④③③
	Bar Boulud	French	②②③
	Chabrot Bistrot d'Amis	"	③①③
	The Chelsea Brasserie	"	④④④
	La Poule au Pot	"	③③①
	Motcombs	International	④④③
	Il Convivio	Italian	③③④
	Olivo	"	③③⑤
	Osteria Dell'Angolo	"	③③⑤
	Sale e Pepe	"	④③③
	Oliveto	Pizza	①③④
	Ishbilia	Lebanese	②④⑤
	Noura	"	③④④
	Hunan	Chinese	①②④
	Ken Lo's Memories	"	②③③
	Quilon	Indian, Southern	①①④
	Mango Tree	Thai	③④④

£40+	Daylesford Organic	British, Modern	④⑤④
	Ebury Wine Bar	"	④❸❸
	The Orange	"	❸❸❷
	The Queens Arms	"	❸❸❸
	Smith Square	"	– – –
	Le Cercle	French	❷❷❷
	The Ebury	"	④④❸
	Browns	International	⑤④④
	Bumbles	"	❸❷④
	City Café	"	④❸④
	Giraffe	"	⑤④④
	Grumbles	"	⑤④④
	Caraffini	Italian	❸⓪❷
	Como Lario	"	⑤④❸
	Gran Paradiso	"	④❸④
	Ottolenghi	"	⓪❸❸
	2 Amici	"	④④④
	Uno	"	④④④
	About Thyme	Mediterranean	❷⓪④
	Goya	Spanish	④④④
	Baker & Spice	Sandwiches, cakes, etc	❸❸❷
	Beiteddine	Lebanese	❸④⑤
	Ranoush	"	❷④④
	Kazan	Turkish	❷❷❸
	The Grand Imperial	Chinese	④❸④
	Made in China	"	④④④
	Salloos	Pakistani	❷❸④
£35+	Tinello	Italian	❷⓪❷
£30+	Seafresh	Fish & chips	❸④⑤
	Jenny Lo's	Chinese	❸⓪④
	Wagamama	Japanese	④❸④
	dim T	Pan-Asian	⑤④❸
	Blue Jade	Thai	❸⓪❸
	Mekong	Vietnamese	❸❷④
£25+	The Vincent Rooms	British, Modern	❸④❸
	Cyprus Mangal	Turkish	❷❸④
£15+	La Bottega	Italian	❸❸❸
	William Curley	Afternoon tea	⓪❸❸

WEST

Chelsea, South Kensington, Kensington, Earl's Court & Fulham (SW3, SW5, SW6, SW7, SW10 & W8)

£120+	Gordon Ramsay	French	④③④
£100+	Tom Aikens	British, Modern	– – –
£90+	The Capital Restaurant	French	③④④
	Rasoi	Indian	③④③
£80+	Blakes	International	④③②
£70+	Launceston Place	British, Modern	②②②
	Bibendum	French	③②②
	Cassis Bistro	"	④④④
	Nozomi	Japanese	④⑤④
	Zuma	"	①③②
£60+	Babylon	British, Modern	④④②
	Clarke's	"	②②③
	Maggie Jones's	British, Traditional	⑤④①
	Bibendum Oyster Bar	Fish & seafood	③②②
	Poissonnerie de l'Av.	"	③③④
	Le Suquet	"	③④④
	Belvedere	French	④③①
	Cheyne Walk Bras'	"	③④③
	L'Etranger	"	③②③
	Racine	"	③②③
	Ilia	Italian	③④④
	Lucio	"	③③③
	Montpeliano	"	④④④
	San Lorenzo	"	④④④
	Scalini	"	④④③
	Locanda Ottomezzo	Mediterranean	④②③
	Min Jiang	Chinese	①②①
	Bombay Brasserie	Indian	③③③
	Benihana	Japanese	④③③
	Yashin	"	②④④
	Mao Tai	Pan-Asian	③④③
£50+	Big Easy	American	④④②
	The Abingdon	British, Modern	③②②
	Bluebird	"	⑤④④
	Brinkley's	"	⑤④③
	The Enterprise	"	③②②
	Kensington Place	"	③③④
	Kitchen W8	"	①②②
	Manson	"	①④③
	Marco	"	④⑤⑤
	Tom's Kitchen	"	④⑤④
	Bistro K	French	④④④
	Le Colombier	"	③②②
	Galoupet	"	①②③
	Foxtrot Oscar	International	④③④
	Gallery Mess	"	④④④

273

Medlar	"	❶❷❸	
Wine Gallery	"	❹❸❷	
The Ark	Italian	❻❸❷	
Cavallino	"	– – –	
Daphne's	"	❸❷❷	
El leven Park Walk	"	❸❹❹	
La Famiglia	"	❸❸❸	
Frantoio	"	❹❸❸	
Manicomio	"	❸❹❸	
Osteria dell'Arancio	"	❸❸❸	
Pellicano	"	❸❸❹	
Timo	"	❷❶❹	
Venosi	"	❹❷❹	
Ziani's	"	❸❷❷	
Cambio de Tercio	Spanish	❷❷❷	
Gaucho	Steaks & grills	❸❹❸	
Kings Road Steakhouse	"	❹❹❹	
PJ's Bar and Grill	"	❹❹❸	
Aubaine	Sandwiches, cakes, etc	❹❹❹	
Pasha	Moroccan	❺❹❷	
Good Earth	Chinese	❸❸❺	
Chutney Mary	Indian	❷❷❷	
The Painted Heron	"	❶❷❸	
Zaika	"	❶❷❸	
Awana	Malaysian	❹❹❹	
Eight Over Eight	Pan-Asian	❷❸❷	

£40+	Bodean's	American	❹❺❹
	Sticky Fingers	"	❹❹❸
	Admiral Codrington	British, Modern	❸❹❸
	The Anglesea Arms	"	❸❹❷
	Brompton Bar & Grill	"	❹❸❸
	The Builders Arms	"	❸❸❷
	The Cadogan Arms	"	❸❹❸
	Eighty-Six	"	❹❺❸
	Harwood Arms	"	❷❷❷
	The Henry Root	"	❹❷❸
	Jam Tree	"	❹❷❸
	Joe's Brasserie	"	❸❸❸
	Lots Road	"	❸❷❹
	The Mall Tavern	"	❸❸❷
	The Phene	"	❹❹❷
	The Phoenix	"	❹❺❸
	The Sands End	"	❷❸❷
	Vingt-Quatre	"	❹❹❹
	White Horse	"	❸❸❸
	Whits	"	❸❶❸
	Bumpkin	British, Traditional	❺❹❸
	Ffiona's	"	❹❷❶
	Chez Patrick	Fish & seafood	❸❷❸
	Geales Chelsea Green	"	❸❸❹
	L'Art du Fromage	French	❸❷❹
	La Bouchée	"	❸❹❷
	La Brasserie	"	❺❹❸
	The Pig's Ear	"	❸❸❶
	Tartine	"	❸❹❸
	Sushinho	Fusion	❹❸❷
	Balans West	International	❹❸❸

			Rating
Giraffe	"		⑤④④
The Kensington Wine Rms	"		④②②
Falconiere	Italian		④③⑤
Frankie's Italian Bar & Grill	"		⑤⑤④
Nuovi Sapori	"		❷⓿❹
Ottolenghi	"		❶❸❸
Il Portico	"		❸⓿❷
Riccardo's	"		④④④
Rossopomodoro	"		❸④④
Santa Lucia	"		❸④❸
Vicino	"		❸❸❸
The Atlas	Mediterranean		❷❸❸
Del'Aziz	"		④⑤❷
Polish Club	Polish		⑤④❸
Madsen	Scandinavian		④④④
Black & Blue	Steaks & grills		④④④
Sophie's Steakhouse	"		④❸❸
Saf	Vegetarian		❷④④
Geales	Fish & chips		❸❸④
(Ciro's) Pizza Pomodoro	Pizza		④④❷
Baker & Spice	Sandwiches, cakes, etc		❸❸❷
Fulham Wine Rooms	"		④❸❸
Rodizio Rico	Brazilian		⑤④⑤
Maroush	Lebanese		❷④④
Randa	"		❸❸④
Ranoush	"		❷④④
Ken Lo's Memories	Chinese		❶❷❸
Mr Wing	"		❸④❷
Royal China	"		❷④④
Haandi	Indian		❷❷④
kare kare	"		❸❸④
Malabar	"		❷❷❸
Star of India	"		❷④❸
Thali	"		❷❷④
Patara	Thai		❷❸❸
Sukho Fine Thai Cuisine	"		❶❷❸
£35+ Butcher's Hook	British, Modern		❸❸❸
Côte	French		④❸❷
Rôtisserie Bute Street	"		❸④④
The Scarsdale	International		④❸❷
Aglio e Olio	Italian		❸❸❸
Buona Sera	"		❸⓿⓿
Da Mario	"		④❷❸
Made in Italy	"		❷❸❷
Napulé	"		❸④❸
Gessler at Daquise	Polish		④❷❸
Capote Y Toros	Spanish		– – –
Casa Brindisa	"		❸④❸
Lola Rojo	"		❷❸❷
Tendido Cero	"		❸❸❷
Tendido Cuatro	"		❷❷❷
Haché	Steaks & grills		❸❸❸
Bluebird Café	Sandwiches, cakes, etc		⑤⑤④
Troubadour	"		⑤❸⓿
Beirut Express	Lebanese		❷④④
Choys	Chinese		④④④
Khan's of Kensington	Indian		❸❸❸

Noor Jahan	"		② ② ④
Bangkok	Thai		② ② ③
Thai Square	"		④ ③ ③
£30+	Kensington Square Kitchen	British, Modern	③ ② ③
	The Windsor Castle	International	④ ④ ❶
	Il Pagliaccio	Italian	④ ③ ❶
	Pappa Ciccia	"	③ ③ ④
	Rocca Di Papa	"	④ ③ ③
	Byron	Burgers, etc	③ ③ ③
	Basilico	Pizza	② ③ ④
	La Delizia Limbara	"	③ ③ ③
	Firezza	"	② ③ ④
	Benugo	Sandwiches, cakes, etc	④ ⑤ ③
	Best Mangal	Turkish	③ ③ ③
	New Culture Rev'n	Chinese	③ ④ ④
	Taiwan Village	"	❶ ❶ ③
	The Greedy Buddha	Indian	③ ② ③
	Masala Zone	"	③ ③ ③
	Memories of India	"	③ ④ ④
	Monty's	"	③ ③ ④
	Itsu	Japanese	④ ④ ④
	Wagamama	"	④ ③ ④
	Addie's Thai Café	Thai	② ② ③
£25+	Costa's Grill	Greek	④ ③ ④
	Chelsea Bun Diner	International	③ ② ③
	The Chelsea Kitchen	"	④ ③ ③
	Mona Lisa	"	④ ❶ ②
	Stock Pot	"	⑤ ④ ④
	Kulu Kulu	Japanese	④ ④ ⑤
	Churchill Arms	Thai	② ③ ②
£20+	Napket	Afternoon tea	④ ④ ③
	Stick & Bowl	Chinese	③ ③ ③
	Café 209	Thai	③ ② ②
£15+	La Bottega	Italian	③ ③ ③

Notting Hill, Holland Park, Bayswater, North Kensington & Maida Vale (W2, W9, W10, W11)

£90+	The Ledbury	British, Modern	❶ ❶ ②
£70+	Notting Hill Brasserie	British, Modern	③ ④ ③
	Angelus	French	② ❶ ③
£60+	Beach Blanket Babylon	British, Modern	⑤ ⑤ ❶
	supperclub	"	④ ④ ❶
	Assaggi	Italian	② ② ③
	Edera	"	② ❶ ③
£50+	Julie's	British, Modern	④ ④ ❶
	The Warrington	"	⑤ ⑤ ⑤
	Le Café Anglais	French	③ ③ ③
	202	International	④ ③ ③
	Dragoncello	Italian	④ ② ③
	Essenza	"	③ ③ ④

			Rating
	Mediterraneo	"	❸❸❸
	Osteria Basilico	"	❸❸❷
	E&O	Pan-Asian	❷❸❷
£40+	All Star Lanes	American	④⑤❸
	Lucky Seven	"	❸❸❷
	The Cow	British, Modern	❸④❷
	Daylesford Organic	"	④⑤④
	The Dock Kitchen	"	❸❸❶
	First Floor	"	❸❷❶
	Formosa Dining Room	"	❸④❸
	The Frontline Club	"	❸❷❷
	The Ladbroke Arms	"	❷❸❷
	The Waterway	"	④⑤❷
	The Westbourne	"	❸④❷
	Bumpkin	British, Traditional	⑤④❸
	Hereford Road	"	❷❷④
	The Summerhouse	Fish & seafood	④④❶
	Electric Brasserie	French	④④❷
	La Sophia	"	❷❷④
	Halepi	Greek	❸❶❸
	Giraffe	International	⑤④④
	L'Accento Italiano	Italian	❸❷❸
	The Oak	"	❷❸❶
	Ottolenghi	"	❶❸❸
	Portobello Ristorante	"	❸④④
	Rossopomodoro	"	❸④④
	Cochonnet	Mediterranean	❸❷❸
	The Red Pepper	Pizza	❷❸④
	Baker & Spice	Sandwiches, cakes, etc	❸❸❷
	Casa Malevo	Argentinian	④④④
	Rodizio Rico	Brazilian	⑤④⑤
	Crazy Homies	Mexican/TexMex	❸④❶
	Al-Waha	Lebanese	❷❸④
	Maroush	"	❷④④
	Ranoush	"	❷④④
	Royal China	Chinese	❷④④
	Seventeen	"	❷❷❸
	Bombay Bicycle Club	Indian	– – –
	Bombay Palace	"	❷❷⑤
	Inaho	Japanese	❶⑤⑤
£35+	Paradise, Kensal Green	British, Modern	❷❷❶
	Côte	French	④❸❷
	Café Laville	International	④④❶
	Ida	Italian	❸❷❷
	Nottingdale	"	❷④❷
	Raoul's Café & Deli	Mediterranean	④⑤④
	Pizza East Portobello	Pizza	– – –
	Beirut Express	Lebanese	❷④④
	Kateh	Persian	❸❷❸
	Mandarin Kitchen	Chinese	❷④⑤
	Pearl Liang	"	❶❷❷
	Noor Jahan	Indian	❷❷④
	Satay House	Malaysian	❸❸④
	Uli	Pan-Asian	❸❶❸
	The Walmer Castle	Thai	❸❷❷

£30+	Galicia	Spanish	③④③
	El Pirata de Tapas	"	③②②
	Firezza	Pizza	②③④
	Tom's Deli	Sandwiches, cakes, etc	③④③
	Taqueria	Mexican/TexMex	④④③
	Magic Wok	Chinese	③③⑤
	New Culture Rev'n	"	③④④
	Leong's Legends	Chinese, Dim sum	④④③
	ping pong	"	④④③
	Masala Zone	Indian	③③③
	Itsu	Japanese	④④④
	Banana Tree Canteen	Pan-Asian	③②③
£25+	Otto Pizza	Pizza	②②③
	Gail's Bread	Sandwiches, cakes, etc	③③④
	Alounak	Persian	③④③
	Mandalay	Burmese	③③⑤
	Fortune Cookie	Chinese	②④⑤
	The Four Seasons	"	②④⑤
	Kiasu	Indonesian	③④④
£20+	Fresco	Lebanese	③②③
	Khan's	Indian	③④③
	Fitou's Thai Restaurant	Thai	②③④
£15+	C&R Cafe	Thai	③④⑤
£5+	Lisboa Pâtisserie	Sandwiches, cakes, etc	②③④

Hammersmith, Shepherd's Bush, Olympia, Chiswick, Brentford & Ealing (W4, W5, W6, W12, W13, W14, TW8)

£70+	Hedone	British, Modern	②④④
	The River Café	Italian	②②③
£60+	La Trompette	French	❶❶②
£50+	Charlotte's Bistro	French	④④④
	Le Vacherin	"	③③③
	The Meat & Wine Co	Steaks & grills	④❶④
£40+	The Anglesea Arms	British, Modern	②④②
	The Carpenter's Arms	"	③④④
	Duke of Sussex	"	③②②
	Ealing Park Tavern	"	③③④
	The Havelock Tavern	"	②④②
	High Road Brasserie	"	④④②
	Hole in the Wall	"	③④③
	The Jam Tree	"	④②③
	Pissarro	"	④④③
	Princess Victoria	"	②②②
	The Roebuck	"	③②②
	Sam's Brasserie	"	④③③
	Charlotte's Place	French	③③③
	Annie's	International	④②②
	Balans	"	④③③
	Giraffe	"	⑤④④

			Ratings	
	Michael Nadra	"	1 3 4
	Carvosso's	Italian	5 4 3
	Cibo	"	3 3 4
	Jamie's Italian	"	4 3 4
	Cumberland Arms	Mediterranean	3 3 3
	Del'Aziz	"	4 5 2
	The Cabin	Steaks & grills	4 4 4
	Popeseye	"	1 2 3
	The Gate	Vegetarian	2 3 4
	Lola & Simón	Argentinian	3 2 3
	Quantus	South American	3 2 3
	Indian Zing	Indian	1 2 3
	Charm	Thai	3 3 2
	Saigon Saigon	Vietnamese	2 2 3
£35+	Queen's Head	British, Modern	4 2 2
	Tatra	East & Cent. European	4 4 4
	Côte	French	4 3 2
	The Real Greek	Greek	5 5 4
	Raoul's Café & Deli	Mediterranean	4 5 4
	The Swan	"	2 3 2
	Fire & Stone	Pizza	4 3 3
	Chella	Persian	3 2 3
	North China	Chinese	2 2 3
	Brilliant	Indian	1 2 3
	Karma	"	2 1 4
	Madhu's	"	2 3 3
	Busaba Eathai	Thai	3 3 2
£30+	Albertine	French	4 2 1
	Canta Napoli	Italian	3 3 4
	Patio	Polish	3 2 1
	Byron	Burgers, etc	3 3 3
	Firezza	Pizza	2 3 4
	Benugo	Sandwiches, cakes, etc	4 5 3
	Azou	North African	3 3 2
	Sufi	Persian	3 2 4
	Best Mangal	Turkish	3 3 3
	Maxim	Chinese	3 4 4
	Anarkali	Indian	3 2 3
	Monty's	"	3 3 4
	Sagar	"	2 2 4
	Shilpa	Indian, Southern	1 3 5
	Kiraku	Japanese	1 2 3
	Okawari	"	3 3 4
	Tosa	"	3 4 4
	Esarn Kheaw	Thai	1 3 4
	Fat Boy's	"	3 4 3
	Pho	Vietnamese	2 3 3
£25+	Santa Maria	Pizza	2 2 2
	Gail's Bakery	Sandwiches, cakes, etc	3 3 4
	Wahaca	Mexican/TexMex	4 3 3
	Adams Café	Moroccan	3 1 2
	Chez Marcelle	Lebanese	1 5 5
	Alounak	Persian	3 4 3
	Faanoos	"	3 3 3
	Mohsen	"	2 3 5

	Atari-Ya	*Japanese*	❶❷④
	Jom Makan	*Malaysian*	④⑤⑤
	Hare & Tortoise	*Pan-Asian*	❸❸❸
	Bedlington Café	*Thai*	④❷⑤
£20+	Franco Manca	*Pizza*	❶❸❸
	Chiswick House Cafe	*Sandwiches, cakes, etc*	④⑤❸
	Abu Zaad	*Syrian*	❸❸④
	Gifto's	*Indian*	❷❸④
	Mirch Masala	*Pakistani*	❷④④
	Old Parr's Head	*Thai*	④④❸
£15+	Tortilla	*Mexican/TexMex*	❸❸④
	Comptoir Libanais	*Lebanese*	④⑤④
£10+	Kerbisher & Malt	*Fish & chips*	❷❸④

NORTH

Hampstead, West Hampstead, St John's Wood, Regent's Park, Kilburn & Camden Town (NW post-codes)

£70+	Landmark (Winter Gdn)	British, Modern	④❸❷
£60+	Gilbert Scott	British, Traditional	④❷❷
	Shaka Zulu	South African	⑤④❷
	Kaifeng	Chinese	❷❷④
	Gilgamesh	Pan-Asian	❸④❷
£50+	Bradley's	British, Modern	④④❸
	Odette's	"	❷❷❷
	St Pancras Grand	"	⑤⑤④
	L'Aventure	French	❷❷❶
	Oslo Court	"	❷❷❷
	Villa Bianca	Italian	④❷❸
	York & Albany	"	④④④
	Gaucho	Steaks & grills	❸④❸
	Rôtisserie	"	④❸④
	Manna	Vegetarian	⑤④④
	Good Earth	Chinese	❸❸⑤
£40+	The Engineer	British, Modern	④④❷
	Freemasons Arms	"	⑤④❷
	The Horseshoe	"	④❸❸
	The Lansdowne	"	❸❸❷
	Market	"	❸❸④
	The North London Tavern	"	❸④❸
	The Wells	"	❸❷❷
	The Wet Fish Cafe	"	❸❷❷
	Bull & Last	British, Traditional	❶❷❷
	Holly Bush	"	❸❸❶
	La Cage Imaginaire	French	④❷❸
	Cocotte	"	④④❸
	Mill Lane Bistro	"	❸❷④
	Lemonia	Greek	⑤❷❷
	Retsina	"	❸❷❸
	The Arches	International	④❸❷
	Giraffe	"	⑤④④
	Spaniard's Inn	"	❸❸❶
	Artigiano	Italian	④❸④
	Caponata	"	❸❷❷
	La Collina	"	– – –
	Fratelli la Bufala	"	❸④④
	The Salt House	"	❸❸❷
	The Salusbury	"	❸❸❸
	Sardo Canale	"	④④④
	Sarracino	"	❷❷④
	Camden Brasserie	Mediterranean	④❸④
	Del'Aziz	"	④⑤❷
	Queen's Head & Artichoke	"	④④❸
	The Sea Shell	Fish & chips	❸❸❸
	Mestizo	Mexican/TexMex	❷❷④
	Mango Room	Afro-Caribbean	❸❷❷
	Solly's	Israeli	④⑤⑤

	Goldfish	*Chinese*	❷❸④
	Phoenix Palace	*"*	❷❸❸
	Jin Kichi	*Japanese*	❶❷④
	Sushi-Say	*"*	❶❶❸
	Singapore Garden	*Malaysian*	❷❷❸
	XO	*Pan-Asian*	❸④❸
£35+	Belgo Noord	*Belgian*	④④❸
	The Junction Tavern	*British, Modern*	❸❷❷
	The Old Bull & Bush	*"*	⑤⑤❷
	Prince Albert	*"*	❸❸❸
	Rising Sun	*"*	❷❷❸
	Walnut	*"*	❸❷❷
	Kentish Canteen	*British, Traditional*	❸❷❸
	L'Absinthe	*French*	❸❶❷
	Somerstown Coffee House	*"*	④❸❸
	Swan & Edgar	*International*	④④❷
	L'Artista	*Italian*	④④❸
	Marine Ices	*"*	❸❷❷
	Haché	*Steaks & grills*	❸❸❸
	Harry Morgan's	*Burgers, etc*	❷❸❸
	Nautilus	*Fish & chips*	❷❷④
	Skipjacks	*"*	❶❷⑤
	La Brocca	*Pizza*	④④❸
	Sofra	*Turkish*	④④④
	Alisan	*Chinese*	❶❷④
	Gung-Ho	*"*	❸❷❸
	Eriki	*Indian*	❷❶❸
	Woodlands	*"*	❸❸④
	Sushi of Shiori	*Japanese*	❶❶④
	Yuzu	*"*	❷④⑤
£30+	Made In Camden	*British, Modern*	❸❸④
	Carob Tree	*Greek*	④❷④
	Daphne	*"*	❸❶❶
	La Porchetta Pizzeria	*Italian*	❸❸❸
	The Little Bay	*Mediterranean*	④❷❶
	Don Pepe	*Spanish*	❸❷❸
	El Parador	*"*	❷❶❸
	The Diner	*Burgers, etc*	⑤⑤❸
	Fine Burger Company	*"*	④④④
	Basilico	*Pizza*	❷❸④
	Benugo	*Sandwiches, cakes, etc*	④⑤❸
	Beyoglu	*Turkish*	❸④④
	ping pong	*Chinese, Dim sum*	④④❸
	Masala Zone	*Indian*	❸❸❸
	Asakusa	*Japanese*	❶④④
	Bento Cafe	*"*	❷❷④
	Café Japan	*"*	❶❷④
	Wagamama	*"*	④❸④
	The Banana Tree Canteen	*Pan-Asian*	❸❷❸
	dim T	*"*	⑤④❸
£25+	Sea Pebbles	*Fish & seafood*	❸❸④
	Stringray Café	*Mediterranean*	④④④
	Trojka	*Russian*	④④❸
	La Giralda	*Spanish*	❸❷❸
	Chamomile	*Sandwiches, cakes, etc*	❸❷❸

	Gail's Bread	"	❸❸④
	Kenwood (Brew House)	"	④④❷
	Green Cottage	Chinese	❷④⑤
	The Water Margin	"	❸❷④
	Chutneys	Indian	❸❸❸
	Diwana B-P House	"	❸⑤⑤
	Five Hot Chillies	"	❷④⑤
	Great Nepalese	"	❸❷⑤
	Kovalam	"	❷④⑤
	Vijay	"	⓪❷④
	Atari-Ya	Japanese	⓪❷④
£15+	Ali Baba	Egyptian	❸❷❸
	Geeta	Indian	❸⓪⑤
	Sakonis	"	❸④⑤
£10+	Chop'd	Salads	❸❸④
£5+	Ginger & White	Sandwiches, cakes, etc	❸❷❷

Hoxton, Islington, Highgate, Crouch End, Stoke Newington, Finsbury Park, Muswell Hill & Finchley (N postcodes)

£70+	Fifteen Restaurant	Italian	⑤⑤⑤
£60+	Morgan M	French	⓪⓪❸
£50+	Frederick's	British, Modern	④④❷
	The Almeida	French	④❸④
	Bistro Aix	"	❷❷❷
	Fifteen Trattoria	Italian	④⑤④
	Rôtisserie	Steaks & grills	④❸④
£40+	The Albion	British, Modern	④④❷
	Bald Faced Stag	"	❸❷❷
	The Barnsbury	"	❸④❸
	The Clissold Arms	"	④④④
	The Drapers Arms	"	④④❸
	The Duke of Cambridge	"	④④❸
	The Fellow	"	④④④
	The Haven	"	④④④
	Hoxton Apprentice	"	❸④❷
	Mosaica	"	❸❷❸
	The Rose & Crown	"	④④④
	Rotunda Bar & Restaurant	"	④❸❷
	The Marquess Tavern	British, Traditional	❸❸❸
	St Johns	"	❷❷❷
	Chez Liline	Fish & seafood	⓪❷⑤
	Les Associés	French	④❷④
	Fig	"	⓪❷❷
	Banners	International	④④❸
	Browns	"	⑤④④
	The Flask	"	❸❸❷
	Giraffe	"	⑤④④
	Canonbury Kitchen	Italian	❸❷④
	Ottolenghi	"	⓪❸❸
	Homa	Mediterranean	❸❸❸

283

			Rating
	Camino	Spanish	④⑤❸
	Garufa	Steaks & grills	❸④❸
	Il Bacio	Pizza	❸④④
	Rodizio Rico	Brazilian	⑤④⑤
	Sabor	South American	❸⓿❸
	Roots At N1	Indian	❷❷④
	Zaffrani	"	❸❸❸
	Isarn	Thai	❷⓿❸
	Yum Yum	"	❸❸❷
£35+	Charles Lamb	British, Modern	❸❸❷
	The Compass	"	❸④❸
	Juniper Dining	"	❷❸❸
	The Northgate	"	❷❷❸
	La Petite Auberge	French	④❸❷
	Le Sacré-Coeur	"	④❷❸
	The Real Greek	Greek	⑤⑤④
	The Orange Tree	International	❸❸❷
	500	Italian	⓿⓿❷
	Pizzeria Oregano	"	❸❷❸
	Rugoletta	"	❸❸❸
	San Daniele	"	❸❸❷
	Trullo	"	❷⓿❷
	Toff's	Fish & chips	❷❷④
	Two Brothers	"	❷❸④
	Furnace	Pizza	❸❸❸
	Mangal II	Turkish	❸❸④
	Rasa Travancore	Indian, Southern	❷❷❸
	Thai Square	Thai	④❸❸
	Viet Garden	Vietnamese	❸❸④
£30+	S & M Café	British, Traditional	④④④
	Kipferl	East & Cent. European	❸❷❷
	Blue Legume	French	❸④❷
	Vrisaki	Greek	④❸④
	Canta Napoli	Italian	❸❸④
	Pizzeria Pappagone	"	❸❷❸
	La Porchetta Pizzeria	"	❸❸❸
	Byron	Burgers, etc	❸❸❸
	Diner	"	⑤⑤❸
	Fine Burger Company	"	④④④
	Basilico	Pizza	❷❸④
	Firezza	"	❷❸④
	Gallipoli	Turkish	❸④❸
	Izgara	"	❸❷❸
	Petek	"	❷❷❷
	New Culture Rev'n	Chinese	❸④④
	Anglo Asian Tandoori	Indian	❷⓿❷
	Indian Rasoi	"	⓿❷❷
	Masala Zone	"	❸❸❸
	Wagamama	Japanese	④❸④
	dim T	Pan-Asian	⑤④❸
	Khoai Cafe	Vietnamese	❸❸④
£25+	Olympus Fish	Fish & seafood	❷❷④
	Le Mercury	French	④❸❷
	Mem & Laz	Mediterranean	④❷❷
	Stringray Café	"	④④④

	La Bota	Spanish	❸❷❸
	Rani	Indian	❷❸④
	Rasa	Indian, Southern	❶❶❷
	Dotori	Korean	❷❸❸
	Huong-Viet	Vietnamese	④⑤⑤
£20+	Gem	Turkish	❷❶❷
	19 Numara Bos Cirrik	"	❸❸④
	Afghan Kitchen	Afghani	❷④④
	Jai Krishna	Indian	❸❷❸
£15+	Café del Parc	Spanish	❷❷❷
	Tortilla	Mexican/TexMex	❸❸④
£10+	Chilango	Mexican/TexMex	❶❷④
£5+	Euphorium Bakery	Sandwiches, cakes, etc	❸④❸

SOUTH

South Bank (SE1)

£80+	Oxo Tower (Rest')	British, Modern	⑤⑤④
£70+	Oxo Tower (Brass')	Mediterranean	⑤④❸
£60+	Le Pont de la Tour	British, Modern	④❸❷
	Butlers W'f Chop-house	British, Traditional	④④❸
	Roast	"	❸④❸
	Brasserie Joël	French	❷④⑤
£50+	Blueprint Café	British, Modern	❸❸❶
	Cantina Vinopolis	"	④④④
	Magdalen	"	❶❷❷
	Skylon	"	④④❷
	Wright Brothers	Fish & seafood	❷❸❸
	Chez Gérard	French	⑤⑤⑤
	Vivat Bacchus	International	④④⑤
	La Barca	Italian	④❸❷
	Gaucho	Steaks & grills	❸④❸
£40+	Garrison	British, Modern	❸❸❶
	Menier Chocolate Factory	"	⑤④❷
	Mezzanine	"	④❸④
	RSJ	"	❸❷⑤
	The Swan at the Globe	"	④④❷
	The Table	"	④❸❸
	Waterloo Bar & Kitchen	"	④❸④
	Applebee's Cafe	Fish & seafood	❷❸④
	fish!	"	④⑤⑤
	Livebait	"	④④⑤
	Waterloo Brasserie	French	⑤⑤④
	Champor-Champor	Fusion	❷❷❷
	Village East	"	❸❷❷
	Browns	International	⑤④④
	Delfina	"	❸❸❸
	Giraffe	"	⑤④④
	Tate Modern (Level 7)	"	④④❷
	Cantina del Ponte	Italian	⑤④④
	Tentazioni	"	❸❸❸
	Zucca	"	❶❶❷
	Del'Aziz	Mediterranean	④⑤❷
	Baltic	Polish	④④④
	José	Spanish	– – –
	Archduke Wine Bar	Steaks & grills	⑤④④
	Black & Blue	"	④④④
	Constancia	Argentinian	❷❶❷
	Mango Tree	Indian	❷❸④
£35+	The Anchor & Hope	British, Traditional	❶❸❷
	Canteen	"	④④④
	Côte	French	④❸❷
	Real Greek	Greek	⑤⑤④
	The Riverfront	International	❷❷❸
	Tate Modern (Level 2)	"	❸④❸
	La Lanterna	Italian	❸❶❸

	Meson don Felipe	Spanish		④④❷
	Tapas Brindisa	"		❷❸❷
	Bengal Clipper	Indian		❸④❸
£30+	Gourmet Pizza Co.	Pizza		❸❸❸
	Benugo	Sandwiches, cakes, etc		④⑤❸
	Tas	Turkish		④❸❸
	Tas Pide	"		④❷❷
	ping pong	Chinese, Dim sum		④④❸
	Bangalore Express	Indian		④❸❷
	Wagamama	Japanese		④❸④
	dim T	Pan-Asian		⑤④❸
£25+	Mar I Terra	Spanish		❸❷❸
	Masters Super Fish	Fish & chips		❷④⑤
	El Vergel	South American		❷❷❷
	Simply Indian	Indian		❸④④
	Tsuru	Japanese		❸④④
£20+	Konditor & Cook	Sandwiches, cakes, etc		❷❸❸
	Leon	"		❸❸❸
£15+	Tortilla	Mexican/TexMex		❸❸④
£10+	Caffé Vergnano	Sandwiches, cakes, etc		④❸❸
	Monmouth Coffee Co	"		❷❷❷
	Pod	"		❸④④
	Spianata & Co	"		❷❸④

Greenwich, Lewisham, Dulwich & Blackheath (All SE postcodes, except SE1)

£50+	Rivington Grill	British, Modern		❸④④
	Lobster Pot	Fish & seafood		❸❸❸
	The Spread Eagle	French		④④❸
	Buenos Aires	Steaks & grills		❸❸❸
	Gaucho	"		❸④❸
	Buenos Aires Cafe	Argentinian		❸❸❸
£40+	Chapters	British, Modern		④❸④
	Franklins	"		❸④❸
	Inside	"		❷❷④
	Simplicity	"		④❸❸
	The Tommyfield	"		⑤⑤④
	Le Chardon	French		④⑤④
	Joanna's	International		❸❷❷
	The Trafalgar Tavern	"		⑤④❸
	The Yellow House	"		❷❷④
	Babur	Indian		❶❶❷
£35+	The Dartmouth Arms	British, Modern		❸❸❷
	Florence	"		④❸❸
	The Old Brewery	"		④④❷
	The Palmerston	"		❷❷❸
	Brasserie Toulouse-Lautrec	French		④❷❷
	Le Querce	Italian		❶❷❷
	Olley's	Fish & chips		❸❸④
	The Gowlett	Pizza		❷④❷

287

	Zero Degrees	"	③④②
	Angels & Gypsies	Cuban	②③②
	Dragon Castle	Chinese	②④④
	Kennington Tandoori	Indian	③②②
	Tandoori Nights	"	③③③
£30+	Green & Blue	International	④②②
	Rocca Di Papa	Pizza	④③③
	Peninsular	Chinese	②④④
	Everest Inn	Indian	②③②
	Ganapati	"	⓪⓪②
	Mogul	"	③②③
£25+	The Sea Cow	Fish & chips	③③③
	Gandhi's	Indian	③②③
£20+	Frizzante Cafe	Italian	③④③
	Thai Corner Café	Thai	③③③

**Battersea, Brixton, Clapham, Wandsworth
Barnes, Putney & Wimbledon
(All SW postcodes south of the river)**

£60+	Cannizaro House	British, Modern	④④③
	Chez Bruce	"	⓪⓪②
£50+	The Fire Stables	British, Modern	④④②
	Four O Nine	"	③②②
	Ransome's Dock	"	④③④
	Trinity	"	⓪⓪②
	Verta	"	④④④
	Bennett Oyster Bar	Fish & seafood	④⑤④
	Fish Place	"	②②⑤
	Enoteca Turi	Italian	⓪⓪③
	Riva	"	②②④
	San Lorenzo Fuoriporta	"	④⑤④
£40+	Bodean's	American	④⑤④
	The Abbeville	British, Modern	④③②
	Avalon	"	④③②
	The Bolingbroke	"	③③③
	The Brown Dog	"	③②②
	The Depot	"	③②⓪
	Earl Spencer	"	③③③
	Emile's	"	②⓪③
	Entrée	"	③④③
	Harrison's	"	④④③
	Lamberts	"	⓪⓪②
	The Prince Albert	"	④③②
	The Prince Of Wales	"	③④③
	Sonny's	"	④②③
	Tom Ilic	"	②②⑤
	The Victoria	"	③③②
	Fox & Grapes	British, Traditional	③④③
	Bellevue Rendez-Vous	French	②②②
	Brasserie James	"	④③④
	Le Cassoulet	"	③④③

			Rating
	Le Chardon	"	④⑤④
	Gastro	"	④⑤❸
	Upstairs Bar	"	❷⓿⓿
	Cafe Strudel	Hungarian	❸④④
	Annie's	International	④❷❷
	Brinkley's Kitchen	"	④❸❸
	Giraffe	"	⑤④④
	The Light House	"	❸❸❸
	The Ship	"	❸❸❶
	Cantinetta	Italian	④⑤❸
	Donna Margherita	"	❷❸❷
	Isola del Sole	"	❸⓿❷
	Numero Uno	"	❸❷❸
	Piccolino	"	④④④
	The Fox & Hounds	Mediterranean	❷❷❷
	La Mancha	Spanish	❸❷❸
	Butcher & Grill	Steaks & grills	④❸④
	Cattle Grid	"	④④④
	Popeseye	"	⓿❷❸
	Santa Maria del Sur	Argentinian	❷④❸
	Royal China	Chinese	④④④
	Bombay Bicycle Club	Indian	– – –
	Indian Zilla	"	❷⓿❸
	Cho-San	Japanese	❷❸④
	Tsunami	"	⓿④❸
	Suk Saran	Thai	❸④④
	Thai on the River	"	❸④❸
£35+	Belgo	Belgian	④④❸
	Alma	British, Modern	④⑤❸
	Antelope	"	❷❸❷
	The East Hill	"	❸❸❷
	The Fentiman Arms	"	❸❸❷
	The Lighthouse	"	❸❷❷
	Scoffers	"	④⓿❷
	The Tree House	"	④❸❷
	Canton Arms	British, Traditional	❷❷❶
	Côte	French	④❸❷
	Gazette	"	④④❷
	Le P'tit Normand	"	❸❷❸
	Hudsons	International	④④❸
	Telegraph	"	④④❸
	Antipasto & Pasta	Italian	❸❷❸
	Buona Sera	"	❸⓿⓿
	Ost. Antica Bologna	"	❸❸❸
	Pizza Metro	"	❸❸❷
	Valentina	"	❸❸❸
	Putney Station	Mediterranean	④④❸
	Lola Rojo	Spanish	❷❸❷
	Rebato's	"	❷⓿⓿
	Fish Club	Fish & chips	❷❷④
	Al Forno	Pizza	❸❷❷
	Eco	"	❸④❸
	Doukan	Moroccan	❸❷❷
	Bayee Village	Chinese	❸❸❷
	Dalchini	"	❸❸④
	Ma Goa	Indian	❷⓿❸
	Mango & Silk	"	④④❸

	Thai Square	*Thai*	④❸❸
£30+	La Delizia	*Italian*	❸❸❸
	Fish in a Tie	*Mediterranean*	④❷⓪
	The Little Bay	*"*	④❷⓪
	El Rincón Latino	*Spanish*	④❷❷
	Byron	*Burgers, etc*	❸❸❸
	Brady's	*Fish & chips*	❸❸❸
	Basilico	*Pizza*	❷❸④
	Firezza	*"*	❷❸④
	Cochin Brasserie	*Indian*	❷④④
	Indian Moment	*"*	❸❸④
	Nazmins	*"*	❸❷④
	Cocum	*Indian, Southern*	❸❸❸
	Wagamama	*Japanese*	④❸④
	Cah-Chi	*Korean*	❸⓪❸
	The Banana Tree Canteen	*Pan-Asian*	❸❷❸
	Amaranth	*Thai*	❷❷❸
	Fat Boy's	*"*	❸④❸
	Thai Garden	*"*	❸④④
£25+	Gail's Bread	*Sandwiches, cakes, etc*	❸❸④
	Faanoos	*Persian*	❸❸❸
	Chutney	*Indian*	❷❷❸
	Indian Ocean	*"*	❷❸❸
	Sree Krishna	*"*	⓪❷❸
	Fujiyama	*Japanese*	❸❸④
	Slurp	*"*	❸❸⑤
	Hare & Tortoise	*Pan-Asian*	❸❸❸
	The Pepper Tree	*Thai*	❸❸❸
	Talad Thai	*"*	❸❸⑤
	The Paddyfield	*Vietnamese*	❷④❸
£20+	Franco Manca	*Pizza*	⓪❸❸
	Hot Stuff	*Indian*	❷⓪❷
	Lahore Kebab House	*Pakistani*	⓪⑤④
	Mirch Masala SW16	*"*	❷④④
	Mien Tay	*Vietnamese*	⓪④④
£15+	Orange Pekoe	*Sandwiches, cakes, etc*	❸❷❷
	Pantry	*"*	❸❸❸
	Lahore Karahi	*Pakistani*	⓪④④

Outer western suburbs
Kew, Richmond, Twickenham, Teddington

£80+	The Bingham	*British, Modern*	④④❸
£60+	Petersham Hotel	*British, Modern*	❸❷❷
£50+	The Glasshouse	*British, Modern*	⓪⓪❸
	Petersham Nurseries	*"*	❷④⓪
	Rock & Rose	*"*	④❸⓪
	The Wharf	*"*	④❷❷
	Brula	*French*	❷⓪⓪
	Gaucho	*Steaks & grills*	❸④❸
	Kew Grill	*"*	❸❷④

£40+	Plane Food	British, Modern	④③④
	Chez Lindsay	French	④③④
	Ma Cuisine	"	④③④
	A Cena	Italian	❷❷❷
	Scarpetta	"	❸❸④
	don Fernando's	Spanish	❸❷❸
	Four Regions	Chinese	❸❷④
	Tangawizi	Indian	❸❸④
	Matsuba	Japanese	❷❸④
£35+	Brouge	Belgian	④❸❷
	La Buvette	French	❸❷❶
	Palmyra	Lebanese	❸❷④
	Origin Asia	Indian	❷❷❸
£30+	O'Zon	Chinese	❸④④
	Fat Boy's	Thai	❸④❸
£25+	Stein's	German	❸④❷
£15+	William Curley	Sandwiches, cakes, etc	❶❸❸

EAST

Smithfield & Farringdon (EC1)

£70+	St John	British, Traditional	❷❸④
	Club Gascon	French	❷❷❸
	Dans le Noir	International	⑤④❶
	Dose	Sandwiches, cakes, etc	❷⓿④
£60+	Hix	British, Traditional	❷❸❸
	Bleeding Heart	French	❷❷❷
	Portal	Mediterranean	❷❷❷
	Smiths (Top Floor)	Steaks & grills	④④❸
£50+	Bistro du Vin	British, Modern	④❸④
	Chiswell Street Dining Rms	"	❸❷❸
	Malmaison Brasserie	"	④❸❸
	North Road	"	❷❸④
	Smithfield Bar & Grill	"	④④④
	Café du Marché	French	❷❷❶
	Le Saint Julien	"	④❷④
	Alba	Italian	❸❷④
	Gaucho	Steaks & grills	❸④❸
	Smiths (Dining Rm)	"	④④❸
£40+	Ambassador	British, Modern	❸❸❸
	Coach & Horses	"	❷❷❸
	The Larder	"	④❸④
	The Modern Pantry	"	❸❸❸
	The Peasant	"	④❸❸
	The Well	"	❸④❸
	The English Pig	British, Traditional	❷❷④
	The Fox and Anchor	"	❸❷❶
	Bistrot Bruno Loubet	French	❷❷❸
	Comptoir Gascon	"	❷❸❷
	Le Rendezvous du Café	"	❸❷❷
	$	International	④④❸
	Fabrizio	Italian	❷❶④
	Moro	Spanish	❷❷❸
	A La Cruz	Steaks & grills	❸❸④
	Redhook	"	④④❸
	Carnevale	Vegetarian	❸❷④
	Saki	Japanese	❷❸④
	54 Farringdon Road	Malaysian	❸❸④
	Cicada	Pan-Asian	❷❷❸
£35+	Giant Robot	American	❸④❷
	Caravan	British, Modern	❷❷❶
	Vinoteca	"	❸❷❶
	Cellar Gascon	French	❸❸❷
	Santore	Italian	❸❷❸
	Amico Bio	Vegetarian	④④④
	Busaba Eathai	Thai	❸❸❷
	Cây Tre	Vietnamese	❷④④
£30+	La Porchetta Pizzeria	Italian	❸❸❸
	The Little Bay	Mediterranean	④❷⓿
	Pinchito	Spanish	④❸⓿

	Benugo	*Sandwiches, cakes, etc*	④⑤❸
	Tas	*Turkish*	④❸❸
	Pham Sushi	*Japanese*	❶④④
	Tajima Tei	*"*	❶❷④
	Banana Tree Canteen	*Pan-Asian*	❸❷❸
	Pho	*Vietnamese*	❷❸❸
£25+	Smiths (Ground Floor)	*British, Modern*	④④❷
	Cock Tavern	*British, Traditional*	❸④④
	Fish Central	*Fish & seafood*	❷❷❸
	Kolossi Grill	*Greek*	④❷❷
	The Eagle	*Mediterranean*	❸④❶
	Gail's Bakery	*Sandwiches, cakes, etc*	❸❸④
£20+	Morito	*Spanish*	❷❷❷
	Sedap	*Malaysian*	❸④⑤
£15+	Abokado	*Japanese*	④❸④
£10+	Nusa Kitchen	*Sandwiches, cakes, etc*	❷④④
	Pod	*"*	❸④④
	Spianata & Co	*"*	❷❸④
£5+	The Farm Collective	*British, Traditional*	❷❸❸
	Pizzeria Malletti	*Pizza*	❷❸❸

The City (EC2, EC3, EC4)

£80+	Rhodes 24	*British, Modern*	❸❸❸
£60+	1 Lombard Street	*British, Modern*	④④④
	Prism	*"*	④④④
	Vertigo 42	*"*	④❸❶
	Green's	*British, Traditional*	❷❷❷
	Chamberlain's	*Fish & seafood*	❸❸④
	Coq d'Argent	*French*	④⑤④
	Lutyens	*"*	❸❸④
	1901	*"*	④❸❸
	L'Anima	*Italian*	❸❸❸
	Caravaggio	*"*	④④④
	Bonds	*Mediterranean*	④④④
	Goodman City	*Steaks & grills*	❷❷❸
	Bevis Marks	*Kosher*	❸❸❸
	Mint Leaf	*Indian*	❸④❸
£50+	Barbecoa	*American*	④④④
	The Chancery	*British, Modern*	❷❸④
	The Don	*"*	❸❷❸
	High Timber	*"*	❸❷❸
	The Mercer	*"*	❸❷❸
	Northbank	*"*	❸❸❷
	Rivington Grill	*"*	❸④④
	Searcy's Brasserie	*"*	④④❸
	Paternoster Chop House	*British, Traditional*	⑤⑤④
	Catch	*Fish & seafood*	④④④
	Sweetings	*"*	❸❸❸
	Chez Gérard	*French*	⑤⑤⑤

	Sauterelle	"	④❸❸
	Vivat Bacchus	International	④④⑤
	Manicomio	Italian	❸④❸
	Refettorio	"	④④④
	Boisdale of Bishopsgate	Scottish	❸❸❸
	Eyre Brothers	Spanish	❸❸❸
	Gaucho	Steaks & grills	❸④❸
	Hawksmoor	"	❷❷❷
	Kenza	Lebanese	④④❸
	Cinnamon Kitchen	Indian	❷❸④
	City Miyama	Japanese	❷④⑤
	Soseki	"	❷❷❷
£40+	Bodean's	American	④⑤④
	The Hoxton Grill	"	❸❸❷
	Princess of Shoreditch	British, Modern	❷❸❸
	The White Swan	"	❷❸④
	George & Vulture	British, Traditional	⑤④❷
	Gow's	Fish & seafood	④❸❸
	Loch Fyne	"	④④④
	Bar Battu	French	❸❸❸
	Brasserie Blanc	"	❸❸❸
	Luc's Brasserie	"	④❸❷
	Relais de Venise L'Entrecôte	"	❷❸❸
	The Royal Exchange	"	④④❶
	28-50	"	❸❷❸
	Browns	International	⑤④④
	Bertorelli	Italian	⑤⑤⑤
	Osteria Appennino	"	❷④④
	Piccolino	"	④④④
	Taberna Etrusca	"	④④④
	Terranostra	"	❸❷④
	Rocket	Mediterranean	④④❸
	Saf	Vegetarian	❷④④
	Vanilla Black	"	❷❷④
	Goldfish City	Chinese	❷❸④
	Imperial City	"	④❸❸
	Anokha Restaurant	Indian	❷❸❸
	Mugen	Japanese	❸❷❸
	Gt Eastern Dining Room	Pan-Asian	❷❸❷
	Pacific Oriental	"	④❸❸
£35+	Café Below	British, Modern	❸❸❸
	The Fox	"	❸④❸
	London Wall Bar & Kitchen	"	④④❸
	The Restaurant at St Paul's	"	❸④❸
	Ye Olde Cheshire Cheese	British, Traditional	④④❶
	Simpson's Tavern	"	④❸❶
	Côte	French	④❸❷
	Haz	Turkish	❸❸❷
	Chinese Cricket Club	Chinese	❸④⑤
	K10	Japanese	❸❸④
	Kurumaya	"	❷❷④
	Thai Square City	Thai	④❸❸
£30+	Byron	Burgers, etc	❸❸❸
	The Diner	"	⑤⑤❸
	Natural Kitchen	Salads	❸❸❸

	ping pong	Chinese, Dim sum	④④❸	
	Bangalore Express	Indian	④❸❷	
	Wagamama	Japanese	④❸④	
£25+	Hilliard	British, Modern	❷❷❸	
	The Punch Tavern	International	❸④❸	
	The Wine Library	"	❺❸❶	
	Tsuru	Japanese	❸④④	
	Hare & Tortoise	Pan-Asian	❸❸❸	
£20+	Napket	Afternoon tea	④④❸	
	Konditor & Cook	Sandwiches, cakes, etc	❷❸❸	
	Leon	"	❸❸❸	
£15+	Hummus Bros	Mediterranean	❷❷④	
	Tortilla	Mexican/TexMex	❸❸④	
	Abokado	Japanese	④❸④	
£10+	Caffé Vergnano	Sandwiches, cakes, etc	④❸❸	
	Fuzzy's Grub	"	④④④	
	Nusa Kitchen	"	❷④④	
	Pod	"	❸④④	
	Spianata & Co	"	❷❸④	
	Chop'd	Salads	❸❸④	
	Chilango	Mexican/TexMex	❶❷④	

East End & Docklands (All E postcodes)

£90+	Viajante	Fusion	❷❷❸	
£70+	Roka	Japanese	❶❸❷	
£60+	Beach Blanket Babylon	British, Modern	❺❺❶	
	The Boundary	"	❸❸❷	
	Le Bouchon Breton	French	④❺❺	
	Galvin La Chapelle	"	❷❶❶	
	Plateau	"	❺④④	
	Les Trois Garçons	"	❸❸❶	
	Quadrato	Italian	④④❺	
£50+	Bistrotheque	British, Modern	④④❶	
	The Gun	"	❷④❷	
	The Narrow	"	④④④	
	Tompkins	"	❺④④	
	St John Bread & Wine	British, Traditional	❶❷❷	
	Curve	Fish & seafood	❸④④	
	Forman's	"	❷❷④	
	Boisdale of Canary Wharf	Scottish	④④❸	
	Gaucho	Steaks & grills	❸④❸	
	Hawksmoor	"	❷❷❷	
	MPW Steakhouse & Grill	"	④④❺	
	Café Spice Namaste	Indian	❶❶❸	
	Dockmaster's House	"	④④❸	
£40+	All Star Lanes	American	④❺❸	
	The Empress of India	British, Modern	❸❸❷	
	The Morgan Arms	"	❸❷❷	
	The Parlour Bar	"	❺❺❺	

295

Wapping Food	"	③④❶
Albion	British, Traditional	❸❸❷
The Grapes	Fish & seafood	❸❸❷
Brawn	French	❶❷❷
Browns	International	⑤④④
Giraffe	"	⑤④④
The Luxe	"	⑤⑤④
Amerigo Vespucci	Italian	④④❸
Il Bordello	"	❷⓪❷
Jamie's Italian	"	④❸④
Ibérica	Spanish	❸❸❸
Ark Fish	Fish & chips	❶❷④
Pizza East	Pizza	❸④❶
Rocket	"	④④❸
Buen Ayre	Argentinian	❶❸❸
Royal China	Chinese	❷④④
Yi-Ban	"	❸④④
Elephant Royale	Thai	④❸❸
£35+ Whitechapel Gallery	British, Modern	– – –
Canteen	British, Traditional	④④④
Real Greek	Greek	⑤⑤④
LMNT	International	❸❷⓪
La Figa	Italian	❸❷❸
Corner Room	Portuguese	– – –
Fire & Stone	Pizza	④❸❸
Haz	Turkish	❸❸❷
Lotus	Chinese	④④❸
Rasa Mudra	Indian	❷❷❸
£30+ Rochelle Canteen	British, Modern	❷⓪❷
S & M Café	British, Traditional	④④④
Al Volo	Italian	❷④❸
Byron	Burgers, etc	❸❸❸
Gourmet Pizza Co.	Pizza	❸❸❸
Hazev	Turkish	④④④
My Old Place	Chinese	❷⑤④
Shanghai	"	❸❸❶
ping pong	Chinese, Dim sum	④④❸
Memsaheb on Thames	Indian	④❷❸
Itsu	Japanese	④④④
Wagamama	"	④❸④
Rosa's	Thai	❸④❸
Green Papaya	Vietnamese	❷❷❷
Namo	"	❸❸❸
Viet Grill	"	❷④❷
£25+ Frizzante at City Farm	Italian	❸❸❷
Stringray Globe Café	Mediterranean	④④④
Faulkner's	Fish & chips	❷❷❸
Wahaca	Mexican/TexMex	④❸❸
Mangal 1	Turkish	⓪❷❸
Little Georgia Café	Georgian	❸❸❸
Clifton	Indian	❸❸❸
Needoo	Pakistani	⓪❸④
New Tayyabs	"	⓪④❸
Sông Quê	Vietnamese	❷⑤⑤
Viet Hoa	"	❷④④

£20+	Leon	*Sandwiches, cakes, etc*	❸❸❸
	Gourmet San	*Chinese*	❷④⑤
	Lahore Kebab House	*Pakistani*	❶⑤④
	Mirch Masala	*"*	❷④④
	Mien Tay	*Vietnamese*	❶④④
£15+	Tortilla	*Mexican/TexMex*	❸❸④
£10+	E Pellicci	*Italian*	❸❷❶
	Spianata & Co	*Sandwiches, cakes, etc*	❷❸④
	Chop'd	*Salads*	❸❸④
	Sweet & Spicy	*Indian*	❷❷⑤
£5+	Brick Lane Beigel Bake	*Sandwiches, cakes, etc*	❶④⑤

MAPS

MAP 1 – LONDON OVERVIEW

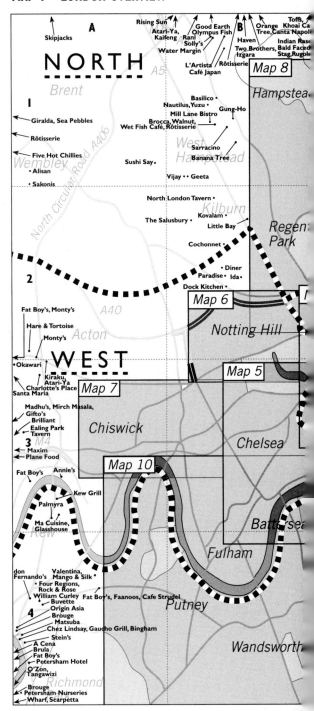

A

Skipjacks

NORTH

Brent

A5

Rising Sun
Atari-Ya, Kaifeng
Good Earth
Rani Olympus Fish
Solly's
Water Margin

B
Orange Tree, Canta Napoli
Toffs, Khoai Ca
Haven
Two Brothers, Izgara
Indian Rasc
Bald Faced
Stag, Rugbel

L'Artista
Café Japan
Rôtisserie

Map 8

Hampstea

I

Giralda, Sea Pebbles

Rôtisserie

Five Hot Chillies
• Alisan

Wembley

North Circular Road A406

• Sakonis

Basilico •
Nautilus, Yuzu
Mill Lane Bistro
Brocca, Walnut,
Wet Fish Café, Rôtisserie

Gung-Ho

West Hampstead

Sushi Say •

Sarracino
Banana Tree

Vijay • • Geeta

North London Tavern •

Kovalam •

Kilburn

The Salusbury •

Little Bay •

Regen Park

Cochonnet •

2

A40

Acton

• Diner
Paradise • Ida •
Dock Kitchen •

Map 6

Notting Hill

Fat Boy's, Monty's

Hare & Tortoise

Monty's

WEST

• Okawari
Kiraku, Atari-Ya,
Charlotte's Place
Santa Maria

Map 7

Map 5

Madhu's, Mirch Masala,
Gifto's
Brilliant
Ealing Park
Tavern

Chiswick

Chelsea

3

M4

← Maxim
← Plane Food

Fat Boy's
Annie's

Map 10

← Kew Grill

Palmyra

Ma Cuisine,
Glasshouse

Kew

Battersea

Fulham

don
Fernando's
Valentina,
Mango & Silk
← Four Regions,
Rock & Rose
← William Curley
Buvette
Fat Boy's, Faanoos, Cafe Strudel

Putney

4

← Origin Asia
← Brouge
← Matsuba
← Chez Lindsay, Gaucho Grill, Bingham
← Stein's
← A Cena
← Brula
← Fat Boy's
← Petersham Hotel
← O'Zon,
Tangawizi

Wandsworth

← Brouge
← Petersham Nurseries
← Wharf, Scarpetta

Richmond

MAP 1 – LONDON OVERVIEW

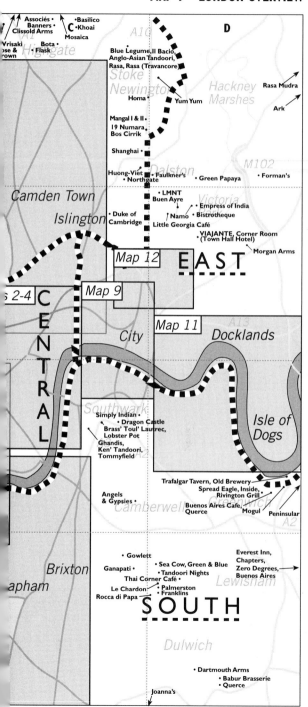

Associés •
Banners •
Clissold Arms
Vrisaki •
ose &
rown
• Bota •
• Flask
Highgate

C • Basilico
• Khoai
Mosaica

D

A10

Blue Legume, Il Bacio,
Anglo-Asian Tandoori,
Rasa, Rasa (Travancore)

Stoke
Newington
• Homa
Yum Yum

Hackney
Marshes
Rasa Mudra →
Ark →

Mangal I & II •
19 Numara,
Bos Cirrik

Shanghai •

Huong-Viet •
• Northgate

Dalston
• Faulkner's
• Green Papaya

M102
• Forman's

Camden Town

Islington

Victoria
• LMNT
Buen Ayre •
↑ Namo • Bistrotheque
Little Georgia Café

• Duke of
Cambridge

• Empress of India

VIAJANTE, Corner Room
• (Town Hall Hotel)
Morgan Arms

Map 12

EAST

s 2-4 C
E
N
T
R
A
L

Map 9

Map 11

City

A13
Docklands

Southwark

Simply Indian •
• Dragon Castle
Brass' Toul' Lautrec,
Lobster Pot,
Ghandis,
Ken' Tandoori,
Tommyfield

Isle of
Dogs

Trafalgar Tavern, Old Brewery
Spread Eagle, Inside,
Rivington Grill
Buenos Aires Cafe,
Querce   Mogul   Peninsular

Angels
& Gypsies •

Camberwell

A2

Brixton

apham

• Gowlett

Ganapati •
• Sea Cow, Green & Blue
• Tandoori Nights
Thai Corner Café •
Le Chardon • • Palmerston
Rocca di Papa • Franklins

Everest Inn,
Chapters,
Zero Degrees, →
Buenos Aires

Lewisham

SOUTH

Dulwich

• Dartmouth Arms
• Babur Brasserie
• Querce

Joanna's

MAP 2 – WEST END OVERVIEW

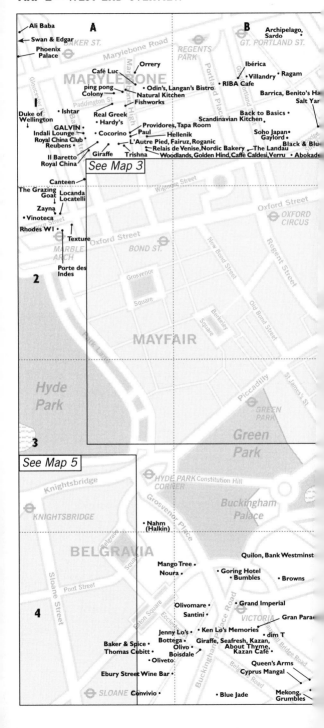

A

Ali Baba
Swan & Edgar
Phoenix Palace

BAKER ST.

Marylebone Road

REGENTS PARK

Orrery

Café Luc

MARYLEBONE

ping pong
Colony
Natural Kitchen
Fishworks

Odin's, Langan's Bistro

Duke of Wellington

Ishtar

Real Greek
Hardy's

GALVIN
Indali Lounge
Royal China Club
Reubens

Cocorino

Providores, Tapa Room
Paul
Hellenik

L'Autre Pied, Fairuz, Roganic
Relais de Venise, Nordic Bakery
Woodlands, Golden Hind, Caffè Caldesi, Verru

Il Baretto
Royal China

Giraffe

Trishna

See Map 3

Canteen

The Grazing Goat
Locanda Locatelli

Zayna

Vinoteca

Rhodes W1

Texture

MARBLE ARCH

Oxford Street

BOND ST.

OXFORD CIRCUS

Grosvenor

2

Porte des Indes

Grosvenor Square

New Bond Street

Old Bond Street

Regent Street

MAYFAIR

Berkeley Square

B

Archipelago, Sardo

GT. PORTLAND ST.

Ibérica
Villandry
Ragam
RIBA Café

Barrica, Benito's Ha
Salt Yar

Back to Basics

Scandinavian Kitchen

Soho Japan
Gaylord
Black & Blu

The Landau
Abokad

Hyde Park

Piccadilly

St James's St.

GREEN PARK

3

Green Park

See Map 5

Knightsbridge

HYDE PARK CORNER

Constitution Hill

Grosvenor Place

KNIGHTSBRIDGE

Buckingham Palace

Nahm (Halkin)

BELGRAVIA

Mango Tree
Noura

Quilon, Bank Westminst

Goring Hotel
Bumbles

Browns

4

Sloane Street

Olivomare
Santini

Grand Imperial

VICTORIA

Gran Para

Jenny Lo's
Bottega
Olivo
Boisdale

Ken Lo's Memories

dim T

Giraffe, Seafresh, Kazan,
About Thyme,
Kazan Café

Baker & Spice
Thomas Cubitt

Oliveto

Ebury Street Wine Bar

SLOANE

Convivio

Queen's Arms
Cyprus Mangal

Mekong,
Grumbles

Blue Jade

MAP 2 – WEST END OVERVIEW

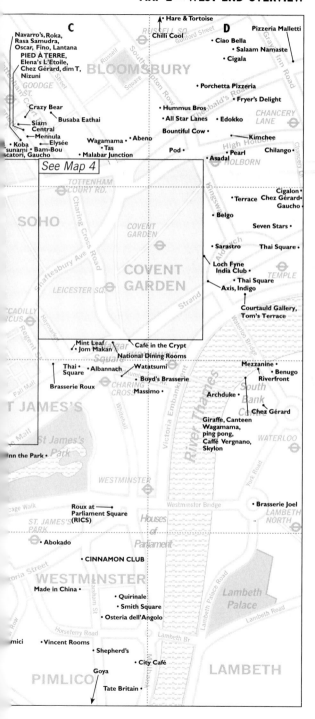

C

Navarro's, Roka,
Rasa Samudra,
Oscar, Fino, Lantana
PIED À TERRE,
Elena's L'Etoile,
Chez Gérard, dim T,
Nizuni

GOODGE
ST.

BLOOMSBURY

Crazy Bear

Siam
Central   Busaba Eathai
Mennula
Elysée
Koba   Bam-Bou
sunami   Wagamama • Abeno
scatori, Gaucho   • Tas
• Malabar Junction

See Map 4

TOTTENHAM
COURT RD.

SOHO

COVENT
GARDEN

Charing Cross Road

COVENT
GARDEN

LEICESTER SQ.

Shaftesbury Ave

D

Pizzeria Malletti

• Chilli Cool
• Ciao Bella
• Salaam Namaste
• Cigala

• Porchetta Pizzeria
• Fryer's Delight
• Hummus Bros
• All Star Lanes   • Edokko

Bountiful Cow •

Pod •

• Hare & Tortoise

CHANCERY
LANE

—Kimchee

• Pearl   Chilango•
• Asadal

HOLBORN

High Holborn

Cigalon •
• Terrace Chez Gérard•
                    Gaucho
• Belgo

Seven Stars •

• Sarastro   Thai Square •

Loch Fyne
India Club •

TEMPLE

• Thai Square
Axis, Indigo

Courtauld Gallery,
Tom's Terrace

Strand

Mint Leaf
• Jom Makan   ` Café in the Crypt

National Dining Rooms

PICCADILLY
CIRCUS

Regent Street

Haymarket

Thai •
Square • Albannach

Brasserie Roux

Watatsumi
Boyd's Brasserie
Massimo •

CHARING
CROSS

Mezzanine •
                • Benugo
                Riverfront

Archduke •

South
Bank

• Chez Gérard

ST JAMES'S

Pall Mall

St James's
Park

nn the Park •

WESTMINSTER

Roux at ——
Parliament Square
(RICS)

Giraffe, Canteen
Wagamama,
ping pong,
Caffè Vergnano,
Skylon

River Thames

Waterloo Bridge

WATERLOO

Victoria Embankment

Westminster Bridge

Houses

• Brasserie Joel

LAMBETH
NORTH

age Walk

ST. JAMES'S
PARK

• Abokado

• CINNAMON CLUB

of

Parliament

oria Street

WESTMINSTER

Made in China •

• Quirinale
• Smith Square
• Osteria dell'Angolo

Marsham St

Horseferry Road

amici • Vincent Rooms

• Shepherd's

PIMLICO

Goya

Tate Britain •

s Row

• City Café

Lambeth Br

Lambeth Palace Road

Lambeth
Palace

Lambeth Road

LAMBETH

MAP 3 – MAYFAIR, ST JAMES'S & WEST SOHO

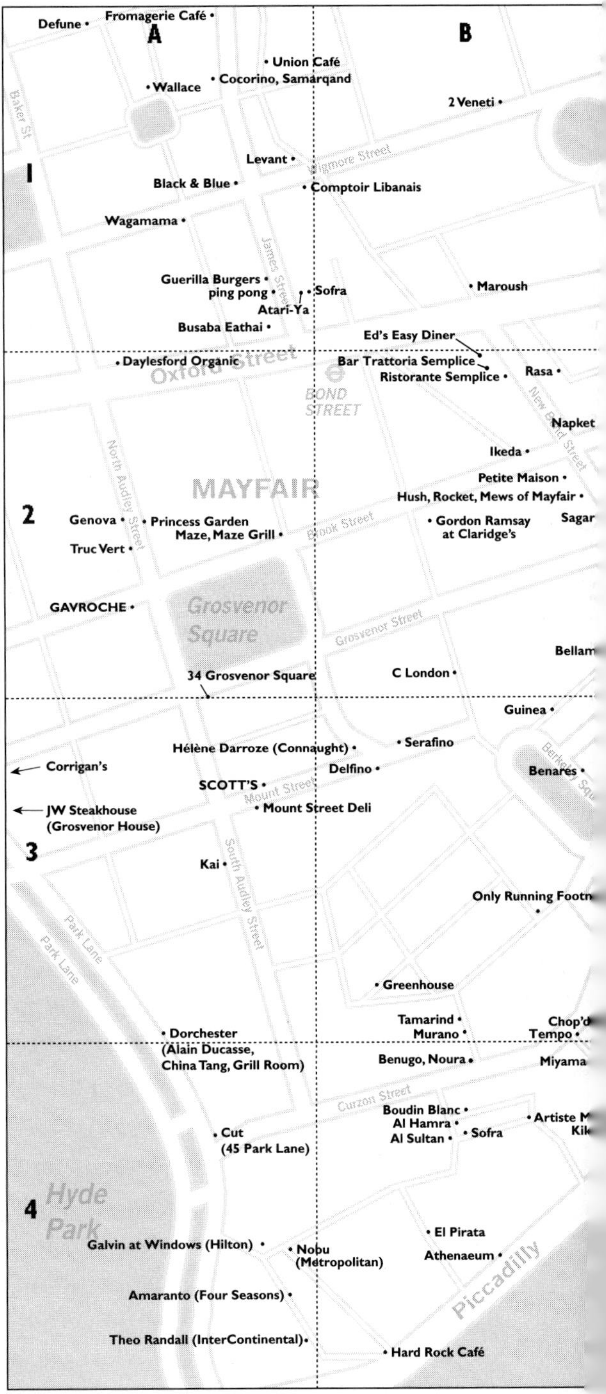

A

B

Defune •

Fromagerie Café •

• Union Café

• Cocorino, Samarqand

• Wallace

2 Veneti •

Levant •

Black & Blue •

• Comptoir Libanais

Wagamama •

Guerilla Burgers •
ping pong • • Sofra

• Maroush

Atari-Ya •

Busaba Eathai •

Ed's Easy Diner

• Daylesford Organic

Bar Trattoria Semplice

Ristorante Semplice • Rasa •

BOND STREET

Napket

Ikeda •

Petite Maison •

MAYFAIR

Hush, Rocket, Mews of Mayfair •

Genova • • Princess Garden

• Gordon Ramsay

Sagar

Maze, Maze Grill •

at Claridge's

Truc Vert •

GAVROCHE •

Grosvenor Square

Bellam

34 Grosvenor Square

C London •

Guinea •

Hélène Darroze (Connaught) •

• Serafino

← Corrigan's

Delfino •

Benares •

SCOTT'S •

← JW Steakhouse
(Grosvenor House)

• Mount Street Deli

Kai •

Only Running Footm

• Greenhouse

Tamarind •

Chop'd

Murano •

Tempo •

• Dorchester
(Alain Ducasse,
China Tang, Grill Room)

Benugo, Noura •

Miyama

Boudin Blanc •

Al Hamra •

• Artiste M

• Cut
(45 Park Lane)

Al Sultan •

• Sofra

Kik

Hyde Park

• El Pirata

Galvin at Windows (Hilton) •

• Nobu
(Metropolitan)

Athenaeum •

Amaranto (Four Seasons) •

Piccadilly

Theo Randall (InterContinental) •

• Hard Rock Café

MAP 3 – MAYFAIR, ST JAMES'S & WEST SOHO

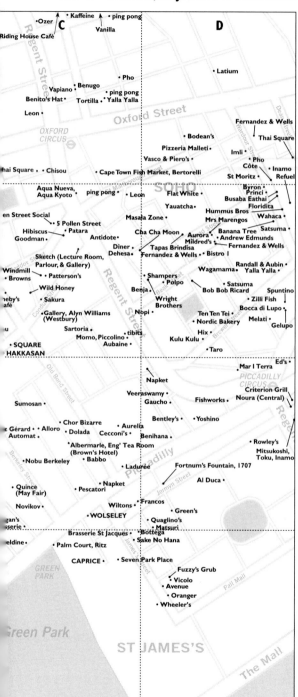

C   **D**

•Ozer   •Kaffeine   •ping pong

Riding House Café   Vanilla

•Pho   •Latium

Vapiano•   •Benugo
Benito's Hat•   •ping pong   •Yalla Yalla
   Tortilla•
Leon •

OXFORD   Oxford Street
CIRCUS

   Fernandez & Wells
   •Bodean's   Thai Square

   Pizzeria Malleti•   Imli •
   Vasco & Piero's•   •Pho
hai Square • • Chisou   •Côte
   • Cape Town Fish Market, Bertorelli   •Inamo
   St Moritz •   Refuel

Aqua Nueva,   SOHO   Byron•
Aqua Kyoto   ping pong•   •Leon   Flat White   Princi•
   Busaba Eathai
   Yauatcha•   Floridita•
en Street Social   Hummus Bros   Wahaca•
   •5 Pollen Street   Masala Zone•   Mrs Marengos
Hibiscus•   •Patara   Banana Tree   Satsuma•
Goodman•   Antidote•   Cha Cha Moon•   Aurora•   Andrew Edmunds
   Diner•   Mildred's•   Fernandez & Wells
   Dehesa•   Tapas Brindisa•   •Bistro 1
Sketch (Lecture Room,   Fernandez & Wells
Parlour, & Gallery)   Randall & Aubin •
Windmill•   •Patterson's   Shampers•   Wagamama•   Yalla Yalla •
•Browns   •Polpo
   •Wild Honey   Benja•   •Satsuma   Spuntino•
neby's   •Sakura   Bob Bob Ricard   Zilli Fish•
afé   Gallery, Alyn Williams   Wright   Bocca di Lupo •
   (Westbury)   Brothers•   Melati •
u   Nopi •   Ten Ten Tei •   Gelupo•
   Sartoria•   •tibits   •Nordic Bakery
   Momo, Piccolino•   Hix •
•SQUARE   Aubaine •   Kulu Kulu •
HAKKASAN   •Taro

   Ed's •
   Mar I Terra •
   Napket•   PICCADILLY
   CIRCUS
   Veeraswamy •   Criterion Grill
Sumosan •   Gaucho •   Fishworks•   Noura (Central) •
   Bentley's •   •Yoshino
 Gérard •   •Chor Bizarre   •Aurelia
Automat•   •Dolada   Cecconi's•   •Rowley's
   Benihana•   Mitsukoshi,
•Nobu Berkeley   •Albermarle, Eng' Tea Room   Toku, Inamo
   (Brown's Hotel)   •Babbo
   •Ladurée   Fortnum's Fountain, 1707
•Quince
(May Fair)   •Napket   Al Duca •
   •Pescatori
Novikov•   Wiltons •   •Francos
gan's   •WOLSELEY   •Green's
sserie •   •Quaglino's
   Brasserie St Jacques •   •Bottega   •Matsuri
eldine •   •Palm Court, Ritz   •Sake No Hana

   CAPRICE •   •Seven Park Place
GREEN   •Fuzzy's Grub
PARK   •Vicolo
   Avenue•
   •Oranger
   •Wheeler's

Green Park   ST JAMES'S   The Mall

MAP 4 – EAST SOHO, CHINATOWN & COVENT GARDEN

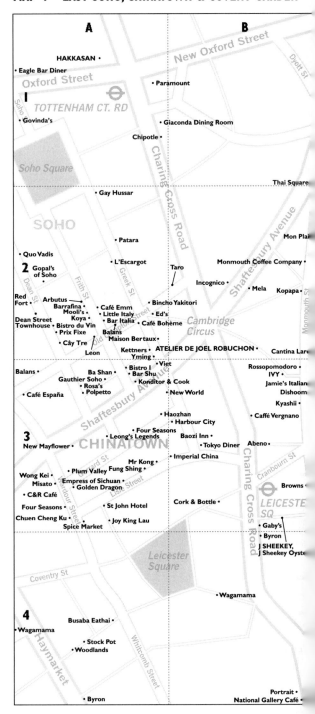

A   **B**

New Oxford Street

Dyott St

• HAKKASAN •

• Eagle Bar Diner

Oxford Street

• Paramount

1

TOTTENHAM CT. RD

• Govinda's

• Giaconda Dining Room

Chipotle •

Charing Cross Road

Soho Square

Thai Square

• Gay Hussar

SOHO

Shaftesbury Avenue

Mon Plai

• Patara

• Quo Vadis

2 Gopal's
     of Soho

• L'Escargot

Taro

Monmouth Coffee Company •

Incognico •

• Mela   Kopapa •

Red
Fort   • Arbutus
     Barrafina •
     Mooli's •   Koya
Dean Street
Townhouse • Bistro du Vin
     • Prix Fixe
     • Cây Tre
           Leon

Greek St

Frith St

Dean St

Monmouth St

• Café Emm
• Little Italy   • Ed's
• Bar Italia • Café Bohème
Balans
Maison Bertaux •
Kettners •
Yming •   ATELIER DE JOEL ROBUCHON •

• Bincho Yakitori

Cambridge
Circus

Cantina Lare

Balans •

Gauthier Soho •
     • Rosa's
• Café España   • Polpetto

Ba Shan •
• Bistro 1
• Bar Shu
• Konditor & Cook
     • New World

• Viet

Rossopomodoro •
     IVY •
Jamie's Italian
     Dishoom

Kyashii •

• Caffè Vergnano

Shaftesbury Avenue

• Haozhan
• Harbour City

3
New Mayflower •

Wardour St

• Four Seasons
• Leong's Legends   Baozi Inn •

CHINATOWN

Mr Kong •

Tokyo Diner

• Imperial China

Abeno •

Charing Cross Road

Cranbourn St

Wong Kei •
Misato •
     • Plum Valley Fung Shing •
• Empress of Sichuan
     • Golden Dragon
• C&R Café

Four Seasons •

Chuen Cheng Ku •
     Spice Market

• St John Hotel

Gerrard St

Newport Street

Cork & Bottle •

• Joy King Lau

Browns •

LEICESTE
SQ

• Gaby's
• Byron

J SHEEKEY,
J Sheekey Oyste

Leicester
Square

Coventry St

• Wagamama

4
• Wagamama

Busaba Eathai •

Whitcomb Street

• Stock Pot
• Woodlands

Haymarket

• Byron

Portrait •
National Gallery Café •

MAP 4 – EAST SOHO, CHINATOWN & COVENT GARDEN

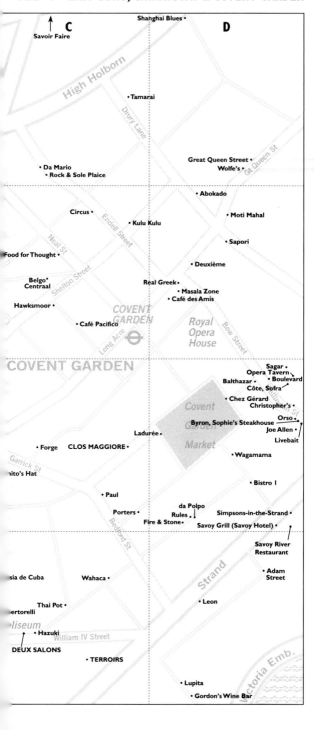

MAP 5 – KNIGHTSBRIDGE, CHELSEA & SOUTH KENSINGTON

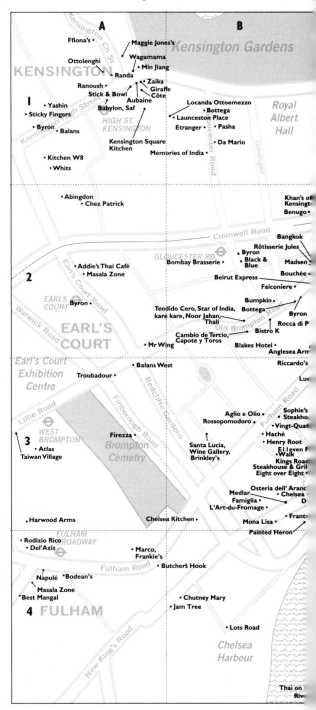

A

B

Kensington Gardens

KENSINGTON

Ffiona's •

• Maggie Jones's

Ottolenghi •

• Wagamama

• Min Jiang

• Randa

Ranoush •

• Zaika

Stick & Bowl •

Giraffe

Côte

Aubaine •

Babylon, Saf •

• Yashin

• Sticky Fingers

• Byron

• Balans

HIGH ST. KENSINGTON

Kensington Square Kitchen

Memories of India •

• Locanda Ottoemezzo

• Bottega

• Launceston Place

Etranger • • Pasha

• Da Mario

Royal Albert Hall

• Kitchen W8

• Whits

• Abingdon

• Chez Patrick

Khan's of Kensingt•

Benugo •

Cromwell Road

Bangkok

GLOUCESTER RD.

• Addie's Thai Café

• Masala Zone

• Byron

Black & Blue

Rôtisserie Jules

Madsen •

EARLS COURT

Byron •

Bombay Brasserie •

Beirut Express •

Bouchée •

Falconiere •

EARL'S COURT

Bumpkin •

Tendido Cero, Star of India, kare kare, Noor Jahan, Thali

Bottega

• Byron

Rocca di P

Bistro K •

Cambio de Tercio, Capote y Toros

Blakes Hotel •

Anglesea Arm

• Mr Wing

Riccardo's

Lu•

• Balans West

Earl's Court Exhibition Centre

Troubadour •

Aglio e Olio •

Rossopomodoro •

Sophie's

• Steakho

• Vingt-Quat

• Haché

• Henry Root

El even F

•Walk

Kings Road Steakhouse & Gril

Eight over Eight •

WEST BROMPTON

• Atlas

Taiwan Village

Firezza •

Brompton Cemetery

Santa Lucia, Wine Gallery, Brinkley's

Osteria dell' Aranc

Medlar • • Chelsea

Famiglia •

L'Art-du-Fromage •

D

• Harwood Arms

Chelsea Kitchen •

Mona Lisa •

Painted Heron

• Frant

• Rodizio Rico

• Del'Aziz

FULHAM ROADWAY

• Marco, Frankie's

Fulham Road

• Butcher's Hook

Napulé •

•Bodean's

Masala Zone

•Best Mangal

4 FULHAM

• Chutney Mary

• Jam Tree

• Lots Road

Chelsea Harbour

Thai on Riv

MAP 5 – KNIGHTSBRIDGE, CHELSEA & SOUTH KENSINGTON

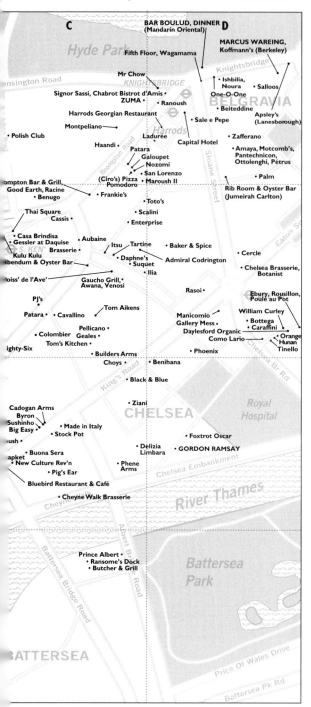

Hyde Park

BAR BOULUD, DINNER D
(Mandarin Oriental)

C

MARCUS WAREING,
Koffmann's (Berkeley)

Fifth Floor, Wagamama

Knightsbridge

Mr Chow

KNIGHTSBRIDGE

• Ishbilia,
Noura   • Salloos
One-O-One

ensington Road

Signor Sassi, Chabrot Bistrot d'Amis •
ZUMA •   • Ranoush

BELGRAVIA

• Beiteddine

Harrods Georgian Restaurant

• Sale e Pepe

Apsley's
(Lanesborough)

Montpeliano

Harrods

• Polish Club

Ladurée

• Zafferano

Haandi •

Capital Hotel

• Amaya, Motcomb's,
Pantechnicon,
Ottolenghi, Pétrus

Patara •
Galoupet
Nozomi
• San Lorenzo

• Palm

ompton Bar & Grill,
Good Earth, Racine
• Benugo

(Ciro's) Pizza
Pomodoro
• Maroush II

Rib Room & Oyster Bar
(Jumeirah Carlton)

• Frankie's

• Toto's

Thai Square

• Scalini

Cassis •

• Enterprise

Eaton S

• Casa Brindisa
• Gessler at Daquise
S. KEN'   Brasserie •
ibendum & Oyster Bar

• Aubaine

Itsu   Tartine
Daphne's
• Suquet

• Baker & Spice
Admiral Codrington

• Cercle

• Chelsea Brasserie,
Botanist

• Ilia

oiss' de l'Ave'

Gaucho Grill,•
Awana, Venosi

Rasoi •

Ebury, Roussillon,
Poule au Pot

PJ's

• Patara • • Cavallino

Tom Aikens

Manicomio
Gallery Mess •

William Curley

• Bottega
• Caraffini

Pellicano •
• Colombier   Geales •
Tom's Kitchen •

Daylesford Organic
Como Lario

• Orange
Hunan
Tinello

ighty-Six

• Builders Arms

• Phoenix

Choys •   • Benihana

King's Road

• Black & Blue

Royal
Hospital

• Ziani

Cadogan Arms
Byron
Sushinho •
Big Easy •

CHELSEA

• Made in Italy
• Stock Pot

• Foxtrot Oscar

oush

apket

• Buona Sera
• New Culture Rev'n

• Pig's Ear

• Delizia
Limbara

• GORDON RAMSAY

Chelsea Embankment

• Phene
Arms

Bluebird Restaurant & Café

• Cheyne Walk Brasserie

River Thames

Prince Albert •
• Ransome's Dock
• Butcher & Grill

Battersea
Park

BATTERSEA

Price Of Wales Drive

Battersea Pk Rd

MAP 6 – NOTTING HILL & BAYSWATER

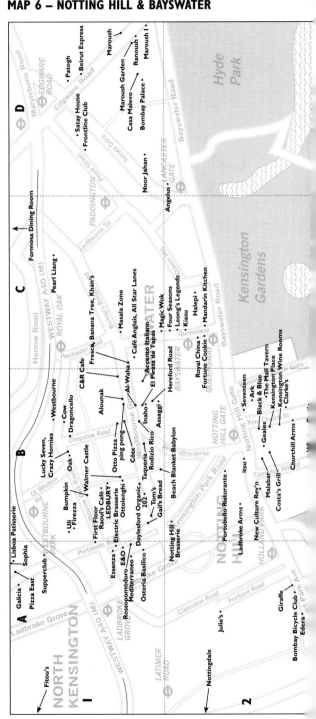

NORTH KENSINGTON

Hyde Park

Kensington Gardens

PADDINGTON

BAYSWATER

NOTTING HILL GATE

NOTTING HILL

Marylebone Road
Edgware Road
EDGWARE ROAD
Sussex Gdns
Harrow Road
WESTWAY A40 (M)
ROYAL OAK
Porchester Rd
Bishops Bridge Rd
Queensway
Bayswater Road
LANCASTER GATE
PADDINGTON
Eastbourne Ter
Praed Street

Maroush
Beirut Express
Ranoush
Maroush 1
Maroush Garden
Patogh
Casa Malevo
Bombay Palace
Satay House
Frontline Club
Noor Jahan
Angus•
Formosa Dining Room
Pearl Liang
Fresco, Banana Tree, Khan's
Masala Zone
Café Anglais, All Star Lanes
Accento Italiano
El Pirata de Tapas
Magic Wok
Four Seasons
Leong's Legends
Kiasu
Halepi
Mandarin Kitchen
Royal China
Fortune Cookie
Hereford Road
C&R Cafe
Al-Waha
Alounak
Inaho
Assaggi
Beach Blanket Babylon
Taqueria
Rodizio Rico
ping pong
Otto Pizza
Côte
Tom's
Gail's Bread
Daylesford Organic
201
Ottolenghi
Electric Brasserie
Raoul's Café
LEDBURY
First Floor
Bumpkin
Uli
Firezza
Oak
Walmer Castle
Lucky Seven, Crazy Homies
Cow
Dragoncello
Westbourne
Essenza
E&O
Rossopomodoro
Mediterraneo
Osteria Basilico
Notting Hill Brasserie
Lisboa Patisserie
Sophia
Galicia
Pizza East
Supperclub
Fitou's
Julie's
Nottingdale
Giraffe
Bombay Bicycle Club
Edera
Ladbroke Arms
Portobello Ristorante
New Culture Rev'n
Costa's Grill
Malabar
Seventeen
itsu
Geales
Ark
Black & Blue
The Mall Tavern
Kensington Place
Kensington Wine Rooms
Clarke's
Churchill Arms
Ladbroke Grove
WESTWAY A40 (M)
LATIMER ROAD
HOLLAND PARK
Clarendon Road
Portland Road
Kensington Park Road
Portobello Rd
Gt Western Rd
Chepstow Road
Pembridge Rd
Westbourne Grove
Notting Hill Gate
Campden Hill Rd
Kensington Church St
Ladbroke Grove

MAP 7 – HAMMERSMITH & CHISWICK

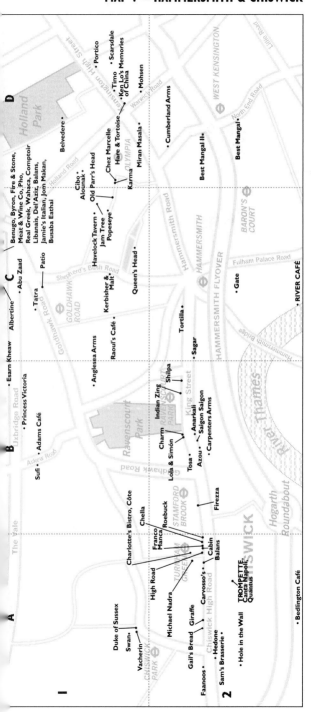

Holland Park

Benugo, Byron, Fire & Stone, Meat & Wine Co, Pho, Real Greek, Wahaca, Comptoir Libanais, Del'Aziz, Balans, Jamie's Italian, Jom Makan, Busaba Eathai

Portico •
• Scarsdale
• Timo
• Ken Lo's Memories of China
• Mohsen

WEST KENSINGTON

Belvedere •

Chez Marcelle •
Hare & Tortoise •
Cibo •
Alounak •
Old Parr's Head •
Karma •
OLYMPIA
Miran Masala •

• Cumberland Arms

Abu Zaad •
Albertine •
• Esarn Kheaw
• Tatra
• Patio

Havelock Tavern •
Jam Tree •
Popeseye •

Best Mangal II •

• Princess Victoria

Suft •
• Adams Café

Kerbisher & Malt •

Queen's Head •

Raoul's Café •

Anglesea Arms •

HAMMERSMITH

Best Mangal II •

Uxbridge Road

GOLDHAWK ROAD

Shepherd's Bush Road

Holland Road

Warwick Road

North End Road

Little Road

Tortilla •

• Gate

HAMMERSMITH FLYOVER

Fulham Palace Road

BARON'S COURT

• RIVER CAFÉ

Shilpa •
Indian Zing •
Charm •
Lola & Simón •
Tosa •
Azou •

King Street

Anarkali •
Saigon Saigon •
Carpenters Arms •

Sagar •

Ravenscourt Park

Askew Road

Goldhawk Road

The Vale

Charlotte's Bistro, Côte
Chella •

Franco Manca
Roebuck •

Firezza •

STAMFORD BROOK

TURNHAM GREEN

High Road

Michael Nadra •

Gail's Bread •
Giraffe •

Faanoos •
Hedone •
Sam's Brasserie •

Carvosso's •
Cabin •
Balans •

TROMPETTE,
Canta Napoli,
Quantus

CHISWICK

Hogarth Roundabout

River Thames

Hammersmith Bridge

• Hole in the Wall

• Bedlington Café

Duke of Sussex •
Swan •

Vacherin •

CHISWICK PARK

Chiswick High Road

MAP 8 – HAMPSTEAD, CAMDEN TOWN & ISLINGTON

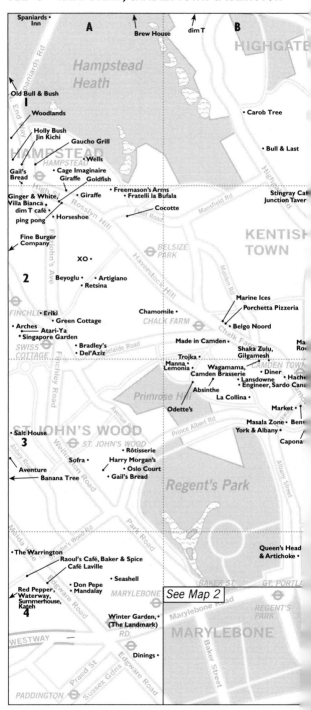

Spaniards • Inn

A

Brew House ↑

↑ dim T

B

HIGHGATE

Spaniards Rd

Hampstead Heath

• Carob Tree

← Old Bull & Bush

Woodlands

North End Rd

HAMPSTEAD

• Bull & Last

Holly Bush
Jin Kichi
Gaucho Grill

• Wells

Gail's Bread

• Cage Imaginaire
Giraffe   Goldfish

Highgate Rd

Stingray Ca
Junction Taver

Ginger & White,
Villa Bianca
dim T café
ping pong

• Giraffe

• Freemason's Arms
Fratelli la Bufala

Mansfield Rd

Rosslyn Hill

• Horseshoe

• Cocotte

KENTISH

BELSIZE
PARK

TOWN

Fine Burger
Company

XO •

Haverstock Hill

1

2

Maiden Rd

Beyoglu •
• Retsina

• Artigiano

Marine Ices
Porchetta Pizzeria

Chamomile •

FINCHLE • Eriki

• Green Cottage

CHALK FARM

Chalk Farm Rd

• Belgo Noord

• Arches
Atari-Ya
• Singapore Garden

SWISS
COTTAGE

Made in Camden •

Finchley Road

• Bradley's
• Del'Aziz

Adelaide Road

Shaka Zulu,
Gilgamesh

Ma
Ro

Trojka •

Manna •
Lemonia

Wagamama,
Camden Brasserie

CAMDEN TOWN

• Diner
• Lansdowne

Hache

• Engineer, Sardo Cana

Primrose Hill

Absinthe

La Collina •

ST. JOHN'S WOOD

Avenue Rd

Prince Albert Rd

Odette's •

Market •

Masala Zone • Ben
York & Albany •

Albany Street

Capona

• Salt House

ST. JOHN'S WOOD

3

Abbey Rd

Wellington Road

St John's Wood Rd

Sofra •

• Rôtisserie

Harry Morgan's •

← Aventure

← Banana Tree

• Oslo Court

• Gail's Bread

Regent's Park

Park Road

Queen's Head
& Artichoke •

• The Warrington

Raoul's Café, Baker & Spice
Café Laville

Maida Vale

St John's Wood Rd

• Don Pepe
• Mandalay

• Seashell

MARYLEBONE

BAKER ST.

GT. PORTLA

See Map 2

REGENT'S
PARK

Red Pepper,
Waterway,
Summerhouse,
Kateh

4

Edgware Road

Winter Garden, •
(The Landmark)

Marylebone Road

MARYLEBONE

RD.

Baker Street

WESTWAY

Dinings •

PADDINGTON

Praed St

Sussex Gdns

MAP 8 – HAMPSTEAD, CAMDEN TOWN & ISLINGTON

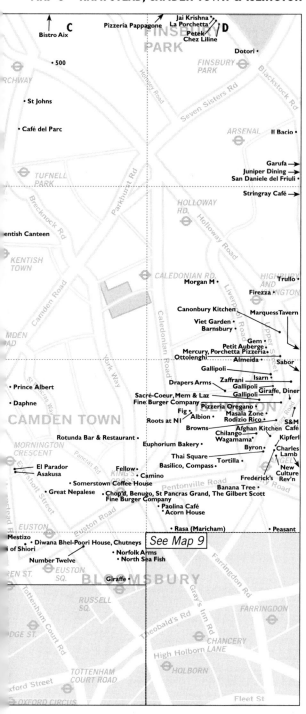

C

Bistro Aix

Pizzeria Pappagone

Jai Krishna
La Porchetta
Petek
Chez Liline

D

FINSBURY PARK

Dotori

• 500

FINSBURY PARK

RCHWAY

Seven Sisters Rd

Blackstock Rd

• St Johns

• Café del Parc

ARSENAL

Il Bacio •

Garufa →
Juniper Dining →
San Daniele del Friuli •

TUFNELL PARK

Holloway Road

Stringray Café →

Brecknock Rd

Parkhurst Rd

HOLLOWAY RD.

entish Canteen

KENTISH TOWN

Camden Road

CALEDONIAN RD.

Morgan M •

HIGHBURY AND NGTON

Trullo •

Firezza •

MDEN AD

York Way

Caledonian Road

Liverpool Road

Canonbury Kitchen

Viet Garden •
Barnsbury •

Marquess Tavern

Gem •
Petit Auberge •
Mercury, Porchetta Pizzeria •
Ottolenghi •

Almeida •

Sabor →

Gallipoli •

Zaffrani

Isarn

• Prince Albert

Drapers Arms •

Gallipoli

• Daphne

Sacré-Coeur, Mem & Laz •
Fine Burger Company •

Gallipoli

Giraffe, Diner

Pizzeria Oregano •

CAMDEN TOWN

Fig •

Albion •

Masala Zone •
Rodizio Rico •

S&M

Roots at N1 •

MORNINGTON CRESCENT

Rotunda Bar & Restaurant •

Browns •

Afghan Kitchen Café

Chilango •
Wagamama •

Kipferl

Euphorium Bakery •

Byron •

Charles Lamb

Thai Square •

Tortilla •

New Culture Rev'n

El Parador •
Asakusa

Fellow •

Basilico, Compass •

Camino

Pentonville Road

Frederick's •

• Somerstown Coffee House

Banana Tree •

• Great Nepalese

• Chop'd, Benugo, St Pancras Grand, The Gilbert Scott
Fine Burger Company

• Paolina Café
• Acorn House

EUSTON

Euston Road

Mestizo •
• Diwana Bhel-Poori House, Chutneys
of Shiori

• Rasa (Maricham)

• Peasant

See Map 9

Number Twelve

• Norfolk Arms
• North Sea Fish

REN ST.

EUSTON SQ.

BLOOMSBURY

Giraffe •

Farringdon Rd

RUSSELL SQ.

Gray's Inn Rd

FARRINGDON

DGE ST.

Theobald's Rd

CHANCERY LANE

xford Street

TOTTENHAM COURT ROAD

High Holborn LANE

HOLBORN

OXFORD CIRCUS

Fleet St

MAP 9 – THE CITY

See Map

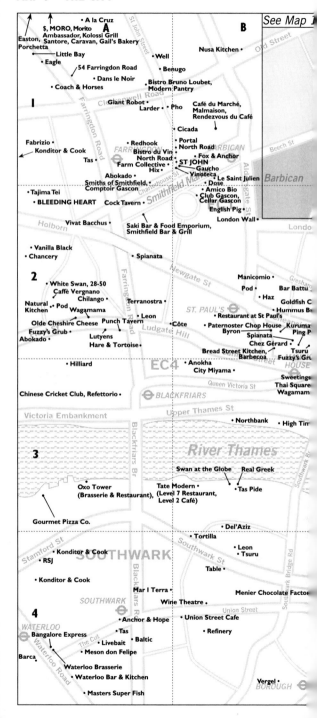

A la Cruz

$, MORO, Morito
Ambassador, Kolossi Grill
Santore, Caravan, Gail's Bakery
Easton,
Porchetta

Nusa Kitchen

Old Street

Little Bay

Eagle

Well

54 Farringdon Road

Benugo

Dans le Noir

Bistro Bruno Loubet,
Modern Pantry

Coach & Horses

Café du Marché,
Malmaison,
Rendezvous du Café

Giant Robot

Larder

Pho

Beech St

Cicada

Fabrizio

Portal
North Road

Konditor & Cook

FARRINGDON

Redhook

BARBICAN

Fox & Anchor

Barbican

Tas

Bistro du Vin
North Road
Farm Collective
Hix

ST JOHN
Gaucho
Vinoteca

Le Saint Julien

Abokado

Dose

Smiths of Smithfield,
Comptoir Gascon

Amico Bio
Club Gascon, Cellar Gascon

Tajima Tei

Smithfield Mkt

English Pig

BLEEDING HEART

Cock Tavern

London Wall

Holborn

Vivat Bacchus

Saki Bar & Food Emporium,
Smithfield Bar & Grill

London

Vanilla Black

Chancery

Spianata

Newgate St

Manicomio

Bar Battu

White Swan, 28-50
Caffè Vergnano
Chilango

Pod

Haz

Goldfish C

Natural
Kitchen

Pod

Wagamama

Terranostra

ST. PAUL'S

Restaurant at St Paul's

Hummus Br

Kuruma

Olde Cheshire Cheese

Punch Tavern

Leon

Côte

Paternoster Chop House
Byron

Ping P

Fuzzy's Grub

Abokado

Lutyens
Hare & Tortoise

Ludgate Hill

Spianata
Chez Gérard

Tsuru
Fuzzy's Gr

Bread Street Kitchen,
Barbecoa

HOUSE

Hilliard

Anokha
City Miyama

EC4

Sweetings
Thai Square
Wagamam

Chinese Cricket Club, Refettorio

BLACKFRIARS

Queen Victoria St

Victoria Embankment

Upper Thames St

Northbank

High Tim

River Thames

Oxo Tower
(Brasserie & Restaurant),

Tate Modern
(Level 7 Restaurant,
Level 2 Café)

Swan at the Globe

Real Greek

Tas Pide

Southwark Br

Gourmet Pizza Co.

Del'Aziz

Stamford St

Tortilla

Konditor & Cook

SOUTHWARK

Southwark St

Leon
Tsuru

RSJ

Konditor & Cook

Table

Southwark Bridge Rd

Menier Chocolate Factor

SOUTHWARK

Mar I Terra

Blackfriars Rd

Wine Theatre

Union Street

WATERLOO

Anchor & Hope

Union Street Cafe

Bangalore Express

Tas

Refinery

Barca

Livebait

Baltic

Meson don Felipe

Waterloo Rd

The Cut

Waterloo Brasserie

Waterloo Bar & Kitchen

Vergel

BOROUGH

Masters Super Fish

MAP 9 – THE CITY

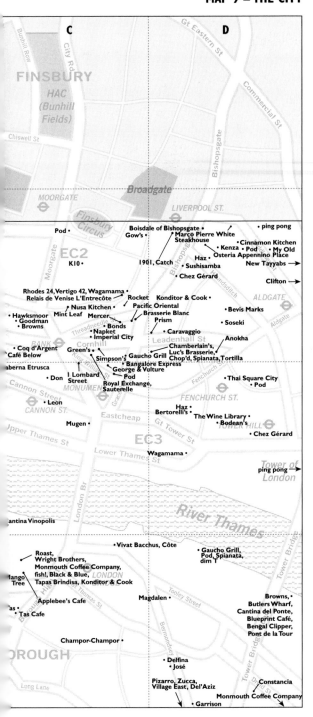

C   D

Gt Eastern St

Bunhill Row

City Road

FINSBURY

HAC
(Bunhill
Fields)

Commercial St

Chiswell St

Bishopsgate

MOORGATE

Broadgate

LIVERPOOL ST.

Finsbury Circus

Pod •

Boisdale of Bishopsgate •
Gow's •

• ping pong

• Marco Pierre White
Steakhouse

• Cinnamon Kitchen
• Kenza • Pod • My Old
Osteria Appennino Place

EC2

Haz •

New Tayyabs →

Moorgate

K10 •

1901, Catch

• Sushisamba

Bishopsgate

Clifton →

• Chez Gérard

Rhodes 24, Vertigo 42, Wagamama •
Relais de Venise L'Entrecôte

ALDGATE

• Rocket

Konditor & Cook •

• Nusa Kitchen •

Pacific Oriental

• Bevis Marks

• Hawksmoor
• Goodman
• Browns

Mint Leaf

Brasserie Blanc
Prism

Aldgate

• Soseki

Threadneedle

• Bonds
• Napket
• Imperial City

• Caravaggio

Mercer •

Anokha

BANK

• Coq d'Argent
Café Below

Green's •

Leadenhall St

Chamberlain's,
Luc's Brasserie,
Chop'd, Spianata, Tortilla

Cornhill

Simpson's • Gaucho Grill •

aberna Etrusca

King William

• Don

I Lombard
Street

Bangalore Express
George & Vulture

MONUMENT

Royal Exchange,
Sauterelle

Pod

Fenchurch

• Thai Square City
• Pod

• Leon

Cannon Street

Gracechurch

FENCHURCH ST.

CANNON ST.

Mugen •

Eastcheap

Haz •
Bertorelli's •

• The Wine Library •
• Bodean's

Gt Tower St

TOWER HILL

Upper Thames St

Lower Thames St

Wagamama •

• Chez Gérard

EC3

Tower of
London

London Br

ping pong →

River Thames

antina Vinopolis

Tower Bridge

• Vivat Bacchus, Côte

• Gaucho Grill,
Pod, Spianata,
dim T

Roast,
Wright Brothers,
Monmouth Coffee Company,
fish!, Black & Blue,
Tapas Brindisa, Konditor & Cook

LONDON

Bankside

Mango
Tree

Applebee's Cafe

Magdalen •

Browns,
Butlers Wharf,
Cantina del Ponte,
Blueprint Café,
Bengal Clipper,
Pont de la Tour

as •
• Tas Cafe

Tooley Street

Bermondsey

Champor-Champor •

OROUGH

• Delfina
• José

Tower Bridge

Long Lane

Pizarro, Zucca,
Village East, Del'Aziz

Druid St

Constancia

Monmouth Coffee Company →

↓ • Garrison

MAP 10 – SOUTH LONDON (& FULHAM)

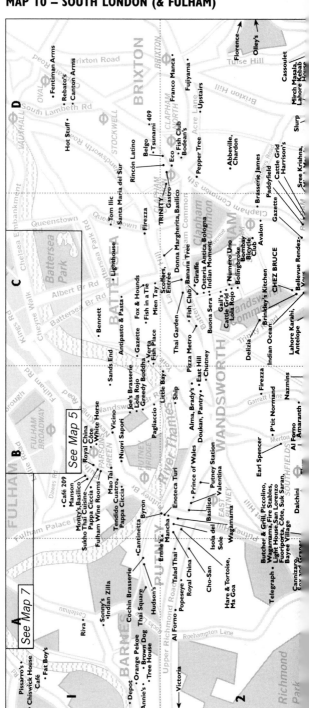

MAP 11 – EAST END & DOCKLANDS

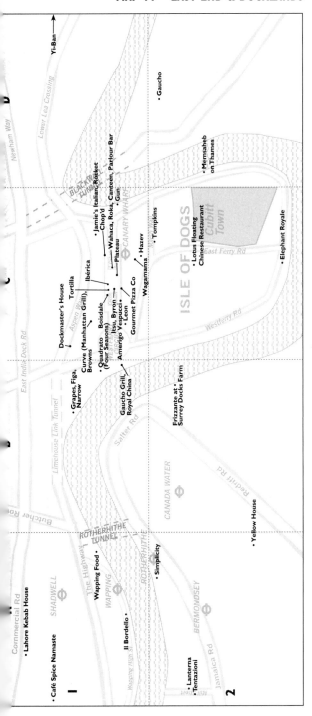

Yi-Ban

Lower Lea Crossing

Newham Way

• Gaucho

BLACKWALL TUNNEL

• Jamie's Italian, Rocket
Chop'd
Wahaca, Roka, Canteen, Parlour Bar
• Gun

Plateau

• Memsaheb
on Thames

CANARY WHARF

Dockmaster's House

Ibérica

Tortilla

Aspen Way

• Hazev
Wagamama •

• Tompkins

ISLE OF DOGS

Cubitt Town

• Lotus Floating
Chinese Restaurant

East Ferry Rd

• Elephant Royale

Curve (Manhattan Grill),
Browns

Quadrato   Boisdale
(Four Seasons)

Itsu, Byron
Amerigo Vespucci •
• Leon
Gourmet Pizza Co

East India Dock Rd

Westferry Rd

• Grapes, Figa,
Narrow

Limehouse Link Tunnel

Gaucho Grill,
Royal China

Salter Rd

Frizzante at •
Surrey Docks Farm

Redriff Rd

Butcher Row

CANADA WATER

ROTHERHITHE
TUNNEL

Commercial Rd

• Café Spice Namaste

• Lahore Kebab House

SHADWELL

The Highway

Wapping Food •

WAPPING

ROTHERHITHE

• Simplicity

• Yellow House

Il Bordello •

Wapping High St

BERMONDSEY

• Lanterna
• Tentazioni

Jamaica Rd

1

2

MAP 12 – SHOREDITCH & BETHNAL GREEN

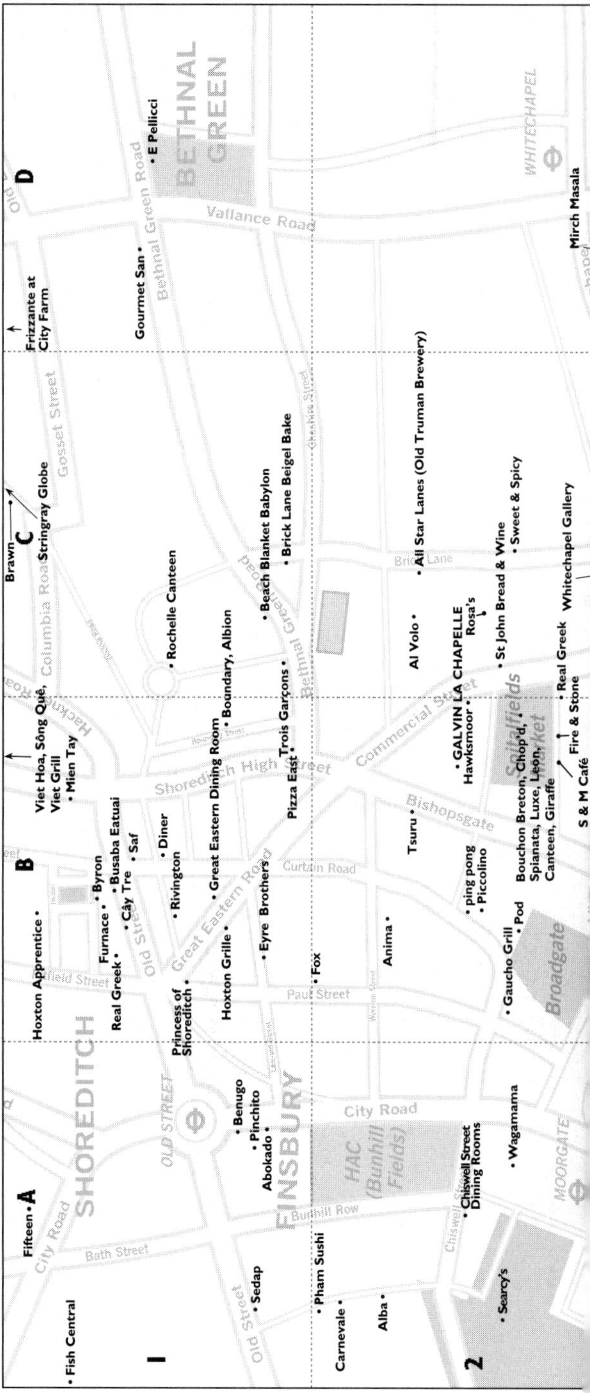

BETHNAL GREEN

SHOREDITCH

FINSBURY

WHITECHAPEL

MOORGATE

Broadgate

HAC (Bunhill Fields)

Spitalfields

Old Street

Columbia Road

Hackney Road

Gosset Street

Vallance Road

Bethnal Green Road

Shoreditch High Street

Great Eastern Street

Commercial Street

Bishopsgate

Curtain Road

Paul Street

City Road

Bunhill Row

Bath Street

Brick Lane

Whitechapel

• E Pellicci

Frizzante at City Farm →

• Gourmet San

Brawn →

Stringray Globe

• Rochelle Canteen

Viet Hoa, Sông Quê
Viet Grill
• Mien Tay

• Beach Blanket Babylon
• Brick Lane Beigel Bake

Hoxton Apprentice •

Real Greek •
Furnace •
• Byron
• Busaba Eatuai
• Cây Tre
• Saf
• Diner
• Rivington

Boundary, Albion

Great Eastern Dining Room

Princess of Shoreditch •

Hoxton Grille •

Eyre Brothers •

Pizza East Trois Garçons •

Al Volo •

• All Star Lanes (Old Truman Brewery)

GALVIN LA CHAPELLE
Hawksmoor •
Rosa's •

• St John Bread & Wine

• Sweet & Spicy

• Real Greek   Whitechapel Gallery

Fire & Stone

S & M Café

• Tsuru

• ping pong
• Piccolino

Bouchon Breton, Chop'd,
Splanata, Luxe, Leon, Net
Canteen, Giraffe

• Fox

Anima •

• Gaucho Grill
Pod

• Mirch Masala

Benugo •
• Pinchito
Abokado •

Fifteen •

• Fish Central

• Sedap
• Pham Sushi

Carnevale •

Alba •

• Searcy's

Chiswell Street Dining Rooms

• Wagamama

HELP FEED
A MALNOURISHED CHILD.
EAT OUT.

This September and October, wherever you see this logo your meal will include a voluntary donation to help feed malnourished children worldwide. Find out more at lovefoodgivefood.org

LOVE FOOD GIVE FOOD

ACTION HUNGER

Registered Charity no. 1047501

CHAMPAGNE TAITTINGER
Reims

delicious.
MAGAZINE

Carluccio's

CLEARCHANNEL

Harden's